METHODS FOR EFFECTIVE TEACHING

Fifth Edition

METHODS FOR EFFECTIVE TEACHING

Meeting the Needs of All Students

Paul R. Burden
Kansas State University

David M. Byrd
University of Rhode Island

Allyn & Bacon

Boston ■ New York ■ San Francisco
Mexico City ■ Montreal ■ Toronto ■ London ■ Madrid ■ Munich ■ Paris
Hong Kong ■ Singapore ■ Tokyo ■ Cape Town ■ Sydney

Series Editor: Kelly Villella Canton
Series Editorial Assistant: Annalea Manalili
Senior Marketing Manager: Darcy Betts Prybella
Production Editor: Cynthia Parsons
Editorial Production Service: Omegatype Typography, Inc.
Composition Buyer: Linda Cox
Manufacturing Buyer: Megan Cochran
Electronic Composition: Omegatype Typography, Inc.
Interior Design: Omegatype Typography, Inc.
Photo Researcher: Annie Pickert
Cover Administrator: Elena Sidorova

For related titles and support materials, visit our online catalog at www.pearsonhighered.com.

Between the time website information is gathered and then published, it is not unusual for some sites to have closed. Also, the transcription of URLs can result in typographical errors. The publisher would appreciate notification where these errors occur so that they may be corrected in subsequent editions.

Library of Congress Cataloging-in-Publication Data

Burden, Paul R.
    Methods for effective teaching : meeting the needs of all students / Paul R. Burden, David M. Byrd— 5th ed.
           p.   cm.
    Includes bibliographical references and indexes.
    ISBN-13: 978-0-13-700804-9 (pbk.)
    ISBN-10: 0-13-700804-X (pbk.)
  1. Teaching   2. Effective teaching.   I. Byrd, David M.   II. Title.

    LB1025.3.B87   2010
    371.102—dc22   2008041400

Printed in the United States of America

10   9   8   7   6   5   4   3   2   1   HAM   12   11   10   09

Credits appear on page 377, which constitutes an extension of the copyright page.

Allyn & Bacon
is an imprint of

www.pearsonhighered.com

ISBN-10: 0-13-700804-X
ISBN-13: 978-0-13-700804-9

About the Authors

Paul R. Burden is an assistant dean and professor in the College of Education at Kansas State University, Manhattan, where he has supervised student teachers and taught courses on teaching methods, classroom management and discipline, foundations of education, and instructional leadership. Previously, he was a middle-level science teacher in Buffalo, New York, and later earned his doctoral degree at Ohio State University. He received the College of Education's Outstanding Undergraduate Teaching Award at Kansas State University in 1999.

His recent publications include *Classroom Management: Creating a Successful K–12 Learning Community* (2010, John Wiley & Sons), *Countdown to the First Day of School* (2006, National Education Association), *Powerful Classroom Management Strategies: Motivating Students to Learn* (2000, Corwin Press), as well as *Establishing Career Ladders in Teaching* (1987, Charles C Thomas). From 1986 to 1997, he served as the editor of the *Journal of Staff Development,* a quarterly journal sponsored by the National Staff Development Council, and he has presented over 70 papers at regional and national educational conferences in addition to authoring 15 articles and four book chapters.

Married with three children, Dr. Burden enjoys traveling with his family and working on genealogy. He can be contacted at Kansas State University, 261 Bluemont Hall, Manhattan, Kansas 66506; (785) 532-5550; burden@ksu.edu.

David M. Byrd is director of the School of Education at the University of Rhode Island (URI). He is a graduate of the doctoral program in teacher education at Syracuse University. Prior to coming to Rhode Island, he was an associate professor at Southern Illinois University. He has a long-term professional and research interest in programs for beginning teachers and teacher professional development.

Dr. Byrd is presently the co-principal investigator for Rhode Island Teacher Education Reform, a five-year, $7.5 million federal grant to support teacher preparation and induction and to build on current efforts in Rhode Island to strengthen the preparation of the next generation of Rhode Island teachers.

Dr. Byrd has authored and co-authored over 30 articles, books, and chapters. He has served as co-editor of the Association of Teacher Educators' *Teacher Education Yearbook* series (2000–2006). Yearbook titles that he edited include *Preparing Tomorrow's Teachers: The Field Experience, Research on the Education of Our Nation's Teachers, Research on Career Long Teacher Education, Research on Professional Development Schools,* and *Research on Effective Models for Teacher Education.* He has served as chairperson of the Research Committee for the Association of Teacher Educators and on the journal board for *Action in Teacher Education.* Dr. Byrd can be contacted at the University of Rhode Island, 706 Chafee Hall, Kingston, Rhode Island 02881; (401) 874-5484; dbyrd@uri.edu.

Brief Contents

Contents

CHAPTER SIX

CHAPTER SEVEN

PART IV   MANAGING INSTRUCTION AND THE CLASSROOM

CHAPTER EIGHT

CHAPTER NINE

Classroom Management   216

CHAPTER TEN

Classroom Discipline   250

PART V   ASSESSING AND REPORTING STUDENT PERFORMANCE

CHAPTER ELEVEN

Assessing Student Performance   276

CHAPTER TWELVE

Grading Systems, Marking, and Reporting   302

PART VI   WORKING WITH OTHERS

CHAPTER THIRTEEN

Working with Colleagues and Families   330

Preface

The fifth edition of *Methods for Effective Teaching* provides research-based coverage of general teaching methods while emphasizing contemporary topics such as learning communities, differentiated instruction, and modifications for student differences. The numerous features, tables, and lists of recommendations ensure that the text is reader friendly and practically oriented. Its unique content includes strategies to promote student understanding, differentiate instruction, manage lesson delivery, apply motivational techniques for instruction and assessment, and work with colleagues and parents. In addition, thorough coverage of classroom management and discipline is provided, along with ways to create a positive learning environment.

INTENDED AUDIENCE

This book is designed primarily as the core textbook for courses in K–12 general teaching methods, secondary/middle teaching methods, or elementary school teaching methods. The content is applicable for teachers at all levels—elementary, middle level, and high school. Additionally, it may be used as a supplementary book for other teaching methods courses. This book would also be appropriate for courses and staff development programs for in-service teachers and as a handbook for teacher reference due to its comprenshensive coverage of current classroom issues and practical teaching applications.

RELATING THIS BOOK TO STANDARDS

A variety of professional standards are listed, correlated to the book, and referenced throughout. Standards are used to guide the development of new teachers, help in-service teachers improve their performance, and assess both teacher preparation and teacher performance. Many teacher education programs are designed around the Interstate New Teacher Assessment and Support Consortium (INTASC) standards. Many states require a passing score on the Principles of Learning and Teaching test (Praxis II) before granting a teaching license. The Praxis III standards and the National Board for Professional Teaching Standards (NBPTS) are used to assess and improve the teaching of in-service teachers. A brief description of these standards is provided here, and tables of these standards can be found on pages xxi–xxiv.

INTASC Standards

The Interstate New Teacher Assessment and Support Consortium (INTASC) is a consortium of state education agencies and national educational organizations dedicated to the reform of the preparation, licensing, and ongoing professional development of teachers. Created in 1987, INTASC's primary constituency is state education agencies responsible for teacher licensing, program approval, and professional development. Its work is guided by one basic premise: *An effective teacher must be able to integrate content knowledge with the specific strengths and needs of students to ensure that all students learn and perform at high levels.* More information can be found at this website: www.ccsso.org/projects/Interstate_New_Teacher_Assessment_and_Support_Consortium.

Praxis Series

The Praxis Series is a set of tests developed and disseminated by the Educational Testing Service (ETS) for assessing skills and knowledge of each stage of a beginning teacher's career, from entry into teacher education to actual classroom performance. More information about the Praxis Series can be found at this website: http://ets.org/praxis/index.html. There are three parts of the Praxis Series:

■ *Praxis I: Pre-Professional Skills Tests (PPST).* These academic skills tests are designed to be taken early in a student's college career to measure reading, writing, and mathematics skills.

■ *Praxis II: Subject Assessments.* There are several assessments available in the Praxis II series, and they measure a teacher candidate's knowledge of the subjects he or she will teach, as well as general and subject-specific pedagogical skills and knowledge. One of these assessments is the Principles of Learning and Teaching (PLT) test, which many states require teachers to pass for their licensure.

■ *Praxis III: Classroom Performance Assessments.* These assessments are conducted for beginning teachers in classroom settings. Assessment of teaching practice is through direct observation of classroom practice, a review of documentation prepared by the teacher, and semistructured interviews. The framework for knowledge and skills for these assessments consists of 19 assessment criteria organized within four categories: planning and preparation, the classroom environment, instruction, and professional responsibilities. Charlotte Danielson's (2007) *Enhancing Professional Practice: A Framework for Teaching* is based on the categories of the Praxis III Classroom Performance Assessments.

Methods for Effective Teaching is not intended to address the preprofessional skills of reading, writing, and mathematics in Praxis I. However, it is designed to address the Praxis II test on Principles of Learning and Teaching and the Praxis III classroom performance criteria areas.

NBPTS Standards

The National Board for Professional Teaching Standards (NBPTS) has established standards for highly accomplished teaching, based on five core propositions. NBPTS has a national voluntary system of certifying teachers who meet the standards in their teaching performance. Teachers meeting all of the standards are certified National Board Certified Teachers. More information about the NBPTS standards can be found at this website: www.nbpts.org.

NEW TO THIS EDITION

We made a number of significant changes in this fifth edition:

- a major revision of Chapter 1 on the teacher as a decision maker, emphasizing the implications of increasing student diversity on all aspects of teaching
- a new emphasis throughout the book on teaching English language learners in all classrooms
- new discussion of the SIOP model (sheltered instruction observation protocol) as a means to guide planning and teaching to meet the needs of English language learners in mainstream classrooms
- new sections in several chapters, including the following topics:

    professional reflections during your program (Chapter 1)

    increasing student diversity and more English language learners (Chapter 1)

    using the concept of backward mapping when planning (Chapter 2)

    applying the SIOP model to planning (Chapter 3)

    expanded discussions about implications for teaching concerning gender, language, and cultural diversity (Chapter 4)

    differentiating instruction with the universal design for learning (Chapter 4)

    applying the SIOP model to instructional strategies (Chapter 7)

    applying the SIOP model to lesson delivery (Chapter 8)

    assessment adaptations for English language learners (Chapter 11)

    working through cultural and language differences with families (Chapter 13)

- a case study in each chapter for reflection and application of chapter concepts
- increased coverage of teacher dispositions
- tables to show how this book addresses professional standards from INTASC, Praxis II Principles of Learning and Teaching, Praxis III, and the standards of the NBPTS

SPECIAL FEATURES

To maintain the reader's interest and to accommodate different learning styles and instructional settings, *Methods for Effective Teaching* contains a variety of pedagogical features.

- *Standards Tables.* Four tables of professional standards can be found on pages xxi–xxiv. These tables feature references to the chapters in this book that address each part of the standards.
- *Objectives.* Each chapter begins with a list of objectives that identify expected reader outcomes.

■ *Chapter Outline.* Each chapter begins with a graphic organizer displaying chapter headings and subheadings to provide an advance organizer for the reader.

■ *Voices from the Classroom.* These features are included in each chapter to provide descriptions by actual elementary, middle school, and high school teachers of ways that they deal with particular topics addressed in the chapter. These teachers come from all parts of the country and different community sizes. There are over 30 Voices from the Classroom features, evenly balanced among elementary, middle, and high school levels.

■ *Sample Standards.* Each chapter has a Sample Standards feature that lists representative knowledge, dispositions, and skills from INTASC standards that relate to the chapter in an effort to direct the reader's attention to important content and characteristics.

■ *Classroom Case Studies.* Each chapter includes a case study describing a situation that a teacher may need to confront. Two or three questions following each case study require the reader to reflect upon and apply chapter concepts.

■ *What Would You Decide?* Several features are placed in each chapter to consider the application of the content. Each feature includes several sentences describing a classroom situation related to an issue in the chapter followed by a few questions asking the reader to make decisions about the application of the concepts.

■ *Creating a Learning Community.* This feature provides a description of a classroom situation followed by three questions asking the reader to think, reflect, and decide on ways to create a learning community.

■ *Spotlight on Technology.* This feature presents specific content about ways that technology can be integrated into instruction. Contemporary uses of computers and technology are highlighted.

■ *Modifications for Diverse Classrooms.* This feature presents a certain issue to illustrate the need to make modifications to help all students learn. Three questions are posed to the reader asking for ways to modify some aspect of the classroom to meet learners' needs.

■ *Key Terms.* A list of key terms at the end of each chapter draws the reader's attention to significant terms. Each term is highlighted in the text.

■ *Major Concepts.* At the end of each chapter, a list of major concepts serves as a summary of the significant concepts.

■ *Discussion/Reflective Questions.* Questions at the end of each chapter promote discussion and reflection in a classroom or seminar in which a number of people are considering the chapter's content.

■ *Suggested Activities.* These activities are listed at the end of each chapter both for clinical (on-campus) settings and for field (school-based) settings to enable the reader to investigate and apply issues addressed.

■ *Further Reading.* An annotated list of recommended readings at the end of each chapter suggests readings for further enrichment.

■ *References.* References cited in the chapters to document the research base of the content are all listed at the end of the book.

SUPPLEMENTS

Instructor's Manual / Test Bank

An instructor's manual to accompany this textbook has been developed by the authors to guide teacher educators on using this book for their courses. This manual includes multiple choice, true/false, short answer, and essay/discussion questions for each chapter. It may be downloaded in PDF from the Instructor Resource Center at the Pearson Higher Education website (www.pearsonhighered.com). Your local Pearson sales representative can help you set up a password for the Instructor Resource Center.

MyEducationLab

Think of MyEducationLab as an extension of the text, where you will find classroom videos and other online resources. MyEducationLab is easy to use! In the textbook, look for the MyEducationLab logo in the margins and follow instructions to access the multimedia assignments in MyEducationLab that correspond with the chapter content. If the access code for MyEducationLab did not come packaged with your book, you may purchase access at www.myeducationlab.com.

ACKNOWLEDGMENTS

Many people provided support and guidance as we prepared this book. A very special acknowledgment goes to our spouses: Jennie Burden and Mary Byrd. Their support kept our spirits up when deadlines were pressing, and their understanding during our absences while preparing the content enabled us to complete the project.

We also appreciate the help from the staff at Allyn and Bacon who provided editorial guidance, facilitated the preparation of the manuscript, and coordinated the production.

A number of classroom teachers provided descriptions of their professional practice, which are included in the Voices from the Classroom features. Their experiences help illustrate the issues and bring life to the content.

Sandi Faulconer provided valuable assistance at Kansas State University in preparing several tables and the permissions log. Finally, we would like to extend our gratitude to the following reviewers who provided constructive feedback for this edition: Karen Paciotti, Texas A & M University–Corpus Christi, and Joan Pedro, University of Hartford.

Paul Burden
David Byrd

INTASC Standards

The following table indicates how the Interstate New Teacher Assessment and Support Consortium (INTASC) standards are addressed in this book.

STANDARDS	CHAPTER COVERAGE
1. Knowledge of Subject Matter	5–6
Understands the central concepts, tools of inquiry, and structures of the subject being taught and can create learning experiences that make these aspects of subject matter meaningful for students.	
2. Knowledge of Human Development and Learning	4–7
Understands how children learn and develop, and can provide learning opportunities that support their intellectual, social, and personal development.	
3. Adapting Instruction for Individual Needs	4–6
Understands how students differ in their approaches to learning and creates instructional opportunities that are adapted to diverse learners.	
4. Multiple Instructional Strategies	4–7
Uses a variety of instructional strategies to encourage students' development of critical thinking, problem solving, and performance skills.	
5. Classroom Motivation and Management	8–10
Uses an understanding of individual and group motivation and behavior to create a learning environment that encourages positive social interaction, active engagement in learning, and self-motivation.	
6. Communication Skills	8–10
Uses knowledge of effective verbal, nonverbal, and media communication techniques to foster active inquiry, collaboration, and supportive interaction in the classroom.	
7. Instructional Planning Skills	2–7
Plans instruction based on knowledge of subject matter, students, the community, and curriculum goals.	
8. Assessment of Student Learning	11–12
Understands and uses formal and informal assessment strategies to evaluate and ensure the continuous intellectual, social, and physical development of the learner.	
9. Professional Commitment	1
Is a reflective practitioner who continually evaluates the effects of his or her choices and actions on others (students, parents, and other professionals in the learning community) and who actively seeks out opportunities to grow professionally.	
10. Partnerships	13
Fosters relationships with school colleagues, parents, and agencies in the larger community to support students' learning and well-being.	

Source: The Interstate New Teacher Assessment and School Consortium (INTASC) standards were developed by the Council of Chief State School Officers and member states. Copies may be downloaded from the Council's website at www.ccsso.org.

Praxis II: Standards for Principles of Learning and Teaching

The following table indicates how the Praxis II standards for the Principles of Learning and Teaching are addressed in this book.

STANDARDS	CHAPTER COVERAGE
1. Students as Learners	
Student development and the learning process	2
Students as diverse learners	4
Student motivation and the learning environment	4, 9–11
2. Instruction and Assessment	
Instructional strategies	4–7
Planning instruction	2–4
Assessment strategies	11–12
3. Communication Techniques	
Basic, effective verbal and nonverbal communication techniques	7, 10
Effect of cultural and gender differences on communications in the classroom	4, 7, 10
Types of communications and interactions that can stimulate discussion in different ways for particular purposes	6–7
4. Profession and Community	
The reflective practitioner	1
The larger community	13

Source: Reprinted by permission of Educational Testing Service, the copyright owner. Permission to reprint the Praxis II materials does not constitute review or endorsement by Educational Testing Service of this publication as a whole or of any other testing information it may contain.

Praxis III: Standards for Classroom Performance Assessments

The following table indicates how the Praxis III standards are addressed in this book.

STANDARDS	CHAPTER COVERAGE
1. Planning and Preparation	
Demonstrating knowledge of content and pedagogy	5–7
Demonstrating knowledge of students	4
Selecting instructional goals	3–4
Demonstrating knowledge of resources	2–3
Designing coherent instruction	2–3
Assessing student learning	11–12
2. The Classroom Environment	
Creating an environment of respect and rapport	9
Establishing a culture for learning	4, 9
Managing classroom procedures	9
Managing student behavior	10
Organizing physical space	9
3. Instruction	
Communicating clearly and accurately	8
Using questioning and discussion techniques	4–5
Engaging students in learning	4–7
Providing feedback to students	4, 11–12
Demonstrating flexibility and responsiveness	4–7
4. Professional Responsibilities	
Reflecting on teaching	1
Maintaining accurate records	8–9, 12
Communicating with families	13
Contributing to the school and district	13
Growing and developing professionally	1
Showing professionalism	1

Source: Reprinted by permission of Educational Testing Service, the copyright owner. Permission to reprint the Praxis III materials does not constitute review or endorsement by Educational Testing Service of this publication as a whole or of any other testing information it may contain.

NBPTS Core Propositions

The following table indicates how the National Board for Professional Teaching Standards (NBPTS) core propositions are addressed in this book.

PROPOSITIONS	CHAPTER COVERAGE
1. Teachers are committed to students and their learning.	4–7
Teachers recognize individual differences in their students and adjust their practice accordingly.	
Teachers have an understanding of how students develop and learn.	
Teachers treat students equitably.	
Teachers' mission extends beyond developing the cognitive capacity of their students.	
2. Teachers know the subjects they teach and how to teach those subjects to students.	2–7
Teachers appreciate how knowledge in their subjects is created, organized, and linked to other disciplines.	
Teachers command specialized knowledge of how to convey a subject to students.	
Teachers generate multiple paths to knowledge.	
3. Teachers are responsible for managing and monitoring student learning.	8–12
Teachers call on multiple methods to meet their goals.	
Teachers orchestrate learning in group settings.	
Teachers place a premium on student engagement.	
Teachers regularly assess student progress.	
Teachers are mindful of their principal objectives.	
4. Teachers think systematically about their practice and learn from experience.	1, 13
Teachers are continually making difficult choices that test their judgment.	
Teachers seek the advice of others and draw on education research and scholarship to improve their practice.	
5. Teachers are members of learning communities.	1, 13
Teachers contribute to school effectiveness by collaborating with other professionals.	
Teachers work collaboratively with parents.	
Teachers take advantage of community resources.	

METHODS FOR EFFECTIVE TEACHING

1 | The Teacher as a Decision Maker

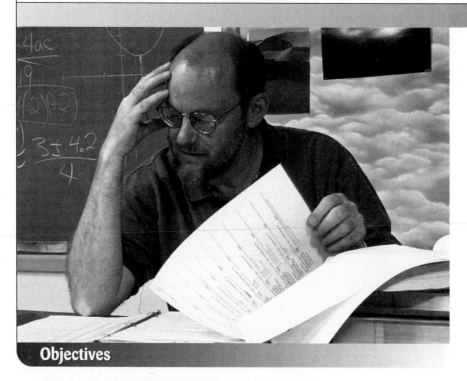

Objectives

This chapter provides information that will help you to:

1. Determine key characteristics of effective teaching.
2. Apply professional teaching standards and understand the purposes they serve.
3. Formulate a plan to use reflection to enhance teacher decision making.
4. Describe ways that instruction of English language learners can be enhanced in all classrooms.

Effective Teaching

- Decisions about Basic Teaching Functions
- Essential Teacher Characteristics
- Expectations for Effectiveness

The Teacher as a Reflective Decision Maker

- Reflective Practice
- Aspects of Instructional Decision Making
- Reflection and a Constructivist Approach to Teaching
- Reflections during Your Program

Standards and Professional Development

- INTASC Standards
- Principles of Learning and Teaching
- Framework for Teaching
- National Board for Professional Teaching Standards

Increasing Student Diversity

- More English Language Learners
- Challenges of English Language Learners
- Teaching English Language Learners in All Classrooms
- The SIOP Model

Your journey to become a teacher continues. You want to be an effective teacher, but what are the characteristics of effective teachers? What do they need to know and do? To a large extent, effective teaching involves making good decisions to help students learn.

Even before instruction takes place, teachers think about and make decisions concerning content, instructional strategies, the use of instructional materials and technology, delivery techniques, classroom management and discipline, assessment of student learning, and a host of other related issues. During instruction, teachers must implement these decisions as they interact with students in a dynamic way.

Decision making involves giving consideration to a matter, identifying the desired end result, determining the options to get to the end result, and then selecting the most suitable option to achieve the desired purpose. Teacher decisions about the issues just mentioned ultimately will influence student learning.

To examine teacher decision making and its relationship to teaching methods, the discussion in this chapter centers on four questions: What is effective teaching? What are the standards used to guide the professional development of teachers? How can a teacher be a reflective decision maker? How can instruction of English language learners (ELLs) be enhanced in all classrooms?

EFFECTIVE TEACHING

What are teachers' responsibilities, and what makes teachers effective in meeting these responsibilities? To answer these questions, it is useful to examine the basic teaching functions, essential teacher characteristics, and expectations for effectiveness.

Decisions about Basic Teaching Functions

Teachers make countless decisions all day long in an effort to promote student learning. When you break the decisions down, they fall into three categories: planning, implementing, and assessing. Some decisions are made at the desk when preparing lesson or unit plans, designing an instructional activity, or grading papers. Other decisions are made on the spot during the dynamic interactions with students when delivering a lesson. Let's briefly examine these three basic teaching functions. Each will be considered in more detail in later chapters.

Planning.   *Planning* involves teacher decisions about student needs, the most appropriate goals and objectives, the content to be taught, instructional strategies, lesson delivery techniques, instructional media, classroom climate, and student assessment. These decisions are made before actual instruction takes place. The goal of planning is to ensure student learning. Planning occurs when teachers are alone and have time to reflect and consider issues such as short-range and long-range plans, student progress, time available, and instructional materials. Planning helps arrange the appropriate flow and sequence of instructional content and events. Planning is considered in more detail in Chapters 2 and 3.

Implementing.   *Implementing* involves the actual enactment of the instructional plans concerning lesson delivery and assessment. Implementation occurs when interacting with students. Teaching skills that support implementation include presenting and explaining, questioning, listening, monitoring, giving feedback, and demonstrating. Additional skills are needed to monitor student behavior, enforce rules and procedures, use instructional technology, exhibit caring and respect, and create a positive learning environment.

As you can see, a multitude of skills are required for implementation of the instructional plans, and teachers make decisions constantly during the delivery of instruction to enact the plans and to promote student learning. Several chapters in this book relate to implementation, including topics such as differentiating instruction for diverse learners, instructional strategies, motivating students, strategies to promote student understanding, managing lesson delivery, and classroom management and discipline.

Assessing.   *Assessing* involves determining the level of student learning. Actually, many aspects of assessment are determined during the planning phase when instructional goals and content are identified. The means to measure student learning include paper-and-pencil tests, portfolios, work samples, projects, reports, journals, models, presentations, demonstrations, and various other types of product and performance assessments. Once assessment data has been gathered, the information is recorded and judgments are made. Assessment is considered in more detail in Chapters 11 and 12.

Teacher decisions about planning, implementing, and assessing matter a great deal. As attempts are made to improve schools and increase student achievement, one constant has remained: Teachers are the most important factor in improving schools. Attempts to reform or improve education depend on the knowledge, skills, and commitment of teachers. This point is made emphatically by Darling-Hammond and Baratz-Snowden (2007) in "A Good Teacher in Every Classroom: Preparing the Highly Qualified Teachers Our Children Deserve." Teachers need to know how to implement new practices concerning the basic teaching functions, but they must also take ownership or the innovation will not succeed.

Essential Teacher Characteristics

When you reflect about the most effective teachers you have had, you may think about their warmth and caring, their creative instructional strategies, their strong command of the content, or their unique presentation skills. When examining effective teachers, the essential teacher characteristics fall into three categories: their knowledge, skills, and dispositions. Let's briefly examine each of these. The descriptions provided here are closely tied to the definitions of those terms provided by the National Council for Accreditation of Teacher Education (2008).

Knowledge.   Effective teachers must know the facts about the content they are teaching. That is vital, but it is not sufficient. Teachers also must have at least three other types of knowledge.

First, they must have professional knowledge related to teaching in general. This includes information about the historical, economic, sociological, philosophical, and psychological understanding of schooling and education. It also includes knowledge about learning, diversity, technology, professional ethics, legal and policy issues, pedagogy, and the roles and responsibilities of the profession of teaching.

Second, teachers must have pedagogical knowledge, which includes the general concepts, theories, and research about effective teaching, regardless of the content area. Thus, it involves general teaching methods.

Finally, teachers must have pedagogical content knowledge. This involves teaching methods that are unique to a particular subject or the application of certain strategies in a special way for a subject. For example, there may be some unique ways to teach map reading skills in a social studies class. This also involves a thorough understanding of the content to teach it in multiple ways, drawing on the cultural backgrounds and prior knowledge and experiences of the students.

Thus, teachers must possess rich knowledge about the content, foundational information about teaching and learning, information about teaching methods in general, and information about teaching techniques unique to particular subjects.

Skills. Teachers also must possess the necessary skills to use their knowledge effectively in the four areas just described to ensure that all students are learning. Teachers must be able to apply these skills as they plan, implement, and assess in diverse teaching settings. In listings of professional standards, the term *performances* is sometimes used instead of the term *skills*.

Dispositions. Teachers also must have appropriate dispositions to promote learning for all students. *Dispositions* include the necessary values, commitments, and professional ethics that influence teacher behaviors. Dispositions are guided by beliefs and attitudes related to values such as caring, fairness, honesty, responsibility, and social justice. Dispositions are affective, thus in the mind of teachers. But dispositions show up in teacher behaviors. For example, a teacher might be willing to use a variety of instructional strategies to promote learning for all students. This disposition could be evidenced by written plans indicating the use of cooperative learning groups, demonstrations, and a role-playing activity and by the actual use of those approaches when instruction took place.

When making decisions, you must have the necessary knowledge, skills, and dispositions to help promote learning for all students. Research has shown that teacher expertise is one of the most important factors that influences student growth and achievement. There is interest in the educational community to develop criteria for the knowledge, skills, and dispositions that teachers need to promote student achievement.

As a prospective teacher, it is important that you identify these essential teacher characteristics (knowledge, skills, dispositions) when you examine the main teaching functions of planning, implementing, and assessing. As the teaching functions are discussed in this book, several chapters have a boxed feature to indicate the knowledge, skills, and dispositions related to the chapter topic using the descriptions provided in the INTASC standards. For example, Chapter 2 on planning will include a box of information about representative knowledge, skills, and dispositions related to planning.

Expectations for Effectiveness

Over the years, there have been calls to improve the quality of teaching, the quality and substance of the K–12 curriculum, and the performance of students on standardized tests. School districts and teachers always feel some degree of pressure from the local school district, the state and federal governments, professional organizations, legislators, and the public in general. Occasionally, there are major education reports with information about student performance, and then there are new calls for improving teacher education and the quality of teaching. Effective teaching is expected.

Measures of Effectiveness. Various approaches have been used to indicate the quality of teaching and the influence on student learning. One approach has been to examine

SAMPLE STANDARDS

Decision Making and Reflection

There are ten INTASC standards (see page xxi), and each standard includes a list of knowledge, dispositions, and performances to indicate more clearly what is intended in the standard.

Since this chapter deals with decision making and reflection, some representative statements for knowledge, dispositions, and performances from INTASC Standard #9 are listed here concerning topics in this chapter.

Knowledge

■ The teacher understands methods of inquiry that provide him/her with a variety of self-assessment and problem-solving strategies for reflecting on his/her practice, its influences on students' growth and learning, and the complex interactions between them.

■ The teacher is aware of major areas of research on teaching and of resources available for professional learning.

Dispositions

■ The teacher is committed to reflection, assessment, and learning as an ongoing process.

■ The teacher is committed to seeking out, developing, and continually refining practices that address the individual needs of students.

Performances

■ The teacher uses classroom observation, information about students, and research as sources for evaluating the outcomes of teaching and learning and as a basis for experimenting with, reflecting on, and revising practice.

■ The teacher draws on professional colleagues within the school and other professional arenas as supports for reflection, problem solving and new ideas, actively sharing experiences, and seeking and giving feedback.

---

student achievement test scores over a three-year time period in a so-called value-added comparison. This value-added concept compares the performance of a student against that same student's performance at an earlier time. The difference in the two assessments is taken as a measure of student learning growth, which can also be conceptualized as the value added by the instructional effectiveness of the teacher. Students' average annual rates of improvement are then used to estimate how much value a teacher has contributed to student achievement (Crane, 2002; Teaching Commission, 2004).

Value-added assessment studies in Tennessee have shown that teacher quality matters. When viewed over a three-year period, students who had highly effective teachers scored meaningfully better on standardized tests, outperforming their peers by approximately 50 percentile points (Sanders & Rivers, 1996). In Texas, researchers have amassed a body of work that validates the importance of teacher quality and its effect on student academic performance (Hanushek, Kain, & Rivkin, 1998).

A second approach to determine the quality of teaching has involved the study of teacher test scores and their relationship to the achievement of their students. A series of studies correlated the teachers' basic skills tests and college entrance exams with the scores of their students on standardized tests. These studies have found that high-scoring teachers are more likely to elicit significant gains in student achievement than their lower-scoring counterparts (Ferguson, 1998; Ferguson & Ladd, 1996).

A third approach to determine the quality of teaching has involved the review of the content knowledge of teachers. A teacher's deep understanding of the content he or she teaches has a positive influence on student achievement (Monk, 1994). This appears especially true for science and mathematics teachers. In a review of research, Michael Allen, program director for the Education Commission of the States Teaching Quality Policy Center, found support for the necessity of teachers being knowledgeable in their subjects and on how best to teach a particular subject (Allen, 2003).

In addition, teaching experience appears to have an influence on student achievement. Teachers with less teaching experience typically produce smaller learning gains in their students compared with more seasoned teachers (Fetler, 1999; Murnane & Steele, 2007). However, most of those studies have also discovered that the benefits of experience level off after the first five or so years of teaching.

No Child Left Behind.   While education is often considered a local and state matter, the federal government in the last decade has increased its involvement in how teachers are prepared and certified. This was undertaken through the "highly qualified" teacher provisions of the *No Child Left Behind Act* (NCLB, 2002). There are several provisions of this act.

1. *Highly qualified teachers.* To be deemed highly qualified, teachers must have a bachelor's degree, have full state certification or licensure, and prove that they know each subject they teach.

2. *State requirements.* NCLB requires that states (a) measure the extent to which all students have highly qualified teachers, particularly minority and disadvantaged students; (b) adopt goals and plans to ensure all teachers are highly qualified; and (c) publicly report plans and progress in meeting teacher quality goals.

3. *Demonstration of competency.* Teachers (in middle and high school) must prove that they know the subject they teach with (a) a major in the subject they teach, (b) credits equivalent to a major in the subject, (c) passage of a state-developed test, (d) state standards for evaluation, (e) an advanced certification from the state, or (f) a graduate degree.

4. *State standards of evaluation.* NCLB allows states to develop an additional way for current teachers to demonstrate subject-matter competency and meet highly qualified teacher requirements. These standards must be high, objective, and uniform throughout the state. Proof may consist of a combination of teaching experience, professional development, and knowledge in the subject garnered over time in the profession.

STANDARDS AND PROFESSIONAL DEVELOPMENT

Each state identifies the licensure requirements for teachers. The states do not arbitrarily select criteria—they often rely on standards proposed by professional educational agencies. The following standards are among those commonly used in the states: (a) INTASC standards, (b) Principles of Learning and Teaching (PLT), (c) a Framework for Teaching, and (d) National Board for Professional Teaching Standards (NBPTS). Each of these standards is outlined in detail on pages xxi–xxiv of this book.

A state may use one of the standards, such as the INTASC standards, and then adapt them somewhat to serve as the basis for the teacher licensure requirements. Once a state establishes its teacher licensure requirements, these become the standards that colleges use to design their teacher education programs. Consequently, you may see that your teacher education program includes many of the topics listed in the standards. Let's examine these four sets of standards.

INTASC Standards

The *Interstate New Teacher Assessment and Support Consortium (INTASC)* asked a committee of teachers, teacher educators, and state agency officials to prepare a set of

---

Voices from the Classroom

Reflections on My Instructional Plans

Sue Garver, third-grade teacher, Riley, Kansas

I find myself constantly evaluating and reevaluating what I do in my classroom on a daily and yearly basis. Being a reflective person has allowed me to grow and improve in my teaching. There are several things that I do on a regular basis that help me be more reflective in my teaching.

First, I meet with other teachers during our breaks or after school in order to compare notes. During this time, we talk, compare ways we teach a subject, share new ideas, and just give each other moral support. This is a time when I reflect on the methods I currently use to present a subject and on ways that I could improve my teaching methods.

Second, I take a few minutes at the end of each day to evaluate the lessons I taught that day. I think this has helped me improve my teaching skills. In addition, I have included a column for

these evaluative and reflective comments right in my plan book next to the plans for each lesson. Throughout the day, I often make notes on a sticky pad concerning the lessons I teach. Then at the end of the day, I transfer those notes to my plan book in the column for my reflections. These are notes concerning the success of the lesson, what I could do differently next time, what could be done to meet the needs of individuals, what I did right in the lesson, and anything else that might be helpful next time I teach that lesson. I keep those lesson plans close by when planning for the following year.

Third, reflecting upon my teaching makes it easier for me to set goals for myself. I have found that I can set goals easily when I make these reflective notes during the school year and when I take time at the end of the school year to reflect on my teaching.

standards for competent beginning teachers. Its report, *Model Standards for Beginning Teacher Licensing, Assessment and Development: A Resource for State Dialogue* (INTASC, 1992), was to serve as a guide for states as they determined teacher license requirements in their own states. Many states found the INTASC standards appropriate and modeled their teacher licensure requirements to be identical to or very similar to the INTASC standards. INTASC (1998) has also examined ways to move toward performance-based licensure in teaching.

As shown on the table of standards on page xxi, there are INTASC standards for knowledge of the subject matter, knowledge of human development and learning, adapting instruction for individual needs, multiple instructional strategies, classroom motivation and management, communication skills, instructional planning skills, assessment of student learning, professional commitment, and partnerships. For each standard, INTASC also outlines the related knowledge, skills, and dispositions deemed essential for beginning teachers. The identification of the dispositions makes the INTASC standards unique when comparing them to standards identified by other agencies.

Principles of Learning and Teaching

The Educational Testing Service (ETS) prepared several Praxis II tests to measure the knowledge of specific subjects that K–12 educators will teach, as well as general and subject-specific teaching skills and knowledge. The three Praxis II tests include Subject Assessments, Principles of Learning and Teaching, and Tests and Teaching Foundations Tests.

The *Principles of Learning and Teaching* (PLT) test assesses general pedagogical knowledge concerning (a) students as learners, (b) instruction and assessment, (c) communication techniques, and (d) profession and community. These topics are outlined in more detail in the PLT standards list on page xxii of this book. Many states require applicants for teaching licenses to take the PLT and report a passing score before granting the teaching license. Because of this, colleges with teacher education programs often give a great deal of attention to the content of the PLT and incorporate the necessary topics into their teacher education programs.

Framework for Teaching

The Educational Testing Service (ETS) developed the Praxis III Classroom Performance Assessments as a means to assess the skills of beginning teachers in classroom settings. The four categories in this assessment are based on empirical studies and theoretical research related to improved student learning. Praxis III Classroom Performance Assessments are designed to assess the skills of beginning teachers in classroom settings. The Praxis III system utilizes three methods to assess the beginning teacher's evidence of successful practice. These include direct observation of classroom teaching, review of teacher documentation regarding planning and teaching, and interviews.

Based on the Praxis III assessment categories, Charlotte Danielson (2007) proposed a framework for teaching in her book *Enhancing Professional Practice: A Framework for Teaching.* The four domains of teaching responsibility described by Danielson are identical to the categories in Praxis III. Danielson's *Framework for*

Teaching provides a useful organizer for examining the important responsibilities of teachers. In her book, Danielson provides rubrics for each item to assess the level of teacher performance. The rubric descriptors for unsatisfactory, basic, proficient, and distinguished provide clarity for the meaning of each item. A detailed outline of Danielson's *Framework for Teaching* (i.e., Praxis III) is displayed on page xxiii of this book.

Many teacher education programs give a great deal of attention to the Framework for Teaching because of its strong research support. As a result, these colleges have incorporated the domains into their teacher education programs. Here is a brief review of the four domains in Danielson's *Framework for Teaching*.

Domain 1: Planning and Preparation.   Planning provides a structure for how content is organized during the process of planning for instruction. Key concepts within this domain are (a) demonstrating knowledge of content and pedagogy, (b) demonstrating knowledge of students, (c) selecting instructional goals, (d) demonstrating a knowledge of resources, (e) designing coherent instruction, and (f) assessing student learning by setting criteria and standards of performance.

myeducationlab

Go to MyEducationLab, select the topic **Effective Teaching and the Effective Teacher,** watch the video entitled "Planning for Instruction," and complete the questions that accompany it.

Domain 2: Classroom Environment.   The classroom environment is more than just the physical space of a classroom. It encompasses the interactions between the teacher and students, as well as the expectations for learning and achievement and the expectations and norms for learning and behavior. Positive classroom environments are associated with a range of important outcomes for students related to motivation, achievement, and safety. Key concepts in this domain are (a) creating an environment of respect and rapport, (b) establishing a culture for learning, (c) managing classroom procedures, (d) managing student behavior, and (e) organizing physical space.

Domain 3: Instruction.   Instruction is the central focus of the teaching/learning act. It is where the teacher and the student move through an instructional sequence. Key concepts within this domain are (a) communicating clearly and accurately, (b) using questioning and discussion techniques, (c) engaging students in learning, (d) providing feedback to students, and (e) demonstrating flexibility and responsiveness.

Domain 4: Professional Responsibilities.   Professional responsibilities focus on those dispositions and skills that the teacher uses not only to be effective in the present but also to ensure future success as a professional. Central to this domain is the ability to reflect accurately on the planning process and the implementation of instruction and then to think deeply about how to improve the teaching–learning process for students. Key concepts within this domain are (a) reflecting on teaching, (b) maintaining accurate records, (c) communicating with families, (d) contributing to the school and district, (e) growing and developing professionally, and (f) showing professionalism.

National Board for Professional Teaching Standards

The *National Board for Professional Teaching Standards (NBPTS)* was initiated in 1987 to establish "high and rigorous" standards for the teaching profession, create a voluntary system to certify accomplished teaching, create professional development opportunities, and increase the status of the teaching profession in America. The National Board's work is guided by five core propositions that articulate what accomplished teachers should know and be able to do (NBPTS, 2005). These core propositions are used as a foundation to assess teaching in a variety of subjects and for teachers working with students at all grade levels.

Details for the five core propositions are outlined on page xxiv. Briefly stated, the NBPTS core propositions are as follows:

- Teachers are committed to students and their learning.
- Teachers know the subjects they teach and how to teach those subjects to students.
- Teachers are responsible for managing and monitoring student learning.
- Teachers think systematically about their practice and learn from experience.
- Teachers are members of learning communities.

These five core propositions describe the knowledge, skills, and dispositions that characterize accomplished teaching. Because of the recognized importance of these criteria, many teacher education programs incorporate features of the five core propositions in their programs.

Experienced teachers choosing to be nationally board certified must prepare portfolios and include a videotape of their teaching, provide samples of student learning products, and provide analyses and reflection on their professional practice. After completion of the portfolio, teachers travel to an assessment center where they answer questions related to the subject area in which they teach. This rigorous process is voluntary. Some school districts provide a financial bonus for teachers who become certified through this process.

THE TEACHER AS A REFLECTIVE DECISION MAKER

An effective teacher draws on education and experience to make decisions on what to teach, how to teach, and how to promote an atmosphere that supports student learning. Thus, effective teachers reflect on the process of teaching and the success of their students. Each of these skills is essential to an effective teacher who is focused on students' achievement and meeting intended learning outcomes. As mentioned, the value added that a teacher brings to the classroom is becoming a primary focus for teacher evaluation and professional development, and value added is measured relative to student gains in achievement while under the direction of the teacher.

Measures of teacher competence are important areas for you to reflect on. Think about effective teachers you have had. Think about their knowledge, skills, and dispositions. Think about what it will take for you to be an effective teacher. A reflective teacher considers what to teach, how to teach, and how to promote an atmosphere that supports student learning (Cooper, 2006; Jensen & Kiley, 2005). Each of these important aspects are described here and represented in Figure 1.1:

1. *What to teach.* Effective teachers have a strong command of the subject matter they are assigned to teach. In addition, they have the ability to make decisions about the selection of materials and examples used to introduce the subject matter to their students.

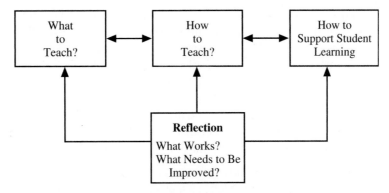

FIGURE 1.1   Effective Teaching and Reflection

2. *How to teach.* Effective teachers have a large collection of teaching strategies that they can draw on to maximize student achievement. Expert teachers recognize that they need to use a variety of methods and strategies to meet the varied learning needs of their students and to capture and maintain student interest and motivation. This is especially important when teachers realize that the strategy they are using has not led to success for all students and that a different strategy needs to be employed.

3. *How to provide an atmosphere that supports student learning.* Knowing the content and knowing about instructional strategies are not sufficient to promote student learning. Effective teachers also must create the necessary classroom conditions to enable student learning; they must create a positive learning community.

A *learning community* is a classroom designed to help all students feel safe, respected, and valued in order to learn new skills. Anxiety, discomfort, and fear are incompatible with the learning process and make teaching and learning difficult. Successful classrooms are those in which students feel supported in their learning, are willing to take risks, are challenged to become fully human with one another, and are open to new possibilities. When creating a learning community, teachers consider issues such as rules and procedures, interpersonal relations, communication, and support and reinforcement for appropriate conduct.

Dispositions toward students and learning are an important part of a teacher's makeup. Teachers must be able to meet the learning needs of students and work to foster a positive atmosphere for student learning. Several key dispositions of professional educators include a caring attitude, a sensitivity to student differences, and a commitment to helping all students learn. According to the National Council for Accreditation of Teacher Education (2008), teacher candidates should be able to work with students, families, and communities to reflect the dispositions of professional educators as delineated in professional, state, and institutional standards.

Reflective Practice

To learn requires that a person reflect on past practice. As a consequence, reflection is a cornerstone of professional competence (York-Barr, Sommers, Ghere, & Montie, 2006).

Reflection can be defined as a way of thinking about educational matters that involves the ability to make rational choices and to assume responsibility for those choices. Reflection requires that the teacher be introspective, open-minded, and willing to accept responsibility for decisions and actions. Reflection facilitates learning and continued professional growth, and it is an important factor in the ability of teachers to be effective throughout their careers (Steffy, Wolfe, Pasch, & Enz, 2000). Educators reflect on their dispositions, objectives, teaching strategies, and the effect each of these has on student achievement.

Minott (2007) points out that reflective teaching leads to a number of positive effects for teachers, including the development of the following:

- self-directed critical thinking inquiry skills
- contextualized knowledge about teaching and learning that can be applied in similar situations (e.g., when to change instructional strategies or lesson pacing)
- a willingness to question, take risks in learning, and try new strategies and ideas
- higher-order thinking skills and the ability to reflect on one's own learning process
- both cognitive (e.g., knowing how to ask questions that help students engage and think deeply) and affective skills (e.g., valuing students as individuals capable of learning)
- an increased ability to react, respond, assess, and revise while teaching
- the ability to implement new activities and approaches on the spot
- improved self-awareness and knowledge
- improved coping strategies (e.g., the ability to redirect student inappropriate behaviors rather than with a response that will escalate the situation)

As reflective practitioners, teachers need to be willing to analyze their own traits and behaviors in relation to the events that take place in the classroom. Teachers, therefore, need to observe and attempt to make sense of situations by checking their insights against prior experience. Information they receive from their students can also be helpful. When viewing a videotape of their instruction, for example, teachers might express a variety of reflective concerns about issues, such as their appearance or mannerisms; techniques, materials, or classroom environment; and ethical and moral issues (Byrd, Foxx, & Stepp, 1990).

Reflective practice is a problem-solving strategy by which individuals or groups can work to improve practice by reviewing routines and the procedures and other aspects of the instructional environment. To engage in reflective practice requires an environment of support. It requires an organizational climate that encourages open communication, critical dialogue, risk taking, and collaboration (Osterman & Kottkamp, 2004).

Pat Roy (2005) introduced the concept of *follow-up* as "the act of repeating or adding to previous action so as to increase effectiveness." Reflectivity has as its goal enhancing the process of follow-up to improve teacher effectiveness. Many activities designated as follow-up are just events that provide an opportunity for focused reflection. For example, if you are trying to implement a new teaching strategy such as cooperative learning, understanding the concept of positive interdependence (i.e., that all students working in a cooperative group will work to ensure that all members of the group will succeed at the learning task) is more important than learning 12 different ways to group students. Therefore, the focus of the follow-up or reflection would target the critical concept of positive interdependence and how to implement the strategy with students. (The concept of cooperative learning will be discussed more in Chapter 6.)

Examples of activities that can provide a focus for reflection include the following:

1. classroom visitations to a master teacher's classroom to view a lesson being taught, along with an opportunity to reflect and debrief
2. reading an article on a new strategy and discussing it with colleagues in a study group
3. reviewing sample lesson plans and adapting them for your classroom
4. co-planning and co-teaching lessons with a coach or knowledgeable peer
5. planning with colleagues to implement new practices, such as students' exhibits of their work
6. videotaping a lesson and requesting collegial review and feedback

Aspects of Instructional Decision Making

The classroom teaching environment is complex and multifaceted, and dealing with complex problem situations is a dominant element in the life of a teacher. The complex life of teachers can be better understood by considering the relationship of teachers' decision making and the conditions and purposes they are trying to address in the classroom. Five aspects of decision making in the teaching environment are worth considering.

First, teachers make decisions to achieve varied academic, social, and behavioral goals. For instance, a teacher might make decisions about monitoring student behavior while working with a single small group of students. At the same time, the teacher might have expectations for students' social and academic performance. Thus, the teacher must consider these varied goals and decide on ways to plan and implement the goals simultaneously.

Second, teachers make decisions to interact with students in a variety of ways in a complex environment. For example, teachers do a number of things to monitor and respond to student off-task behavior. Effective teachers have a high degree of *withitness,* which is their ability to be aware of what is happening in the classroom and to communicate that awareness to the students through their actions (Kounin, 1970). Decisions related to withitness are continually made by teachers.

Third, teachers make decisions when considering multiple perspectives. In fact, teachers may interpret a situation far differently than their students do. For example, a teacher might try to reinforce a student when, in fact, the student might be embarrassed by the attention or comments. Reflective teachers should use their experience, knowledge about effective teaching, intuition, and insight to help understand how events in the classroom influence learning. Beginning teachers, of course, have limited experience and may not have a broad knowledge base when being reflective.

Fourth, teachers make moment-by-moment decisions to adjust their plans to fit the continually changing and uncertain conditions found in classrooms. Teachers learn to make these adjustments through the knowledge they have gained from the context of their classrooms, the interactive nature of their thinking, and their speculations about how these adjustments will affect the classroom environment.

Fifth, teachers make decisions when planning, implementing, and assessing instruction and when creating proper conditions for a positive learning environment. Each step involves multifaceted classroom conditions and student characteristics. When planning for instruction, for example, teachers must decide on goals and objectives, needs assessments, appropriate instructional strategies, materials and technology, and evaluation of student performance. Numerous factors must be considered when making decisions about each step.

Reflection and a Constructivist Approach to Teaching

A related concept to teacher decision making and reflection is constructivist theory. *Constructivist theory* holds that individuals construct meaning and understanding through their prior knowledge and then apply this knowledge in new current situations. In a constructivist classroom, the teacher searches for students' understandings of concepts and then structures learning opportunities for students to refine or revise these understandings by posing contradictions, presenting new information, asking questions, encouraging research, and/or engaging students in inquiries designed to challenge current concepts.

In a constructivist classroom, there are several overarching principles: (1) Teachers seek and value their students' points of view, (2) classroom activities challenge students' suppositions, (3) teachers pose problems of emerging relevance, (4) teachers build lessons around primary concepts and "big" ideas, and (5) teachers assess student learning in the context of daily teaching. As you can see, a tremendous amount of teacher decision making and reflection is needed to establish and maintain a constructivist classroom in an effort to meet the academic needs of the students when using this instructional approach.

Students should be challenged by the activities and stimulated by questions from both the teacher and themselves. A key feature of this model is that students are encouraged to actively seek understanding and knowledge by relating new investigations to previous understandings (Gagnon & Collay, 2006; Marlowe & Page, 2005).

Teachers who reflect on their own practice employ a constructivist perspective. They constantly review significant events that take place in the classroom and try to clarify and improve their understanding of teaching and learning. As you read this text, you will encounter many concepts related to teaching, and you will have the opportunity to reflect on how these concepts can help you become a better teacher and help your students become better learners.

Go to MyEducationLab, select the topic **Instructional Design,** click "simulation," and select "Using Learning Strategies." Execute the simulation and complete the questions that accompany it.

Asking questions about how you structure teaching and learning can be a useful approach for helping to engage in a guided reflective process. Barbara McCombs (2003), working out of the University of Denver Research Institute, conducted research on the effectiveness of asking beginning teachers to reflect on their own beliefs and practices while also asking for their students' perceptions of these same practices. Results showed that learner-centered beginner teachers are more successful in engaging all students in an effective learning process. Beginning teachers reported that the process of reflection and self-assessment assisted them in identifying areas for improvement and implementing practices to be more effective in reaching students.

One major point was that a discrepancy often existed between the learning teachers believed was occurring and what students perceived they were actually learning. Therefore, you should not be afraid to use a guided reflection process to identify areas for improvement nor to question students about what they have learned (McCombs, 2003).

Reflections during Your Program

Teachers may improve their decision making through a variety of means. Several approaches used in teacher education programs are briefly described here:

1. *Reflective teaching.* This procedure provides a person with repeated opportunities to teach and analyze brief lessons developed by program designers specifically for this purpose (Cruickshank, 1985; Phi Delta Kappa, n.d.). Lessons are commonly videotaped, thus enabling replay and critique.

2. *Microteaching.* Microteaching involves a preservice teacher teaching a brief lesson to peers to exhibit specific teaching behaviors, such as nonverbal cues, wait time for questions, and probing questions. The brief lesson is videotaped, and the preservice teacher receives feedback from the instructor and classmates.

3. *Reflective writing.* Reflective writing is a way for preservice teachers to practice critical analysis and reasoning. Journal writing is the most common way to stimulate reflection. With it, preservice teachers keep a daily or regular journal, in which they record their experiences and raise questions about teaching. Journal writing enables prospective teachers to systematically reflect on their development as a teacher and on their actions in the classroom.

4. *Portfolio development.* This involves the development of portfolios, in which preservice and beginning teachers collect and organize materials and artifacts such as lesson plans and examples of students' work, photographs from classrooms, and videotapes of lessons with self-critiques. Purposefully collecting sets of artifacts demonstrates the ability to reflect on important indicators of success.

Voices from the Classroom

Reflective Writing

Sandy Peer, high school math teacher, Wichita, Kansas

The most valuable graduate course I took was one that required me to express my philosophy in writing. I then had to videotape myself and look for evidences of my philosophy. I also had to interview my students to find out, if possible, what they thought about my philosophy of teaching. Students' perceptions of teachers are reality for them. Thus, I make it a personal goal to have their perceptions agree with what I am doing—or at least what I think I am doing. This whole process caused me to be more reflective about decisions I made in my teaching—decisions about planning, instructional strategies, media, the ways I interact with students, evaluation, and other areas.

Classroom Case Study

Improving Teaching through Reflection

Joel Escher is an experienced seventh-grade language arts teacher. After attending a professional development session on reflective teaching, he decided to videotape himself during some of his classes to better understand how to involve more of his students in whole-group discussions.

After watching the videotaped sessions of his recent classes, Mr. Escher noticed that he was neglecting some of his students during class discussions because he tended to stand on one side of the room. Since his posture was directed to only half of his class, he did not notice students outside his field of vision who were raising their hands but not called on to participate in the discussion.

In addition, Mr. Escher recognized that he didn't give students much time to formulate a response after he asked a question. On the videotape, several students appeared to be considering his question, but he called on another student before more students could formulate a response. To resolve this problem, Mr. Escher decided that he would write key questions on the board prior to class and then give students a couple of minutes prior to class discussions to jot down some ideas to share with the whole group.

Focus Questions

1. If Mr. Escher did not have access to video equipment, how else could he have learned why his whole-group discussions were unsuccessful?
2. Reflecting on your own classroom experiences, what recommendations can you make for having successful whole-class discussions?

INCREASING STUDENT DIVERSITY

Students in your classroom will vary in many ways. This *diversity* may be in ethnicity, race, socioeconomic status, gender, exceptionalities, language, religion, sexual orientation, and even geographical area (National Council for the Accreditation of Teacher Education, 2008). Many of these characteristics will be examined in Chapter 4. Of course, this diversity has always been evident in U.S. classrooms. Over the past 25 years, however, the characteristics of the U.S. population have changed, and consequently, the characteristics of the K–12 student population also have changed. The most apparent changes in schools are the increasing number of students from ethnic and racial minority groups and the significant increase in the number of students whose first language is not English. Consider the following facts about the current U.S. student population (most from Kober, 2006, unless noted otherwise):

- Four out of ten public school students are children of color—a proportion that is expected to increase in coming years (57 percent white, 19 percent Latino, 16 percent African American, 4 percent Asian/Pacific Islander, 3 percent Other).

- Children of color make up the majority of public school enrollments in six states and many districts.
- Hispanics, African Americans, and Asians combined make up the majority of the population in 48 of the 100 largest U.S. cities (Macionis, 2007).
- About one in five school-age child is a child of immigrants.
- One in every ten public school students is an English language learner—a student whose first language is not English and who is learning English.
- More than one-third of public school students are from low-income families.
- Almost 14 percent of public school students receive special services because they have a disability. In 2003–2004, three-fourths of these students with disabilities were educated in regular classrooms with other children for a significant part of the schoolday.

More English Language Learners

As just noted, *English language learners* (ELLs) are students whose first language is not English and who need help in learning to speak, read, and write in English. Due to immigration and the higher levels of ethnic diversity in the U.S. student population, it is not surprising that the number of English language learners has also increased significantly in the past 15 to 20 years. There are many different types of ELLs, ranging from students who are very educated to those with limited schooling, from children of professional families to children of migrant workers, from recent arrivals to the United States to those born here. In addition to functioning in two languages, ELLs also navigate two cultures.

According to statistics compiled by the National Clearinghouse for English Language Acquisition (NCELA, 2006), K–12 enrollment in U.S. schools increased by 2.59 percent from the 1994–1995 school year to the 2003–2004 schoolyear. However, ELL enrollments during those same years increased by 61 percent. In some parts of the country, ELL students may comprise as much as 90 percent of the student population. Currently, at least 329 different languages are spoken in the United States, with the most common language groups being Spanish (representing over 79 percent of all ELL students), Vietnamese, Hmong, Chinese, and Korean (NCELA, 2004, 2005).

You should expect to have students in your classroom who are learning English, and you should be prepared to meet their learning needs. In a national study, most new teachers ranked reducing class size and preparing teachers to adapt or vary their instruction to meet the needs of a diverse classroom as the top ways to improve teaching (Public Agenda, 2008).

Challenges of English Language Learners

Imagine what it would be like to have limited knowledge of English when attending school. It would be difficult to understand the teacher and the other students, and it would affect your ability to understand teacher directions, participate in the instructional activities, and complete classroom assessments. Your overall school performance would be affected. In fact, ELL students often experience challenges in school, as indicated by the following facts:

- A dramatic, lingering divide in achievement exists between Caucasian students and those from culturally and linguistically diverse groups on state and national measures of achievement (California Dept. of Education, 2004; Grigg, Daane, Jin, & Campbell, 2003; Kindler, 2002; Siegel, 2002).
- ELLs have some of the highest dropout rates and are more frequently placed in lower-ability groups and academic tracks than language-majority students (Ruiz-de-Velasco & Fix, 2000; Steinberg & Almeida, 2004).
- Only 10 percent of young adults who speak English at home fail to complete high school, but the percentage is three times higher (31 percent) for young adult English language learners (NCES, 2005).

Teaching English Language Learners in All Classrooms

Because of the large number of ELLs in schools today, *all* teachers are teachers of English. There are four major instructional models for serving English language learners, characterized by the degree to which they incorporate a student's native language and the approach they take to delivering academic content (Rothenberg & Fisher, 2007): (1) instructional methods using the native language, (2) instructional methods using the native language as support, (3) instructional methods using English as a second language (ESL), and (4) content-based or sheltered instruction.

The last approach, sheltered instruction, has been widely used in the United States. *Sheltered instruction* is an approach to teaching content to ELLs in strategic ways that make subject-matter concepts comprehensible while promoting the students' English language development. There are two well-known sheltered instruction programs: the cognitive academic language learning approach (CALLA) and the sheltered instruction observation protocol (SIOP).

CALLA is a program that integrates content-area instruction with language development activities and explicit instruction in learning strategies (Chamot & O'Malley, 1994). It helps ELLs become active learners who focus on concepts and meanings, rather than language forms. CALLA teachers develop five-phase lesson plans that include preparation, presentation, practice, evaluation, and expansion. This approach has been used successfully by many teachers in sheltered classes, but some teachers have found the planning to be difficult. In addition, ELLs with low levels of English proficiency and limited background knowledge still struggle to learn grade-appropriate content in English (Freeman & Freeman, 2007). Of the sheltered instruction programs, the SIOP model is widely adopted and is emphasized here.

The SIOP Model

One of the best researched and most highly developed models to teach English language learners is the *sheltered instruction observation protocol (SIOP) Model* (Echevarria, Vogt, & Short, 2008). The SIOP model was originally a lesson plan observation protocol, but it has evolved to be an effective lesson planning and delivery system. It is a way to plan and teach content in a way that is understandable for ELLs and that also promotes their English language development. With increasing student diversity in language, meeting the needs of English language learners can be facilitated by the use of the SIOP model to provide more flexibility in the design and delivery of instruction.

The SIOP model may be used as a lesson planning guide for sheltered content lessons, and it embeds features of high-quality instruction into its design. The model is not an add-on responsibility for teachers but rather a planning framework that ensures that effective practices are implemented to benefit all learners (Echevarria et al., 2008). The SIOP model has eight components and 30 features, as displayed in Figure 1.2. Other than the lesson preparation component being first, there is no particular hierarchy or order to the eight SIOP components. The components and features of the SIOP model are interrelated and integrated into each lesson.

Even students who are not struggling readers or English learners will benefit from a teacher who plans and delivers instruction using the SIOP model (Echevarria et al., 2008). Thus, mainstream teachers at all grade levels can effectively use the SIOP model to benefit all learners in their classrooms. Because of this, various components of the SIOP model will be more fully described in other chapters in this book. For example, information in the SIOP model concerning lesson delivery will be discussed in Chapter 8 on Managing Lesson Delivery. Other topics will be considered in the appropriate chapters to provide guidance in using the SIOP model components to meet the needs of all learners.

Key Terms

Assessing
Constructivist theory
Decision making
Dispositions
Diversity
English language learners (ELLs)
Framework for Teaching
Implementing

Interstate New Teacher Assessment and Support Consortium (INTASC)
Learning community
Microteaching
National Board for Professional Teaching Standards (NBPTS)
No Child Left Behind Act
Planning
Portfolio development

Principles of Learning and Teaching (PLT)
Reflection
Reflective practice
Reflective teaching
Reflective writing
Sheltered instruction
Sheltered instruction observation protocol (SIOP) model
Withitness

Major Concepts

1. Teachers make decisions concerning three basic teaching functions: planning, implementing, and assessing.
2. Essential teacher characteristics fall into three categories: knowledge, skills, and dispositions.

3. Teachers are expected to be effective, and many surveys, reports, and state and federal guidelines address ways for them to achieve this.
4. Professional teaching standards are used to guide the selection of state teaching licensure

FIGURE 1.2   Components of the SIOP Model

Lesson Preparation
- Clearly define, display, and review content objectives with the students
- Clearly define, display, and review language objectives with the students
- Select content concepts that are appropriate for age and educational background of the students
- Use supplementary materials to a high degree, making the lesson clear and meaningful
- Adapt content to all levels of student proficiency
- Provide meaningful activities that integrate lesson concepts with language practice opportunities

Building Background
- Explicitly link concepts to students' background experiences
- Explicitly make links between past learning and new concepts
- Emphasize key vocabulary

Comprehensible Input
- Speak appropriately for students' proficiency levels
- Provide clear explanations of academic tasks
- Use a variety of techniques to make content concepts clear

Strategies
- Provide ample opportunities for students to use learning strategies
- Consistently use scaffolding techniques to assist and support student understanding
- Use a variety of questions or tasks that promote higher-order thinking skills

Interaction
- Provide frequent opportunities for interaction and discussion
- Group students to support language and content objectives of the lesson
- Consistently provide sufficient wait time for student responses
- Give ample opportunities for students to clarify key concepts in their first language

Practice/Application
- Supply hands-on materials for students to practice using new content knowledge
- Provide activities for students to apply content and language knowledge
- Integrate all language skills into each lesson

Lesson Delivery
- Clearly support content objectives by lesson delivery
- Clearly support language objectives by lesson delivery
- Engage students during 90–100% of the lesson
- Appropriately pace the lesson to the students' ability levels

Review and Assessment
- Provide comprehensive review of key vocabulary
- Supply comprehensive review of key content concepts
- Provide regular feedback to students on their output
- Conduct assessments of student comprehension and learning of all lesson objectives throughout the lesson

Source: Adapted from Echevarria, Jana; Vogt, MaryEllen; & Short, Deborah J. (2008). *Making content comprehensible for English learners: The SIOP model.* Boston: Allyn & Bacon.

requirements and the development of teacher education programs at colleges and universities.

5. Teaching is centrally the act of decision making. Teachers plan and act through the process of thought and reflection.

6. Reflection can be defined as a way of thinking about educational matters that involves the ability to make rational choices and to assume responsibility for those choices.

7. The strategies in the SIOP model can be used to reach English language learners in all classrooms.

Discussion/Reflective Questions

1. Which is the most important teaching function: planning, implementing, or assessing? Why?
2. Give some examples of dispositions. Why are dispositions important?
3. How might teacher reflection help teachers improve their practice?
4. What are some of the strengths of the SIOP model?

Suggested Activities

For Clinical Settings

1. Select a significant event from a class you have attended on campus during the last three weeks. Reflect on what worked well using one of the standards tables reviewed in this chapter.
2. Teach a brief lesson to a small group of peers. Write and reflect about a significant event that took place in your lesson. Consider how you could improve the lesson if you were to teach it again.
3. Identify ways that you might apply aspects of the SIOP model into a microteaching lesson.

For Field Experiences

1. Talk with several teachers to explore what they think are the main characteristics of effective teachers.
2. Ask several teachers to describe lessons that they changed after the lesson began. Explore their thinking and decision making.
3. Ask several teachers about how they teach ELLs in their classroom.

Further Reading

Echevarria, J., Vogt, M., & Short, D. J. (2008). *Making content comprehensible for English learners: The SIOP model.* Boston: Allyn & Bacon.

Provides details about each SIOP component, rubric rating forms on SIOP use, lesson plan formats, and guidelines for use.

Osterman, K. F., & Kottkamp, R. B. (2004). *Reflective practice for educators: Professional development to improve student learning* (2nd ed.). Thousand Oaks, CA: Corwin Press.

Explains reflective practice and offers practical strategies to integrate reflective practice into daily work.

Taggart, G. L., & Wilson, A. P. (2005). *Promoting reflective thinking in teachers: Fifty action strategies* (2nd ed.). Thousand Oaks, CA: Corwin Press.

A thorough presentation of strategies for instilling reflective practices in educators. The tasks and tools provided have been specifically designed to facilitate teachers becoming critical thinkers.

York-Barr, J., Sommers, W. A., Ghere, G. S., & Montie, J. (2006). *Reflective practice to improve schools: An action guide for educators* (3rd ed.). Thousand Oaks, CA: Corwin Press.

A very useful guide providing a framework for reflective thinking and acting. Offers examples of strategies to guide individuals, small groups, or schoolwide reflection.

2 The Fundamentals of Planning

Objectives

This chapter provides information that will help you to:

1. Describe the reasons for instructional planning.
2. Identify factors that you might consider when planning for instruction.
3. Describe the two predominant approaches to instructional planning.
4. Identify resources that can be used when planning.
5. Prepare a syllabus and plan to motivate students.
6. Describe changes that teachers often experience in their approach to planning.

What Is Planning?
- Reasons for Planning
- Planning Phases
- Factors Considered in Planning
- Planning and the Standards Movement

Additional Planning Considerations
- Backward Mapping
- Resources for Planning
- Teacher–Student Planning
- Team Planning
- Preparing a Syllabus
- Planning to Use Academic Time Wisely

Approaches to Planning
- The Linear-Rational Model
- The Mental-Image Approach

Planning for instruction is a critical element in the instructional process. Carefully designed, comprehensive plans will have a positive effect on student learning. To help you to understand and be prepared to plan for instruction, this chapter will examine the planning process, approaches to planning, and related planning issues. The chapter ends with a discussion about how teachers really plan.

WHAT IS PLANNING?

Planning for instruction refers to decisions that are made about organizing, implementing, and evaluating instruction. Planning is one of the most important tasks that teachers undertake. It allows teachers to deeply reflect about the subject matter and the content they teach (Shen, Poppink, Cui, & Fan, 2007).

When making planning decisions, you also need to consider who is to do what, when and in what order instructional events will occur, where the events will take place, the amount of instructional time to be used, and resources and materials to be used. Planning decisions also deal with issues such as content to be covered, instructional strategies, lesson delivery behaviors, instructional media, classroom management, classroom climate, and student evaluation.

The goal of planning is to ensure student learning. Planning, therefore, helps create, arrange, and organize instructional events to enable that learning to occur. Planning helps arrange the appropriate flow and sequence of instructional events and also manage time and events.

The amount of time spent on planning varies greatly by individual teachers. It is influenced by factors such as pupil needs, the complexity of the teaching assignment, facilities and equipment, and the experience of the teacher. Some teachers estimate that they spend 10 to 20 percent of their time in planning (Clark & Yinger, 1987).

To more fully understand instructional planning, it is useful to consider the reasons for planning, the phases in which planning occurs, and factors that are considered while planning.

Reasons for Planning

When looking at the entire schoolyear, planning is needed for the year, each term, each unit, each week, and each lesson. Written weekly plans are typically required by school districts, and these plans for beginning teachers are often reviewed by the school principal. Plans for the year, term, and units are not commonly reviewed by the principal. There are a number of reasons to prepare thorough plans for all the time frames, with some plans written in detail and some not so thoroughly written (Freiberg & Driscoll, 2005).

Planning can help you to do the following:

- Gain a sense of direction, and through this, a feeling of confidence and security. Planning can help you stay on course and reduce your anxiety about instruction.
- Organize, sequence, and become familiar with course content.
- Collect and prepare related instructional materials, and plan to use various types of instructional media. This planning will help when ordering instructional supplies.
- Use a variety of instructional strategies and activities over time.
- Prepare to interact with students during instruction. This may include preparing a list of important questions or guidelines for a cooperative group activity.
- Incorporate techniques to motivate students to learn in each lesson.
- Take into account individual differences and the diversity of students when selecting objectives, content, strategies, materials, and requirements.
- Arrange for appropriate requirements and evaluation of student performance.
- Become a reflective decision maker about curriculum and instruction.
- Provide substitute teachers and members of a teaching team with a specific plan to follow if you are absent.
- Show other members of a teaching team what you are doing and how you are doing it.
- Satisfy administrative requirements. Teachers are often required to turn in their weekly plans for review by their principal.
- Use written plans as resources for future planning.

Planning Phases

There are four phases in the planning process (Freiberg & Driscoll, 2005). Each phase has a function in the planning process, and key decisions are made at each level, which in turn affects subsequent decisions in the next planning phase:

1. *Preplanning* is a time when a mental plan is made before instruction actually begins.
2. *Active planning* is a time when decisions are made about instruction and a commitment to a specific plan is made. This occurs before instruction and is the time when written plans are prepared.
3. *Ongoing planning* occurs during instruction itself and involves fine-tuning the plan based on events that take place during instruction.
4. *Postplanning* occurs after instruction takes place and involves evaluation of the instruction that just took place. This reflective time after instruction can help you to evaluate strengths and weaknesses of the planned lesson and consider how to improve instruction.

Classroom Case Study

Good Lesson Plan, Poor Results

Carla Ramirez, a third-grade teacher, has some concerns about her ability to carry out her lesson plans as the first half of the year is coming to a close. At the beginning of the schoolyear, Ms. Ramirez asked her students to fill out a questionnaire regarding their interests and the types of activities they like. She planned to use the student responses to come up with ideas for her lessons to meet students' interests and to engage them in the learning process.

Since the majority of her students indicated that they enjoy cooking and/or baking with adults, Ms. Ramirez decided to incorporate recipes and food measurements in her math lesson today on fractions. She also made a note of all of the resources she would need and made sure the materials were gathered and available for the lesson. Prior to teaching the lesson, she wrote a detailed lesson plan, including a list of anticipated student questions and corresponding responses.

During instruction, Ms. Ramirez found that most of the students answered her questions with ease. While she anticipated that a number of concepts in the lesson would be challenging for the students, many students appeared to have previous experience with these topics and grasped them effortlessly. Ms. Ramirez continued with her lesson as planned, but she became anxious when a group of students who completed the activity early become talkative and distracting.

Focus Questions

1. What were the strengths of Ms. Ramirez's planning process? Her weaknesses?
2. What would you suggest that she do to improve her lessons in the second half of the year?

SAMPLE STANDARDS

Planning

There are ten INTASC standards (see page xxi), and each standard includes a list of knowledge, dispositions, and performances to indicate more clearly what is intended in the standard.

Since this chapter deals with planning, some representative statements for knowledge, dispositions, and performances from INTASC Standard #7 are listed here concerning topics in this chapter.

Knowledge

- The teacher understands learning theory, subject matter, curriculum development, and student development and knows how to use this knowledge in planning instruction to meet curriculum goals.
- The teacher knows how to take contextual considerations (instructional materials, individual student interests, needs and aptitudes, and community resources) into account in planning instruction that creates an effective bridge between curriculum goals and students' experiences.

Dispositions

- The teacher believes that plans must always be open to adjustment and revision based on student needs and changing circumstances.
- The teacher values planning as a collegial activity.

Performances

- As an individual and a member of a team, the teacher selects and creates learning experiences that are appropriate for curriculum goals, relevant to learners, and based upon principles of effective instruction.
- The teacher plans for learning opportunities that recognize and address variation in learning styles and performance modes.

Factors Considered in Planning

When making plans for instruction, you will need to take into account factors related to your beliefs about teaching and the role of teachers, the instructional activities, your own personal and professional characteristics, and your reflections on your practice. Taken together, these factors will affect the decisions that you make about your instructional plans.

Factors Related to Instructional Activities. Instructional activities are the basic means through which teachers interact to present concepts and skills to students. There are a number of factors which you may consider when you plan any given instructional activity.

1. *Content.* *Content* refers to the knowledge, skill, rule, concept, or creative process that you wish students to learn. Students are expected to achieve school district goals stated in curriculum guides, and you select content related to the goals. While you have some autonomy, you are expected to teach and deal with content that is consistent with the district-approved goals.

Planning for content varies with the level of instruction, whether it be an advanced course, general content, or remedial material. Also, the nature of the content may affect teachers' planning decisions. For example, you might plan and teach in different ways for mathematics, reading, laboratory-related content, and social studies. Thus, what is taught determines to a great extent how you might plan and teach your lessons.

2. *Materials.* *Materials* are the tangible written, physical, or visual stimuli that are used in instruction. Textbooks, workbooks, computers, videotapes, software, and websites are some materials that you might use.

The availability of these materials influences your planning decisions. For example, when planning a lesson in which the students are painting with watercolors, an art teacher would need to be sure that certain materials are available. If the materials are not available, the teacher would need to make alternative plans. Teachers also need to consider how closely matched the materials are to the instructional objectives. For example, when considering using a film in a lesson, you would need to check on the nature and level of the content and also be sure the equipment is available when needed.

3. *Instructional strategies.* Selecting a variety of instructional strategies used to teach content is a central planning decision for teachers. These instructional strategies will be reviewed more thoroughly in Chapters 5 and 6. Briefly, though, you might use lectures, demonstrations, questions, recitations, practice, and drills, or you could use discussions, panels and debates, or small groups. You might also select inquiry and discovery approaches through the use of gaming, role-playing and simulation, laboratory work, or computer-assisted instruction.

4. *Teacher behaviors.* Teachers do a number of things during a lesson to conduct the lesson and to help engage students in learning activities; these will be discussed in Chapter 8 on managing lesson delivery. Briefly, though, you need to make plans to state expectations, provide a set induction, maintain a group focus, provide smooth transitions, clearly present lesson content, provide closure and a summary, and handle other aspects of conducting a lesson.

5. *Structure of the lesson.* *Structure of the lesson* refers to actions that take place at certain points in the class period or the lesson presentation, and you need to plan for the structure of a lesson. For example, at the start of the class period you may provide directions, pass out materials, or direct students to new locations. As the lesson proceeds, students might be reading, discussing, writing, or be participating in a particular instructional strategy. At the end of the class, students may return to their seats, clean up, or collect materials. These phases of a lesson are more thoroughly discussed in Chapter 8 on managing lesson delivery. When delivering lesson content, you might use a certain sequence of actions reflecting a certain approach to instruction.

6. *Learning environment.* When planning for instructional activities, consider the type of learning environment you would like to create. While many factors need to be taken into account, several issues warrant special attention. First, an effective classroom management system needs to be planned for and established, dealing with issues such as establishing classroom rules and procedures, reinforcing desired behaviors, holding students academically accountable, and creating a positive classroom climate (all discussed in Chapter 9). Second, a plan of dealing with misbehavior needs to be established (see Chapter 10). Third, you need to plan for ways to provide for individual differences (see Chapters 4 and 8). Fourth, you need to plan for ways to motivate students to learn (see Chapters 4 and 11). All of these issues contribute to the learning environment, and you need to plan for ways to address them.

7. *Students.* When planning for instructional activities, consider characteristics of the particular students you have in your classroom. Take into account students' motivational needs, academic needs, cultural backgrounds, and physical and psychological needs. Furthermore, consider how students will be grouped for instruction (i.e., whole group, small group, independent work), and consider which particular students will be in groups. As you plan, take into account the ability levels of the students and the ways in which students might be grouped to achieve instructional objectives. In addition, take into account the number of students who are involved in the instructional activities.

8. *Duration of the lesson.* Make plans for the time that is available or allocated. Instructional activities tend to last from 10 to 60 minutes. In a kindergarten class, 10 minutes of an activity may be the limit of student concentration and attention. Class lengths in primary and intermediate elementary grades are commonly up to the discretion of the teacher, but they often last no longer than 20 to 30 minutes. Classes in middle schools, junior high schools, and high schools commonly have predetermined lengths, ranging from 45 to 60 minutes or as much as 90 minutes in a block schedule. Within the time available, teachers need to use a variety of activities and resources to achieve lesson objectives and maintain student motivation. You need to be a good time manager to ensure that students have the opportunity to achieve the goals of the lesson during this time period.

9. *Location of the lesson.* When planning for instructional activities, plan for where the lesson will take place. The location of an activity may change based on the need for (a) space to work on a set of materials (i.e., a computer station or a learning center); (b) additional new references, materials, or experiences (i.e., the library, a field trip); or (c) a different social structure (i.e., a debate, a play, or any activity in which students work together).

Teacher Characteristics. Planning decisions about instructional activities and instructional routines are affected by the characteristics of the teachers themselves:

1. The amount of teaching experience you have influences planning decisions. Previous experiences provide you with a more complete mental image of lessons and thus your initial lessons need less adjustment.

2. Your philosophy of teaching and learning will have an effect on planning decisions.
3. Your knowledge of content also affects planning decisions. Teachers who know their content usually can plan more varied and flexible lessons because they can readily use and arrange information.
4. Your organizational style affects planning decisions. This style is reflected by your need for structure, planning routine, and style of solving problems.
5. Expectations that you set for your classes, for student learning, and for your own teaching also influence your planning and lesson images.
6. General feelings of security and control about teaching play an influential role in the planning process. When you feel secure in all dimensions of teaching, teaching plans tend to be less rigid. When teachers are not so secure, they tend to be more structured and plan in greater detail.

In summary, your characteristics serve as a filter through which instructional activities and routines are considered.

Planning and the Standards Movement

The standards movement has led to the development of standards or criteria for student performance. Beverly Falk (2002) maintains that standards-based assessment and instruction can stimulate both teachers and their students to "get clear about their purposes, to develop coherent goals for learning, and to make use of a range of instructional strategies to support students' varying approaches to learning" (p. 613). These *standards* are especially helpful when you are considering the content, materials, and instructional strategies outlined in the preceding section.

The standards movement began with the development of content standards in areas such as mathematics (National Council of Teachers of Mathematics, 1989), science (American Association for the Advancement of Science, 1993) and English (National Council of Teachers of English & International Reading Association, 1996). A central feature of this process has been to involve education stakeholders (e.g., policy makers, educators, parents, students, and community members) in the identification of what students should know and be able to do to be productive citizens.

myeducationlab

Go to MyEducationLab, select the topic **Concepts: Strategies for Teaching,** click "simulation," and select "Content Standards." Execute the simulation and complete the questions that accompany it.

The standards address what should be taught, and the performance assessment indicates the level of performance that students should demonstrate. The goal of these new standards is to benchmark or match these assessments to those of other countries whose students achieve highly on international assessments. The tests include a mix of traditional test items and performance tasks that ask students to use their knowledge to solve complex problems.

The National Assessment of Educational Progress (NAEP) is the only nationally representative, continuing assessment of what U.S. students know and can do in various subject areas. As such, the NAEP is often called the Nation's Report Card. Assessment has taken place since 1969. As the only measure given over time to assess educational achievement, the NAEP plays a primary role in evaluating the progress of the nation's educational system. Currently, the commissioner of education statistics, the head of the National Center for Education Statistics (NCES) in the U.S. Department of Education, is responsible for administering and reporting on the NAEP assessments. The National Assessment Governing Board, appointed by the secretary of education but independent of the department, governs the program.

APPROACHES TO PLANNING

Planning is continually connected to the overall instructional cycle. Planning occurs before instruction, prior to student assessment, and after student assessment (see Figure 2.1). Therefore, during the act of planning, you will consider the instructional effectiveness of your lesson, keeping in mind factors such as students' prior knowledge, your knowledge of the subject matter, and the difficulty of the subject being taught. You will then consider how to assess student progress. After the assessment has been administered and reviewed, you plan for remediation, introduction of higher-order concepts, or new instructional material. Often planning and decision making occur spontaneously while teaching, usually due to an unforeseen impediment to student learning (Arends, 2007).

There are two prominent approaches to instructional planning. The linear-rational model involves sequential decisions about goals, objectives, needs assessment, strategies, and evaluation. The mental-image approach involves forming mental images of lessons you plan to teach after considering factors related to instructional activities and instructional routines.

The Linear-Rational Model

The type of planning taught most often in teacher education programs is a sequential process based on clear goals and objectives. The *linear-rational model* of instructional

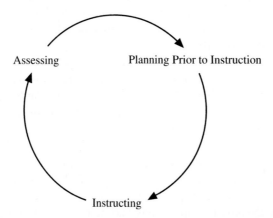

Assessing   Planning Prior to Instruction

Instructing

FIGURE 2.1   Planning for Instruction and Assessment

planning involves sequential decisions about the (a) formulation of goals, (b) specification of objectives, (c) assessment of student needs relative to the stated goals and objectives, (d) selection of strategies and learning activities linked to the objectives, and (e) evaluation of student performance (see Figure 2.2).

It is a logical and organized way to plan for instruction. With this model, you build on the knowledge gained from each step. Insights gained in one step lead to changes in other steps. In this way, objectives, methods, and evaluation are logically linked and given consideration in the initial planning. For example, you must think about evaluation even when making decisions about objectives, activities, content, and sequence.

The rational model is sometimes referred to as *instructional design* or the *systems approach* to planning. It requires the analysis of the components of planning in a logical order with an orderly but flexible sequence. Each of the five steps in the linear-rational model for instructional planning is discussed in the following sections.

Formulation of Aims and Goals.   The first step of the linear-rational model of instructional planning involves the formulation of goals. Educational goals are the broad statements of purpose that educators use to provide a direction for the courses they plan. The purposes of education are stated at a number of levels: nation, state, school district, subject, grade level, unit plan, or lesson plan. The terms *aims, goals,* and *objectives* are commonly used to identify the educational purposes at each of these levels.

Aims.   The term *aim* refers to broad statements about the intent of education. Aims are often written by national or state panels, commissions, or policy-making groups. Aims express a philosophy of education and concepts about the social role of schools and the needs of children. They guide our schools and give educators direction.

The terms *philosophy, aims,* or *goals* are often used interchangeably in reference to any statement associated with the broad purposes of education. As a rule, statements of philosophy and aims are the most abstract and general statements for the purposes of education. Furthermore, statements of philosophy are often written in paragraph form, with short statements of aims following them to further clarify and delineate the educational mission.

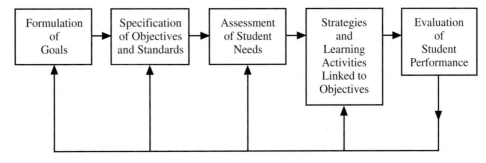

FIGURE 2.2   **The Linear-Rational Model for Planning**

Historically, aims of education have changed very little. For example, the "Seven Cardinal Principles of Secondary Education," written by the Commission on the Reorganization of Secondary Education in 1918, include many beliefs found in current statements of educational philosophy, aims, or goals. The seven principles include (a) health, (b) command of the fundamental processes, (c) worthy home membership, (d) vocation, (e) citizenship, (f) worthy use of leisure time, and (g) ethical character.

Goals.   Educators need to translate general aims into statements that will describe what schools are expected to accomplish. These translations of aims into more specific, subject-related terms are called *goals.*

Goals are more definite than aims. Goals are nonbehavioral and provide direction for educators, but they do not specify achievement levels. Goals are often written by professional associations and state and local educational agencies to serve as guidelines for school and curriculum guides for what all students should accomplish over their entire school career. General school goals are then written by school district personnel in more specific terms for each subject area in curriculum guides.

A number of school districts now use outcomes-based education, which affects goal statements and the subsequent translation into objectives and the evaluation of student performance. *Outcomes-based education (OBE)* involves focusing and organizing all the school's programs and efforts with an emphasis on clearly defined outcomes which all students must demonstrate upon exit from the course, program, or grade level. With OBE, there is more emphasis on the product of learning instead of the process as well as more emphasis on individualized learning. Various labels are used to describe OBE. *Master learning* and *total quality performance* are terms that are sometimes used to describe these same ideas. A curriculum guide reflecting OBE would state the content and also what the student should be able to demonstrate.

Subject-specific educational goals are written as a bridge to even more explicit learning objectives. Luckily, the task of translating general school goals to subject-area goals is not left solely on the shoulders of the individual teacher. Most school districts have curriculum guides that the district prepares, adopts, and makes available for teachers to use. These curriculum guides are based on goals selected by the district.

Curriculum guides commonly include subject-specific course goals, a fairly detailed outline of curricular content, and recommended instructional activities and materials. Curriculum guides are prepared by teachers in the district and are formally adopted by the school board. The guides ensure that the goals have proper coverage at appropriate grade levels. Teachers are expected to use these curriculum guides in their planning.

In summary, aims are translated into general school goals, which in turn are translated into subject-specific course goals. These course goals are in the curriculum guides that are made available to teachers. You would use the course goals in the curriculum guide to identify learning objectives for unit and weekly plans. When you prepare daily lesson plans, you translate the learning objectives into performance objectives. As displayed in Figure 2.3, general aims undergo a series of translations and ultimately result in a number of specific performance objectives used in daily lesson plans.

Textbooks, student workbooks, and other published instructional materials have great influence on the interpretation of aims and goals and on the curriculum in schools.

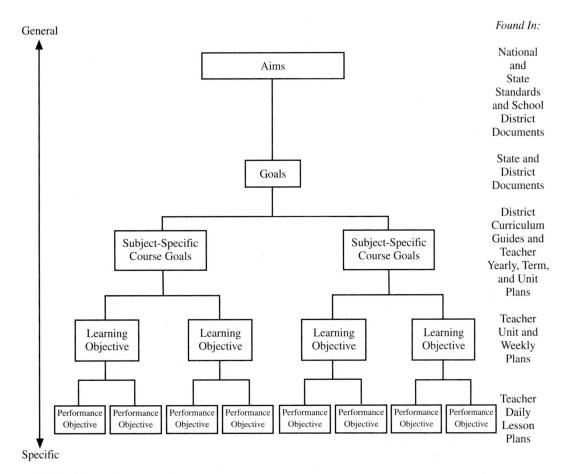

FIGURE 2.3 **Aims, Goals, and Objectives**

When preparing the content of printed materials and textbooks, publishing companies seek input from teachers through surveys and interviews. The companies also take into account goals for courses that have been developed by the state departments of education. Teachers, especially new teachers, tend to rely heavily on curriculum guides and textbooks for a large portion of their planning.

Teachers should keep in mind the students' cultural backgrounds when selecting printed materials and textbooks. In the case of a diverse classroom, James Banks (2007) recommends that teachers infuse different cultural elements—for example, heroes and holidays—into their lesson plans. Banks points out that this is an effective way to incorporate multicultural content into their lessons.

Specification of Objectives. When preparing unit plans, teachers commonly look at the subject-specific course goals and curriculum content in the curriculum guide for their subject. They then translate that material into learning objectives for unit or weekly plans. When preparing daily lesson plans, unit learning objectives are translated into performance objectives (see Figure 2.3).

Subject-specific course goals are more specific translations of district goals and are stated in curriculum guides. Subject-specific course goals can be translated and broken down into more specific learning objectives used in unit or weekly plans (Gronlund & Brookhart, 2009). *Learning objectives* are statements of what is hoped that students will achieve through instruction, and they are narrower in scope than subject-specific goals. For example, a subject-specific course goal concerning increasing student literacy might lead to a more narrow and specific learning objective about students writing a well-organized business letter.

To write learning objectives, look at the subject-specific course goals that are printed in the curriculum guide for the subject being taught. Then translate these subject-specific course goals into more specific learning objectives, which are included in your unit and weekly plans. From these learning objectives, you can then write more specific performance objectives for daily lesson plans.

Performance objectives are written for daily lesson plans and are stated in behavioral terms to indicate what is to be observed and measured. When writing performance objectives, you need to consider the parts of the stated objective and the learning domains represented. These issues are considered next.

Assessment of Student Needs.   The next step in the linear-rational model of planning is *needs assessment* or *diagnosis*. Diagnosis means looking at a situation to fully understand it and to find clues for deciding what to do. Successful diagnosis reveals (a) the students' aptitudes, aspirations, backgrounds, problems, and needs; (b) the level of learning your students have reached; and (c) where your students are weak and strong.

This information will help you make a number of planning decisions about both curriculum and instruction. With this information, you will be able to capitalize on students' strengths and intrinsic motivation and to help correct their deficiencies. This information also can serve as the basis for placing students in appropriate groups and for adjusting assignments; this is especially useful when assigning students to groups, such as for cooperative learning. Information obtained through diagnosis also helps you make decisions about curricular material to be covered. Areas of need can vary widely within the same classroom and therefore you need to be aware of both the general needs of your students and the specific needs of individual students.

The process of diagnosis involves seeing what the situation is and what should be done next. The steps of diagnosis are (a) assess the situation; (b) determine if there is any difficulty; (c) if there is any difficulty, identify what it is, determine its cause, and search for factors in the situation that would help you to make your teaching more effective and eliminate the difficulty and its cause; (d) make a final estimate of the situation in view of the information obtained in the earlier steps; and (e) make decisions on the basis of the final estimate of the situation.

Information for needs assessment or diagnosis comes from a variety of sources. A number of printed records are available, such as the cumulative record folder kept for each student, test results, anecdotal records, and even reports of physical exams. Indirect contacts also provide information. These include contacts with parents, other teachers who have had involvement with the student, the guidance counselor, and others. Direct contacts with the students also provide very useful information. This can be done through personal observations, through student autobiographies or questionnaires, or through diagnostic, formative, or summative tests.

What Would You Decide?   *Assessing Students' Prior Knowledge*

Before selecting specific content and instructional activities for a unit, it is useful to find out what students already know about the content in the unit.

1. If you were teaching about the electoral process in the state and federal government,

how would you assess your students' current knowledge?

2. What are some alternative assessment approaches that would bring novelty and variety to the class?

Strategies and Learning Activities.   In the linear-rational model to instructional planning, teachers formulate goals, specify objectives, and assess students' needs before getting to the point where they select strategies and learning activities. After carefully selecting the precise performance objectives in different levels of the learning domains, you need to select strategies and learning activities that will help students achieve those objectives.

There are many instructional strategies that the teacher could select to achieve the instructional objectives for a particular lesson. These include lectures, demonstrations, practice and drills, reviews, group and discussion methods, inquiry approaches, discovery learning and problem solving, role-playing, community involvement, and other approaches. Instructional strategies will be considered in detail in Chapters 5 and 6.

Here, it is useful to consider an important aspect in the delivery of the content and the choice of instructional strategies—planning for the sequence of instructional tasks. Sequencing has two basic purposes (Orlich, Harder, Callahan, Trevison, & Brown, 2007). First, it can be used to isolate knowledge (a fact, concept, generalization, or principle) so that students can understand the unique characteristics of the selected information or to isolate a thinking process so that students can master the process under varying conditions. This makes learning more manageable. Second, sequencing can be used to relate the knowledge or process being taught to the larger organized body of knowledge. This makes learning more meaningful. A sequence is process related in that it establishes a schedule for learning the various parts of the related content.

There are several principles that apply to all kinds of sequencing (Orlich et al., 2007):

1. Start with a simple step. Structure the presentation so the students can easily identify content. It is helpful to provide numerous examples.
2. Proceed to the concrete. This means that you should illustrate the objective or content with materials, models, simulations, or artifacts.
3. Plan to structure a lesson or learning sequence so that it becomes more complex. This means that you might introduce additional variables, generate new sets of

criteria, or establish relationships between the content of the lessons and other content.

4. You may introduce abstractions in which students are asked to generalize, predict, or explain information generated.

Evaluation of Student Performance.   The last step in the linear-rational model of instructional planning involves evaluating student performance. The issue of student evaluation will be thoroughly covered in Chapter 11, including selecting instruments of evaluation and preparing and administering teacher-made tests. But you need to make decisions about evaluating student performance even *before instruction occurs,* and thus it should be considered when making planning decisions.

While details about establishing a framework for evaluation will be covered in Chapter 11, it is useful to examine aspects of evaluation that need to be addressed when planning for instruction. The reasons for evaluation must first be determined. A classroom test, for instance, can serve a variety of purposes such as judging student mastery, measuring growth over time, ranking students, and diagnosing difficulties. Different purposes lend themselves to various evaluation measures. Evaluation measures include tests, observations, discussions, interviews, work samples, experience summaries, rating instruments, questionnaires, and other approaches.

Course content which is to be evaluated must be specified, and general objectives (learning objectives at the unit level of planning) must be identified. Then performance objectives need to be prepared in the cognitive, affective, and psychomotor domains. A table of specifications (discussed in Chapter 11) then must be created with the content and objectives placed within a grid. All these steps for evaluation need to be done before instruction occurs. Therefore, you need to plan for the evaluation of student performance when you are preparing your instructional plans.

The Mental-Image Approach

Despite the logic of using the linear-rational model for instructional planning, many teachers do not use that approach. Instead, they tend to develop mental images about how they think a particular lesson or activity ought to unfold (Clark & Yinger, 1987). This approach is called the *mental-image approach* to instructional planning, and it involves teachers forming mental images of the lessons they plan to teach after considering instructional routines and other factors (Morine-Dershimer, 1977, 1979).

Teachers think about and visualize lessons in greater detail than is generally written in a plan book. Teachers realize they must take into consideration their past experiences, goals for the children, the topics or content that need to be covered, materials available, the length of time available, and many other factors when they plan. When considering these factors, many teachers go through a cycle of comprehension, planning and preparation, teaching, evaluation, and reflection. This cycle is influenced by many factors including their level of experience; beliefs about teaching, learning, and classroom management; philosophy of education; materials available; and the particulars of the setting or context in which they teach.

Features of the Mental-Image Approach.   The mental-image approach to instructional planning is portrayed in Figure 2.4. Each component of the mental-image approach is described in the following sections.

1. *Factors related to instructional activities and routines.* When making mental images of a lesson, teachers often give primary consideration to the instructional activities and instructional routines described earlier in this chapter. Based on their mental review of these factors, teachers make tentative decisions about the instructional plans.

2. *Teacher characteristics.* The tentative planning decisions are affected by the characteristics of the teacher, as described earlier in this chapter. These characteristics serve as a filter through which the instructional activities and routines are considered. Thus, your tentative instructional plans may be modified as you reflect on your teaching experience, philosophy, knowledge of the content, and collective life experiences.

3. *Mental images of lessons.* Teachers begin to form mental images of lessons after they have considered the factors related to instructional activities and instructional routines, and these decisions are filtered by the characteristics of the teachers. Effective teachers usually plan by thinking of long-term and short-term plans at the same time. To plan effectively, teachers must consider specific, daily, and short-term plans simultaneously as they consider how semester goals and long-range planning will be accomplished.

A teacher's *lesson images* will commonly take into account objectives, materials, content, instructional strategies, instructional behaviors, and the like. The mental image will also include plans for weekly and longer-term planning. Once a teacher develops

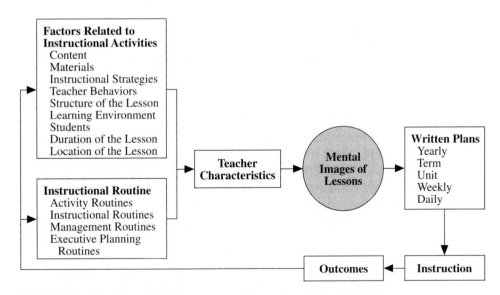

FIGURE 2.4   The Mental-Image Approach to Instructional Planning

the mental image, then the plans can be written but usually not in the degree of detail that was in the teacher's mental image.

While the arrows in Figure 2.4 indicate a regular sequence of events, teachers develop a personal approach to considering the factors related to instructional activities and instructional routines. This personal approach to addressing all these factors is affected by the teacher's thought processes.

4. *Written plans.* As teachers become more experienced, they have more to draw on as they create mental images of plans. As a result, experienced teachers tend to write fewer detailed plans than beginning teachers. Written plans include yearly, term, unit, weekly, and daily plans. An experienced teacher may have just a few notes or statements in the written plan, whereas the teacher's mental image of the plan may be rich in detail.

Principals commonly review teachers' weekly plans, especially those of beginning teachers. It is also important to have written weekly plans in the event that a substitute teacher is needed. While you may write yearly, term, unit, and daily plans, they are commonly not reviewed by the principal.

5. *Instruction.* After mental images of lessons have been developed and plans have been written, instruction takes place one lesson at a time. Thus, teachers actually implement the plans they developed after taking into account the factors related to instructional activities and instructional routines. Teachers use instructional strategies in an effort to have students meet instructional objectives.

Once again, the teacher's plan is not intended to be a rigid script but rather a flexible framework for the lesson. You may need to make a number of changes from the intended plan due to student interest and performance, the relative success of the instructional delivery, and other factors.

6. *Outcomes.* After instruction, the teacher needs to assess student learning, which is one gauge of the success of the planning. In addition, teachers assess many aspects of the lesson to determine whether it was successful. For example, you might reconsider the factors related to the instructional activities and the instructional routines. The experience of teaching the lesson provides additional information to draw upon when creating mental images of lessons in the future.

7. *Adjusting plans.* Planning establishes a proposed course of action that serves as the teacher's guide. Appropriate deviations from this plan can be made as instruction takes place. Teachers anticipate what is likely to happen during a lesson, but they may realize that the lesson needs to be changed somewhat as the events unfold during instruction. For instance, student enthusiasm, attention, and interest may cause you to make changes from the original plan. In addition, you may change the structure and sequence for ending class activities such as cleaning up, returning materials, returning to seats, and summarizing.

Good teachers expect to adjust their plans as they go along, and they plan alternatives so they are prepared to do so. Even during instruction, teachers might need to call on their mental images of lessons and alternative lessons to deal with the changing conditions of the classroom. The ability to adjust plans and instruction is a combination of forethought, insight, experience, and common sense. Middle-level and secondary teachers often have several sections of the same course. This enables them to modify a lesson and teach it differently in the same day. In doing so, they can make adjustments to the lesson, teach it to the next class that comes in, and see the effects immediately.

myeducationlab

Go to MyEducationLab, select the topic **Planning: Lessons and Units,** and read the lesson entitled "Strategy: Mini-lesson—Mrs. Armstrong Teaches Visualizing to Her Fourth Graders."

It is very helpful to write your reactions to lessons and suggestions for modification directly in the plan book. In that way, you can take these reactions into account when planning to teach the lesson the next time. By saving your lesson plans and weekly plans from one year to the next, you can refer back to the plans and the extra notations when planning the lesson in the new year.

ADDITIONAL PLANNING CONSIDERATIONS

In addition to the fundamentals of planning already discussed, there are a few other issues that you should consider as you plan for your instruction.

Backward Mapping

Backward mapping, which is sometimes referred to as *backward design,* is a planning tool that prompts you to begin planning by asking the following questions: What intended learning outcomes or goals do you have for your students? How will students demonstrate their achievement or understanding of these learning outcomes?

Asking what students are going to learn at the start of planning ensures that your lessons will be directly related to what you want your students to know and be able to do. You have worked backward, in effect, to design instructional activities that focus on learning outcomes. Therefore, what students should ultimately take from instruction drives planning, rather than occuring as an afterthought (Wiggins & McTighe, 2006).

The following steps illustrate the process of planning using the concept of backward mapping:

1. Select and then analyze the outcome or standard to be achieved.
2. Design or select an assessment through which students can demonstrate mastery of the standards; determine the required performance level, if it is not already given.
3. Identify what students must know and be able to do to perform well on the assessment.
4. Plan and deliver instructional activities that include direct instruction and teacher–student interaction. This process helps all students gain the knowledge and skills identified in the standards.

5. Provide all students with adequate opportunities to learn and practice the necessary skills and knowledge.
6. Assess students and examine their results to plan further instruction or individual support, if needed. If appropriate, give a grade or other feedback.

Backward mapping starts with your expected result: What do your students need to know to meet the performance expectation? If you want your students to do a culminating activity, such as using a PowerPoint presentation to outline the similarities and differences between *West Side Story* and *Romeo and Juliet,* then they will need to know many things. For example, they will need to know how to use PowerPoint, how to collaborate on a project, and what certain vocabulary words mean. They will also need to have a working knowledge of textual analysis, character traits, dialect recognition, and reading skills/strategies specific to drama and dialogue. Each of these areas of knowledge will be part of both assessments and instructional activities. By identifying where and how each assessment will occur and how students will receive feedback, then remediating as necessary, you can assist students to successfully meet the instructional goal.

Resources for Planning

Teachers can consult a number of resources when they begin planning for the schoolyear and for each unit and lesson. Many of these resources relate to the *curriculum,* which is the content to be taught. Resources are also available concerning how you go about instruction and how you might take into account related issues such as meeting the diversity of student needs, guiding student study, using instructional media, and evaluating student learning. Many resources commonly used by K–12 teachers are outlined here:

Voices from the Classroom

Working Backward When Planning

Rob Cohen, middle school language arts teacher, Franklin Lakes, New Jersey

For the first few years of my teaching, I found there often was a big gap between what I intended to do in my classroom and the things that actually happened. When planning day by day and week by week, I sometimes overlooked the final end-of-the-year goals that I wanted my students to achieve.

Finally, I changed my planning approach to first look at what I wanted my students to achieve by the end of the year. It then became more obvious what the intermediate steps should be to help lead up to the final goals. I could then more easily select the sequence of projects, novels, or other activities that would help lead to the end-of-the-year goals. By working backward when planning, I have been more effective in my long-range planning and in building the connections between the various units. I view this planning as a type of narrative that unfolds across a schoolyear but that is constructed in a deliberate way knowing from the beginning where you wanted to go.

1. *Curriculum guides.* A *curriculum guide* is a document that identifies the objectives and content to be included in a given grade level for a given subject. Not all districts have curriculum guides available. But for those that do, the curriculum guides are approved by the local school board, and teachers are expected to help students master that material during the schoolyear.

Curriculum guides commonly include subject-specific course goals, a fairly detailed outline of curricular content, recommended instructional activities, an annotated bibliography, and an annotated list of films, filmstrips, videotapes, computer software, and other instructional resources. Curriculum guides are often revised every few years, and teachers in the district who teach in the subject area of the curriculum guide usually have an opportunity to serve on revision committees.

2. *Curriculum bulletins or materials published by the state department of education or by professional organizations.* The state department of education in each state may have additional curricular materials available such as curriculum bulletins, suggested curriculum guides for the various subject areas, and related materials concerning the content. You could contact the state department of education in your state to inquire about materials that might be available in the subject area that you teach.

Many professional organizations prepare materials that relate to the middle-level and secondary curriculum. These materials may include resource books on the particular subject matter but also may include thorough descriptions of objectives, outcomes, and content for the various grade levels. The National Council of Teachers of Mathematics (NCTM), for example, has prepared comprehensive documents that outline and describe standards for K–12 mathematics instruction. These are significant resources for teachers of mathematics. In varying degrees, professional organizations in the other subject areas have similar resources available about curriculum and instruction.

3. *The teacher's edition of the textbook being used or instructor's manuals.* Most textbook companies provide a teacher's edition for each textbook that is used by students. The teacher's edition often includes chapter objectives, suggested activities and resources, suggested time frames for each chapter, lists of vocabulary words, suggested questions, and other guides. It may also include transparencies, lists of suggested test questions, and other resources.

4. *Other textbooks for the course.* In addition to the textbook that you use for your course, there probably are several textbooks for that course available from other companies. Even though the material might be slightly different, these books and their accompanying teacher's editions can be a good source of additional information. You might be able to use suggested activities, resources, or test questions listed in the teacher's edition, or you might be able to use photocopies of certain tables or figures.

5. *Professional journals and publications.* Most subject fields have a professional organization that produces journals, books, monographs, videotapes, and other resource materials that relate to the curriculum and instruction of that discipline. These organizations include the National Council of Teachers of English, the National Council for the Social Studies, the National Association of Biology Teachers, the Home Economics Education Association, and the National Art Education Association.

6. *Other sources.* Additional resources may be obtained from a variety of sources. Many public and private agencies have prepared materials that are suitable for middle-level and secondary instruction. For example, the National Dairy Council can be contacted about nutrition-related content and instructional materials. Similarly, many state and national governmental agencies have materials available. The extension departments of many public universities provide materials on request. Museums may have some curricular materials, and resources may be available from many community agencies. Parents and other teachers should not be overlooked as resources for additional information about curriculum and instruction.

Teacher–Student Planning

Teacher–student planning means that the teacher does not make all the decisions about the curriculum and instruction and that students are involved in some degree in the planning and decision making. The amount of freedom that you give students in cooperative planning will depend on many things, such as student maturity, student ability levels, the subject area, your educational philosophy, and the students' previous experience with cooperative planning. Teacher–student planning may not be suited to every teacher or every subject area.

There are several ways that students might be involved in this cooperative planning. One way is to present alternative plans to the students and allow them to select the plans they prefer. For example, you might give students the choice of several activities related to the unit objectives and let students select which activities will be used. Second, you might let students, individually or as a whole class, select their goals from a list of behavioral objectives. Third, you could propose a plan of action and then ask students for their suggestions and approval. It is best to start by giving students limited choices and to have successful experiences with those choices before moving to approaches involving more student freedom.

Team Planning

Teachers in some schools plan together, but that does not necessarily mean that they also are involved in team teaching. *Team planning* occurs when two or more teachers collaboratively prepare instructional plans. Planning procedures that a group of teachers use are often similar to the steps you might take when planning alone. The success of teams can be enhanced through the use of team-building activities and clarification of team roles and procedures. Time to plan and the authority to make changes are issues related to team collaboration.

There are two ways that team planning may occur. First, all teachers who teach the same course may get together to plan cooperatively. For example, all teachers of algebra may meet on a regular basis to plan a common curriculum for the students going through that course. These teachers may agree to a common set of course objectives, activities, and outcomes. They may even meet on a weekly basis to share ideas about weekly and daily lesson plans. This type of team planning for the same course occurs most often at the junior and high school levels where there may be several teachers teaching a given course.

Second, teachers from several different subject areas may meet to arrange for *interdisciplinary planning,* which involves planning and coordinating instructional activities and assignments for each subject area represented by the teachers. Thus, an interdisciplinary team may consist of the teachers of social studies, mathematics, English or language arts, science, and perhaps teachers in other subject areas. The team may meet several times a week. This type of planning is more common at the middle level where there may be blocked courses involving investigation of an issue from the perspective of several subject areas.

There are several advantages of team planning. First, groups can help complement the talents of each team member. Each person has strengths and weaknesses, and ideas coming from others in the group may help cover a weakness of an individual member. For example, one teacher on the team may not be very familiar with the computer software available for the unit under discussion. Collectively, other team members may be able to provide this information that the teacher would not have had. Second, team planning can help teachers address the interdisciplinary nature of the content they teach. Further, team planning can enhance classroom management. Teams may plan common rules and procedures that are consistently implemented and enforced by all team members. Finally, teams can help establish collegiality among teachers, which provides support and encouragement for all team members.

Voices from the Classroom

Student Input to Teacher Planning

Sue Watson, high school history teacher, Columbus, Georgia

I begin each course and each unit by asking the students to identify Why we need to study this particular subject and What we expect to learn. While I have already selected my goals and objectives, I will often find a way to tie in their ideas into the course or unit. I can add some of their ideas into the course and also can better understand what their interests are. This is particularly helpful when it is a required course that they are not excited about taking.

I encourage the students to write down the Whys and the Whats that we identified at the start. I want them to refer back to these ideas to see if we have met the goals that we set for ourselves. This What and Why procedure helps me to stay in tune with the students' interests and to tailor the course to the students.

Preparing a Syllabus

A *syllabus* is a written statement about the content, procedures, and requirements of a particular course. A course syllabus can serve the following purposes (Kellough & Kellough, 2008):

- states requirements, rules, expectations, and other policies and thus helps eliminate misconceptions about the course
- serves as a plan to be followed by the teacher and the students
- helps students feel at ease by providing an understanding of what is expected of them
- helps students organize, conceptualize, and synthesize their learning experiences
- serves as documentation about the course for those outside the classroom (e.g., the principal, parents, other teachers)
- serves as a resource for members of a planning team (In fact, each team member should have a copy of each other member's syllabus.)

Many teachers prepare a course syllabus before the schoolyear begins and give it to the students on the opening day of school and thoroughly discuss it at that time. Some teachers, however, prefer to provide students with an opportunity for input into the course syllabus. To do so, you could provide time for students to meet in small groups sometime in the opening days of the schoolyear. Have them brainstorm the development of their course syllabus; you might mention some issues that are commonly included in a course syllabus to guide their discussion. Each group could report its ideas, and consensus could be developed for the content of the syllabus. You could then prepare a copy of the syllabus that was agreed on and provide each student with a copy.

Whether developed only by yourself or in cooperation with your students, a course syllabus typically has the following information (e.g., Kellough & Kellough, 2008):

- *General information about the course.* List the teacher's name, course title, class period, beginning and ending times, and room number. This may include times when you are available for a conference, and perhaps your phone number.
- *Course description.* Describe the course, and mention how students will profit from it. This may also include a list of course goals and expected outcomes.
- *Materials required.* Mention the textbook, notebook, or other supplies needed by the student. Indicate what is provided by the school and what the student should provide. Mention what should be brought to class each day.
- *Instructional approaches and activities.* Indicate the type of instructional approaches you plan to use during the course, and also mention any special events or activities that are planned (field trips, experiments, guest speakers, special projects).
- *Course requirements and evaluation procedures.* Indicate the means of evaluating student learning: tests, quizzes, homework, projects, group work, work samples, and so on. Indicate the point value or relative weight for each of these items when the report-card grade is determined.

- *Policies on various issues.* Include your policy on late homework or papers, tardiness, absenteeism, extra credit, makeup work, plagiarism, rules for classroom behavior, procedures for completing work, procedures for various classroom tasks, and others.
- *A course outline of content.* Provide an outline of the content to be covered in the course. This should include some headings to reveal some details about the course.

What Would You Decide?   *Developing A Syllabus*

A course syllabus includes much useful information for the students concerning course content, procedures, and requirements.

1. Would you want your students to participate in the preparation of your course syllabus? Why or why not?

2. Would the grade level or the subject of the course that you teach make a difference in your decision about student involvement?

3. How might you accommodate student learning style differences as you develop your syllabus?

Planning to Use Academic Time Wisely

When considering how to use academic time wisely, it is first useful to examine the time that actually is available for instruction. Students are in school for several hours a day, yet much of that time is used for lunch, time between classes, and homeroom or announcement times. Of the allocated time, some time is used for announcements, collecting or distributing papers and supplies, transitions between activities, and other noninstructional events. Thus, the actual academic time is less than the allocated time.

Some students may be daydreaming or be off task, so the time spent in learning is less than the allocated time. The time students are actually paying attention and are engaged in action is called *time-on-task. Academic learning time* refers to the amount of time a student engages in learning tasks that yield fairly high rates of success. What really counts is for students to be successful during that allocated time. As you can see, the amount of engaged time is much less than the time students are in school.

To illustrate this, consider a 45-minute class. Within this allocated time, 5 minutes may be spent on taking attendance and making announcements, 5 minutes on describing an activity and giving directions, and 5 minutes for cleanup and preparation to finish the class. That leaves 30 minutes of actual academic time, but students may not even be fully engaged during all that time. Furthermore, their engagement during this time may not be entirely fruitful.

The amount of time students are engaged in learning academic content is positively related to their achievement in that content area. A student who is continually off task will not achieve as well as one who remains on task. Students often are off task in rather obvious ways, such as getting out of their seats, reading notes or materials, or talking to other students. Off-task behavior can often manifest itself in daydreaming or other forms of mental or emotional disengagement that may be difficult to detect.

To engage students in the learning process, you could (a) elicit the desired behavior; (b) provide opportunities for feedback in a nonevaluative atmosphere; (c) use group and individual activities as motivational aids when necessary; (d) use meaningful verbal praise; and (e) monitor seatwork and check it (Borich, 2007). You can begin and end lessons precisely on time, reduce transition time between tasks and activities in a lesson, and minimize waste time in an effort to maximize time-on-task and student engagement. The time available for instruction increases when you (a) follow schedules; (b) begin and end activities on time; (c) facilitate transitions from activity to activity; and (d) assign scheduled activities first priority rather than engaging in spontaneous alternative activities.

Effective classroom management and scheduling can lead to increased learning and a reduction of discipline problems. Good and Brophy (2008) indicate that time-on-task is important, but the task itself must be relevant, appropriate, lead to a reasonably successful outcome (such as designing the difficulty of the assignment to enable the student to have at least 80 percent of the problems correct), and be followed by timely feedback. Instructional time should be allocated in relation to the importance of the academic task.

Key Terms

Academic learning time	Learning objectives	Performance objectives
Active planning	Lesson images	Planning for instruction
Aims	Linear-rational model of planning	Postplanning
Backward mapping	Materials	Preplanning
Content	Mental-image approach to	Standards
Curriculum	planning	Subject-specific course goals
Curriculum guide	Motivation	Syllabus
Diagnosis	Needs assessment	Teacher–student planning
Goals	Ongoing planning	Team planning
Interdisciplinary planning	Outcomes-based education (OBE)	Time-on-task

Major Concepts

1. Planning for instruction refers to decisions teachers make about organizing, implementing, and evaluating instruction.
2. Planning is needed for the schoolyear, each term, each unit, each week, and each lesson.
3. The linear-rational model of instructional planning emphasizes planning in a linear sequence when formulating goals, specifying objectives, assessing student needs, developing strategies and learning activities, and evaluating student performance.
4. Aims are translated into general school goals, which are translated into subject-specific course goals. These course goals are in curriculum guides and are used by teachers when they translate the course goals into more specific learning objectives.

These, in turn, are translated by teachers into performance objectives for daily lesson plans.

5. Diagnosis of student needs provides information about student abilities, needs, interests, and backgrounds.
6. Plans for evaluation of student performance need to be made prior to instruction to be sure that objectives and content covered in instruction match those measured in the final assessment.
7. The mental-image approach to instructional planning involves teachers forming mental images of lessons they plan to teach after considering the factors related to instructional activities and instructional routines. With this approach, teachers think about and visualize

lessons in greater detail than is written in a plan book.

8. Additional considerations for planning include backward mapping, resources for planning, teacher–student planning, team planning, preparing a syllabus, and planning to use academic time wisely.

Discussion/Reflective Questions

1. Select one class session you recently experienced. Identify and discuss factors that the instructor might have taken into account when planning the lesson.
2. What are the merits for beginning teachers of using the linear-rational model for instructional planning?
3. Why should you consider aspects of student evaluation even before instruction takes place?

4. What does the term *lesson image* mean to you? What are the merits of using the mental-image approach to instructional planning?
5. What might be the merits and disadvantages of involving your students in instructional planning? What factors might affect your decision about involving students in planning?

Suggested Activities

For Clinical Settings

1. Select a course you are now taking and consider how content was sequenced in several class sessions. Consider why content was sequenced in that way. Describe alternative ways to successfully sequence the content.
2. List possible merits and disadvantages for both the linear-rational model and the mental-image approach to instructional planning.
3. Examine the course syllabi for several courses that you have taken. Identify features and content that contribute to an effective course syllabus. What information was missing on any of these syllabi that would have been useful to you?

For Field Experiences

1. Examine several curriculum guides that are produced by the district. Look at the goals, objectives, content outline, recommended activities, instructional materials, and other features of the curriculum guides.
2. Ask several teachers how they planned for instruction during their first year of teaching. Ask them to describe how their approach to planning might have changed as they became more experienced. How do they plan now?
3. If there are teachers in the school who are team planning, ask one or more of them to discuss the planning procedures they use and to identify the strengths of this process as well as any problems with it.

Further Reading

Morrison, G. R., Ross, S. M., & Kemp, J. E. (2007). *Designing effective instruction* (5th ed.). New York: John Wiley & Sons.

Designed for prospective educators, this book presents a 10-element model of instructional design. Includes real-life examples to reinforce concepts.

Posner, G. J., & Rudnitsky, A. N. (2006). *Course design: A guide to curriculum development for teachers* (7th ed.). Boston: Allyn & Bacon.

Examines how to develop courses with consideration of the content, strategies, assessment, and other factors.

3 | Types of Teacher Planning

Objectives

This chapter provides information that will help you to:

1. Describe ways that yearly, term, unit, weekly, and daily plans contribute to the planning process.
2. Describe the reasons for planning, the resources and factors to consider, the steps in the planning process, and the products for yearly, term, unit, weekly, and daily planning.
3. Identify the components of a daily lesson plan.
4. Prepare instructional objectives.
5. Select a format for your weekly plans and your daily lesson plans.
6. Apply the SIOP model to planning instruction for English language learners.

Types of Teacher Plans
- Course Planning
- Term Planning
- Unit Planning
- Weekly Planning
- Daily Planning

Components of a Daily Lesson Plan
- Identifying Course Information
- Objectives for the Lesson
- Procedures
- Materials
- Evaluation of Students
- Other Possible Items

Applying the SIOP Model to Planning
- Lesson Preparation
- Building Background

Comprehensive planning is needed for effective teaching in all grade levels. When making plans for instruction, teachers typically think of the big picture first—the entire course. Then, their planning is broken down into successively smaller subparts—into each marking term, each unit, each week, and finally each lesson.

When preparing a daily lesson plan, you need to make decisions about the instructional objectives, the standards that students are to meet, the activities and procedures that are designed to help students meet the objectives, instructional materials and resources, the means of evaluating students, and other related issues. You will also need to select a format for your weekly and daily plans that is functional for you. Finally, you will need to address the needs of English language learners when preparing your instructional plans.

TYPES OF TEACHER PLANS

Planning is a critical function to ensure student learning, and you will likely plan for two reasons. First, the planning process will help you organize the curriculum and address the complex classroom variables that are constantly blending during a typical

49

day as you make instructional decisions. These are variables such as available time, appropriate teaching strategies, available materials, and the level of student need or motivation. Second, the planning process will provide you with a sense of direction and a feeling of confidence and security.

Experienced teachers develop written plans for the course, term, unit, week, and day. Shen, Poppink, Cui, and Fan maintain that "careful lesson planning takes place at both the macro and micro level" (2007, p. 250). This means that a teacher should start by planning an entire semester, then plan units, and finally plan daily lessons. See Figure 3.1 for an illustration showing plans of different duration.

Plans for an entire course are more general than plans for each particular lesson. But course plans serve as a framework for term plans, just as term plans serve as a framework for unit plans. Thus, you will likely refer to earlier general plans as you proceed to more specific plans for each unit, week, and lesson. Teacher plans are more specific at the unit and daily levels, and teachers tend to deviate less from unit and daily

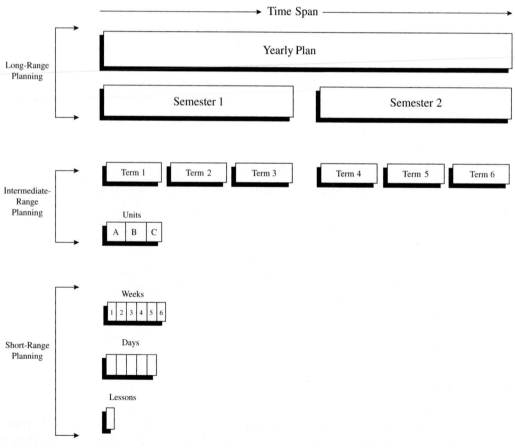

FIGURE 3.1   **Plans of Different Durations**

plans than from course or term plans. In addition, most teachers give equal importance to the planning they do mentally and to their written plans.

Course Planning

A *course* is a complete sequence of instruction that includes a major division of the subject matter. Courses in middle schools, junior high schools, and high schools vary in length. Some courses, such as required courses in English, social studies, and mathematics, may run the entire schoolyear. Other courses are completed within a semester, a trimester, or a quarter.

Course planning involves organizing and scheduling the content to be taught during the time allotted for the course, whether that time is for a year, semester, trimester, or quarter. School districts break up the schoolyear in various ways and have the courses completed within these time frames. When the schoolyear is broken up into two parts, each part is called a *semester*. When the school year is broken up into three parts, each part is called a *trimester*. When the schoolyear is broken up into four parts, each part is called a *quarter*.

Reasons for Course Planning.   There are several reasons for planning for an entire course:

- to become familiar with the content to be taught
- to determine the sequence in which the content will be taught
- to incorporate any changes in materials, textbooks, or content that may have been made since the last time you taught a particular topic
- to develop a rough schedule of when various topics will be taught during the course
- to make additions, deletions, and adaptations to the curriculum, taking into account your own particular circumstances and the needs of your students
- to plan classroom routines

Resources and Factors for Course Planning.   Several resources can be useful when preparing course plans. If available, the curriculum guide for the course may include objectives, an outline of content, and a proposed timetable for the amount of time to spend on each unit. The textbook for the course and the accompanying teacher's edition, if one is available, provide information about goals and content. The school calendar also needs to be taken into account when planning for the course because it indicates the vacation days, holidays, and other days that school is not in session as well as the grading-term weeks and other special events.

If you have taught the course before, the unit file folders that you have prepared are commonly full of useful information and materials that can aid in course planning. These unit file folders often include lecture notes, handouts, worksheets, audiovisual aids, quizzes, tests, lists of guest speakers, and other resources used in previous years. Teachers usually keep a unit file folder for each unit they teach for the course. Thus, the folders can be a rich resource when planning for a course.

Voices from the Classroom

Preparing Long-Range Plans

Sandra Clark, middle school mathematics teacher, Pueblo, Colorado

As a lead mathematics teacher in the district for the past three years, I have helped develop and update curriculum guides. Through that process, I realized more than ever before that I should use the district curriculum guide when preparing my long-range plans.

I now print monthly calendars and then write down important concepts on a daily, weekly, and monthly basis, and I use that calendar as an organizer when planning units and lessons. I intersperse the state testing preparation activities on the calendar, and add in dates for reporting grades for each grading period. This long-range planning calendar has also helped me get photocopies of instructional materials ready on time.

Steps in Course Planning.   There are several steps to course planning that can lead to useful results (e.g., Kellough & Carjuzaa, 2009):

1. Determine the course goals (to indicate what you plan for students to learn from the course) and the principal supporting objectives.
2. Decide on course content that is related to the course goals. This includes selecting the topics to be studied, arranging them into an appropriate sequence, and deciding how much emphasis to place on each topic.
3. Decide how much time to spend on each topic.
4. In view of the goals and topics you selected, determine your approach in the course, including basic strategies, major assignments, texts, and so on. A course syllabus is one of the products of this step.
5. Make plans to order special supplies, books, videotapes, computer software, and other materials and also to arrange for special speakers or for collaborative planning when conducting term, unit, or weekly planning.
6. Determine procedures for evaluating student attainment of course objectives.

The Products of Course Planning.   Course planning commonly takes the form of a general outline of content with specific ideas noted within the outline concerning course content, methods, and evaluation. Other accompanying materials are also produced as a result of course planning. You could keep these materials in separate notebooks for each course or subject area that you teach. When you prepare your plans for the term, unit, and week, you will likely need to refer to these materials:

1. *A list of course goals.* Using the steps in course planning as a guide, a list of course goals would be the first product you would prepare. You may determine these

goals after careful review and consideration of the goals that are in the curriculum guide, the teacher's edition of the textbook, state department of education guidelines, and other sources.

2. *An outline of course content.* For many teachers, this outline is a listing of the various units within a course and the chapter numbers and titles within each unit. This outline of units, in fact, may be the same as what is in the textbook that you use, or you might decide to change the sequence of the units.

3. *Notations for time to be spent on each unit.* Using that content outline as a base, you indicate how much time you plan to spend on each particular unit. For example, you could make notations in your outline that the first unit, consisting of four chapters, will be covered from the start of the schoolyear to the middle of October. Similar notations would be made for each unit.

4. *A course syllabus.* This is the printed material that you would give your students concerning general information about the course, the course description, materials required, instructional approaches and activities to be used, course requirements and evaluation procedures, policies on various issues, and an outline of course content. It is especially important that you decide about course requirements and evaluation procedures before the course begins and include detailed information about these issues in the syllabus so students are well informed.

5. *Notes about ordering supplies and other instructional resources.* You may immediately need to order special supplies, books, videotapes, computer software, or other materials, or you might make notes to yourself to order these items at a later point in the course. Similarly, you might need to arrange for special speakers or for collaborative planning at that time, or you could make notes to yourself to do this at a later point closer to the time the unit will actually be conducted.

Term Planning

A *term* is the amount of time the school district designates for the length of a marking period (typically 8 to 10 weeks) for report cards. *Term planning* involves the preparation of more detailed outlines of the content to be covered within a marking period or term. They are elaborations of course-planning outlines and indicate which units will be covered during that term. Term plans help you arrange for handling specific issues related to the curriculum and instruction of each unit; they will be useful resources when preparing your unit plans.

Term plans are commonly broken down into weeks, with an outline indicating instructional activities and materials to be included each week. The balance of content, goals, and time are important considerations when preparing term plans. Curriculum guides may include a recommended number of weeks to cover each part of the content outline. This is very helpful, especially for beginning teachers, when making decisions about the pace of content coverage.

Unit Planning

A *unit* is a major subdivision of a course involving planned instruction about some central theme, topic, issue, or problem for a period of several days to a maximum of three weeks. Essentially, *unit planning* involves developing a sequence of daily plans that addresses the topic of the unit in a cohesive way. Unit planning is considered by many teachers to be the most important phase of planning.

Unit plans have more detail than term plans and are often linked directly to major themes or concepts within the curriculum (e.g., exploration in social studies, fractions in mathematics, poetry in English, nutrition in science). A unit plan should provide increased organization and ensure that the material presented is accurate, thorough, and comprehensive.

Reasons for Unit Planning.   There are several reasons for unit planning. First, planning for units allows you to organize and sequence a related body of material into a series of lesson plans. Next, unit planning allows you to decide on the specific activities that you will use to teach the content. Finally, unit planning helps you gather and make the materials that are necessary for the various activities throughout the unit.

Teachers usually begin planning their units several weeks before they intend to teach them. In this way, you have sufficient time to develop your plans and take any needed actions resulting from your plans prior to the first lesson of the unit. For example, you may need to schedule a field trip, arrange for a guest speaker, develop a cooperative learning activity, or prepare handouts some time in advance of the first lesson.

Resources and Factors in Unit Planning.   When planning a unit, you will likely use some of the same materials used in course planning, such as unit file folders, the curriculum guide, the textbook, and the calendar. At this point, you need to give special attention to planning and selecting instructional resources. You might need to order or schedule certain videotapes, films, or guest speakers, or you might need to prepare various instructional materials. In addition, you will likely take into account your previous experiences with the unit, student interest, and other issues when planning a unit:

Steps in Unit Planning.   After selecting the unit topic, there are several steps that are commonly taken when planning a unit:

1. *Select the overall goals and the more specific objectives for the unit.* Since a unit involves a central theme or topic, one or more overall goals are appropriate. Each goal then will have several related, specific objectives. In unit plans, make plans to teach the course content at an appropriate level of complexity for the students. The appropriate level of complexity is considered in terms of the ability of students to (a) understand the material in its present form and (b) build on their understanding for future learning.

2. *State the rationale for the unit.* This step encourages you to be thoughtful and reflective during the planning process and helps link learning experiences to unit goals.

SAMPLE STANDARDS

Planning

There are ten INTASC standards (see page xxi), and each standard includes a list of knowledge, dispositions, and performances to indicate more clearly what is intended in the standard.

Since this chapter deals with planning, some representative statements for knowledge, dispositions, and performances from INTASC Standard #7 are listed here concerning topics in this chapter.

Knowledge

- The teacher understands learning theory, subject matter, curriculum development, and student development and knows how to use this knowledge in planning instruction to meet curriculum goals.
- The teacher knows when and how to adjust plans based on student responses and other contingencies.

Dispositions

- The teacher values both long-term and short-term planning.
- The teacher believes that plans must always be open to adjustment and revision based on student needs and changing circumstances.

Performances

- The teacher creates lessons and activities that operate at multiple levels to meet the developmental and individual needs of diverse learners and help each progress.
- The teacher creates short-range and long-range plans that are linked to student needs and performance, and adapts the plans to ensure and capitalize on student progress and motivation.

This rationale can help connect the unit content to the course as a whole. Also, sharing the rationale for the unit with the students enables them to see the importance of the material in their lives.

3. *Outline or organize the content.* Outlining the content helps you clarify the subject matter and provides organization to the unit. It helps you consider the most appropriate order of the content and examine the interrelationships among the content.

4. *Plan a sequence of daily lessons with appropriate instructional activities.* The lessons throughout the unit should enable your students to reach the goals and objectives of the unit. There are three types of lessons to consider in this sequence (Kellough & Carjuzaa, 2009). There should be some *introductory lessons* that identify the reasons for studying this unit, provide for preassessment and diagnostic activities, set the tone for the lessons to follow, and generally motivate the students. Next, there should be *developmental lessons* that build the learning that makes up the unit objectives and content. Many instructional strategies can be used, including lectures, questions, practice, group and discussion methods, and inquiry and discovery methods (see Chapters 5 and 6). Finally, there should be *culminating lessons* that tie together what has been learned in the developmental lessons. These may include review lessons, student reports, and some type of student evaluation such as a test.

5. *Plan and prepare for ways that students will be evaluated.* Student learning can be assessed in a variety of ways including tests, observation tools, work samples, logs, portfolios, and other approaches (see Chapter 11). Any assignments or other requirements should be included in the course syllabus.

6. *Gather and prepare the materials needed for instruction.* You may need to gather and prepare many materials for the unit. Materials to be prepared for students may include handouts, study guides, bibliographies, project guideline sheets, books and resource materials for the students, and various supplies and equipment. In addition, you may need to gather and prepare materials for yourself that will help you prepare for instruction or that you will use during instruction. These may include transparencies, notes, resources, texts, posters, maps, computer programs, or other items.

The Products of Unit Planning. Unit planning will likely result in several products. First, there will be a list of goals and objectives for the unit, a statement of the rationale for the unit, and an outline of unit content. Next, there will be a written sequence of daily lessons with appropriate instructional activities. The daily lesson plans that you prepare later will have more details than the brief descriptions of the lesson plans that are within the unit plan. Further, the materials needed for instruction will be prepared and gathered (e.g., handouts, study guides, various supplies). In addition, the materials needed for student evaluation will be prepared (e.g., worksheets, tests). Finally, the material that you need for yourself for instruction will be gathered and prepared (e.g., transparencies, posters, notes).

Strategies Leading to Successful Implementation of Unit Plans. It is one thing to successfully plan a unit by choosing objectives or standards, selecting content and materials, and sequencing lessons. Yet it is another thing to actually incorporate learning strategies that help students to learn (Marzano, Pickering, & Pollock, 2005). Some strategies that can be used to successfully implement your unit plans include the following:

1. Set clear learning goals for students, and let them personalize and record their own learning goals.
2. Provide students with corrective feedback and the criteria used in grading to help them to assess their own progress. Ask students to reflect on their own learning, effort, and achievement. Celebrate meaningful progress.
3. Provide an environment in which students are expected to articulate what they know about topics in the unit. Help students to link the information that they know

to the new information that they will be learning. Have students keep notes on what they are learning.

4. Vary instructional strategies and have students work both individually and as members of collaborative groups.

5. Assign homework that allows students to practice, review, and apply what they have learned. Then provide feedback on their performance.

6. Involve students in long-term projects.

7. Ask students to represent what they have learned in paragraph form and by drawing figures, comparison charts, and outlines.

8. Provide clear assessment of student progress concerning the learning objectives and standards and have students compare these assessments to their own self-assessments using the same rubric or criteria. Ask students what they have learned about the content and themselves as learners.

Weekly Planning

Weekly planning involves laying out the week's activities within the framework of the daily schedule throughout the week. While the degree of detail that teachers write in weekly plans varies, weekly plans for each class period may include a list of the instructional objectives, the instructional activities, resources and materials (e.g., the page numbers in the textbook, the title of the videotape), and student assignments. Many school districts require beginning teachers to submit weekly lesson plans to the principal for review, sometimes several days before instruction is to begin.

Consider student performance during the preceding weeks as you identify content to be covered and determine the pace of instruction. Identify what you expect the students to complete and how you will evaluate student progress. Interruptions and any special events (e.g., field trips, assemblies, holidays) should be noted in the weekly plans. The completeness of the plans and mesh of activities with goals are important considerations in weekly plans.

Using a Plan Book for Weekly Plans.   A *plan book* is used to display weekly plans in a brief way, commonly on a two-page grid format. In commercially prepared plan books, the days of the week are often labeled on the top of the grid and the class period or subject area is labeled on the left of the grid. Consequently, there is only about a 1½-by 1½-inch box to write the planning notes for each class period to be taught in that week. A sample plan book format for weekly plans is displayed in Figure 3.2. This sample format indicates the plans in the order of the class periods for each day throughout the week.

School districts often provide teachers with commercially prepared plan books to display their weekly plans. Due to the limited amount of space in the boxes of the plan books, you might prefer to develop your own format in a separate notebook. Regardless of the format that you use, it is important to prepare the weekly plans and write them in a plan book for your own use, for review by your school administrator, and for use by a substitute teacher in case you are absent.

FIGURE 3.2   Sample Plan Book Format for Weekly Plans: Version A

PERIOD SUBJECT GRADE	TEACHER _____ ROOM NO. _____ WEEK OF _____				
	MONDAY	**TUESDAY**	**WEDNESDAY**	**THURSDAY**	**FRIDAY**

It is possible that you will teach several subjects and need to prepare plans for each subject. For example, you might have two classes of algebra, two classes of geometry, and one class of trigonometry. If you use the format shown in Figure 3.3, you will need one page of that format for each subject area that you teach. You may prefer this format because it provides more space for your plans as compared to the format shown in Figure 3.2.

Daily Planning

A *lesson* is a subdivision of a unit, usually taught in a single class period or, on occasion, two or three successive periods. *Daily planning* involves preparing notes about objectives, materials, activities, evaluation, and other information for a lesson for a particular day but in more detail than in the weekly plan. Several useful resources provide additional guidance when preparing lesson plans (Karges-Bone, 2000; Price & Nelson, 2007; Schoenfeldt & Salsbury, 2009; Skowron, 2006).

Reasons for Daily Planning.   As discussed more thoroughly in Chapter 2, there are a number of reasons for planning, and many of these reasons apply specifically to preparing written daily lesson plans. Written daily plans help you clarify the instructional objectives of a particular lesson, precisely identify the content, determine the

FIGURE 3.3   Sample Plan Book Format for Weekly Plans: Version B

TEACHER _____   CLASS PERIOD(S) _____

WEEK OF _____   GRADE LEVEL AND COURSE TITLE _____

ROOM NUMBER _____   UNIT TOPIC _____

DAY	DATE	OBJECTIVES	PROCEDURES	MATERIALS	ASSIGNMENT	COMMENTS
MONDAY						
TUESDAY						
WEDNESDAY						
THURSDAY						
FRIDAY						

instructional activities and the specific means about how the activities will be conducted, and arrange for appropriate evaluation of student learning.

Written daily plans give you a sense of direction and a feeling of confidence and security about what you are doing. They help you organize, sequence, and become familiar with the lesson's content. The preparation of the plans also sparks your preparation or collection of the necessary instructional materials needed for the lesson.

To be able to plan effective lessons takes practice in developing the skills and knowledge necessary to structure lessons that are standards based, motivational, and built on students' prior knowledge and skills. Numerous sample lessons are available on the Web—some of them of excellent quality. However, individual isolated lessons that are not tied to the flow and structure of your instructional goals and objectives will add little to student understanding and skill building. Therefore, it is imperative that you gain the skills to develop your own lessons.

There is no single best format for a lesson plan, but the best plans incorporate many of the aspects listed in the following examples. Keep in mind that a good lesson plan is a way of communicating a pathway for student learning. Good lessons communicate; poor lessons do not. Lesson plans also help organize content, materials, teaching strategies, and assessment activities. As time goes on you will get better at the art and skill of planning based in large part on the feedback you receive from students, parents, and colleagues.

How Detailed?   The degree of detail that teachers include in daily lesson plans varies considerably. Experienced teachers prepare their weekly plans in a plan book and may not prepare any additional, detailed plans for each particular lesson. Therefore, an experienced teacher may write the objective(s) that he or she wants students to achieve, the content standard that students will be working on, and some short notations about activities and materials. From these short notes, the experienced teacher knows exactly how to conduct the lesson, whereas a novice teacher may need to write out an explicit step-by-step outline that includes the following:

- *Objectives/standards:* What will your students know and be able to do as a result of this lesson? Which national or state content standards are targeted in this lesson?
- *Instructional materials and resources:* What materials, texts, manipulatives, or resources will you need for this lesson? What technological resources will you need?
- *Learner factors:* How does this lesson accommodate different developmental levels of students? How does this lesson accommodate individual differences in approaches to learning, create connections between subject matter and student experiences, and/or include provisions for students with particular learning differences or needs?
- *Environment factors:* What student groups will be used? What changes will you need to make in the classroom arrangement due to the instructional strategy that you are using?
- *Assessment activities:* How will you determine what the students know and are able to do during and as a result of the lesson? (Is there a direct relationship with the objectives and the content standards that students are asked to meet?)

Lesson Plan Formats.   Throughout your teacher education program but especially during student teaching, you will be expected to prepare a detailed lesson plan for each lesson that you teach. The main purpose of this activity is to ensure that you have a clear representation of how you expect the lesson to progress. This outline can be invaluable as you reflect on the success of the lesson relative to both student performance and your ability to implement a plan successfully. If the lesson is not as successful as you would like, a detailed plan can help you to decide if the problem was in the plan

Classroom Case Study

Improving Lesson Planning

Terrell Green is an eighth-grade science teacher who has been teaching for two years. While he knows his content well, his lesson plans still lack organization. To spark intrigue and interest in his students, he likes hands-on and fun activities. Last year, Mr. Green's students worked in teams to create pop rockets with effervescing antacid tablets. To increase student interest, he added incentives by rewarding the team whose rocket flew the highest. However, he did not bring enough effervescing antacid tablets for one class, putting them a day behind. Also, his lessons took longer than he expected, and his closing activities were rushed and poorly executed. His students began side conversations when they realized that Mr. Green wasn't going to have enough time to finish the lesson. Further, students were not required to submit lab reports and were graded only on class participation. This left students wondering about the main goals of the assignment and did not provide them with closure.

Mr. Green has revisited his lesson plans and is having trouble finding the problem. He has a good mental image of his lesson plans and briefly outlines his objectives and developmental activities on paper. He puts little consideration into the circumstances under which his students will perform activities, however. He is looking for some guidance.

Focus Questions

1. What factors contributed to the problems in the science lesson?
2. What specific suggestions do you have for Mr. Green to improve his lesson planning and to increase the effectiveness of the lessons?
3. How might Mr. Green put more emphasis and accountability on students' assessment of their own learning?

or its implementation. As a beginning teacher, it is wise to continue writing lesson plans. As you become more experienced, you may find that you do not have to write such detailed descriptions of your lesson plans.

No single lesson plan format is used by all teachers, nor is there a list of universally adopted components of a lesson plan. As a result, you need to decide on the type of information that you would like to include in your lesson plans and then display this information in a format that suits your needs and preferences. Two sample lesson plan formats are displayed in Figures 3.4 and 3.5.

Some common categories of information are included in each of the sample formats. You may want to adapt these formats or use a different layout that is better suited to your specific philosophy, your teacher education program, or the content area that you teach. For example, if you have lessons in which you pose a number of questions to students, you might want to adapt the layout of Figure 3.5 by adding an extra column to the right side of the procedures list to show the main questions that you plan to ask during the lesson.

FIGURE 3.4   **Sample Lesson Plan Format: Version A**

TEACHER _____	DATE _____
TITLE OF LESSON _____	GRADE LEVEL _____
CLASS _____	UNIT TOPIC _____

OBJECTIVES AND STANDARDS What will your students know and be able to do as a result of this lesson? Which standards are targeted with this lesson?	
INSTRUCTIONAL MATERIALS AND RESOURCES What materials, texts, etc., will you need for this lesson? What technological resources (if any) will you need?	
LEARNER FACTORS How does this lesson accommodate different developmental levels of students? How does this lesson accommodate individual differences in approaches to learning, create connections between subject matter and student experiences, and/or include provisions for students with particular learning differences or needs?	
ENVIRONMENT FACTORS What student groups will be used? What changes will you need to make in the classroom due to instruction, materials, etc.?	
ASSESSMENT ACTIVITIES How will you determine what the students know and are able to do during and as a result of the lesson?	
LESSON PLAN OUTLINE[a] Introductory activities Developmental activities Closing activities Extended practice activities	

[a]In this section, you give an overview of the lesson introduction, development, and closing activities. These form the outline for a detailed lesson plan, in which activities and tasks are fully described.

FIGURE 3.5   Sample Lesson Plan Format: Version B

ROOM NUMBER _____   COURSE TITLE _____

CLASS PERIOD(S) _____   UNIT TOPIC _____

DATE _____   LESSON TOPIC _____

OBJECTIVES/STANDARDS	PROCEDURES (AND THE NUMBER OF MINUTES)
A.	A-1
	A-2
	A-3
B.	B-1
	B-2
	B-3
C.	C-1
	C-2
	C-3

Instruction Materials and Resources

Evaluation of Students

Assignment

Comments about the Lesson and Ideas for Revision

In any case, you will need to create a format for the lessons that you develop. You will probably create a master format on your computer so you can simply copy the file and type the detailed information about the lesson that you are working on. In this way, you have a computer file for each lesson, making it easier to read, print, and modify the next time you teach the lesson. It is helpful to keep lessons filed or organized by unit topic.

Beginning teachers generally benefit from writing down detailed, well-organized lesson plans and from the experience of conducting these lessons. As you become more experienced, you may be able to write your plans in less detail, knowing that in your mind you have made decisions about some parts that are not written in detail.

Parts of an Effective Lesson.   Take into account the three parts of an effective lesson as you make planning decisions about the content and sequence of events within the lesson. Many planning experts recommend that each lesson have introductory, developmental, and closing activities:

1. *Introductory activities.* These activities are designed to introduce the content to the students, capture student attention and interest, and set the stage for the developmental activities that follow. It is important to have activities at the start of the lesson to capture the interest of the students as a means to motivate them to learn that particular content. Introductory activities serve these purposes. Relating the lesson to aspects of students' lives, reviewing previous key points from lessons and stating the objectives and their purpose, and finding our what prior knowledge students retain are the types of activities often used at the beginning of a lesson (Serdyukov & Ryan, 2008).

This introductory overview of the lesson helps students understand what they will be studying, how the lesson is related to previous lessons, and how the lesson fits into the larger framework of the course content. This brief introduction about the lesson's objectives and about your expectations of the students is very important. Telling students in advance what they are going to learn, what the key points will be, and what the students should know by the end of the lesson has been positively related to student achievement.

2. *Developmental activities.* These activities address the content and are the vehicles for student learning. As discussed in Chapters 5 and 6, there are many instructional strategies to use, including lectures, questions, practice, group and discussion methods, and inquiry and discovery approaches. Furthermore, there are various ways to group the students for instruction, including whole-group instruction, small-group instruction, and independent work.

The instructional strategies selected must help students be successful in meeting the instructional objectives for the lesson. It is often helpful to plan for the sequential use of several different types of instructional strategies during a lesson to add instructional variety, to take into account students' attention spans, and to accommodate students' different learning styles.

For example, a lesson in a tenth-grade literature class might begin with a brief lecture about the parts of a short story. Next, the class may view a videotape about short stories and then work in pairs to analyze and identify the parts of a particular short story they recently read as a class assignment. The class might end with a whole-class discussion about these issues and perhaps a listing on the board of the key concepts. This lesson has four major segments with each part requiring a different type of activity and student role in the activity.

3. *Closing activities.* These are activities that are designed to provide a summary of the lesson's content and to allow the students time to prepare to leave the classroom. Effective teachers plan to stop the developmental part of the lesson a few minutes before the end of the class period to provide sufficient time for the content closing and the procedural closing of a lesson.

The *content closing* of a lesson includes a summary of the main points in the lesson. This helps reinforce the content that was covered in the lesson and helps students see how the content fits with the context of the other information in the unit and the course. The *procedural closing* of a lesson involves actions that help students get ready to move on to the next subject or class at the appropriate time. Students might use the time during the procedural closing to write down the homework assignment, put away materials and supplies, turn in papers, and get ready leave the classroom.

Some additional considerations in managing lesson delivery are addressed in Chapter 8.

Making Ongoing Changes.   You may have three classes of world history and prepare only one daily lesson that would be used for each class. Yet no two classes are the same; each has its own characteristics that will likely affect how you actually go about instruction. In one class, for example, you might have some students who have traveled to a country that you are covering in the lesson, and you might want to draw on these particular students during the lesson. Another class may work better with cooperative learning activities. Consequently, even before instruction begins, you may modify your daily lesson somewhat after taking into account the unique characteristics of each class.

In another case during actual instruction, you might find that the lesson is not working out in the way that you had planned. Students may have difficulty grasping the concepts, they may have little interest in the topic, or participation may not be what you expected. For these and other reasons, you might find that you need to alter the lesson during instruction. You might decide to alter the approach of an activity to have students work in pairs instead of individually, or you might shorten one activity and add in something entirely different. If things do not work as you had planned, you should change the type of activity or the manner of delivery in some way.

Tips for Daily Planning.   As you become more experienced at daily planning, you will automatically take into account a number of factors as you design each lesson. As a starting point, several tips are offered here as you prepare your daily lesson plans:

1. Keep all your notes and daily plans for a unit in your unit file folder as a resource the next time you teach that material.
2. Have some additional backup plans if something unexpected happens, such as a guest speaker not arriving in time or any equipment not working.

Voices from the Classroom

Changing Your Daily Lesson Plan

Edward Gamble, third-grade teacher, Jamestown, Rhode Island

Sometimes even the best prepared plans for a day may have to be changed because an educational opportunity may arise which needs to be seized. This happened last week in my classroom. We had a special assembly which was a sheep shearing demonstration.

The assembly was fantastic! Two people from a nearby farm sheared a sheep, carded and spun the wool, and discussed raising sheep. Another woman used a loom to demonstrate how the yarn is woven. They had brought five sheep with them, including two lambs.

I thought to myself, "Why should I stop this excitement when I get back to class?"

When we got back to class, we discussed what we had learned, and I tried to tie the discussion to content in our existing curriculum. I wrote some of the words the farmers had used on one chalkboard and questions I had come up with on another board. Then I had the class answer these questions in complete sentences.

I initially had not planned on following up on the content of the assembly. But I got some of the best discussion and work during that week because I was willing to change my plans when I felt it was called for.

3. Seek help from other teachers when planning; they can be a rich source of ideas and support.
4. Have the lesson's objectives tie in directly to the unit and course goals.
5. Be sure that each instructional activity addresses a lesson objective.
6. Plan for a variety of instructional activities within each lesson as well as varied use of instructional media.
7. Build motivational strategies into the lesson.
8. Arrange for a suitable amount of time for each instructional activity.
9. Provide extended practice activities to ensure students have opportunities for independent practice and skill building.

myeducationlab

Go to MyEducationLab, select the topic **Planning: Lessons and Units Lesson,** read the case study entitled "Early Reading," and review the sample lessons and activities.

COMPONENTS OF A DAILY LESSON PLAN

Written lesson plans might be displayed in various formats, but regardless of the format, the plans typically have the following information: identifying course information, objectives for the lesson, procedures, materials, and evaluation. You may want to add some categories of information or modify these components in some way. Some alternative formats for displaying this information in written lesson plans are provided later in this chapter.

Identifying Course Information

Certain information about the course, subject, and lesson is needed at the top of each lesson plan. This information can include the name of the teacher, the course title, the grade level, the room number, the name of the unit, the topic of that particular lesson, and the date of the lesson. Certainly, you will know this information, but anyone else reading your lesson plans will need it. Substitute teachers, for example, will need that information in order to use the appropriate lesson plan that you briefly described in your weekly plans. Your principal or members of your planning team also will also need to see that information on the plan sheet.

Objectives for the Lesson

Each lesson will have one or more objectives. An *objective* is a statement of the intended learning outcomes. Objectives commonly describe what the student will be able to do when instruction has been completed.

Stating Objectives.   As suggested by Mager (1997), each *performance objective* should include (a) an *action statement* identifying the action that the teacher expects the student to perform (e.g., Write an essay describing the process of selection of members of the House of Representatives); (b) a *conditions statement* identifying the conditions under which the action occurs (e.g., using information found in the textbook); and (c) a *criterion statement* identifying the criteria or level of performance expected of the student (e.g., All five major steps central to the election process listed in the text must be present).

Placing each of these parts together, we have a complete performance objective: "Write an essay describing the process of selection of members of the House of Representatives (ACTION), incorporating the five major steps central to the election process (CRITERION) listed in the textbook (CONDITION)."

Here's another example: "After practicing the concept during class in small work groups (CONDITION), the student will underline the key information needed to solve each of 10 word problems (ACTION) with 80 percent accuracy (CRITERION)." It is useful to examine each part of the performance objective in more detail.

Action Statements.   The action statement in a performance objective is always stated in terms of what the student is expected to know or do. This central action or performance by the student is observable by the teacher, and through observation or assessment of the performance, the teacher knows whether the student has learned the content or skill under study. To select a particular behavior, analyze the goals of the course, the content and materials available for teaching, the learning task prepared for students, and the skills or knowledge you hope they will retain for future use in school or work environments. After reflecting on these issues, identify an action verb. This action verb describes the student behavior you will observe as the student successfully completes the learning task.

Performance objectives are intended to give students clear statements about what they are to do or complete in the learning situation. Often, when first thinking about what students should be able to know and do, words open to many interpretations come to mind (e.g., *to know, understand, appreciate, enjoy,* or *believe*). Instead, words open to limited interpretations are desired (e.g., *to write, recite, identify, differentiate, contrast, list,* or *compare*). For example, it is very appropriate to have student appreciation of literature as an instructional goal, but that is an abstract goal. Thus, you should write performance objectives in observable terms, rather than with abstract terms open to many interpretations. Action verbs need to be selected that are specific and that clarify what is expected of students.

Conditions Statements.   Another important part of a performance objective is the statement of conditions or circumstances under which the students are to perform the task or assignment given to them by the teacher. These conditions or circumstances may include (a) materials given to students (e.g., with a calculator, without using the text), (b) time limits for the completion of the task (e.g., in 15 minutes, in a two-week period of time), and (c) the location for the task to be performed (e.g., at the student's desk, in small groups, in the library).

For example, if students are asked to list the states that border their own state, it matters a great deal whether they can use a map to answer the question or if they are expected to respond from memory. In another example, you might ask, "What rights does the First Amendment to the Constitution of the United States of America give to the citizens of this country?" It is important for students to know if they should turn to the Bill of Rights in their textbooks or if they are to respond from memory, and the performance objective should be written accordingly.

Students also should have the opportunity to master content in the form that will be asked on the test. If the textbook is not to be used during the test, students should be made aware of that before the day of the exam.

Criterion Statements.   The third component of a behavioral objective is the standard by which students' successful completion of the objective is measured. This level, sometimes referred to as the *standard of performance,* sets the level of acceptable performance for the objective. Some examples of criterion statements include the following:

- Five out of five parts of the definition
- 80 percent of the given problems will be answered correctly
- Write a topic sentence and at least three supporting sentences
- With 90 percent accuracy

While this level of performance is often thought of as the minimum level of acceptable performance, it should *not* be thought of only in terms of the traditional grading scale: A = 90 or above, B = 80 through 89, C = 70 through 79, D = 65 through 69, and F = 64 and below. Instead, you may want your students to master a given objective at a higher rate than simply a grade of D. The belief that students need higher than minimal levels of competence can be based on any number of related factors.

For example, the material may have been covered in the past, but it is essential for students to be confident in their understandings since the material is a building block to new concepts or skills. Material of this type is often referred to as *prerequisite information,* or information that is essential or required for successful completion of the next or related learning task. Without near complete understanding of this information, the student has little chance of successfully mastering the new concept or skill and subsequent related skills. Many teachers like to give students a pretest before a unit to make sure student needs are served by the objectives.

What Would You Decide? *Writing Instructional Objectives*

Lesson plan objectives should include the criterion or standard by which the student's completion of the objective will be measured.

1. If you were a physical education teacher and the lesson concerned effective passing in basketball, what kind of criterion statements would be appropriate?

2. How might you take into account the various levels of students' experiences in basketball and overall physical coordination?

Learning Domains.   One way of translating goals into learning objectives and performance objectives is to categorize the desired outcomes into a classification system. A *taxonomy* is a classification system that enables educators to precisely organize learning objectives in an effort to achieve specific outcomes (Anderson & Krathwohl, 2001; Bloom, 1984). Bloom's taxonomy of objectives is hierarchical, and there is a relationship among the levels of the classification system. Thus, the higher levels of a taxonomy are more complex than the lower levels, and each of the lower levels is built on to form the next higher level.

Bloom's (1984) classification system has three *learning domains,* which are categories for organizing the logically related purposes of the learning objectives. The three learning domains are (a) cognitive, which refers to mental or intellectual thinking skills and abilities; (b) affective, which classifies student attitudes toward learning; and (c) psychomotor, which involves physical movement and related skills. Each of these areas has a classification system to aid in the process of describing and designing the learning activities. Perhaps as much as 80 percent of what is learned is in the cognitive domain, with the balance in the other two domains.

Carefully consider the performance objectives when preparing lesson plans, because the objective will dictate the nature of the content to be taught. Furthermore, if you want to have students achieve a particular learning objective at a particular level of understanding, then you should assess the student only for that level.

The objective selected should guide your selection and presentation of content. For example, if students are expected to describe the reasons for Columbus's voyage, then more than dates and a calendar of events need to be presented. Also, the test over this material should be in line with the objective and content covered (i.e., test questions should deal with the reasons for the voyage if the objectives and content were about reasons for the voyage). In short, a taxonomy allows the cross-checking of objectives, instructional processes, and evaluation instruments to ensure that content is taught, practiced by students, and evaluated at the same level of complexity.

Teachers often select several objectives for a lesson, and information about the cognitive complexity of an objective can help you decide on appropriate teaching strategies to help students achieve these objectives. In this regard, you can use question prompts as a strategy to encourage higher-order thinking by students. For example, after reading from a text or source material, you can ask students to provide information on who, what, when, where, and why? From this simple technique, students can also be taught to use a list of question stems to form higher-level questions about the material they are studying. The following are examples:

How are _____ and _____ alike?
What is the main idea of _____?
What do you think would happen if _____?
What are the strengths and weaknesses of _____?
In what way is _____ related to _____?
How does _____ affect _____?
Which one is the best _____ and why?
What are some possible solutions for the problem of _____?
What do I (you) still not understand about _____?

Cognitive Domain.   The classification system most often used for the *cognitive domain* is Bloom's taxonomy of educational objectives (Bloom, 1984). Using Bloom's taxonomy, there are six levels of the cognitive domain dealing with mental or intellectual thinking skills and abilities. Descriptions of each level are presented here along with sample objectives that teachers might write for daily lesson plans. The sample objectives do not include conditions and the intended degree of success; these would be added by the teacher.

1. *Knowledge.* Included at this level are objectives related to (a) knowledge of specifics such as terminology and facts; (b) knowledge of ways and means of dealing with specifics such as conventions, trends and sequences, classifications and categories, criteria, and methodologies; and (c) knowledge of universals and abstractions such as principles, generations, theories, and structures. Examples include:

- The student will be able to identify the capitals of each state.
- The student will be able to write the formula for sulfuric acid.
- The student will be able to list the principal parts of a speech.
- The student will be able to state the quadratic formula.

2. *Comprehension.* Objectives at this level include (a) translation, (b) interpretation, and (c) extrapolation of materials. Examples include:

- The student will be able to identify transitive verbs.
- The student will be able to describe photosynthesis in his or her own words.

outlined in Chapter 1, there are eight components of the model, and two components relate to planning: lesson preparation and building background (Echevarria, Vogt, & Short, 2008). While these strategies were originally designed for use with ELLs, they are also helpful in meeting the needs of all learners in the classroom.

The excellent information from Echevarria, Vogt, and Short (2008) serves as the organizer for much of the content in this section.

Lesson Preparation

When planning lessons, teachers should consider factors such as content and language objectives, depth of content, supplementary materials, adaptations for the learners, and instructional activities that promote understanding of the content and also promote language development. Take the following factors into account as you make your planning decisions:

1. *Clearly define, display, and review content objectives with the students.* Content objectives should be written in terms of what the students will learn or do, be stated simply, and tied to specific grade-level content. It also is important to write the objectives on the board and to state them orally. It may be necessary to limit the content objectives to only one or two per class period to reduce the complexity of the learning task.

2. *Clearly define, display, and review language objectives with the students.* Language objectives should also be written on the board and stated orally. Recognize that acquiring a new language is a process, so sequence the objectives to give students an opportunity first to explore and then to practice before demonstrating mastery of an objective. Language objectives, for example, may relate to vocabulary, listening, reading comprehension, the writing process, spelling, and grammar, even while teaching a social studies lesson.

3. *Select content concepts that are appropriate for the age and educational background of the students.* When planning lessons, consider students' first language, second-language proficiency, and reading ability, along with the cultural and age appropriateness of the second-language materials and the difficulty level of the materials to be read. You may need to find reading materials that will provide the scaffolding students need to understand the content concepts. If students do not have much prior knowledge about the subject, you can provide a small-group minilesson that precedes the regular whole-class lesson. In some cases, you may also need to provide extensive background building.

4. *Use supplementary materials to a high degree, making the lesson clear and meaningful.* Information that is embedded in context allows ELLs to understand and complete more cognitively demanding tasks. You should use many supplementary materials that support the core curriculum and contextualize learning. Plan for supplementary materials that will enhance meaning and clarify confusing concepts, making lessons more relevant. Examples of supplementary materials include hands-on manipulatives, real-life objects, pictures and photographs, graphs, maps, bulletin board displays, multimedia, and demonstrations.

5. *Adapt content to all levels of student proficiency.* Make the text and other resource materials accessible for all students, adapting them so the content concepts are left intact. Be cautious about selecting reading materials suited to earlier grades; students may object to them, and the necessary content may not be included. Instead, adapt content through the use of graphic organizers, outlines (with some spots empty, to be filled in by the student), various study guides designed for learners of varied reading ability, highlighted texts, taped texts, jigsaw reading, and marginal notes.

6. *Provide meaningful activities that integrate lesson concepts with language practice opportunities for reading, writing, listening, and/or speaking.* Students are more successful when they are able to make connections between what they already know and what they are learning by relating classroom experiences to their own lives. These meaningful experiences represent a reality for the student, since they mirror what actually occurs in the learner's world. Authentic, meaningful experiences are especially important for ELLs because they are learning to attach labels and terms to things already familiar to them. Examples of meaningful activities include interviews, letter writing, simulations, and models.

Building Background

When planning lessons, take into account the students' background experiences, prior knowledge, and vocabulary level to design effective lessons to enable learning. Information about these factors will influence your planning decisions concerning content and delivery of instruction:

1. *Explicitly link concepts to students' background experiences.* A student's knowledge of the world provides a basis for understanding, learning, and remembering facts and ideas. This prior knowledge helps the student organize and learn new related information. When students have limited prior knowledge, three instructional interventions may be used:

- Teach vocabulary as a prereading step. In a SIOP lesson, teachers select words that are critical for understanding the text or the material and provide a variety of ways for students to learn, remember, and use those words. In this way, students develop a core vocabulary over time.
- Provide meaningful experiences for students. Connect students' prior knowledge and experiences to new content through authentic experiences.

■ Introduce a conceptual framework that will enable students to develop appropriate background information. This can be accomplished through teaching techniques such as graphic organizers and chapter previews.

2. *Explicitly make links between past learning and new concepts.* Build a bridge from previous lessons and the new content; students do not automatically make these connections. Learning is enhanced when new information is integrated with material, vocabulary, and concepts students already know. This connection to previous lessons can be accomplished by referring to outlines, charts, maps, time lines, and graphic organizers or by asking questions such as "How does this idea relate to what we learned in the last chapter?"

3. *Emphasize key vocabulary.* Vocabulary development is strongly related to academic achievement for all learners, but it is especially critical for English language learners. Systematic and comprehensive vocabulary development is necessary, and it should be included as a priority in planning lessons. Vocabulary related to lesson content should be introduced, written, repeated, and highlighted for students to see and use.

Key Terms

Action statement
Affective domain
Closing activities
Cognitive domain
Conditions statement
Content closing
Course
Course planning
Criterion statement
Culminating lessons

Daily planning
Developmental activities
Developmental lessons
Introductory activities
Introductory lessons
Learning domain
Lesson
Objective
Performance objective
Plan book

Procedural closing
Psychomotor domain
Taxonomy
Term
Term planning
Unit
Unit planning
Weekly planning

Major Concepts

1. The planning process helps you organize the curriculum and address complex classroom variables and also provides you with a sense of direction and a feeling of confidence and security.
2. Plans need to be written for each course and for each marking period, unit, week, and lesson within each course.

3. Weekly planning involves laying out the week's activities within the framework of the daily schedule throughout the week. A plan book is used to display your plans in a brief way.
4. Daily planning involves preparing notes about objectives, materials, activities, evaluation, and other information for a lesson for a

particular day but in more detail than in the weekly plan.

5. Performance objectives include (a) an action statement identifying the action that the teacher expects the student to perform; (b) a conditions statement identifying the conditions under which the action occurs; and (c) a criterion statement identifying the criteria or level of performance expected of the student.

6. Learning objectives can be written in three learning domains: (a) cognitive, which refers to mental or intellectual thinking skills, (b) affective, which classifies student attitudes toward learning, and (c) psychomotor, which involves physical movement and related skills.

7. When planning for instructional activities and procedures, select introductory, developmental, and closing activities within the lesson.

8. You need to decide what type of information you would like in your lesson plans and then display that information in a format that suits your needs and preferences.

9. The SIOP model can be used when planning to meet the needs of English language learners.

Discussion/Reflective Questions

1. Why is the preparation of a series of daily lesson plans not sufficient when planning for an entire course?

2. What are the benefits of unit planning? What might be some consequences if you did not conduct unit planning?

3. What is the rationale for novice teachers to prepare detailed lesson plans?

4. Should all objectives that you write be at the upper three levels of the cognitive domain? Why or why not?

5. How do *all* students benefit from use of the SIOP model in planning?

Suggested Activities

For Clinical Settings

1. Obtain a textbook for a course that you might teach. Select a unit within the text, and outline the introductory, developmental, and culminating lessons that you would include in the unit.

2. Write at least five performance objectives concerning content in this chapter representing different levels of the cognitive domain. Also consider if objectives in the affective and psychomotor domains are appropriate for this chapter.

3. After considering the information that you want to include in your daily lesson plans, design a lesson plan format that you would like to use.

For Field Experiences

1. Examine the curriculum guide for one course, and compare it to the textbook that is used. In what ways would the curriculum guide help you in your planning?

2. Ask several teachers to look at their weekly plans. Ask the teachers to describe how they

prepared those weekly plans and to identify factors they took into account when planning.

3. Ask several teachers about ways they plan to meet the needs of English language learners.

Further Reading

Gronlund, N. E., & Brookhart, S. M. (2009). *Gronlund's writing instructional objectives* (8th ed.). Upper Saddle River, NJ: Pearson/Prentice-Hall.

A thorough, practical guide that examines how to prepare instructional objectives in each learning domain. Considers performance objectives. Includes many examples and summary charts.

4 | Differentiating Instruction for Diverse Learners

Objectives

This chapter provides information that will help you to:

1. Describe multiple ways in which diversity is exhibited in student characteristics.
2. Select instructional approaches and ways to interact with students that take into account their characteristics to promote student learning.
3. Identify ways to differentiate instruction.
4. Describe ways to differentiate with the universal design for learning.

Implications for Diverse Classrooms

Sources of Student Diversity

- Cognitive Area
- Affective Area
- Physical Area
- Learning Styles
- Gender
- Language
- Cultural Diversity
- Exceptionalities
- Students at Risk
- Socioeconomic Status

Creating an Inclusive, Multicultural Classroom

- Create a Supportive, Caring Environment
- Offer a Responsive Curriculum
- Vary Instruction
- Provide Assistance When Needed

Differentiating Instruction

- Elements of the Curriculum That Can Be Differentiated
- Student Characteristics That Teachers Can Differentiate
- Instructional Strategies That Facilitate Differentiation
- Differentiating with the Universal Design for Learning

Just think about the diversity apparent in a typical urban classroom. There may be a wide range of student cognitive and physical abilities. Students may have different degrees of English proficiency, and some may have a disabling condition such as a hearing disorder. A wide range of ethnic characteristics may be evident, and various socioeconomic levels are likely to be represented. The students may prefer to learn in different ways, such as in pairs, in small groups, or independently. Some may prefer written work; others may learn best when performing an activity.

These examples are just a few of the human and environmental variables that create a wide range of individual differences and needs in classrooms. Individual differences need to be taken into account when instructional methods and procedures are selected. What are the sources of student diversity? How can our understanding of these student characteristics help teachers to create an inclusive, multicultural classroom? How can you differentiate your instruction to meet the learning needs of all students? These issues are explored in this chapter.

IMPLICATIONS FOR DIVERSE CLASSROOMS

Students who are in the classroom affect classroom management and instruction. Schools in the United States are very diverse and have students from different economic, cultural, ethnic, and linguistic backgrounds. In addition, you may find that your classroom has students with a range of ability levels or achievement, groups of students with skills below grade level, and students with special needs. All of these factors contribute to the diversity in your classroom.

For you and your students to be successful, you may need to make adjustments in instructional and management practices to meet the needs of different groups in your class. For example, you may find a wide variety of academic ability in your classroom and consequently need to vary your curriculum, instruction, and assessments. You also may have several students whose primary language is not English, and similar adjustments may need to be enacted. Your job is to enhance student learning, and adjustments based on student characteristics will be necessary.

Your understanding of your students will likely influence your decisions about ways that you will organize the physical environment, manage student behavior, create a supportive learning environment, facilitate instruction, and promote safety and wellness. To be an effective classroom manager in a diverse classroom, you should make a commitment to do these things:

- Get to know all of your students.
- Create an inclusive classroom by making instructional and management modifications based on an understanding of your students.
- Create a classroom environment that promotes positive behavior and enhances student learning.

SOURCES OF STUDENT DIVERSITY

Individual differences abound, and adapting instruction to student differences is one of the most challenging aspects of teaching. The first step in planning to address the diversity of students is to recognize those differences. This section explores differences in cognitive, affective, and physical areas; differences due to gender, ethnicity, learning style, language, or creative potential; differences due to exceptionalities and at-risk characteristics;

and others (Gollnick & Chinn, 2009). In the classroom, students rarely fall cleanly into one category or another and may exhibit characteristics from several categories.

Cognitive Area

Cognitive activity includes information processing, problem solving, using mental strategies for tasks, and continuous learning. Children in a classroom will differ in their cognitive abilities to perform these tasks. Thus, there may be a range of low-academic-ability to high-academic-ability students in a classroom. *Intelligence* involves the capacity to apprehend facts and their relations and to reason about them; it is an indicator of cognitive ability.

Howard Gardner (1983, 1995, 1999) believes that all people have multiple intelligences. He has identified eight independent intelligences: linguistic, musical, logical–mathematical, spatial, bodily kinesthetic, naturalistic, interpersonal, and intrapersonal. According to this theory, a person may be gifted in any one of the intelligences without being exceptional in the others. Gardner proposes more adjustment of curriculum and instruction to individuals' combinations of aptitudes. Do not expect each student to have the same interests and abilities or to learn in the same ways.

The work of Gardner and other cognitive psychologists provides ideas for teachers when selecting instructional techniques and differentiating instruction. When considering the cognitive differences of your students, you should do the following:

1. Expect students to be different.
2. Spend the time and effort to look for potential.
3. Realize that student needs are not only in deficit areas. Development of potential is a need, too.
4. Be familiar with past records of achievement.
5. Be aware of previous experiences that have shaped a student's way of thinking.
6. Challenge students with varied assignments, and note the results.
7. Use a variety of ways of grading and evaluating.
8. Keep changing the conditions for learning to bring out hidden potential.
9. Challenge students occasionally beyond what is expected.
10. Look for something unique that each can do.

There are many useful resource guides about addressing the diversity of students by applying the multiple intelligences to lesson activities (e.g., Campbell, 2008; Campbell, Campbell, & Dickinson, 2004; Fogarty & Stoehr, 2008; Lazear, 2003).

Struggling Learners.   A student who is considered a *struggling learner* cannot learn at an average rate from the instructional resources, texts, workbooks, and materials that are designated for the majority of students in the classroom (Bloom, 1982). This student often has a limited attention span and deficiencies in basic skills such as reading, writing, and mathematics. He or she needs frequent feedback, corrective instruction, special instructional pacing, instructional variety, and perhaps modified materials (Educational Research Service, 2004).

For the struggling learners in your class, you should (a) frequently vary your instructional technique; (b) develop lessons around students' interests, needs, and experiences; (c) provide for an encouraging, supportive environment; (d) use cooperative learning and peer tutors for students needing remediation; (e) provide study aids; (f) teach content in small sequential steps with frequent checks for comprehension; (g) use individualized materials and individualized instruction whenever possible; (h) use audio and visual materials for instruction; and (i) take steps to develop each student's self-concept (e.g., assign a task where the student can showcase a particular skill).

Gifted or Talented Learners.   *Gifted or talented learners* are those with above-average abilities, and they need special instructional consideration. Unfortunately, some teachers do not challenge high-ability students, and these students just "mark time" in school. Unchallenged, they may develop poor attention and study habits, form negative attitudes toward school and learning, and waste academic learning time. This problem is illustrated in Figure 4.1, which reproduces a real note that a middle school teacher received concerning the need to challenge the class. Many resources for teaching gifted students are available (e.g., Karnes & Stephens, 2008; Smutny & von Fremd, 2009).

For these students, you should (a) not require that they repeat material they already have mastered; (b) present instruction at a flexible pace, allowing those who are able to progress at a productive rate; (c) condense curriculum by removing unneeded assignments to make time for extending activities; (d) encourage students to be self-directing and self-evaluating in their

myeducationlab

Go to MyEducationLab, select the topic **Special Needs and Differentiating Instruction,** click "videos," and select "Challenging Gifted Students." Watch the video and answer the questions that accompany it.

The petition provided here is real. It was left on the desk of a middle school math teacher by a student who had become frustrated with his math class. The teacher was able to figure out that it was written by an identified gifted student. The student attended a large middle school in a small city in the Midwest. Twenty other students also signed the petition before it was given to the teacher.

WANTED: WORK

I, as a concerned and bored student, am protesting against you underestimating our abilities. I'm sorry to say that I'm writing this in class, but what we do in here is really not worth working on. Review, review, that's all we do. This class is no challenge. If I've learned anything in this class, it would be boredom. I want work. We want work. I have no intention to do anything in this class except twiddle my thumbs. I've found no enjoyment in sitting here listening to my teacher repeat things I've learned in the fifth grade. I'm sure others feel the way I do. Please, we want a challenge.

Sincerely,

Bob

FIGURE 4.1   A Petition to Be Challenged

work; (e) use grading procedures that do not discourage students from intellectual risk taking or penalize them for choosing complex learning activities; (f) provide resources beyond basal textbooks; (g) provide horizontal and vertical curriculum enrichment; (h) encourage supplementary reading and writing; and (i) encourage the development of hobbies and interests.

Affective Area

Education in the *affective area* focuses on feelings and attitudes. Emotional growth is not easy to facilitate, but sometimes the feelings students have about their skills or the subject are at least as important as the information they learn (Slavin, 2009). Self-esteem, time management, confidence, and self-direction are typical affective education goals.

While affective goals have played a secondary role to cognitive goals in school, they should be given an important place when planning and carrying out instruction. Love of learning, confidence in learning, and cooperative attitudes are important objectives that teachers should have for students. You may find a range of affective characteristics exhibited in the classroom, from low to high self-esteem, confidence, cooperation, self-direction, and the like.

Physical Area

Perhaps the best place to observe the wide range of physical differences among students is the hallway of any junior high or middle school. Tall and short, skinny and heavy, muscular and frail, dark and fair, active and quiet describe just a few of the extremes one can see there.

Physical (psychomotor) differences among students have sometimes been overlooked by teachers who are not involved in physical education (Woolfolk-Hoy, 2007). *Psychomotor skills* involve gross motor skills and fine motor skills, such as dribbling a basketball and drawing a fine line. These skills are integral parts of most learning activities. Indeed, psychomotor and affective objectives often overlap.

Physical demands on learning are obvious in areas of handwriting, industrial arts, sewing, typing, art, and driver education. However, they must not be minimized in less obvious areas such as science labs, computer classes, speech and drama, and music. Vision and hearing deficiencies also contribute to individual differences. You should recognize the importance of physical skills to the total learning program and explore the possibilities for including psychomotor development activities in classroom objectives.

Learning Styles

A *learning style* is an individual's preferences for the conditions of the learning process that can affect one's learning (Woolfolk-Hoy, 2007), including where, when, and how learning takes place, and with what materials. These styles may play an integral role in determining how the student perceives the learning environment and responds to it. Therefore, knowledge about learning styles can allow teachers to provide options in the classroom that would enhance students' learning.

Theories and research studies about learning styles are tentative and ongoing, but several promising areas of instructional assistance have emerged. These include cognitive style, brain hemisphericity, and sensory modalities. Students' learning styles can be addressed by using differentiated instructional techniques (Gregory, 2005).

SAMPLE STANDARDS

Differentiating Instruction

There are ten INTASC standards (see page xxi), and each standard includes a list of knowledge, dispositions, and performances to indicate more clearly what is intended in the standard.

Since this chapter deals with differentiating instruction, some representative statements for knowledge, dispositions, and performances from one or more of the INTASC standards are listed here concerning topics in this chapter.

Knowledge

- The teacher understands how students' learning is influenced by individual experiences, talents, and prior learning, as well as language, culture, family, and community values. (INTASC #3)
- The teacher recognizes factors and situations that are likely to promote or diminish intrinsic motivation, and knows how to help students become self-motivated. (INTASC #5)
- The teacher understands how cultural and gender differences can affect communication in the classroom. (INTASC #6)

Dispositions

- The teacher believes that all children can learn at high levels and persists in helping all children achieve success. (INTASC #3)
- The teacher appreciates and values human diversity, shows respect for students' varied talents and perspectives, and is committed to the pursuit of "individually configured excellence." (INTASC #3)
- The teacher is committed to the continuous development of individual students' abilities and considers how different motivational strategies are likely to encourage this development for each student. (INTASC #5)

Performances

- The teacher identifies and designs instruction appropriate to students' stages of development, learning styles, strengths, and needs. (INTASC #3)
- The teacher makes appropriate provisions (in terms of time and circumstances for work, tasks assigned, communication and response modes) for individual students who have particular learning differences or needs. (INTASC #3)
- The teacher analyzes the classroom environment and makes decisions and adjustments to enhance social relationships, student motivation and engagement, and productive work. (INTASC #5)

Cognitive Style.   Cognitive style should be considered in planning. *Cognitive style* refers to the way people process information and use strategies in responding to tasks. Conceptual tempo and field dependence/field independence are two categories of cognitive style that educators may consider when planning instruction.

First, *conceptual tempo* deals with students being impulsive or reflective when selecting from two or more alternatives. For example, impulsive students look at alternatives only briefly and select one quickly. They may make many errors because they do not take time to consider all the alternatives. However, not all cognitively impulsive students are fast *and* inaccurate. On the other hand, reflective students deliberate among the alternatives and respond more slowly.

Second, *field dependence/field independence* (sometimes referred to as *global/analytic style*) deals with the extent to which individuals can overcome effects of distracting background elements (the field) when trying to differentiate among relevant aspects of a particular situation. You can expect field-dependent students to be more people oriented, to work best in groups, and to prefer subjects such as history and literature. Field-independent students would prefer science, problem-solving tasks, and instructional approaches requiring little social interaction (Slavin, 2009). Field-dependent students respond more to verbal praise and extrinsic motivation, while field-independent students tend to pursue their own goals and respond best to intrinsic motivation.

Brain Hemisphericity.   *Brain hemisphericity* is another aspect of student preferences for learning environments. The two halves of the brain appear to serve different functions, even though they are connected by a complex network which orchestrates their teamwork (Sousa, 2006). Each side is dominant in certain respects. Left-brain-dominant people tend to be more analytical in their orientation, being generally logical, concrete, and sequential. Right-brain-dominant people tend to be more visually and spatially oriented and more wholistic in their thinking.

Teacher presentations focusing on left-hemisphere activity include lecture, discussion, giving verbal clues, explaining rules, and asking yes–no and either–or questions in content areas. Useful materials include texts, word lists, workbook exercises, readings, and drill tapes. To develop left-hemisphere functions, teachers should (a) introduce and teach some material in the linear mode, (b) sequence the learning for meaning and retention, (c) conduct question-and-answer periods, (d) emphasize the meanings of words and sentences, and (e) increase student proficiency with information-processing skills such as note taking, memorization, and recall.

Teacher presentations featuring right-hemisphere activity involve demonstration, experiences, open-ended questions, nonverbal clues, manipulations, and divergent thinking activity. Useful materials for these activities include flashcards, maps, films, audiotapes for main ideas, drawings, and manipulatives. To develop right-hemisphere functions, teachers should (a) encourage intuitive thinking and "guess-timating," (b) allow for testing of ideas and principles, (c) introduce some material in the visual/spatial mode, (d) use some nonsequential modes for instruction, and (e) integrate techniques from art, music, and physical education into social science, science, and language arts disciplines.

Voices from the Classroom

Learning Styles

Loraine Chapman, instructional technology training, Tucson, Arizona

Shortly after I began teaching, I noticed that students react differently to learning tasks. For example, Kelly stated that unless she can hear the words she reads, she has difficulty comprehending. Delila needs complete silence when she reads and will even put her fingers in her ears when reading to make it quieter. When given the option, some students always select a partner for work, while others work alone.

After gathering more information about learning styles, I began to incorporate that information into my lesson plans and developed strategies to take into account the various cognitive learning styles of my students. For example, sometimes I let students choose from a list of activities that all fulfill the lesson's objectives, but each activity involves a different type of learning experience reflecting the various learning styles.

I also believe that students need to learn to stretch and use all learning styles. So within a class, or over a few days or a week, tasks using all learning styles will be incorporated into the lessons, and each student must complete each activity, no matter what the learning style.

Sensory Modality. Sensory modality is a third factor in students' preferences for a learning environment. A *sensory modality* is a system of interacting with the environment through one or more of the basic senses: sight, hearing, touch, smell, and taste. The most important sensory modalities for teachers are the visual, auditory, and kinesthetic modes. Information to be learned is first received through one of the senses. The information is either forgotten after a few seconds or, after initial processing, is placed in short-term or long-term memory. Learning may be enhanced when the information is received through a preferred sensory modality. Use a variety of instructional approaches that enable the students to receive the content through one or more of the basic senses.

Gender

There are obviously differences between males and females, and some of those differences influence students' performance at school. Researchers have found that females generally are more extroverted, anxious, and trusting; are less assertive; and have slightly lower self-esteem than males of the same age and background. Females' verbal and motor skills also tend to develop faster than those of males (Berk, 2008, 2007; Sadker & Silber, 2007).

Gender differences are caused by a combination of genetics and environment. These differences are examined in *Boys and Girls Learn Differently* (Gurian & Henley, 2001), which includes discussions concerning elementary, middle, and high school classrooms. Concerns about boys' performance in school are examined in sources such as *The Minds of Boys* (Gurian & Stevens, 2005) and *Teaching the Male Brain* (James, 2007).

In a study by Auwarter and Aruguete (2008), teachers' perceptions and expectations for students were shaped by students' gender and socioeconomic status (SES). Teachers rated high-SES boys more favorably than low-SES boys but low-SES girls more favorably than high-SES girls. Teachers perceived that low-SES students have less promising futures than do high-SES students. Findings suggest that teachers are likely to develop negative attitudes toward low-SES students in general but especially boys. The study did not find that all teachers have these preconceived attitudes but suggests that teachers should be cautious about holding differing expectations for students based on gender or SES.

There are also gender differences in career preparation and career choice. Teachers should keep both boys and girls academically motivated, especially in science, technology, engineering, and math areas, where gender-based differences in career choices still exist. To address this, you can do these things (Tsui, 2007):

- Provide students with a mix of successful male and female role models.
- Make sure that girls take an active part in math and science classes, especially given boys' tendency to be more assertive in such settings.
- Use more hands-on experiments and group activities and less teaching by telling and lecturing.
- Allow students to investigate real-world problems, both large and small.
- Encourage students to see that academic achievement is more a product of effort than of natural ability.
- Help parents recognize the importance of having gender-neutral expectations for their children's education.

What can you do to prevent gender inequity in your classroom? First, be aware that you may have stereotypical attitudes that influence the ways you interact with boys and girls. Research indicates that teachers interact with boys more often and ask them more questions; boys are also more likely to ask questions and volunteer comments about ideas being discussed in class (Good & Brophy, 2008). These patterns can lead to girls being less involved in learning activities and ultimately having lower achievement.

You can make your classroom more gender friendly for all students by following these guidelines: (a) incorporate movement in instruction, (b) make learning visual, (c) give students choice and control, (d) provide opportunities for social interaction, (e) find ways to make learning real, (f) blend art and music into the curriculum, (g) connect with your students, (h) promote character development for the benefit of the individuals and the classroom environment, and (i) encourage equal participation (Gurian, Stevens, & King, 2008; James, 2007).

Language

Some students come from homes where English is not the primary language or is not spoken at all. They may have limited proficiency in English. In descending order, Spanish, French, German, Italian, and Chinese are the top five languages spoken at home other than English. This fact has a bearing on teachers' decisions about management and work.

There are four major instructional models for serving English language learners (Rothenberg & Fisher, 2007), each varying in the degree to which it incorporates the student's first language and the approach it takes in delivering academic content:

1. instructional methods using the student's first language (which are transitional programs)
2. instructional methods using the first language as support
3. instructional methods using English as a second language
4. content-based instruction or sheltered instructional methods

Presently, one in nine students in U.S. public schools, or over 5 million students, have limited English proficiency. This is an increase of 150 percent over the last decade. Some estimates claim that by 2025, one in four public K–12 students will come from a home where a language other than English is spoken (NCELA, 2005, 2006). Many students will have limited English proficiency when they begin school, and some will remain less than completely fluent for years (Goldenberg, 2008).

As an educator, it is increasingly likely that you will have English language learners in your classes. To help address the learning needs of ELLs, apply the following principles:

1. *Instruction in the primary language aids achievement.* Academic instruction in the student's home language should be part of the educational program of an ELL when possible. The National Literacy Panel conducted a meta-analysis of experimental studies and concluded that teaching reading skills in the first language is modestly more effective in terms of second-language achievement than immersing children in English (August & Shanahan, 2006).

2. *Good instruction for English language learners is similar to good instruction for other English-speaking students.* Primary-language instruction is often not feasible for various reasons, including the fact that over 400 different languages are spoken in the United States (Capps, Fix, Murray, Passel, & Herwantoro, 2005). The best evidence researchers have suggests that ELLs learn much the same way as other students and that good instruction for students in general tends to be good instruction for ELLs in particular. Thus, English language learners benefit from (a) clear goals and objectives, (b) well-designed instructional routines, (c) active engagement and participation, (d) informative feedback, (e) opportunities to practice and apply new learning and transfer it to new situations, (f) periodic review and practice, (g) opportunities to interact with other students, and (h) frequent assessments, with reteaching as needed (Marzano, 2007).

3. *English language learners require instructional accommodations.* While general principles of effective instruction should be the basis for instructing ELLs, these students need certain accommodations. The National Literacy Panel found that the impact of instructional interventions is weaker for English learners than it is for English speakers, suggesting that additional supports or accommodations are needed for ELLs to derive as much benefit from effective instructional practices. These additional supports or accommodations include the following:

- using the primary language strategically
- providing predictable, clear, and consistent instructions, expectations, and routines

- offering extended explanations and additional opportunities for practice
- providing redundant information, such as visual cues and physical gestures
- focusing on the similarities/differences between English and the native language
- building on students' knowledge and skills in the native language
- identifying and clarifying difficult words and passages
- consolidating text knowledge through summarization
- providing extra practice in reading words, sentences, and stories
- providing opportunities to have students work in pairs or small groups with tutors
- discriminating and manipulating the sounds of the language (phonemic awareness)
- decoding words (phonics)
- targeting vocabulary and checking comprehension frequently
- paraphrasing students' remarks and encouraging expansion

Providing instruction in English language development and opportunities to extend oral English skills are critical for ELLs. Every lesson should target both course content and English language development. Students must make rapid progress in their oral English skills if they are to enter the educational mainstream and derive maximum benefit from classroom instruction delivered in English. To do so, they must have a supportive learning environment (Goldenberg, 2008; Slavin, Cheung, Groff, & Lake, 2004).

Classroom Case Study

Adjustments for English Language Learners

Jason Kulpinski teaches high school history in an urban school in which 25 percent of the students are Hispanic and many are English language learners. To introduce his classes to some of the major events and themes of U.S. history, Mr. Kulpinski uses short texts: texts that can be read in one sitting and that combine both words and pictures to tell a story. He has found that all the students in his classes have benefited from reading the short texts.

The short texts provide ELLs with background knowledge on the content they will learn in the course. Without this background, many students would have no prior knowledge as a reference point for learning new content in the unit. With the design of words and pictures providing context clues, the short texts help struggling readers and English language learners to negotiate meaning from the material.

Mr. Kulpinski has seen many of his hesitant readers grow in confidence after they have read several short texts and been able to comprehend the content. Class discussions also have been enhanced by the use of short texts.

Focus Questions
1. How does Mr. Kulpinski's strategy of using short texts help him to teach diverse learners?
2. How do all learners in the classroom benefit from this strategy?

Cultural Diversity

Cultural diversity is reflected in the wide variety of values, beliefs, attitudes, and rules that define regional, ethnic, religious, and other culture groups. Minority populations wish their cultures to be recognized as unique and preserved for their children. The message from all cultural groups to schools is clear: Make sure that each student from every cultural group succeeds in school.

Culturally responsive teaching is instruction that acknowledges cultural diversity (Gay, 2000, 2005). It attempts to accomplish this goal in three ways: (a) accepting and valuing cultural differences, (b) accommodating different cultural interaction patterns, and (c) building on students' cultural backgrounds. Culturally responsive teachers use the best of what is known about good teaching, including strategies such as these (Irvine & Armento, 2001):

■ connecting students' prior knowledge and cultural experiences with new concepts by constructing and designing relevant cultural metaphors and images
■ understanding students' cultural knowledge and experiences and selecting appropriate instructional materials
■ helping students to find meaning and purpose in what is to be learned
■ using interactive teaching strategies
■ allowing students to participate in planning
■ using familiar speech and events
■ helping learners construct meaning by organizing, elaborating, and representing knowledge in their own way
■ using primary sources of data and manipulative materials

In a culturally relevant classroom, the student's culture is seen as a source of strength on which to rely, not as a problem to be overcome or as something to be overlooked (Ladson-Billings, 1997). Teachers can weave a range of cultural perspectives throughout the curriculum to make education more relevant for students who see their cultures recognized. In doing so, teachers need to be aware of a variety of cultural experiences to understand how different students may learn best (Moje, Collazo, Carillo, & Marx, 2001). Learning about the various cultures is important. Resources such as *Through Ebony Eyes* (Thompson, 2004) and *Up Where We Belong* (Thompson, 2007) provide information about helping African American and Latino students in school.

Each cultural group teaches its members certain lessons about living. Differences exist among cultures in the way members conduct interpersonal relationships, arrive on time, use body language, cooperate with group members, and accept directions from authority figures. You need to treat each student as an individual first, because that student is the product of many influences. Many resources are available concerning cultural diversity (e.g., Banks, 2006; Gollnick & Chinn, 2009). As you consider individual differences produced by cultural diversity, you should do the following:

1. Examine your own values and beliefs for evidences of bias and stereotyping.
2. Regard students as individuals first, with membership in a culture group as only one factor in understanding that individual.
3. Learn something about students' family and community relationships.
4. Consider nonstandard English and native languages as basic languages for students from culturally diverse populations to support gradual but necessary instruction in the majority language.
5. Allow students to work in cross-cultural teams and facilitate cooperation while noting qualities and talents that emerge.
6. Infuse the curriculum with regular emphasis on other cultures, rather than providing just one unit a year or a few isolated and stereotyped activities.

What Would You Decide?   *Your Culture Is Different*

Many classrooms have students from a variety of ethnic and cultural backgrounds. It is possible that you will feel disconnected from your students because you have a different ethnicity or different cultural background from your students.

1. What can you do so that you and your students feel comfortable with one another?
2. What can you do so that the different backgrounds do not contribute to misunderstandings and off-task behavior?

Exceptionalities

Exceptional students include those who need special help and resources to reach their full potential. Exceptionalities include both disabilities and giftedness.

More than 10 percent of students in the United States are identified as having disabling conditions that justify placement in a special education program (Turnbull & Turnbull, 2007). This figure increases to 15 percent when gifted children are counted as special education students. Categories for special education services include learning disabilities, speech or language impairment, mental retardation, emotional or behavioral disabilities, other health impairment, multiple disabilities, hearing impairment, orthopedic impairment, visual impairment, deafness or blindness, traumatic brain injury, and autism spectrum disorder.

myeducationlab

Go to MyEducationLab, select the topic **Planning: Lessons and Units,** click "simulation," and select "Instructional Accommodations." Execute the simulation and complete the questions that accompany it.

The Individuals with Disabilities Education Act (IDEA) committed the United States to a policy of mainstreaming students who have handicapping conditions by placing them in the least restrictive environment in which they can function successfully while having their special needs met. The degree to which they are treated differently is to be minimized. The *least restrictive environment* means that students with special needs are placed in special settings only if necessary and only for as long as necessary; the regular classroom is the preferred least restrictive placement.

Students with Learning Disabilities in the Regular Classroom

Linda Innes, seventh-grade language arts teacher, Kansas City, Missouri

I teach one class that is labeled a class-within-a-class, which means that students identified as being learning disabled (LD) are placed in the same class with regular middle school students. To help meet state standards required for LD students, the learning disability teacher co-teaches the class with me. To meet the students' needs in this class, I do several things to be very clear and specific when teaching or giving directions.

First, I give directions in various ways. I have two or three other students repeat the directions I just gave. Also, it is helpful to have the students write down the directions, especially for homework.

Second, I give instruction thoroughly and slowly. When the students are taking notes, I speak in a slower manner, write out the notes word for word on the overhead projector, repeat what I have written and spoken several times, and monitor the room and the notes of the students to make sure that they are getting them copied down correctly. There are times when I or the LD teacher actually write the notes for some of the students or provide a photocopy due to the severe writing handicaps or slow processing skills.

Third, I place each LD student next to an academically strong student who can provide help whenever necessary. I have found that the stronger students benefit as well as the LD students. LD students get the personalized attention they require, and the regular student has the opportunity to explain the information and in the process learn it more thoroughly.

Teachers often make accommodations and modifications to their teaching to meet the learning needs of students with exceptionalities (Haager & Klingner, 2005). An *accommodation* is an adjustment in the curriculum, instruction, learning tasks, assessments, or materials to make learning more accessible to students. For example, a student might have an adapted test with fewer test items. The student may also have the same test but take it orally in a one-on-one situation with the teacher, or he or she might be given extra time to take a test. Different materials might be used to teach the same content, or additional practice or various instructional approaches may be used. In any case, accommodation is *not* a watering down or change in the content or a change in expected learner outcomes.

A *modification* is a change in the standard learning expectations so that they are realistic and individually appropriate. The curriculum or instruction is altered as needed. Modifications are used for students for whom all possible accommodations have been considered and who still need additional measures to help them progress. For example, students with skill deficits in reading or math may need modifications in assignments or the level of the content and reading materials, or they may need an alternative assignment or test.

Students at Risk

Other environmental and personal influences may converge to place a student at risk. *Students at risk* are children and adolescents who are not able to acquire and/or use the skills necessary to develop their potential and become productive members of society. Conditions at home, support from the community, and personal and cultural background all affect student attitudes, behaviors, and propensity to profit from school experiences. Students potentially at risk include children who face adverse conditions beyond their control, those who do not speak English as a first language, talented but unchallenged students, those with special problems, and many others. At-risk students often have academic difficulties and thus may be low achievers.

Students at risk, especially those who eventually drop out, typically have some or all of the following characteristics (Ormrod, 2008): (a) a history of academic failure, (b) older age in comparison with classmates, (c) emotional and behavioral problems, (d) frequent interaction with low-achieving peers, (e) lack of psychological attachment to school, and (f) increasing disinvolvement with school.

Here are some general strategies to support students at risk (Ormrod, 2008):

- Identify students at risk as early as possible.
- Create a warm, supportive school and classroom atmosphere.
- Communicate high expectations for academic success.
- Provide extra academic support.
- Show students that they are the ones who have made success possible.
- Encourage and facilitate identification with school.

Socioeconomic Status

Socioeconomic status (SES) is a measure of a family's relative position in a community, determined by a combination of parents' income, occupation, and level of education. There are many relationships between SES and school performance (Woolfolk-Hoy, 2007). SES is linked to intelligence, achievement test scores, grades, truancy, and dropout and suspension rates.

Students' school performance is correlated with their socioeconomic status: Higher-SES students tend to have high academic achievement, and lower-SES students tend to be at greater risk for dropping out of school (Books, 2004; Lee & Bowen, 2006; Ormrod, 2008). As students from lower-SES families move through the grade levels, they fall further and further behind their higher-SES peers. Students from higher-SES families, however, may face pressure from their parents to achieve at a high level, leading to anxiety and depression.

To better address the learning needs of students living in poverty, some educators seek to understand the characteristics of the students and their culture and then make appropriate decisions about curriculum and instruction. In *A Framework for Understanding Poverty,* Ruby Payne (2005, 2008) strongly advocates seeking this understanding. However, others have been critical of this approach as stereotyping students of poverty (e.g., Bomer, Dworin, May, & Semingson, 2008; Gorski, 2008).

Taking these factors into account, you should (a) capitalize on students' interests; (b) make course content meaningful to the students and discuss the practical value of the material; (c) make directions clear and specific; (d) arrange to have each student experience some success; (e) be sure that expectations for work are realistic; and (f) include a variety of instructional approaches, such as provisions for movement and group work.

CREATING AN INCLUSIVE, MULTICULTURAL CLASSROOM

Understanding the sources of student diversity is not enough. You must use this information as the basis of many classroom decisions when creating a positive learning environment, selecting a responsive curriculum, determining instructional strategies, and providing assistance. A number of useful resources offer guidance about these issues, including *Culturally Proficient Instruction* (Robins, Lindsey, Lindsey, & Terrell, 2006), *Building Culturally Responsive Classrooms* (Gaitan, 2006), and *How to Teach Students Who Don't Look Like You* (Davis, 2006).

Create a Supportive, Caring Environment

How students feel about the classroom can make a big difference in how they participate. Your attitude toward the students and the curriculum can influence these student feelings. To create a supportive, caring environment, you should translate your attitude into the following actions:

1. *Celebrate diversity.* Student diversity exists in many ways, as reviewed earlier in this chapter. Students do not want to be criticized because they have some characteristic that is different from others. Through your actions, recognize that each student contributes to the rich variety of ideas and actions in the classroom. Show that you appreciate and value the diversity that is reflected in the students in the classroom. In turn, students will feel appreciated, rather than different, and this will make them feel more comfortable in the classroom.

2. *Have high expectations for students and believe that all students can succeed.* Teachers may sometimes consider certain sources of student diversity—cognitive ability, language, disabilities, socioeconomic status, for example—as having a negative effect on student performance. Thus, teachers may lower expectations and adjust the content and activities accordingly. However, this is a disservice to the students when they are not given the opportunity to address meaningful and challenging content and to develop their knowledge and skills. It is important to hold high expectations for all students and to believe that all students can succeed. Students appreciate the challenge and will find the classroom more stimulating and worthwhile as compared to a classroom with lowered expectations.

3. *Encourage all students.* Students who perform well academically often receive words of praise, reinforcement, and encouragement from teachers. There may be many students in a classroom who do not perform at the highest academic levels, but they would appreciate hearing encouraging statements as well. Encouraging words and guiding suggestions will help all students to feel that they are being supported in their efforts.

4. *Respond to all students enthusiastically.* When students see that their teacher is welcoming and enthusiastic about each student, they feel more comfortable in the classroom and more willing to participate fully. Warm greetings when students enter the classroom, conversations with individual students, and positive reactions when students contribute to classroom discussion are just a few ways that enthusiasm might be expressed. The main thing is that each student needs to feel valued and that each sees this through enthusiastic teacher responses.

5. *Show students that you care about them.* When students know that you care for them and that you are looking out for them, it makes all the difference in the world. Students then feel valued, regardless of their characteristics, and are more likely to actively participate in the classroom. Even when the teacher needs to deal with a student concerning a problem, the student recognizes that the teacher's actions are well intentioned.

Offer a Responsive Curriculum

Students feel that they are valued when the curriculum is fair and relevant and when the content and curriculum materials reflect the diversity of learners in the classroom.

1. *Use a fair and relevant curriculum.* Teachers can make decisions to ensure that the curriculum is inclusive, relevant, and free of bias. Using the district-approved curriculum guide as a starting point, teachers can select appropriate instructional content to demonstrate that their students are valued as people and that they offer a challenging, culturally relevant curriculum. This content may involve integrating subject areas from diverse traditions, and the content may even arise out of students' own questions so that they can construct their own meaning.

2. *Consider differentiating curriculum materials.* Curriculum materials must also reflect the diversity of learners in the classroom. Books and other instructional materials should be free of bias, and they should provide the voices and perspectives of diverse people.

Once appropriate curriculum materials have been selected, teachers may allow students options in the use of these materials. Learning activity packets, task cards, and learning contracts are examples of *differentiated materials* that address individual differences by providing curriculum options. Learning centers, for example, include differentiated materials with several kinds and levels of goals and activities. Centers, packets, and cards can be made for a particular student's needs and then stored until another student has need of them. When prepared properly, the materials will accommodate different rates of learning and different cognitive styles.

Vary Instruction

To meet the needs of diverse students, instruction cannot be one-dimensional. A variety of instructional approaches is needed to challenge all students and to meet their instructional needs. Several ways to vary your instruction are highlighted here.

1. *Challenge students' thinking and abilities.* Students have various learning styles, and they may learn best with their preferred learning style. However, should teachers always try to match student preferences and instructional methods? Probably not.

You should (a) start where the learner is (i.e., in concert with the pupil's level of development), (b) then begin to mismatch (i.e., use a different approach than what the student prefers) by shifting to a slightly more complex level of teaching to help the student to develop in many areas, and (c) have faith that students have an intrinsic drive to learn. These practices complement the recommendations of Lev Vygotsky, Lawrence Kohlberg, and others to nudge students beyond comfort zones of learning into just enough cognitive dissonance to facilitate growth.

2. *Group students for instruction.* Grouping makes differentiation of instruction more efficient and practical. When each group is challenged and stimulated appropriately, students are motivated to work harder. Differentiated materials can be used more easily. On the other hand, labeling can be stigmatizing if grouping is based on variables such as ability or achievement. Grouping too much and changing groups too infrequently can obstruct student integration and cooperation.

With the proper planning, structure, and supervision, grouping is a useful way to provide for individual differences. When using grouping arrangements, you should follow these guidelines:

- Make liberal use of activities that mix group members frequently.
- Adjust the pace and level of work for each group to maximize achievement. Avoid having expectations that are too low for low groups. Students tend to live up or down to teachers' expectations.
- Provide opportunities for gifted students to work with peers of their own level by arranging cross-age, between-school, or community-based experiences.

- Form groups with care, giving attention to culture and gender.
- Structure the experience and supervise the students' actions.
- Prepare students with the necessary skills for being effective group members, such as listening, helping, cooperating, and seeking assistance.

3. *Consider differentiated assignments. Alternative* or *differentiated assignments* can be provided by altering the length, difficulty, or time span of the assignment. Alternative assignments generally require alternative evaluation procedures.

Enrichment activities qualify as alternative assignments when directed toward the individual student's needs. There are three types of enrichment activities. First, relevant enrichment provides experiences that address the student's strengths, interests, or deficit areas. Second, cultural enrichment might be pleasurable and productive for the student even if not particularly relevant to his or her needs. An example would be an interdisciplinary study or a global-awareness topic. Third, irrelevant enrichment might provide extra activity in a content area without really addressing student needs.

4. *Consider individualized study. Individualized study* can be implemented through learning contracts or independent studies as a means to address individual needs. Such plans are most effective when developed by the student with your assistance. Individualized study facilitates mastery of both content and processes. Not only can the student master a subject, but he or she can also master goal setting, time management, use of resources, self-direction, and self-assessment of achievement. Independent study is ideal for accommodating student learning styles. Individual ability is nurtured, and students often learn more than the project required.

Independent study encourages creativity and develops problem-solving skills. It can be used in any school setting and all curricular areas. Most important, this method of learning approximates the way that the student should continue to learn when no longer a student in school.

This method requires varied, plentiful resources, and it may not provide enough social interaction. The student may spend too long on the study, and parents may complain that nothing is being accomplished.

When considering individualized study, you should do the following:

- Include the student in all phases of planning, studying, and evaluating.
- Encourage the student to ask higher-order questions (analysis, synthesis, evaluation) as study goals.
- Encourage the student to develop a product as an outcome of the study.
- Provide the student with an opportunity to share the product with an interested audience.
- Emphasize learner responsibility and accountability.

5. *Give opportunities for students to try different types of activities.* Although certain class activities and instructional strategies may seem well suited for a particular student, it is important to involve the student in many different types of activities to challenge the student and the student's thinking and understanding.

6. *Use authentic and fair assessment strategies.* Some students demonstrate their learning better through certain types of assessment. Since there are many types of students in classrooms, a variety of methods for evaluating student learning should be used. Using a variety of approaches—such as written or oral tests, reports or projects, interviews, portfolios, writing samples, and observations—will circumvent bias. In addition, evaluation of student learning should be at several levels: recall, comprehension, application, analysis, synthesis, and evaluation.

Provide Assistance When Needed

Many classrooms include students who can benefit from special assistance in their learning. When creating an inclusive, multicultural classroom, these students must not be overlooked, because they may not advance in their learning without such assistance.

1. *Provide special individualized assistance to all students.* Teachers often provide individualized assistance to students who have difficulty learning. This assistance can make a big difference in helping students to overcome hurdles and can lead to better understanding. However, other students can benefit from this type of assistance as well. By providing assistance to all types of diverse learners, teachers express their interest in the student, provide support for student learning, and have the opportunity to challenge the student in new ways.

2. *Work with students with special needs.* As a first step, teachers need to know district policies concerning students with special needs and what their responsibilities are for referrals, screening, and the preparation of individualized educational plans (IEPs). Learning materials and activities can be prepared commensurate with the abilities of students with special needs. Positive expectations for student performance are a means to promote student learning.

DIFFERENTIATING INSTRUCTION

How might teachers differentiate their instruction? As Figure 4.2 indicates, *differentiation* can take place when planning, grouping students, using instructional activities and materials, identifying assignments, and determining the assessments to use. The discussion of the vehicles of differentiation is organized in three areas: the curriculum, student characteristics, and instructional strategies.

Elements of the Curriculum That Can Be Differentiated

The curriculum can be differentiated in three ways: (1) the content—the curriculum and the materials and approaches used for students to learn the content, (2) the process—the instructional activities or approaches used to help students to learn the curriculum,

Teachers employ several strategies to help students to attain the concepts. Inductive approaches include concept attainment strategies, inquiry lessons, and projects, reports, and problems.

- *Social instructional approaches* have students working together in various ways to gather, process, and learn the information or skills. The teacher acts as a facilitator, rather than the information provider. Social approaches include discussions, cooperative learning, panels and debates, role playing, simulations, and games.
- *Independent instructional approaches* allow students to pursue content independently with less teacher direction than other lessons. Students sometimes are permitted to pursue their own interests. Independent approaches include learning centers, contracts, and independent work.

All these instructional strategies are discussed in more detail in Chapter 5 and 6. When deciding on a particular teaching strategy for a lesson, weigh the advantages and disadvantages of the various strategies along with the objectives of the intended lesson. Effective teachers use many different strategies throughout a unit and the school year as a means to differentiate their instruction and be more responsive to student needs.

Differentiating with the Universal Design for Learning

Teachers at any grade level can use the *universal design for learning (UDL)* to meet the needs of all students by adapting the curriculum and delivery of instruction. UDL is an instructional approach that helps meet the challenge of diversity by suggesting flexible instructional materials, techniques, and strategies that empower educators to meet students' varied needs (Center for Applied Special Technology, 2008; Council for Exceptional Children, 2005). To create the flexible design and delivery of instruction in UDL, teachers must provide multiple means of representation, expression, and engagement.

Multiple Means of Representation.   Teachers should provide multiple means of representation to give learners various ways of acquiring information and knowledge. Students differ in the ways they perceive and comprehend information presented to them. For example, students with learning disabilities or language or cultural differences may require different ways of approaching content.

There is no single means of representation that is optimal for all students. Providing options in representation is essential:

1. *Provide options for perceiving the content.* To be effective in diverse classrooms, curricula must be presented in ways that are perceptible to all students. To reduce barriers to learning, teachers can (a) provide the same information through different sensory modalities (e.g., vision, hearing, or touch) and (b) provide information in a format that will allow for adjustability by the student (e.g., text that can be enlarged, sounds that can be amplified). For example, when the same information is presented in both speech and text, the complementary representations enhance comprehension for most students. To facilitate the perception of content, provide options that (a) customize the display of information, (b) provide alternatives for auditory information, and (c) provide alternatives for visual information.

2. *Provide options for language and symbols.* Students vary in their facility with different forms of representation, both linguistic and nonlinguistic. A graph that illustrates the variables between two concepts may be helpful to one student but puzzling to another. Similarly, vocabulary may clarify concepts to one student but not another. Inequities arise when information is presented to all students through one approach. Provide alternative representations for accessibility, clarity, and comprehensibility for all students. To vary the use of language and symbols, provide options that (a) define vocabulary and symbols, (b) clarify syntax and structure, (c) help with decoding text or mathematical notations, (d) promote cross-linguistic understanding, and (e) illustrate concepts nonlinguistically.

3. *Provide options for facilitating comprehension.* In addition to perceiving the information, students need to use information-processing skills, such as integrating new information with prior knowledge, using strategic categorization, and practicing active memorization. Since students differ in information processing skills, teachers can provide cognitive "ramps" that will help all students gain access to the information. To facilitate comprehension, use options that (a) provide or activate prior background knowledge, (b) highlight critical features, big ideas, and relationships, (c) guide information processing, and (d) support memory and transfer.

Multiple Means of Expression.   Teachers should also provide multiple means of *expression* to provide learners with alternatives for demonstrating what they know. Students differ in the ways they can navigate a learning environment and express what they know. For example, students with attention-deficit disorder or those who have language barriers may approach learning tasks and demonstrate mastery very differently. Some may be able to express themselves in writing but not in oral speech, and vice versa.

There is no single means of expression that will be optimal for all students. Again, providing options for expression is essential:

1. *Provide options for physical action.* A textbook or workbook in a print format provides limited means of navigation or physical interaction (e.g., turning the pages, writing in a workbook). Navigating and interacting in limited ways may be a barrier for some students, such as those who are physically disabled, blind, or have other disorders. Provide options in the (a) mode of physical response, (b) means of navigation, and (c) way to access tools and assistive technologies.

2. *Provide options for expressive skills and fluency.* There is no medium of expression that is equally suited for all students. Also, there are some types of media that may be poorly suited for some kinds of expression and for some kinds of students. A student with dyslexia, for example, might excel at storytelling in conversation but have a difficult time writing the story. Alternative approaches to expression should be used. Provide options in the (a) media of communication, (b) tools for composition and problem solving, and (c) scaffolds for practice and performance.

3. *Provide options for long-term goal setting.* Higher-level brain functioning permits people to overcome impulsive, short-term reactions to their environment and instead set long-term goals, plan effective strategies for reaching those goals, monitor their progress, and modify strategies as needed. The UDL approach involves efforts to expand these executive functions by scaffolding lower-level skills to promote higher levels of development. Provide options that (a) guide effective goal setting, (b) support planning and strategy development, (c) facilitate managing information and resources, and (d) enhance capacity for monitoring progress.

Multiple Means of Engagement.   Teachers should provide multiple means of *engagement* to tap learners' interests, offer appropriate challenges, and increase motivation. Students differ markedly in the ways in which they can be engaged or motivated to learn. Some students are highly engaged by spontaneity and novelty, while other students are not affected by these aspects.

No single means of representation will be optimal to engage students in learning. Providing multiple options for engagement is essential:

1. *Provide options for recruiting interest.* Students do not learn information that does not attract their attention or engage their understanding. Also, students differ significantly in what attracts their attention and engages their interest. Provide options that (a) increase individual choice and autonomy, (b) enhance relevance, value, and authenticity, and (c) reduce threats and distractions.

2. *Provide options for sustaining effort and persistence.* Many kinds of learning require sustained attention and effort. However, students differ considerably in their ability to self-regulate due to their initial motivation, their capacity and skills for self-regulation, their susceptibility to interference, and other reasons. Provide options that (a) heighten the importance of goals and objectives, (b) vary levels of challenge and support, (c) foster collaboration and communication, and (d) increase mastery-oriented feedback.

3. *Provide options for self-regulation.* The ability to *self-regulate*—to modulate one's emotional reactions to increase effectiveness at coping and engaging with the environment—is a critical aspect of human development. Students benefit from self-regulation. It can be promoted by providing alternatives to support learners with very different aptitudes and prior experiences in learning how to regulate themselves. Provide options for self-regulation that (a) guide personal goal setting and expectations, (b) scaffold coping skills and strategies, and (c) develop self-assessment and reflection.

Key Terms

Accommodation	Cognitive style	Exceptional students
Advanced learners	Conceptual tempo	Field dependence/independence
Affective area	Content	Gifted or talented learners
Alternative or differentiated assignments	Cultural diversity	Independent instructional approaches
Brain hemisphericity	Differentiated materials	Individualized study
Cognitive activity	Differentiation	Inductive instructional approaches
	Direct instructional approaches	

Instructional strategy
Intelligence
Learning profile
Learning style
Least restrictive environment
Modification

Process
Products
Psychomotor skills
Readiness
Sensory modality
Social instructional approaches

Socioeconomic status (SES)
Struggling learner
Students at risk
Universal design for learning (UDL)

Major Concepts

1. Individual differences need to be taken into account when instructional methods are selected and procedures are determined.
2. Diversity can be due to influences of learning style, creative potential, gender, language, cultural diversity, disabilities, conditions placing the student at risk, and socioeconomic factors.
3. Information about the sources of student diversity can be used as the basis of classroom decisions to create a supportive, caring learning environment.
4. A variety of instructional approaches is needed to challenge all students and to meet their instructional needs.
5. Differentiation is simply attending to the learning needs of a particular student or group of students, rather than the more typical pattern of teaching the class as though all individuals in it were basically alike.
6. Teachers can adapt one or more of the curricular elements (the content, the learning process, and the products students prepare) based on student characteristics (readiness, interests, and learning profiles) at any point in a lesson or unit using a range of instructional and management strategies.
7. There is a continuum of instructional strategies ranging from teacher-centered, explicit approaches to student-centered, less-explicit approaches.
8. Universal design for learning (UDL) is a way to adapt the curriculum and the delivery of instruction to meet the needs of all learners.

Discussion/Reflective Questions

1. What types of student diversity were evident in classrooms in your own K–12 schooling experience? In what ways did your teachers take these student characteristics into account in the selection of content and the use of instructional approaches?
2. Are you enthusiastic or skeptical about the relevance of learning style theory and brain hemisphere research for classroom instruction? Why?
3. What are some challenges that you might experience in dealing with students with limited English proficiency? What could you do to overcome these challenges to promote student learning?
4. What challenges might teachers face when trying to differentiate the curriculum and the techniques of delivering the content?
5. What are the merits and disadvantages of offering students choices in instructional tasks and requirements?

Suggested Activities

For Clinical Settings

1. Make a list of 10 or more questions that you would like to ask an effective teacher about addressing the diversity of students.
2. Examine a unit from a textbook you might use, and identify ways that you might differentiate elements of the curriculum.
3. Make a list of several ways that you could provide accommodations when students take a test.

For Field Experiences

1. Using the categories of differences addressed in this chapter as a guide, ask several teachers to describe individual differences that they notice in their students. How do the teachers take these differences into account?
2. Talk to several teachers to identify the types of instructional strategies they use in the classroom. Determine why they selected these various strategies. Ask for recommendations about effective use of these strategies.
3. Ask several teachers to identify students at risk and to discuss any measures taken to work with these students.

Further Reading

Center for Applied Special Technology. (2008). *Universal design for learning guidelines.* Wakefield, MA: Author. Retrieved on July 30, 2008, from www.cast.org/publications/UDLguidelines/version1.html

Describes the three principles of universal design and provides examples to apply them in teaching.

Gollnick, D. M., & Chinn, P. C. (2009). *Multicultural education in a pluralistic society* (8th ed.). Boston: Allyn & Bacon.

Examines differences in students based on class, ethnicity and race, gender, exceptionality, religion, language, and age. Considers ways that education can be multicultural.

Howard, G. R. (2007). As diversity grows, so must we. *Educational Leadership, 64*(6), 16–22.

Discusses five phases of professional development for staff in schools that are experiencing rapid demographic shifts.

Tomlinson, C. A. (2005). *How to differentiate instruction in mixed-ability classrooms* (2nd ed.). Upper Saddle River, NJ: Pearson Prentice-Hall.

Describes ways that teachers can differentiate content, process, and product according to the student's readiness, interests, and learning profile.

Villegas, A. M., & Lucas, T. (2007). The culturally responsive teacher. *Educational Leadership, 64*(6), 28–33.

Offers guidelines for teaching students from diverse cultural and linguistic backgrounds to engage them as capable learners.

5 | Direct Instructional Strategies

Objectives

This chapter provides information that will help you to:

1. Identify the characteristics of deductive and inductive teaching strategies.
2. Describe features of direct instruction.
3. Identify guidelines for the effective use of presentations, demonstrations, questions, and recitations.
4. Describe effective techniques when using practice, drills, reviews, guided practice, and homework.

Deductive and Inductive Strategies

Direct Instructional Approaches
- Direct Instruction
- Presentations
- Demonstrations
- Questioning
- Recitations
- Practice and Drills
- Reviews
- Guided Practice and Homework

Now that you see the need for differentiating your instruction, you need to examine the various specific instructional strategies. First, it is useful to consider the ways that deductive and inductive strategies can be used to aid in your instructional differentiation. Then you should consider a number of direct, teacher-centered instructional approaches.

DEDUCTIVE AND INDUCTIVE STRATEGIES

Students learn in various ways, and you should vary your use of instructional strategies so that you can relate to their learning styles and needs. One way to vary instruction is to use deductive and inductive instructional strategies. Deductive strategies are more direct and straightforward and lend themselves to direct instructional approaches, whereas inductive strategies are intended to tap into the interests and thinking abilities of the students. Let's look at some examples.

117

Deductive strategies are instructional approaches that start with a known principle and then attention moves to the unknown. *Inductive strategies* are instructional approaches that start with an unknown principle and then attention moves to a known. The differences in these strategies can be illustrated in the way that a teacher might teach the concept of a topic sentence.

A teacher using a deductive approach might give students the following definition of a topic sentence: "A topic sentence is usually the first sentence in a paragraph. This sentence provides the reader with a sense of the writer's purpose. The rest of the paragraph contains specific details related to this purpose." With this deductive approach, the teacher next might give students some examples of topic sentences and finish the lesson by having students write their own topic sentences. The teacher could then review these sentences and give feedback on the students' performance.

The strengths of the deductive strategy are the directness and specific focus of the teaching strategy and the tight linkage between the teacher's examples and the task required of students. The lesson began with known principles (i.e., what is a topic sentence) and then led to examples of this principle. It was a fairly direct, straightforward way of addressing the lesson objective.

In contrast, a teacher using an inductive approach might give students sample paragraphs with the topic sentences underlined. With this strategy, the teacher would not tell students at the start that they are studying topic sentences, nor would the teacher provide a definition of a topic sentence. Instead, students would study the paragraphs and answer questions posed by the teacher. For example, the teacher might ask, "What do the underlined sentences in these paragraphs have in common?" And after receiving a series of answers, the teacher may ask a second question: "Can anyone provide a name for the underlined sentences?" From these two questions, many ideas might be generated.

The teacher would need to focus students' comments toward the concept of topic sentences, while also being aware that students may introduce other interesting concepts. By asking "What do the sentences have in common?" the teacher anticipates that students will give the attributes or characteristics of a topic sentence: (1) it is the first sentence in the paragraph and (2) it seems to tell what the paragraph will be about. Thus, this inductive lesson used examples and questions that helped students to recognize the fundamental principle of topic sentences. This inductive approach is more indirect, but it can be very effective because students interact with the content to make meaning.

Sometimes, you may want to have fairly direct presentation of the content and thus would use deductive teaching approaches. Other times, you may want to start out with examples and then lead to the main concept through the use of inductive approaches. This chapter discusses a variety of indirect instructional approaches, many of which lend themselves to inductive strategies. It also examines direct instructional approaches, those that are often teacher directed in a whole-class format. Deductive teaching strategies can be used effectively to promote student learning.

DIRECT INSTRUCTIONAL APPROACHES

As discussed in Chapter 4, there are many ways to differentiate your instruction. Figure 4.3 displayed a continuum of instructional strategies going from direct, teacher-centered approaches at one end to indirect, student-centered approaches at the other end. This chapter examines many of the direct, teacher-centered approaches, including direct instruction, presentations, demonstrations, questions, and several other directed strategies.

SAMPLE STANDARDS

Instructional Strategies

There are ten INTASC standards (see page xxi), and each standard includes a list of knowledge, dispositions, and performances to indicate more clearly what is intended in the standard.

Since this chapter deals with instructional strategies, some representative statements for knowledge, dispositions, and performances from one or more INTASC standards are listed here concerning topics in this chapter.

Knowledge

- The teacher understands how learning occurs—how students construct knowledge, acquire skills, and develop habits of mind—and knows how to use instructional strategies that promote student learning. (INTASC #2)
- The teacher knows how to enhance learning through the use of a wide variety of materials as well as human and technological resources. (INTASC #4)

Dispositions

- The teacher appreciates multiple perspectives and conveys to learners how knowledge is developed from the vantage point of the knower. (INTASC #1)
- The teacher is disposed to use the students' strengths as a basis for growth and their errors as an opportunity for learning. (INTASC #2)

Performances

- The teacher carefully evaluates how to achieve learning goals, choosing alternative teaching strategies and materials to achieve different instructional purposes and to meet student needs. (INTASC #4)
- The teacher develops a variety of clear, accurate presentations and representations of concepts, using alternative explanations to assist students' understanding and presenting diverse perspectives to encourage critical thinking. (INTASC #4)

Direct Instruction

Direct teaching strategies are instructional approaches in which the teacher structures lessons in a straightforward, sequential manner. The teacher is clearly in control of the content or skill to be learned and the pace and rhythm of the lesson. Generally, direct strategies allow the teacher to introduce new skills or concepts in a relatively short period of time. Direct instructional strategies are academically focused, with the teacher clearly stating the goals for the lesson to the students. The teacher closely monitors student understanding and provides feedback to students on their performance.

Direct instruction has four key components:

1. clear determination and articulation of goals
2. teacher-directed instruction
3. careful monitoring of students' outcomes
4. consistent use of effective classroom organization and management methods

Direct instruction is effective because it is based on behavioralistic learning principles, such as obtaining students' attention, reinforcing correct responses, providing corrective feedback, and practicing correct responses. It also tends to increase the academic learning time, or the amount of instructional time during which students are attending to the task and performing at a high success rate. Many studies have found that students learn basic skills more rapidly when they receive a greater portion of their instruction directly from the teacher.

Two well-known direct instruction approaches are examined in the next sections: (1) explicit teaching, proposed by Barak Rosenshine, and (2) instructional theory into practice (ITIP), proposed by Madeline Hunter.

Explicit Teaching.   *Explicit teaching* calls for the teacher to gain student attention, reinforce correct responses, provide feedback to students on their progress, and increase the amount of time that students spend actively engaged in learning course content. Its objective is to teach skills and help students to master a body of knowledge. Ten general principles apply when developing an explicit teaching lesson (Rosenshine, 1987, p. 76):

1. Begin a lesson with a short statement of goals.
2. Begin a lesson with a short review of previous prerequisite learning.
3. Present new material in small steps, with student practice after each step.
4. Give clear and detailed instructions and explanations.
5. Provide a high level of active practice for all students.
6. Ask many questions, check for student understanding, and obtain responses from all students.
7. Guide students during initial practice.
8. Provide systematic feedback and corrections.

9. Provide explicit instruction and practice for seatwork exercises, and when necessary, monitor students during seatwork.
10. Continue practice until students are independent and confident.

Based on studies of explicit teaching, Rosenshine (1987) identified six teaching functions:

1. *Daily review.* The purpose of daily review is to determine if the students have obtained the necessary prerequisite knowledge or skills for the lesson. Typically, an effective teacher will begin the lesson by reviewing previously covered material, correcting homework, or reviewing prior knowledge relevant to the day's lesson.

What Would You Decide?   *Conducting a Daily Review*

Let's say that you are teaching an art lesson concerning painting styles (e.g., impressionistic, modern). As part of your daily review, you want to know if the students can identify the names of the various styles, representative painters, and characteristics of each style that you have covered in the previous three class sessions.

1. What strategies might you use to conduct your daily review in this case?
2. How might you incorporate the use of technology into the daily review?

---

2. *Presenting new material.* Effective teachers spend more time presenting new material and guiding practice than do less effective teachers. To begin a lesson, effective teachers capture the students' attention by explaining the learning objectives to be covered during the lesson. In this way, students are able to better focus on the lesson's purpose without being distracted by extraneous material.

After the lesson's introduction, effective teachers continue by teaching one point at a time. Each point consists of a short presentation utilizing many examples. The examples provide concrete experiences or knowledge by which the students can process the new material. It is important that these presentations be clear and concise. The clarity of the presentation avoids any misunderstanding by the students. As the lesson progresses, effective teachers periodically assess student understanding of the material. They may assess the students by asking them questions or by having them summarize the main points of the lesson up to that point.

Based on his review of experimental and correlational research, Rosenshine (1987) lists the following suggestions for an effective presentation:

- Organize material so that one point can be mastered before the next point needs to be introduced.
- State lesson goals.
- Give step-by-step directions.
- Focus on one thought at a time, completing one point and checking for understanding before proceeding to the next.
- Model behaviors by going through the directions.

3. *Conducting guided practice.* The purpose of guided practice is to supervise the students' initial practice of a skill and to provide the reinforcement necessary to progress new learning from short-term into long-term memory. Little research exists concerning the appropriate length of the presentation prior to the guided practice. But shorter segments of presentation appear to be more effective with less able students and with new material.

The frequency of guided practice is an important variable in the success rate of students learning new material. Continually reinforcing new material helps students to retrieve the information from long-term memory. In addition to the frequency of guided practice, the percentage of correct student responses is also significant. Rosenshine (1987) reports that the most effective teachers appear to have a 75 to 80 percent success rate during guided practice, suggesting that effective teachers combine success and challenge.

4. *Provide feedback and correctives.* During guided practice, it is important to give process feedback to the students. Process feedback provides the student with an additional explanation that is sometimes needed when the student is correct but hesitant about how he or she arrived at the answer. For example, you might say, "Yes, the answer is correct" and then proceed to explain the process for arriving at the correct answer.

When a student has made an error, it is inappropriate to simply provide the correct answer. This does not provide you with an opportunity to determine how the student made the incorrect response and robs the student of a learning opportunity. Rather, when a student has made an error, it is appropriate to simplify the question and to then probe for the correct answer. Often this is done by providing clues or reteaching the material. It is important that errors not go uncorrected.

5. *Conduct independent practice.* After conducting guided practice, it is important to have the student do independent practice. Independent practice provides the additional review and reinforcement necessary to become fluent in a particular skill. Independent practice differs from guided practice in that you do not provide the cues that you gave during guided practice. The independent practice should involve identical material as that covered during guided practice. It is appropriate for you to cover the material before the students take it home.

Students are more engaged during seatwork when teachers spend more time circulating around the room and supervising and monitoring their work. Effective teachers also provide sufficient and clear explanations prior to the independent practice.

6. *Weekly and monthly review.* Much of the previous discussion about the teaching functions has suggested frequent review and reinforcement of new material for the students. Teachers could review the previous week's work every Monday and the previous month's work every fourth Monday.

The Hunter Model. Instructional theory into practice (ITIP) is a method for planning and implementing instruction developed by Madeline Hunter (1976, 1981, 1984, 1994). ITIP is essentially a lesson design process that considers relevant factors in making instructional decisions. Furthermore, it is a teacher-directed approach to instruction. Robin Hunter (2004) provided an update of Madeline Hunter's mastery teaching.

According to Hunter, three categories are basic to lesson design. First, teachers decide what content to teach within the context of the grade level, student ability, and the lesson rationale. Next, teachers must decide what students will do to learn and to demonstrate that they have learned. Finally, teachers must decide which research-based teaching behaviors will most effectively promote learning.

Hunter is perhaps best known for her seven elements of a lesson (see Figure 5.1, which is adapted from Hunter, 1984). To implement the three categories mentioned previously, Hunter maintains that the seven elements be used. Hunter asserts that these seven elements should be considered in planning a lesson and then included or excluded for a reason. Each lesson does not need every element, nor are they steps that necessarily are taken in sequence.

Hunter's ITIP has been widely adopted and adapted by many school districts. Unfortunately, problems arise when the model is used beyond its intended purpose. ITIP is intended to serve as a planning tool, but many districts inappropriately view the model as a solution to instructional problems if all teachers use the seven elements. Hunter has

FIGURE 5.1   Hunter's Elements of Lesson Design

1. *Anticipatory Set*
   a. Focus the students' attention on content to be learned.
   b. Provide tie with prior learnings if appropriate.
   c. Develop readiness for learning.
2. *The Objective and Its Purpose:* Learners usually should know what they will be learning and why it is important to them.
3. *Instructional Input*
   a. Present material in achievable steps.
   b. Present varied and specific examples.
4. *Modeling*
   a. Visual or kinesthetic input accompanied by verbal input.
   b. Criteria for a correct performance are known.
5. *Monitoring to Check for Understanding*
   a. Sampling: Question whole group and take responses from individuals.
   b. Signaled responses.
   c. Private response: Written or whispered to teacher.
6. *Guided Practice:* The initial practice stage in which the response of the learner must be monitored by the teacher to make certain that it is accurate.
7. *Independent Practice:* The student can perform the task without major errors, discomfort, or confusion and with a minimum of teacher supervision.

Source: Adapted with permission from the author. Hunter, M. (1984). Knowing, teaching, and supervising. In P. L. Hosford (Ed.), *Using what we know about teaching* (pp. 169–192). Alexandria, VA: Association for Supervision and Curriculum Development. Reprinted with permission of the Association for Supervision and Curriculum Development. Copyright © 1984 by the Association for Supervision and Curriculum Development. All rights reserved.

maintained that they are not steps, but they are sometimes used this way. Some districts even evaluate teachers on how well they demonstrate ITIP principles. The problem lies in using ITIP as a teaching checklist instead of a planning tool.

Presentations

A *presentation* is an informative talk that a more knowledgeable person makes to less knowledgeable persons. There may be little or no student participation by questioning or discussion. Presentations can be used to disseminate information in a short time, to explain difficult ideas, to stimulate student desire to learn, to present information in a certain way or adapt it to a particular group, or to introduce or explain learning tasks.

Presentations should not be used when (a) objectives other than knowledge acquisition are sought; (b) the information is complex, abstract, or detailed; (c) learner involvement is important; higher cognitive learning is sought; or (d) students are below average in ability. Presentations often do not actively engage students in learning or permit passive learning and generally do not give the teacher opportunities to check student understanding. You should thoroughly plan and prepare presentations, know the content like an expert, limit the length of the presentation to the tolerance levels of the particular age group, present in a way that is interesting to students, provide appropriate levels of structure and sequence, maintain flexibility, provide organizers, use the presentation in combination with other methods, use instructional media and materials, summarize the content, and provide follow-up activities.

Good and Brophy (2008) suggest that the attention span of students needs to be taken into consideration when preparing a presentation. Certainly, the age and maturity level of the students need to be taken into account. Few students can sustain their interest when a teacher talks for over 20 minutes. After presenting for a short time, you could add variety by asking a series of questions that would be the focus of large-group or small-group discussions. Then you could return to the presentation. It is useful to alternate class time with various presentation techniques that require active involvement by students. Some teachers minimize presentations and use more interactive discussion; they often teach by asking questions.

Based on a review of the research, Rosenshine and Stevens (1986) describe several useful guidelines for delivering clear presentations: (a) clearly state goals and main points, (b) provide step-by-step presentations, (c) use specific and concrete procedures, and (d) check for students' understanding. In addition, teaching behaviors such as clarity, enthusiasm, and smooth transitions are all necessary for the presentation if the students are to be motivated and learn the material. Some teachers like to provide students with a note-taking outline to help students to follow the lecture and fill in selected information.

Also take these guidelines into account as you plan for and conduct presentations:

1. Present the lesson objectives to the students.
2. Use an advance organizer to introduce the topic and capture the students' interest.
3. Present the information in an organized, step-by-step manner.

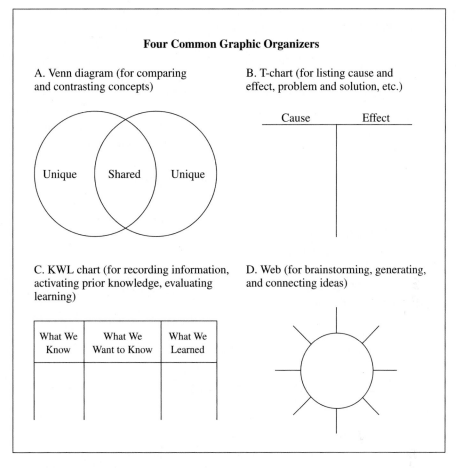

FIGURE 5.2   **Four Common Graphic Organizers**

4. Expect student interaction in the form of questions and comments.
5. Move from general to specific ideas and information.
6. Use a graphic organizer (see Figure 5.2) or other aids to promote learning.
7. Use good explanations and examples.
8. Encourage students to reflect on and apply what they have learned.
9. Check for student understanding.

Demonstrations

A demonstration is similar to a lecture in its direct communication of information from teacher to students. A *demonstration* involves a visual presentation to examine processes, information, and ideas. The demonstration allows students to see the teacher as an active learner and a model. It allows for students to observe real things and how they work.

myeducationlab

Go to MyEducationLab, select the topic **Concepts: Strategies for Teaching,** watch the video entitled "Demonstrating as a Method," and complete the questions that accompany it.

There may be pure demonstrations, demonstrations with commentary, or participative demonstrations with students. In many cases, a teacher demonstrates a certain action or activity prior to having the students perform the activity individually, such as the teacher locating certain points on a map before students are asked to do so. For many students, this teacher demonstration provides a model of the actions and establishes expectations. Demonstrations can be used to illustrate points or procedures efficiently, stimulate interest in a particular topic, provide a model for teaching specific skills, and provide a change of pace.

To carry out effective demonstrations, follow these guidelines:

1. Carefully plan the demonstration.
2. Break down complex procedures into separate components that can be adequately demonstrated.
3. Practice the demonstration.
4. Develop an outline to guide the demonstration.
5. Make sure that everyone can see the demonstration.
6. Introduce the demonstration to focus attention.
7. Describe the procedure at the same time that you demonstrate it. Repeat as needed.
8. Ask and encourage questions.
9. Permit students to practice the procedure if they are expected to use the procedure.
10. Provide individual corrective feedback.
11. Plan a follow-up to the demonstration.

Questioning

Questioning is a critical instructional tool, but there are many facets to successful questioning. Guidance about questioning falls into two categories: the kinds of questions and questioning techniques. Useful guidelines for improving classroom questions are provided by Chuska (2003) and Walsh and Sattes (2005).

Kinds of Questions.   When using questions, consider the level of question, the use of convergent and divergent questions, and the type of question:

1. *Questions for the learning domains.* Most questions focus on the cognitive domain, as discussed in Chapter 3. Questions can be developed for each level of the cognitive domain (see Table 3.1, p. 72): knowledge, comprehension, application, analysis, synthesis, and evaluation. The first three levels are considered to require low-level questions because they emphasize primarily the recall and moderate use of the information. The upper three levels of the cognitive domain require high-level questions that go beyond memory and partial recall; they deal with abstract and complex thinking.

2. *Convergent and divergent questions.* Two types of answers might be required from questions. *Convergent questions* tend to have one correct or best answer (e.g.,

What is the capital of Illinois? Who is the author of *Moby Dick*?). These questions may be phrased to require either low- or high-level thinking. *Divergent questions* are often open ended and usually have many appropriate but different answers (e.g., Why is it important that we continue to explore space? What would be a good title for this story?).

3. *Types of questions.* There are different types of questions for different purposes:

- *Focusing questions* are used to focus students' attention on the day's lesson or on material being discussed. They may be used to determine what students have learned, to motivate and arouse students, to generate interest at the start of or during a lesson, or to check for understanding during or at the close of a lesson (Moore, 2007). You may need to prompt students when asking questions.
- *Prompting questions* include hints and clues to aid students in answering questions or to assist them in correcting an initial response. A prompting question is usually a rewording of the original question with clues or hints included.
- *Probing questions* may be needed when a student does not answer the question completely. In this case, you may stay with the same student by asking one or more probing questions that are intended to seek clarification and to provide guidance students to more complete answers (e.g., What do you mean by that? Could you explain that more fully? What are your reasons for that?).

Questioning Techniques.   Once instruction begins, you need to use effective questioning techniques to get the desired results. You will need to consider a number of factors when selecting questions. Based on a research review, Wilen (1991) outlined fundamental questioning techniques (see Figure 5.3). In addition, use the following questioning technique guidelines:

1. *Use random selection when calling on students.* Calling on students in a prearranged format often leads to boredom and disruptive behavior for those who have already answered a question. Calling on students at random helps to keep them more attentive. Teachers tend to call on higher-achieving students rather than their lower-achieving peers. However, you should call on students at all achievement levels. In addition, it is important to create an environment that encourages success for everyone. You will want to ask the lower-achieving students questions that allow them to be successful.

2. *Use variety and unpredictability in asking questions.* Students should know that they may be called on at any time, regardless of what has gone on before. You need to be cautious about using predictable patterns, such as calling only on students who raise their hands, always calling on someone in the first row first (or another particular area), taking questions in the same order as in the textbook, and not questioning a student again after he or she has answered one question.

3. *Ask the question before calling on a particular student.* Asking the question before calling on someone allows all students more time to consider the question and a possible answer, creates greater interest, and increases attentive behavior. If one student is named before asking the question, others may not pay attention to what follows because they realize they will not have to perform.

FIGURE 5.3   Questioning Techniques

1. *Plan key questions to provide lesson structure and direction.* Write questions into lesson plans, at least one for each objective, especially higher-level questions necessary to guide discussions. Ask spontaneous questions based on student responses.
2. *Phrase questions clearly and specifically.* Avoid vague or ambiguous questions such as "What did we learn yesterday?" or "What about the heroine of the story?" Ask single questions; avoid run-on questions that lead to student confusion and frustration. Clarity increases the probability of accurate responses.
3. *Adapt questions to student ability level.* This enhances understanding and reduces anxiety. For heterogeneous classes, phrase questions in natural, simple language, adjusting vocabulary and sentence structure to students' language and conceptual levels.
4. *Ask questions logically and sequentially.* Avoid random questions lacking clear focus and intent. Consider students' intellectual ability, prior understanding of content, topic, and lesson objective(s). Asking questions in a planned sequence will enhance student thinking and learning, particularly during discussions.
5. *Ask questions at a variety of levels.* Use knowledge-level questions to determine basic understandings and diagnose potential for higher-level thinking. Higher-level questions provide students opportunities to use knowledge and engage in critical and creative thinking.
6. *Follow up student responses.* Develop a response repertoire that encourages students to clarify initial responses, expand their responses, lift thought to higher levels, and support a point of view or opinion. For example, "How would you clarify that further?" "How can you defend your position?"
7. *Give students time to think when responding.* Increase wait time after asking a question to three to five seconds to increase the frequency and duration of student responses and to encourage higher-level thinking. Insisting on instantaneous responses, particularly during discussions, significantly decreases the probability of meaningful interaction with and among students.
8. *Use questions that encourage wide student participation.* Distribute questions to involve the majority of students in learning activities. For example, call on nonvolunteers, using discretion regarding the difficulty level of questions. Be alert for reticent students' verbal and nonverbal cues, such as perplexed looks or partially raised hands. Encourage student-to-student interaction. Use circular or semicircular seating to create an environment conducive to participation, particularly during discussions.
9. *Encourage student questions.* This promotes active participation. Student questions at higher cognitive levels stimulate higher levels of thought, essential for inquiry. Give students opportunities to formulate questions and carry out follow-up investigations of interest.

Source: Wilen, W. W. (1991). *Questioning skills, for teachers* (3rd ed.) (pp. 10–11). Washington, DC: National Education Association. Reprinted with permission.

4. *Wait at least three to five seconds after asking the question before calling on a student.* After asking a question, the average teacher waits for less than one second before calling on a student or answering the question himself or herself. This short amount of time may be fine when using a lower-order question that deals with recall. However, one second or even three seconds do not provide the student with enough time to reflect on a complex question and formulate an appropriate answer.

Voices from the Classroom

Using Wait Time When Questioning

Susan Bosco, fourth-grade teacher, East Greenwich, Rhode Island

I made the decision to practice wait time during a social studies lesson. *Wait time* is the amount of time that a teacher waits between asking a question and calling on students. I realize that I have not always practiced enough wait time. Therefore, I asked some higher-order questions and waited a while before calling on students. Wondrous things happened!

In a review of a unit entitled "The Northeastern States," by my asking complex questions and waiting for responses, I had students talking to each other about the questions. Also, a greater number of students were willing to answer questions. By waiting for a longer time after asking my questions, students were able to think about the material more completely, and I had better answers and more involvement by students.

While five seconds does not seem like a long time, research indicates that many possible benefits can be gained from waiting that amount of time. Increasing your wait time to five seconds can result in an increase in the length of students' responses, the number of unsolicited but appropriate responses, students' confidence, the number of students' questions, lower-achieving students' contributions, students' proposals, the variety of students' responses, and also increased evidence to support answers.

5. *Have students respond to classmates' answers.* It is important that all students attend to their classmates' responses to the teacher's questions. This can be accomplished by occasionally asking other students to comment on another's answer. After one student finishes giving reasons for the United States to maintain membership in the United Nations, for example, you might ask others if they agree with that answer or if they might elaborate on these reasons. This strategy not only results in increased attentiveness but also encourages additional student–student interaction.

6. *Do not consistently repeat student answers.* Teachers do this for a variety of reasons, but most commonly it is done to make sure that all students hear the answer. Although the motive for this behavior is meant to be positive, it often results in students believing that they do not need to listen to their fellow students' answers and that the individual answering the question does not need to speak loudly.

7. *Ask questions that relate to students' own lives or similar situations.* Students will find learning more meaningful when it can be related to their own lives and interests. Useful questions might include "Have you ever felt this way?" "Do you believe it is right to . . . ?" and "How would your parents feel about this?"

8. *Vary the types of questions being asked.* Questions might be convergent (leading to a single correct answer: "What is the capital of Florida?") or divergent (there may be

Have Key Questions Ready

Richard Schwartz, high school social studies teacher, Whippany, New Jersey

When preparing a lesson plan, it is not enough to write *discussion* in your plan book. Based on my experience, you must select at least three good discussion questions ahead of time that will advance student understanding.

These key questions can guide meaningful discussion in class. To be effective, the questions should include the words *how* and *why*. Also, you could ask students to explain their views, citing material from what has been covered in class. You may want to provide your students with a preview of the key questions by posting them on the whiteboard, chalkboard, or projector screen early in the class or just before the segment of the class when the material is addressed.

a number of possible answers: "What are the consequences of sex role stereotyping in K–12 textbooks?"). In addition, questions should be asked at various levels of the cognitive domain.

Recitations

A *recitation* involves a teacher asking students a series of relatively short answer questions to determine if they remember or understand previously covered content. You might use recitations as a means to diagnose student progress. The typical interaction pattern is teacher question, student response, and teacher reaction. Questions often deal with who, what, where, and when. Recitation is highly structured, with the teacher clearly in control of directing the learning. It is important to direct questions to both volunteering and nonvolunteering students.

Teachers usually ask known information questions during recitations. Thus, you ask questions to find out if the student knows the answer, not to get information. Recitation is frequently used in middle and secondary schools. It has flexible use because it can be tailored to the amount of time and the number of students. The most common uses of recitation are in review, introduction of new material, checking answers, practice, and checking understanding of materials and ideas.

Practice and Drills

Practice involves going over material just learned. Practice is intended to consolidate, clarify, and emphasize what the student has already learned. Practice sessions are more meaningful when spread out over time (not just the day before a test), when conducted in context, when whole issues are examined rather than parts, and when used in different activities.

Drilling involves repeating information on a particular topic until it is firmly established in the students' minds. It is used for learning that needs to be habitualized or to be retained a long time (e.g., multiplication tables). Many teachers find that drills work best at a certain point in the lesson, such as at the beginning of class.

Practice and drills involve repetition that is intended to help students to better understand and recall the information. They are useful in developing speed and accuracy in the recall of facts, generalizations, and concepts. They could be used, for example, when learning certain information, such as dates and events in history, chemical symbols, or translations in foreign language. Practice and drills help the long-term retention of facts.

Reviews

A *review* is an opportunity for students to look at a topic another time. A review differs from practice and drill in that it does not require drill techniques. It does involve reteaching and is intended to reinforce previously learned material and to sometimes give new meaning to the material. Reviews can be in the form of summaries at the ends of lessons, units, or terms; quiz games; outlines; discussions; questioning sessions; and other approaches.

A daily review at the start of a class will help you to determine if your students have the necessary prerequisite knowledge or skills for the lesson. Weekly and monthly reviews help to check student understanding, ensure that the necessary prior skills are adequately learned, and also check on the teacher's pace.

Guided Practice and Homework

Another teacher-directed instructional approach is the use of techniques through which the students use and practice the knowledge and skills being addressed in class. The use of guided practice in class and homework are the two most common techniques.

Guided Practice.   Although teachers commonly use seatwork for guided practice, there are additional approaches such as teacher-led practice and student cooperative practice.

Seatwork.   *Seatwork* involves students working on in-class assignments, often independently. Students in grades 1 through 7 spend more time working alone on seatwork than on any other activity; approximately 50 to 75 percent of their time involves seatwork (Rosenshine & Stevens, 1986). Therefore, it is important to learn how to maintain student engagement during seatwork.

Successful independent practice requires both adequate preparation of the students and effective teacher management of the activity. In addition to the guidelines

Classroom Case Study

Questioning Strategies

Teachers use questioning in the classroom for a variety of instructional purposes. In Abby Lebowitz's high school social studies class, questioning is used to promote students' critical-thinking and problem-solving skills. In a discussion on global warming, the two sample interactions listed below between Ms. Lebowitz and her students illustrate different degrees of effectiveness when using questions.

Sample 1

Ms. Lebowitz: Global warming is such a huge issue. As a concerned citizen, what are some things I can do to be more environmentally conscious?

Joshua raises his hand immediately.

Ms. Lebowitz: Joshua, what do you have in mind?

Joshua: Well, you could start by buying a more fuel-efficient car.

Ms. Lebowitz: I could buy a more fuel-efficient car. Yes. That is a good idea.

Joshua: You can also decrease the amount of time you spend driving by carpooling or taking a bus.

Ms. Lebowitz: Yes. Carpooling and taking a bus are both great examples. Morgan, what else can I do?

Morgan: Um . . .

Ms. Lebowitz: Can anyone help Morgan out?

Chris: You can use energy-saving light bulbs—

Maria *(interrupting)*: —I don't think those things make any big difference.

Ms. Lebowitz: You don't think the energy-saving bulbs make a difference?

Maria: Nope.

Maria rolls her eyes.

Sample 2

Ms. Lebowitz: Global warming is such a huge issue. As a concerned citizen, what are some things I can do to be more environmentally conscious?

Three students raise their hands right away. Ms. Lebowitz waits until half of the students show they are ready to respond.

Ms. Lebowitz: Joshua, what do you have in mind?

Joshua: Well, you could start by buying a more fuel-efficient car.

Ms. Lebowitz: Yes. That is a good idea, but what if I can't afford to buy a new car?

Ms. Lebowitz looks around the classroom to see who else has his or her hand raised. She calls on Kaya.

Kaya: You can decrease the amount of time you spend driving by carpooling or taking a bus.

Ms. Lebowitz: Those are both great examples, Kaya. Does anyone have anything to add?

Chris raises his hand. Ms. Lebowitz makes eye contact with him and nods.

> **Chris:** You can use energy-saving light bulbs—
> **Maria** *(interrupting)*: —I don't think those things make any big difference.
> **Ms. Lebowitz:** Maria, I am glad that you want to contribute, but please let Chris finish his thought. You will have time to respond when he is finished.
>
> **Focus Questions**
> 1. Which dialogue sample illustrates better questioning techniques? Why?
> 2. How can you prepare yourself for effective questioning in lessons that you will teach?

described previously for identifying and introducing assignments, the following suggestions from the research are ways to improve student engagement during seatwork (Rosenshine & Stevens, 1986):

1. Circulate around the classroom during seatwork, actively explaining, observing, asking questions, and giving feedback.
2. Have short contacts with individual students (i.e., 30 seconds or less).
3. For difficult material in whole-class instruction, have a number of segments of instruction and seatwork during a single class period.
4. Arrange seats to facilitate monitoring the students (i.e., face both small-group and independently working students).
5. Establish a routine to use during seatwork activity that prescribes what students will do, how they will get help, and what they will do when they have completed the exercises. (p. 388)

What Would You Decide?   *Seatwork*

You often plan time at the end of math class for students to work on problems independently while you monitor the students and provide assistance.

1. What routines would you establish for students during this seatwork?
2. How might you use peer tutoring as part of this seatwork time?

Teacher-Led Practice.   *Teacher-led practice* is often in the form of repetition drills and question-and-answer sessions. Drill is the intensive repetition of content to ensure swift, accurate responses. It is intended to establish associations that are available without "thinking through" each time that the associations are needed. Drill is useful for skill learning and intellectual skills; it is not effective on complex principles and appreciations.

Student Cooperative Practice.   Another type of in-class supervised study is *student cooperative practice,* in which students help each other during seatwork. In some cases, the students in the groups prepare a common product, such as an answer to a drill sheet, and in other situations the students study cooperatively to prepare for competition that takes place after the seatwork.

Homework.   *Homework* is study that students do when they are not under the direct supervision of their teachers, such as study at home, in the library, or in study hall. Homework does not include (a) in-school guided study, (b) home study courses delivered through the mail, television, or on audio- or videotape, or (c) extracurricular activities such as sports teams and clubs (Cooper, 2007).

There are four types of homework assignments: (a) practice, to help students to master specific skills and to reinforce material presented in class; (b) preparation, to prepare students for upcoming lessons; (c) extension, to go beyond the information obtained in the classroom and to transfer new skills and ideas to new situations; and (d) creative, to offer students the opportunity to think critically and engage in problem-solving activities.

Use these guidelines as you make decisions about homework for your students.

1. *Recognize that homework serves different purposes at different grade levels.*   For younger students, homework should be used to foster positive attitudes toward school and better academic-related behaviors and character traits, not to improve subject matter achievement measurably. As students grow older, the function of homework should change toward facilitating the acquisition of knowledge in specific topics.

2. *Have a mixture of mandatory and voluntary homework.*   Some homework should be mandatory at each grade level. A mixture of mandatory and voluntary assignments may be most beneficial to students. Voluntary assignments are probably most helpful for producing intrinsic motivation.

3. *Use homework to address topics previously covered, those covered on the day of the assignment, and those yet to be covered.*   In this way, students are reinforced for topics previously covered, address topics covered on the day of the assignment, and became familiar with topics soon to be covered.

4. *Have homework focus on simple skills and material or on the integration of skills already possessed by the student.*   Do not use homework to teach complex knowledge and skills. Also be sure that the assignments and directions are very clear since students will be working on the homework independently.

5. *Select an appropriate amount of homework for the grade level.*   While much will depend on the individual community, teacher, and student, general guidelines can be offered. After reviewing research on homework, Cooper (2007) has made recommendations for the frequency and duration of assignments. Grades 1 to 3 may have one to three mandatory assignments each week, each lasting no more than 15 minutes. Each week, grades 4 to 6 may have two to four mandatory assignments; grades 7 to 9, three to five; and grades 10 to 12, four to five. At all grade levels, additional voluntary assignments may be presented at the discretion of the teacher.

It is important to note that these time recommendations represent the total of all assignments from all subject areas at a given grade level. For example, each teacher of a ninth-grade subject should not assign three to five homework assignments of 45 to 75 minutes each week; instead, all the subject areas combined can come up to this time recommendation.

6. *Select a process for providing feedback and grading homework.* Different strategies for providing feedback differ little in their influence. Cooper (2007) suggests that the practice of grading homework be kept to a minimum, especially if the purpose of homework is to foster positive attitudes toward the subject matter (as in the lower grades). He proposes that the purpose of homework should be to diagnose individual learning problems and provide feedback, rather than to test students. You should collect homework, check it for completeness, and give intermittent instructional feedback.

7. *Do not use homework as punishment.* Using homework as punishment conveys an inappropriate message about the value of academic work. If a student misbehaves and punishment is needed, nonacademic consequences should be selected.

8. *Clearly communicate your homework policy to students.* Students need to know the procedures and policy for homework. The importance of doing homework must be carefully explained. Students' motivation for doing homework is enhanced when they recognize the value of it and its place in the academic program.

9. *Show students ways to overcome distractions.* The most prominent disturbances for students studying and doing homework at home are the phone, television, family members, and the radio. You can provide guidance for ways to minimize, overcome, or respond to these distractions. These include selecting a quiet study place and using a regular study time.

10. *Teach homework skills to students.* Students can improve homework skills by establishing appropriate places and times for studying, previewing the material, focusing attention, reading carefully and thinking about the concepts covered, casting what is learned in different forms, self-testing, and taking notes effectively.

Key Terms

Convergent questions	Focusing questions	Questioning
Deductive strategies	Homework	Recitation
Demonstration	Inductive strategies	Review
Direct teaching strategies	Practice	Seatwork
Divergent questions	Presentation	Student cooperative practice
Drill	Probing questions	Teacher-led practice
Explicit teaching	Prompting questions	

Major Concepts

1. Deductive strategies are instructional approaches that start with a known principle and then attention moves to the unknown. Inductive strategies are instructional approaches that start with an unknown principle and then attention moves to a known.
2. Direct teaching strategies are instructional approaches in which the teacher structures lessons in a straightforward, sequential manner.

3. There are a number of direct, teacher-centered instructional strategies. These include presentations, demonstrations, questions, recitations, practice and drills, reviews, guided practice, and homework.

Discussion/Reflective Questions

1. What are the merits and possible disadvantages of using direct, teacher-centered instructional strategies, such as lectures, demonstrations, practice, and reviews?
2. What type of instructional approaches did you prefer as a student? Why?

3. Why might some teachers prefer a direct approach to instruction? Why might some teachers prefer other approaches that are more student centered?
4. What skills does a teacher need to effectively conduct a whole-class discussion?

Suggested Activities

For Clinical Settings

1. Select a unit topic and prepare a two-week unit plan that includes several types of direct, teacher-centered strategies throughout the unit.
2. Prepare a description of how you will use seatwork as part of your instructional approach. What types of tasks will you include in seatwork? How often will you require it? Will every item be assessed, and how? What weight will homework carry in the report card grade?

For Field Experiences

1. Talk to several teachers to explore how they make presentations. Ask them to offer you guidelines for planning and delivering effective presentations.
2. Talk to several teachers to explore how they use questions during instruction. Ask them for recommendations for the effective use of questions.

Further Reading

Chuska, K. R. (2003). *Improving classroom questions: A teacher's guide to increasing student motivation, participation, and higher-level thinking* (2nd ed.). Bloomington, IN: Phi Delta Kappa.

Provides concise, practical guidance for asking better questions, using questions as motivators, designing questions, and using specific questioning strategies.

Cooper, H. M. (2007). *The battle over homework: Common ground for administrators, teachers, and parents* (3rd ed.). Thousand Oaks, CA: Corwin Press.

Provides useful guidance about the purposes and types of homework assignments. Research evidence is reviewed.

Harmin, M., & Toth, M. (2006). *Inspiring active learning: A complete handbook for teachers.* Alexandria, VA: Association for Supervision and Curriculum Development.

Provides very practical suggestions and guidance about selecting and using instructional strategies, organizing the classroom, handling homework and testing, and producing meaningful learning.

Walsh, J. A., & Sattes, B. D. (2005). *Quality questioning: A research-based practice to engage every learner.* Thousand Oaks, CA: Corwin Press.

Provides very detailed and useful guidance when formulating and using questions to promote student thinking.

6 | Indirect Instructional Strategies

Objectives

This chapter provides information that will help you to:

1. Design lessons that involve inductive instructional approaches, such as concept attainment, inquiry lessons, and projects and reports.

2. Design lessons during which students work cooperatively in groups.

3. Identify ways to effectively use discussions, panels, debates, and other social instructional approaches.

4. Determine ways to have students learn through independent means with learning centers, contracts, and other approaches.

Inductive Approaches
- Concept Attainment Approaches
- Inquiry Lessons
- Projects, Reports, and Problems

Independent Approaches
- Learning Centers or Stations
- Contracts and Independent Work

Social Approaches
- Discussions
- Cooperative Learning
- Panels and Debates
- Role-Playing, Simulations, and Games

As you consider your students' abilities, interests, and needs, you will want to differentiate your instruction. One way to differentiate is by your selection of instructional approaches. There is a continuum of instructional approaches to use. At times, you may want to use some of the more direct, teacher-centered instructional approaches discussed in Chapter 5. At other times, you will want to use some strategies that are less direct and more student centered. A number of these indirect instructional strategies are discussed in this chapter, including inductive approaches, social approaches, and independent approaches.

INDUCTIVE APPROACHES

Inductive instructional approaches often begin with exploratory activities and then lead to students discovering a concept or generalization. There are various ways to use inductive approaches; some have a higher degree of teacher-directed activity, and others have students more actively involved in planning and designing their instructional activities. Some of the more common inductive instructional approaches are concept attainment strategies; inquiry lessons; and projects, reports, and problems.

Concept Attainment Approaches

Concepts serve as the building blocks for student higher-level thinking. In general, concepts are main ideas used to help us to categorize and differentiate information. Therefore, when you ask students to place things together or to classify them, you are asking students to use concepts. Robert Gagné (1985) believes being able to label or classify things demonstrates an understanding of concepts and that combinations of concepts can be joined together into rules. He takes this a step further to say that the understanding of concepts and rules is what allows students to problem solve.

According to Jensen and Kiley (2005), three types of concepts are incorporated into the concept attainment model. First, *conjunctive concepts* address steady, unchanging content. For instance, the sun always rises in the east and sets in the west. Second, *disjunctive concepts* take alternate forms of the topic being considered. For example, the form of government may be democratic, aristocratic, or theocratic. Third, *relational concepts* describe the relationship between two or more concepts. When discussing the concept of driving, for example, the relationship between the driver, the mode of transportation, and the environment needs to be considered. It's essential that teachers categorize these concepts correctly, because understanding the concept type shapes the way the concepts are processed and learned. Consequently, it should also influence teachers' organizational behaviors regarding methods of instruction implementation and instructional strategy choice.

Concepts are central to the curriculum in every classroom. Table 6.1 lists a number of common concepts that students are asked to understand in various content areas. As demonstrated in the table, concepts can be simple, such as *verb,* or difficult, such as *evolution.* Many strategies designed to help students understand concepts call for students to identify similarities and differences. This can be accomplished through a number of research-based methods.

Concept attainment is an instructional strategy in which students are provided both examples and nonexamples of a concept. For instance, you might list a series of words containing some examples of, or attributes of, the concept that you want students

TABLE 6.1   Typical Curricular Concepts

LANGUAGE ARTS	SCIENCE	SOCIAL STUDIES	MATHEMATICS
Summarize	Technology	Cities	Congruent
Metaphor	Density	Democracy	Fractions
Perspective	Energy	NATO	Patterns
Verb	Motion	Terrorism	Equations
Audience	Evolution	Representative	Estimate
Context	Ecosystems	Manifest destiny	Predict
Theme	Diversity	Power	Triangle
Grammar	Genes	Distribution of wealth	Area
Essay	Cells	Culture	Volume
Point of view	Climate	Citizenship	Relationship

TABLE 6.2   Concept Lesson

Elections	Yes	Volume	No
Snowstorms	No	Closure	No
Right to vote	Yes	Majority decision making	Yes
Osmosis	No	Freedom	Yes
Participation	Yes		

to recognize. Table 6.2 shows a list of words, and each word is followed by a yes or a no. The yes answers form the concept under study. Can you guess the concept?

Based on the work of Bruner (1966), Joyce and Weil (2009) suggest that the following process be used for indirect concept learning:

1. You prepare labeled examples.
2. Students compare attributes of positive and negative examples.
3. Students put forward possible concepts.
4. Students provide a definition based on the essential attributes of the concept. From the attributes listed in Table 6.2, for example, students might define a *democracy* as follows: "A country with a government that has been elected freely and equally by all its citizens."
5. Add examples, and call on students to indicate a yes or no descriptor for each label.
6. You confirm student hypotheses, name the concept, and have students come up with a common definition.
7. Students generate examples.
8. Students describe their thought processes and discuss the role of hypotheses and attributes.

A variation of this approach would involve your providing students with a list of examples of countries that practice democracy in the first column and countries that do not in the second column. Since we are discussing indirect models in this chapter, concept-based lessons can take either a direct or indirect form. In using the indirect form, you would not label the columns as democratic or totalitarian countries, rather, you would let students reflect on what similarities the words share and have the students respond with concepts that they feel join the examples together.

Concept learning activities can also take a number of other forms. Some of the most productive concept attainment approaches are based on a rich line of research (Marzano, Pickering, & Pollock, 2005) in four key areas: comparisons, classifications, metaphors, and analogies.

Comparisons.   *Comparing* involves identifying similarities and differences between concepts. Students can only compare if they have deep understanding of the topics or concepts they are comparing. Comparing is a complex process that students need to practice to use skillfully (Marzano, Norford, Paynter, Pickering, & Gaddy, 2005). A key to success with this teaching strategy is to provide models of comparisons for students.

For example, Figure 6.1 uses a Venn diagram to provide a comparison of life before and after creation of the U.S. Constitution. A *Venn diagram* is a type of graphic organizer

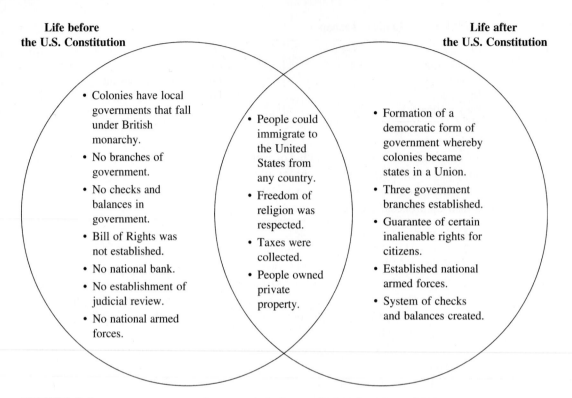

**Life before
the U.S. Constitution**

**Life after
the U.S. Constitution**

- Colonies have local governments that fall under British monarchy.
- No branches of government.
- No checks and balances in government.
- Bill of Rights was not established.
- No national bank.
- No establishment of judicial review.
- No national armed forces.

- People could immigrate to the United States from any country.
- Freedom of religion was respected.
- Taxes were collected.
- People owned private property.

- Formation of a democratic form of government whereby colonies became states in a Union.
- Three government branches established.
- Guarantee of certain inalienable rights for citizens.
- Established national armed forces.
- System of checks and balances created.

FIGURE 6.1   Venn Diagram Explaining Life before and after Creation of the U.S. Constitution

or visual tool that can be used to visually represent concepts you want to compare. Similarities are listed in the intersection between the circles, and differences are listed in the areas of the circles that do not intersect. Therefore, similarities in life between colonists before the U.S. Constitution was ratified and after include open immigration patterns, freedom of religion, the collection of taxes, and ownership of private property.

Venn diagrams and other graphic organizers can be used in two ways: (a) *indirectly* by asking students to create the diagrams and fill in the information and (b) more *directly* when you as the teacher develop the diagram. If you choose the indirect approach and have students create their own diagrams, it is helpful to start with content that is familiar to them. Once familiar with the process, students can then move to unfamiliar or more challenging material.

The feedback you give to students on the diagrams they create is very important. You can comment on important characteristics that are being compared, on the accurate identification of similarities and differences, and on student explanations for their decisions. Be cautious, however, about students waiting to hear the ideas from you or the other students. You can increase the probability of student involvement in these ways:

1. Give students sufficient time to think and reflect about the issue before asking for responses.

2. Ask for completed work from all students.

3. Have students work in small cooperative groups.

Another method that can be used to represent similarities and differences is a simple matrix. For example, you could have students who are investigating various expeditions throughout history fill out a matrix for the concept of *exploration*. A basic start would be for them to fill in a matrix that compares various explorers based on key concepts, such as personal information, goal for exploration, resources, and accomplishments. Table 6.3 represents a matrix for comparing Neil Armstrong, the first human to walk on the moon, and Richard Byrd, polar explorer. A matrix allows you to design lessons so that your students respond to set categories of information.

Classifications.   *Classifying* is the grouping of ideas or concepts into categories or groups based on similar characteristics. A useful method for showing the organizational structure of major concepts is by creating concept webs or maps. The Iroquois League of Nations before 1492, for example, could be organized into a web to illustrate the key concepts that represented these native peoples' way of life. A web representing the economy, housing, and social structures of the Iroquois League of Nations is shown in Figure 6.2.

Through organized representation, students can link concepts they already know to new concepts being considered. Students either can be given a web to work with, or they can be asked to produce their own.

TABLE 6.3   Comparison Matrix Exploration

COMPARISON (similarities and differences)	CONCEPT TO COMPARE: EXPLORERS		CHARACTERISTICS FOR COMPARISON
	Neil Armstrong	*Richard Byrd*	
Similarities			Personal information
Differences			
Similarities			Goals for exploration
Differences			
Similarities			Resources
Differences			
Similarities			Accomplishments
Differences			

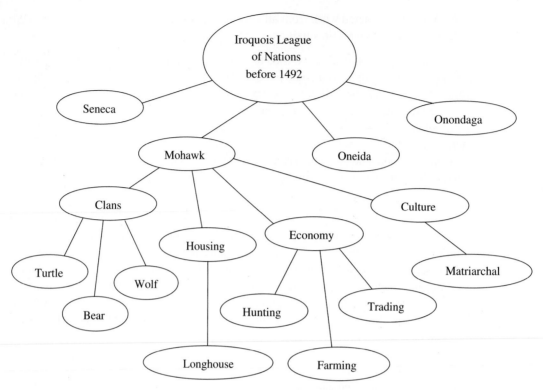

FIGURE 6.2   **Concept Web for the Iroquois League of Nations**

Metaphors.   A *metaphor* is a figure of speech, often used in poetry, to make an implicit comparison or connection between two unlike things (e.g., He was a rock through all this; She is a pillar in the community; I have a song in my heart). The two seemingly unrelated things, however, on examination, share a relationship on an abstract level. For example, a rock is literally solid and hard to break; on an abstract level, someone is strong and resilient in a difficult situation; and, therefore, on a literal level, some people appear to remain unmoved and stay tough during hard times.

Beyond their role as a figure of speech, metaphors can be used as instructional strategies to help your students to understand abstract patterns and convey the meaning of complex concepts or ideas in simpler terms. To prepare your students for identifying metaphors, you can warm them up with a discussion of a familiar topic, such as being moody. First, ask students to volunteer words that relate to being moody and record the words so everyone can see. Then, state another concept, such as a thunderstorm. Next, relate traits of a thunderstorm that line up with the traits the students identified for being moody. Thunderstorms may be loud and then quiet, or they may be bright and then dark.

Similar metaphors can be identified with other concepts. A chameleon changes colors with changes in conditions, and moods may change in a similar way. A thermometer records hot and cold temperatures, as moods may be hot and cold. Or the roll of dice is unpredictable, and moods may be the same way. Practicing the use of metaphors is helpful, and students will be more prepared when you want to identify metaphors with the content in the curriculum.

Another way to use metaphors in the classroom is to ask students to take the topic that you are studying, talk about it in literal terms, and then create a metaphor, or an abstract method of discussing it. For example, in science, you can ask students to create a metaphor for the role that arteries and veins play in the circulatory system. The students could use streets and highways to explain how blood moves through the body. In geology, students could say that Earth's crust is a cake to explain the various layers in its crust.

Analogies.   An *analogy* is a comparison between two similar things and can be used to explain something or to make it easier to understand. Analogies are often represented by asking students to identify pairs of concepts. When students can fill in the appropriate word, they demonstrate comprehension of the concept that they are studying.

Analogies are represented in the following relationship: A is related to B in the same way that C is related to D. Consider these examples:

Galaxy is to Star as Beach is to	(Sand)
Deciduous is to Maple as Evergreen is to	(Pine)
Blood is to Vein as Water is to	(Pipe)
Shakespeare is to Hamlet as J. K. Rowling is to	(Harry Potter)

Inquiry Lessons

Inquiry, discovery, and problem-solving approaches allow students to become involved in the process of discovery by enabling them to collect data and test hypotheses. As such, these approaches are inductive in nature. Teachers guide students as they discover new meanings, practice the skills, and undergo the experiences that will shape their learning. Generally, inquiry, discovery, and problem-solving approaches are student centered and less explicit than direct-teaching approaches. Several common inquiry and discovery approaches are considered here.

Inquiry is an open-ended and creative way of seeking knowledge. One of the strengths of this approach is that both the lesson content and the process of investigation are taught at the same time. The steps of inquiry essentially follow John Dewey's (1933) model of reflective thinking. The common steps include the following: (a) identify and clarify a problem; (b) form hypotheses; (c) collect data; (d) analyze and interpret the data to test the hypotheses; and (e) draw conclusions.

myeducationlab

Go to MyEducationLab, select the topic **Questioning Strategies,** click "videos," and select "Inquiry Learning." View the video and reflect.

Dewey, along with Jean Piaget and Lev Vygotsky, was instrumental in developing a major concept central to understanding the power of inquiry learning. This concept is referred to as *constructivism.* Through studies of how children think and develop, Piaget confirmed that children strive to construct understandings of the world in which they live. Vygotsky held that individuals develop intellectually when they confront new and puzzling events that they try to understand by linking this new knowledge to knowledge that they already possess in an effort to create new meanings.

Therefore, a *constructivist approach* involves students constructing meaning out of information that they have been exposed to through active engagement and investigation.

Voices from the Classroom

Students as Active Participants in Inquiry

Leo Harrison, middle school mathematics teacher, Louisville, Kentucky

Teacher-oriented, passive-student approaches to instruction are outdated. Especially in the middle school, we cannot effectively conduct our classes as if students were sponges who sit passively and absorb attentively. I base my approaches on the philosophy that the teacher is a coach of students. Thus, I view the student as having an active role in learning, and I serve as a guide in the pursuit of knowledge. This approach to instruction makes all gained knowledge more valuable, well learned, and better retained.

For students to care, the knowledge must be provocative, valuable, and reality based. Therefore, instruction should have much problem solving, research, and cooperative investigations. This doesn't mean that we eliminate standard lectures or guided practice. In fact, guided practice becomes essential to reinforce learning of useful knowledge. Overall, I have included a variety of instructional approaches in my teaching to help students to learn things that are important to them.

Constructivism promotes (a) the student point of view, (b) teacher–student interaction, (c) questioning to promote student thought, and (d) the importance of nurturing student reflection and thought, rather than a primary focus on a single correct answer or product. Useful resources are available, such as *Creating and Sustaining the Constructivist Classroom* (Marlowe & Page, 2005) and *Constructivist Learning Design* (Gagnon & Collay, 2006).

A constructivist approach provides students with the opportunity to investigate concepts and assists students in understanding new information by providing an environment of student-based discussion and investigation. You should ensure that your students are challenged by the instructional activities and stimulated by their own questions and the questions that you also might offer. Encourage your students to actively seek understanding and knowledge and to use prior knowledge to help them to understand new material.

Several approaches to inquiry may be used. *Guided inquiry* involves the teacher providing the data and then questioning the students in order to help them inductively to arrive at an answer, conclusion, generalization, or solution. *Unguided,* or open-ended, *inquiry* has the students take more responsibility for examining the data, objects, or events; these investigations are commonly done individually. Guided and unguided inquiry approaches may involve discussion and question sessions, guided or controlled discussions, projects, and research projects.

An inquiry problem-solving lesson typically consists of these five components:

1. *Students are presented with a problem* that is socially important and personally meaningful to them. The problem should be authentic, one that stimulates and motivates the students by having them seek solutions to meaningful problems that exist in the world. Problems often have an interdisciplinary focus that encourages students to investigate and apply many subjects—science, math, economics, government. A cooperative learning approach, in which students work in pairs or small groups, is often used in an inquiry problem-solving lesson.

2. *Students describe what is creating the problem* or the barriers barring its solution.

3. *Students identify solutions* for overcoming constraints and hypothesize which solution is likely to work. Students should feel free to brainstorm regarding the hypotheses. At this point, there is no right answer, so no hypotheses should be rejected. All hypotheses should be recorded either within individual student groups or as a whole class on the board.

4. *Students gather data and try solutions* to solve the problem. During this stage, the students, not the teacher, should do the thinking.

5. *Students analyze the data,* compare the results to the earlier generated hypotheses, and decide if they want to test another solution or hypothesis. Students construct exhibits or reports that represent their solutions. These could take many forms, from an experiment in science to a mock debate in social studies (Arends, 2007; Marzano, Pickering, & Pollock, 2005).

What Would You Decide?   *A Discovery Learning Activity*

In your science class, you want the students to participate in a discovery learning activity concerning the characteristics of various rocks and minerals. You haven't had your students do an activity like this before.

  1. What preparations would you need to make to ensure the success of this activity?

  2. How might your preparations be different if you were to have the students work independently as compared to working in small groups?

  3. How might you include the students in your preparations?

Problem solving involves the application of knowledge and skills to achieve certain goals. There are several components for problem-solving skills (Slavin, 2009). First, means–ends analysis is a problem-solving technique that encourages identifying the goals (the ends) of a problem, the current situation, and what needs to be done (the means) to reduce the difference between the two conditions. Second, creative problem solving involves cases for which the answers are not very clear or straightforward.

Projects, Reports, and Problems

Project-based lessons flow naturally in a problem-solving environment. Students often work either independently or cooperatively on projects related to the objectives of the unit being covered. A *project* is an activity that involves investigation about the facts of a particular issue and the reporting of these facts in various ways. Projects may include research reports, surveys, or case studies that have a particular purpose or objective. Problem-based instruction is essentially a project-based approach. Projects provide students with the opportunity to work somewhat independently from the teacher, have positive academic experiences with their peers, develop independent learning skills, become especially knowledgeable in one area of the subject matter, and develop skill in reporting this knowledge.

The degree of teacher direction can vary with projects. For a given unit, you may ask all students to prepare a report on one particular topic, or you may give a choice of several topics. You may ask students to work independently or in small groups, or you could let each student select the grouping that he or she would prefer. It is often helpful to provide written guidelines and time lines for the outlines, drafts, and completed projects. Criteria for evaluation of the project should be clearly stated.

After receiving initial guidelines, students decide on the tasks to be done, such as conducting library research or interviewing, and then collect the information in a cohesive way to report their findings and conclusions that they have drawn. Provide sufficient class time over a number of days to enable students to plan their actions, gather the information, and organize and prepare their report. After providing the initial project guidelines, your role will be to assist, advise, and facilitate student learning.

SOCIAL APPROACHES

Another indirect, student-oriented approach to instruction involves *social instructional approaches,* which permit students to interact with each other in various ways to help each others' learning. Some common social approaches include discussions, cooperative learning, panels and debates, and role-playing, simulations, and games.

Discussions

A group discussion is a powerful indirect instructional strategy, since students learn and remember when they participate. No matter what the format of the discussion—whole group, small group, or other opportunities for interaction—students have the opportunity to think out loud about concepts, giving them practice that they can then apply to other concepts. As instructional strategies go, discussions are generally less explicit and less teacher centered than other strategies. The class setting may range from informal to formal, with the teacher having a dominant to nondominant role.

Whole-Class Discussions.   A *discussion* is a conversation among several people having a particular purpose or objective. A *whole-class discussion* involves all students in the class discussing a topic with guidance from the teacher. When conducting a whole-class discussion, you must be able to clearly focus the discussion, keep it on track by refocusing, and encourage all participants to listen carefully to all points of view.

Teachers often direct whole-class discussions. Whole-class discussions may go astray when the class drifts from the main objectives of the discussion. Thus, prior to the discussion, it is important to plan key questions to be used so that the discussion is more likely to remain focused on the objectives. Useful resources are available for leading student-centered discussions (Hale & City, 2006).

Before beginning a whole-class discussion, make sure that students have an adequate knowledge base about the subject. A discussion cannot take place if students do not know much about the topic. Sometimes a discussion can be used before instruction as a means to generate interest, but the information must still be presented to students at some point.

Take the following guidelines into account when planning and implementing effective discussions (e.g., Borich, 2007; Jacobsen, Eggen, & Kauchak, 2009). These eight guidelines apply to whole-class and small-group discussions, as well as to panels and debates:

1. *Consider the goals of the discussion.* The goals of the lesson should structure the discussion. If the objective is to focus on cognitive development, then questions dealing with concepts and ideas are appropriate. If the discussion is to focus on the affective domain, then questions dealing with values and personal experiences are appropriate.

2. *Consider the experience and development of the students.* Younger and/or inexperienced students may need more direction during the discussion. The directions and questions may need to be more explicit, and the discussion itself may need to be shorter than it might be with an older group of students. As students become more mature and gain experience in discussions, they can take on more direction themselves.

3. *Study the issues.* Be familiar with the issues and/or material to be discussed during the lesson. This may appear too obvious to mention, but too often, teachers have not prepared themselves by learning about all the various issues surrounding a topic and thereby allow the discussion to drift during presentation.

4. *Orient the students to the objective of the discussion.* Explaining the objectives of the discussion to the students provides a road map for them and gives students a better idea of what to expect during the lesson.

5. *Provide a supportive classroom environment.* If a classroom discussion is to be successful, students must believe that they can contribute to the discussion without fear of embarrassment or ridicule. The effective teacher creates an environment where all ideas are welcome and where students give and receive constructive criticism in a supportive climate.

6. *Provide new or more accurate information when it may be necessary.* At times, it may be necessary for you to contribute information to the discussion. This allows the discussion to remain focused on the objectives.

7. *Review, summarize, or weave opinions and facts into a meaningful relationship.* At times, restate the major themes emerging from the discussion in order to provide a needed structure to the lesson. This permits the students to see how ideas are interrelated.

8. *Use humor.* Some discussions can cause tension within the class. Depending on the topic, students may not always agree with the opinions of their classmates. Students say something, without realizing it, that might offend another student. You can reduce the tension in the classroom by interspersing humor into the discussion.

Small-Group Discussions. *Small-group discussions* can meet the goal of increased student participation by allowing more students to become involved in the discussion. Groups of four to five students are most appropriate for small-group work. In addition to promoting higher-level thinking skills, small-group discussions help to promote the development of communication skills, leadership ability, debate, and compromise.

Students involved in small-group discussions often get off task easily. Careful organization can help these discussions to run more smoothly. There are at least four things that you can do to effectively conduct small-group discussions:

1. Carefully monitor the activity by moving around the room and checking with each group to make sure it remains focused on the discussion's objectives.
2. Make sure that students have enough background knowledge to effectively contribute to the discussion. Thus, small-group discussions should follow a lesson focusing on content and should build on topics previously developed.
3. Plan for relatively short discussions. If you see that the students are interested and are on task, the discussion can be allowed to continue. If a time limit is specified at the beginning of the lesson, the students are encouraged to remain on task.

Voices from the Classroom

Stimulating Classroom Discussions

Hildie Brooks, seventh- and eighth-grade health teacher, Manhattan, Kansas

Stimulating a discussion in the classroom is often a challenge for most teachers. The challenge is to include all the students. Many times the same 5 or 6 students enter a discussion and the other 15 to 20 students start to daydream. I have a terrific strategy that encourages all the students to participate in some manner. The form of the discussion is called the *discussion continuum,* which is intended to allow students to identify their own opinion by literally standing up for their opinion on the imaginary continuum line from one side of the room to the other side. If students choose to explain the reasons for their own opinion, they simply need to raise their hand. By having the students place themselves on the imaginary line, students are actively participating in the discussion.

I place two signs on opposite ends of the room: one states AGREE and the other states DISAGREE. I explain to the students what a continuum is and emphasize that there are no right or wrong answers, just their opinions. After a statement is read, students move to a point on the continuum that represents their own position on the statement. If a student is uncertain about his or her opinion, agrees with both sides of the issue, or does not choose to share his or her opinion, then, for any of these reasons, the student can stand in the middle of the continuum. Students may change their opinions at any time as they listen to each other. Thus, students may move themselves along the continuum as the discussion progresses.

In the seventh-grade drug education curriculum, I use this type of discussion approach when considering issues such as drinking alcohol, legalizing marijuana, and dealing with the rights of nonsmokers. In the eighth-grade class, which includes sex education, I use this format when discussing abortion and AIDS. The students enjoy using the discussion continuum.

4. Give students precise directions for the activity. If the students realize specifically what they are to do during the discussion, they are more than likely to remain on task. At the conclusion of the small-group activity, each group should report its results to the class. This can be accomplished by a written report or by having a representative from the group give an oral report to the class.

Cooperative Learning

Cooperative learning involves students working together in small, mixed-ability learning teams to address specific instructional tasks, thus aiding and supporting each other during the learning process. It is a popular instructional approach. The teacher presents the group with a problem to solve or task to perform. Students in the group then work among themselves, help one another, praise and criticize one another's

SAMPLE STANDARDS

Instructional Strategies

There are ten INTASC standards (see page xxi), and each standard includes a list of knowledge, dispositions, and performances to indicate more clearly what is intended in the standard.

Since this chapter deals with instructional strategies, some representative statements for knowledge, dispositions, and performances from INTASC Standard #4 are listed here concerning topics in this chapter.

Knowledge

- The teacher understands the cognitive processes associated with various kinds of learning (e.g., critical and creative thinking, problem structuring and problem solving, invention, memorization and recall) and how these processes can be stimulated.
- The teacher understands principles and techniques, along with advantages and limitations, associated with various instructional strategies.

Dispositions

- The teacher values the development of students' critical thinking, independent problem solving, and performance capabilities.
- The teacher values flexibility and reciprocity in the teaching process as necessary for adapting instruction to student responses, ideas, and needs.

Performances

- The teacher uses multiple teaching and learning strategies to engage students in active learning opportunities that promote the development of critical thinking, problem solving, and performance capabilities and that help students assume responsibility for identifying and using learning resources.
- The teacher varies his or her role in the instructional process in relation to the content and purposes of instruction and the needs of students.

contributions, and often receive a group performance score (Gillies, 2007; Jolliffe, 2007).

For example, you might divide the class into cooperative groups of four and assign each group to prepare a report on a different country in South America. Within each group, students agree to take on various responsibilities: leader–organizer, recorder of discussions, timekeeper, or other needed roles. Each group also decides on strategies to divide up the work—for example, who will be responsible for (a) collecting information, (b) organizing the information collected from various group members, (c) preparing the report, and (d) presenting the report to the class as a PowerPoint presentation. You would serve as a resource for the students in each group.

Collaborative learning generally occurs in three different ways:

1. Students have specific responsibilities within a larger group task or project.
2. Students work together on a common project or task.
3. Students take responsibility for all group members' learning.

Research indicates that cooperative learning approaches lead to higher academic achievement than strategies that call for students to complete similar tasks as individuals or to compete against each other (Marzano, Pickering, & Pollock, 2005). In addition, cooperative learning has been shown to have a positive effect on student attitudes. Students in cooperative learning groups have (a) better interpersonal relationships and (b) more positive attitudes toward subjects studied and the overall classroom experience (Johnson & Johnson, 1999).

Cooperative learning works best with heterogeneous groupings of students. Having students work in groups generally has a positive effect on their achievement when compared to their work as individuals. However, the findings become more complex when comparing the achievement of low-ability students who worked in homogeneous groups to that of low-ability students who were grouped heterogeneously. Low-ability students actually perform significantly worse when placed in homogeneous groups (Lou, Abrami, Spence, Paulsen, Chanvers, & d'Apollonio, 1996).

Through cooperative learning, students understand that they are responsible not only for their own learning but also for the learning of their team members. Cooperative learning approaches are often used to supplement other instructional practices. Research conducted by Lou and colleagues (1996) reported that cooperative learning works best when used in a weekly, systematic fashion.

Johnson and Johnson (1999) outline cooperative learning in three different styles: informal groups, formal groups, and base groups.

Informal Groups. *Informal groups* are short term, often accomplished by asking students to "turn to a neighbor," and used to clarify information, focus students on objectives, or bring about closure on a topic. These groups usually take place after lectures or other direct-teaching strategies. There are numerous types of informal groupings, but a feature central to all informal groups is that students are encouraged to actively participate and stay engaged by sharing their solutions with others.

Classroom Case Study

Using Cooperative Learning

Eric Johansson is a third-grade teacher who uses literature circles when his students read *Charlotte's Web,* by E. B. White. *Literature circles* are groups made up of four to six students in which students work together to discuss a piece of literature. While in literature circles, students may read the novel aloud to each other and/or respond to questions about it. Mr. Johansson believes that working in literature circles is a productive way for his students to gain a firmer grasp of a piece of literature by learning from each other.

After getting to know his students, Mr. Johansson formed several heterogeneous groups based on students' reading and cognitive abilities coupled with their individual learning styles, personality traits, and interests. Thus, Mr. Johansson created well-balanced, five-member groups that provide opportunities for students to learn from one another's differences while utilizing one another's strengths.

Each group must summarize five key plot developments in *Charlotte's Web,* and each student is responsible for summarizing one key plot development. The students then combine their work to create a brief plotline of the entire story. Students must interact with each other to ensure the main plot points are covered. When finished, groups will have the opportunity to share their summaries with the entire class.

Focus Questions

1. Based on this example, what are some of the positive factors associated with cooperative learning?
2. What factors would you consider when selecting which students to place in each group?
3. How would you use this strategy to enhance your teaching?

All activities start with the teacher asking students a question or giving them a problem to work on. During *think–pair–share,* students initially work independently but then move to pairs to discuss their answers. To conclude, you would call on students to report. In a *round-robin* activity, you place students in groups of three or four and have them share their answers with others in their group.

Formal Groups.   *Formal groups* are carefully designed so that a heterogeneous mix of students works together on specific learning tasks. Several common types of cooperative learning techniques are described in this section. Robert Slavin and his associates developed the first four; these rely on student team-learning methods, which include team rewards, individual accountability, and equal opportunities for success (Slavin, 1995).

1. *Student teams–Achievement divisions* (STAD) involves four-member learning teams that are mixed in performance level, gender, and ethnicity. After the teacher presents a lesson, students work within their teams to make sure that all members have mastered the lesson. Students then individually take a quiz, and their scores are based on the degree to which they meet or exceed their earlier performances. These points are then totaled to form team scores. Teams that meet certain criteria may earn certificates or other awards. If students want their team to earn rewards, they must help their teammates to learn the material. Individual accountability is maintained since the quiz is taken without the help of teammates. Because team scores are based on each student's improvement, there is equal opportunity for all students to be successful.

2. *Teams–games–tournaments (TGT)* uses the same teacher presentations and teamwork as in STAD. In TGT, however, students demonstrate individual subject mastery by playing academic games. Students play these games in weekly tournaments in which they compete with members of other teams who have similar past records in the subject. The competition takes place with three students at each tournament table. Since the tables include students of similar ability (i.e., high-achieving students are at the same table), all students have the opportunity to be successful. High-performing teams earn certificates or other team-based awards. Individual accountability is maintained during competition since teammates cannot help each other.

3. *Team accelerated instruction (TAI)* is a combination of individualized instruction and team learning. With TAI, students again work in heterogeneous teams, but each student studies individualized academic materials. Teammates check each other's work from answer sheets. Team scores are based on both the average number and the accuracy of units completed by team members each week.

4. *Jigsaw* involves six-member teams working on academic material that has been broken down into sections. Each team member reads his or her section. Then members of different teams who have studied the same sections meet in "expert groups" to discuss their section. Next the students return to their teams and take turns teaching their teammates about their sections. Since the only way students can learn about sections other than their own is to carefully listen to their teammates, they are motivated to support and show interest in each other's work.

5. *Learning Together* is a cooperative approach in which students are organized into teams that include a cross section of ability levels (Johnson & Johnson, 1999). Each team is given a task or project to complete, and each team member works on a part of the project that is compatible with his or her own interests and abilities. The intent is to maximize strengths of individual students to get a better overall group effect. Each team is responsible for gathering the information and materials needed to complete its assigned task or project. Final assessment is based on the quality of the team's performance. Each student on the team receives the same grade. This encourages students to pool their talents so each student makes the greatest possible contribution to the effort.

Base Groups.   *Base groups* are long-term, heterogeneous groups that stay together across tasks throughout the year. Base groups provide student-to-student support and a sense of routine in the classroom. Students in these groups build long-term relationships and a support system that encourages academic progress.

In elementary schools, base groups might meet in the morning and again at the end of the day. Morning tasks might include taking a lunch count, making sure everyone in the group has completed the homework, getting materials ready for the day, and catching up on outside activities. Afternoon meetings would allow groups to make sure that everyone has the correct homework assignment, share insights into the assignments and tasks, and focus on a question that brings closure to the day's activities.

After working with various students in cooperative learning groups, you will gain a sense of how to get the most out of all participants, how much time is needed for groups to complete their work, and how to transition to other activities. You should move around the room as groups work so that you can assess learning and plan follow-up activities.

What Would You Decide?   *Cooperative Learning Groups*

Before starting cooperative learning groups, it is important to show students how to work together as a supportive group. You should provide clear written directions and opportunities for students to receive feedback on their academic performance and the group's success in working together.

1. What additional orientation or training will enable students to work effectively in cooperative learning groups?

2. How might this orientation be different for second-graders as compared to tenth-graders?

3. How might you accommodate the different knowledge and skills of the students in their roles within the groups?

Panels and Debates

Panels, symposiums, task forces, and debates all involve a group of students becoming informed about a particular topic, presenting information to the class, and interacting in discussion. Each approach has unique characteristics. Panels and debates are designed to help students to understand several points of view related to a topic or issue. They combine prepared activities and statements with the give and take of discussions. They are useful in large-class activities when more informal whole-class or small-group discussions are not feasible.

myeducationlab

Go to MyEducationLab, select the topic **Questioning Strategies,** click "videos," and select "Debate." View the video and reflect.

A *panel* is a fairly informal setting in which four to six participants with a chairperson discuss a topic among themselves while the rest of the class listens. Later, there is give and take with the class. Each participant makes an opening statement. A round table is an informal version of a panel.

A *symposium* is very similar to a panel, but it involves a more formal presentation of information by each panel member. A *task force* is also like a panel, but it involves thorough investigation of a particular problem prior to the presentation to the rest of the class about the problem investigated. A *debate* is a formal discussion approach consisting of set speeches by participants of two opposing teams and a rebuttal by each participant. Panels and debates are conducted for the benefit of the whole class, which becomes involved through question and answer sessions upon the panel's completion.

Role Playing, Simulations, and Games

Role playing is a student-directed activity in which students act out or dramatize a particular situation, circumstance, or idea. The teacher structures and facilitates the role-playing and conducts the follow-up discussion. The majority of the class will be involved in observing and analyzing the enactments. Role playing can be successfully used at both the middle and secondary levels.

Role playing is particularly useful in helping students to understand the perspectives and feelings of other people concerning a variety of personal and social issues. In addition, role playing can be used to clarify and demonstrate attitudes and concepts, plan and test solutions to problems, help students to prepare for a real situation, and deepen understanding of social situations.

Joyce and Weil (2009) suggest that a nine-step process be used to maximize students' role-playing performance and learning:

1. *Warm up the group.* The warm-up centers on introducing students to the problem and making sure that they comprehend the problem. Next you provide examples of the problem. These examples can come from a variety of sources, including classroom situations (e.g., how to deal with situations that students often face with peers, such as use of cigarettes, alcohol, or drugs or a friend asking to copy homework) or historical problems without an ending or resolution disclosed. Examples can also come from students' life experiences, films, texts, newspapers, or other source materials. The final phase of the warm-up is for you to ask students questions to make sure that they understand the problem and that they are ready to start predicting various scenarios and outcomes: "What would you do in this situation?" "What are some possible ways this story could end?"

2. *Select the participants.* In this phase, you and your students describe the various characters or roles: What are they like? How do events affect different characters in different ways? How might a specific character act? What would they do and say? Students must want to play a particular role. As the teacher, you should ensure that students are well matched to their roles and understand the complexities these roles bring.

3. *Set the stage.* Ask students to outline the scene and set aside a place for the action to take place.

4. *Prepare the observers.* Several students without roles should be asked to act as observers. They should analyze the enactment relative to its realism, logical sequence of effects, and whether the actors covered the full range of their characters' likely feelings and perceptions.

5. *Enact.* The players start to role play, responding to the situation and to each other as realistically as possible. This first enactment should be kept short, and you should stop it when the major points have been made and the purpose of the enactment is clear. You can ask other students to provide a second enactment to fully investigate the issue.

6. *Discuss and evaluate.* You focus the discussion on what motivated the actors and what would be likely to occur should the scene continue. Alternative scenarios should be investigated.

7. *Reenact.* Reenactments can take place to ensure that students have opportunities to bring in new interpretations. Reenactments and discussion should alternate freely. Cause and effect should be investigated. For example, how does a change in one player's interpretation change the behavior of other players?

8. *Discuss and evaluate.* Repeat this step as needed.

9. *Share experiences and generalize.* As the teacher, you should help students to clarify their perceptions and relate the experience to other real-life problems or historical situations.

Simulations are exercises that place students in situations that model a real-life environment. They require students to assume roles, make decisions, and face consequences. Through the simulated experience, the goal is for students to understand the important factors and how to behave in real situations. Students will also benefit by seeing how others behave in real situations. Although the roles for the students in the simulation are clearly defined, student responses are impromptu.

Games are designed to involve students in competition as the primary means to achieve a learning goal. Games can be used to teach a wide variety of skills, including problem solving and decision making. (See the section on cooperative learning earlier in this chapter for specific strategies.) Of course, you need to select a game to fit the desired objectives. An instructional game has rules, a structure for playing the game, and a method for determining the winners and losers. You structure the setting, facilitate conducting the game, and supervise the students. Educational games can be useful in an interdisciplinary thematic unit.

INDEPENDENT APPROACHES

Independent instructional approaches are those in which students work by themselves on some project or at a learning center or learning station in the classroom. The teacher may be involved in some way in the identification and design of the particular instructional tasks. However, there is often considerable latitude for students with independent instructional approaches.

Learning Centers or Stations

A *learning center* is a designated place within the room where a student goes to pursue either required or optional activities on a given topic. It is a self-contained environment that includes all materials that students will need. Learning centers or learning stations are used to provide enrichment and reinforcement opportunities for students. Learning centers can be used to motivate students and provide a variety of instructional activities designed to meet the various ability levels and learning styles of the students.

Teachers often design and prepare a number of instructional tasks that the student can perform while in the learning center. These tasks typically accommodate a range of academic abilities and a variety of student interests. Students usually are not required to complete all tasks at a center, but may select the ones that they prefer based on their ability, interests, or other factors.

Contracts and Independent Work

Learning *contracts* provide a structure that allows a student and teacher to agree on a series of tasks to be completed in a given time frame. Many contracts are designed to allow students to work independently through a body of required content or to carry out an individual project. Most contracts entail specific assignments drawn from the regular curriculum and optional activities either drawn from the curriculum or planned around student interest.

It is not necessary that all students have learning contracts. Contract activities may be pursued during any independent work time, such as when other students are involved in skills instruction, when other assignments have been completed, or at any other time designated by the teacher as being appropriate for independent work.

Key Terms

Analogy	Formal groups	Project
Base groups	Games	Role playing
Classifying	Guided inquiry	Simulations
Comparing	Inductive instructional approaches	Small-group discussion
Concept attainment	Informal groups	Social instructional approaches
Constructivist approach	Inquiry	Symposium
Contracts	Learning center	Task force
Cooperative learning	Metaphor	Unguided inquiry
Debate	Panel	Venn diagram
Discussion	Problem solving	Whole-class discussion

Major Concepts

1. Inductive instructional approaches often begin with exploratory activities and then lead to students discovering a concept or generalization. Some inductive approaches have a higher degree of teacher-directed activity, and others have students more actively involved in planning and designing their instructional activities.

2. Examples of inductive instructional approaches include concept attainment strategies, inquiry lessons, and projects, reports, and problems.

3. Social instructional approaches are indirect, student-oriented strategies that permit students to interact with each other in various ways to help each other's learning. Some common social approaches include discussions, cooperative learning, panels and debates, and role-playing, simulations, and games.

4. Cooperative learning involves students working together in small, mixed-ability learning teams to address specific instructional tasks while aiding and supporting each other during the learning process.

5. Independent instructional approaches are those in which students work by themselves on some project or at a learning center or learning station in the classroom. The teacher may be involved in some way in the identification and design of the particular instructional tasks, but there is often considerable latitude for students in independent instructional approaches.

Discussion/Reflective Questions

1. Why should you be competent in the use of a variety of indirect instructional strategies?
2. Why might some teachers prefer more student-centered approaches?
3. What skills does a teacher need to effectively conduct a whole-class discussion?
4. What are the advantages and possible disadvantages of using cooperative learning, inquiry, and concept-based instructional strategies?
5. How might the subject area that you are teaching affect your selection of the instructional strategy to be used in a lesson? How might the age and maturity of the students affect this decision?

Suggested Activities

For Clinical Settings

1. Select a unit topic and prepare a two-week unit plan that includes inquiry strategies, cooperative learning, discussion methods, and group activities throughout the unit.
2. Explore computer software and other computer-assisted technology that is available. Evaluate this material and determine how you can use it in your instruction.
3. Prepare a list of guidelines and procedures for how you would use cooperative learning groups, problem solving, and independent work in your classroom.

For Field Experiences

1. Talk to several teachers to identify the types of indirect instructional strategies they use in the classroom. Determine why they selected these various strategies. Ask for recommendations for the effective use of these strategies.
2. Talk to several teachers to explore how they use discussion during instruction. Ask them for recommendations for effectively holding discussions.
3. Examine a school's computer equipment, software, and facilities. What procedures are established for teachers and students to use the computers? How do teachers in the school use computers and related technology to assist instruction?

Further Reading

Gillies, R. M. (2007). *Cooperative learning: Integrating theory into practice.* Thousand Oaks, CA: Sage.

   Discusses key components of cooperative groups, including ways to form groups, assign student roles, promote student thinking and learning, use strategies to promote student discourse, and assess student learning.

Johnson, D. W., & Johnson, R. T. (1999). *Learning together and alone: Cooperative, competitive, and individualistic learning* (5th ed.). Boston: Allyn & Bacon.

   Thoroughly examines the goals and elements of cooperative, competitive, and individualistic approaches to learning. Well written and organized to facilitate application.

Joyce, B., & Weil, M. (2009). *Models of teaching* (8th ed.). Boston: Allyn & Bacon.

   Provides an overview of different approaches to instruction, including many indirect instructional strategies.

7 Strategies That Promote Student Understanding

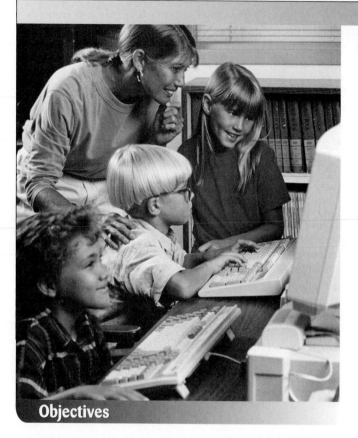

Objectives

This chapter provides information that will help you:

1. Identify instructional strategies that have a high probability of enhancing student achievement.
2. Identify the research-based generalizations about the use of each of the strategies.
3. Describe ways that each strategy can be used in the classroom.
4. Describe how strategies can be used for English language learners.

GENERATING AND TESTING HYPOTHESES

The process of generating and testing hypotheses involves the application of knowledge, and two generalizations can be made from the research in this area. First, hypothesis generation and testing can be approached through inductive and deductive approaches. *Inductive approaches* require students first to discover the principles and then to generate the hypotheses. With a *deductive approach,* a teacher would first present the principle and then ask students to generate and test hypotheses based on this principle. When discussing the scale of hardness for rocks and minerals, for example, a teacher may use an inductive approach by giving students various mineral samples and asking them to try scratching the materials to see what conclusions or principles they might draw. However, with the deductive approach, the teacher would first describe the principle and then ask the students to use the mineral sample to test out the principle.

Second, teachers should ask students to explain their hypotheses and their conclusions clearly. This can be done in various ways, such as providing students with templates for reporting their work, providing sentence stems for students to help them articulate their explanations, and providing rubrics so students know the criteria that will be used to evaluate their explanations.

Set aside time for students to verbally explain their hypotheses and conclusions. This will assist in ELLs' verbal language development and will also help them develop academic knowledge.

Teachers can use six types of tasks to engage students in generating and testing hypotheses:

1. *Systems analysis.* Students study many systems across the disciplines, such as ecosystems, weather systems, and systems of government. One way to enhance students' understanding of these systems is to ask them to generate hypotheses that predict what would happen if some aspect of a system were to change. For example, what would happen if there were not a Supreme Court in the United States? Systems analysis would involve several steps. First, explain the purpose of the system and the parts and functions of each part. Second, describe how the parts affect each other. Third, identify a part of the system, describe a change, and then hypothesize what would happen because of this change. Finally, test the hypothesis whenever possible.

2. *Problem solving.* Students are often asked to solve structured problems with specific goals and conditions. However, asking students to solve unstructured problems involves generating and testing hypotheses. *Unstructured problems* do not have clearly defined goals or constraints, and there is more than one way to solve the problem. Problem solving involves several steps. Identify the goal you are trying to accomplish, describe the constraints or conditions in reaching the goal, identify different solutions and hypothesize which solution is likely to work, try the solution, and then explain whether the solution was correct.

3. *Historical investigation.* Students are engaged in historical investigation when they investigate plausible scenarios for events from the past about which there is no general agreement. For example, there has been considerable public debate about whether President George W. Bush had justification to take the United States to war in Iraq. Historical investigation involves several steps. Clearly describe the historical event to be examined. Identify what is known or agreed on and what is not known or about which there is disagreement. Based on the students' understanding about the situation, offer a hypothetical scenario. Finally, seek out and analyze evidence to determine whether the hypothetical scenario is plausible.

4. *Invention.* The process of invention involves generating and testing hypotheses. To do so, students must hypothesize what might work, develop an idea, and then conduct tests to determine whether their idea does work. Invention often involves generating and testing multiple hypotheses until one of them proves effective. We need invention in situations when we ask "Shouldn't there be a better way to . . . ?"

5. *Experimental inquiry.* Experimental inquiry involves making observations, generating explanations, making predictions, and testing them. While experimental inquiry is often associated with science classes, it can be effectively used in all subject areas.

6. *Decision making.* Using a structured decision-making framework can help students examine hypothetical situations, especially those requiring them to select what is the most or least of something or what is the best or worst of something. In a literature class, for example, you might ask students to examine the characters in two books read in class and to identify which character best fulfills the civic responsibilities of a good citizen. Students might select various characters. But the results might be different if you identified a structured decision-making framework in which several criteria were identified and a rating system was established for the criteria as students considered the main characters. Using a decision-making process to test their prediction requires students to reflect on and use a broad range of knowledge related to the topic.

SPOTLIGHT on Technology

Computer Software for Diagramming and Outlining

Software is available for students to create concept maps, webs, and other graphic organizers using pictures and text to represent concepts and relationships and then to convert those concepts and images easily into an outline format, or vice versa. This helps strengthen students' critical thinking skills, comprehension, and writing skills across the curriculum. *Inspiration* is one such program for grades 6–12, and *Kidspiration* is available for grade K–5 (see www.inspiration.com).

Consider the following for use of this concept-mapping software.

1. How might you use this software to apply the strategies discussed in this chapter?
2. What advantages might you experience with the use of this software?
3. What disadvantages or problems might exist?

CUES, QUESTIONS, AND ADVANCE ORGANIZERS

myeducationlab

Go to MyEducationLab,
select **Direct Instruction,**
click "videos," and select
"A Lesson on Fractions."
View the video and
reflect.

Cueing and questioning are at the heart of classroom practice. *Cues* are explicit hints concerning what students are about to experience. *Advance organizers* are organizational frameworks that teachers present to students prior to teaching new content to prepare students for what they are about to learn. Taken together, cues, questions, and advance organizers help students understand and make connections to the content.

Cues and Questions

Here are several guidelines for using cues and questions:

■ *Focus cues and questions on what is important, not on what is unusual.* Questions designed to help students obtain a deeper understanding of the content will eventually increase their interest in the topic.

■ *Use explicit cues.* Cues are more effective when they relate to specific content and purposes.

■ *Use higher-level questions because they promote deeper understanding.* Questions that require students to analyze information produce more learning than do questions that simply require students to recall or recognize information.

■ *Wait briefly before accepting responses from students to increase the depth of students' answers.* Wait time involves pausing several seconds after asking a question to give students time to think before being called on for an answer. Wait time promotes more student discourse and more student-to-student interaction.

■ *Use questions before a learning activity to establish a mental set for the learning experience.* Questions after a learning activity are useful, but they should be supplemented with questions before the learning activity.

Advance Organizers

Advance organizers provide a preview of the content that is to be addressed. They take the surprise out of what is to come, help students retrieve what they already know about a topic, and focus them on the new information. Advance organizers are most useful with information that is not well organized; using an advance organizer helps students recognize the important information and put it in context with related information.
     Several types of advance organizers can be used:

■ *Use expository advance organizers.* Expository advance organizers are straightforward descriptions of the new content that students will be learning. The descriptions can be written or oral, should focus on the important information, and may include text and pictures. The objectives of the lesson may be stated within this advance organizer.

Graphic organizers also can be effectively used as an advance organizer to provide a preview of the lesson.

■ *Use narrative advance organizers.* Narrative advance organizers are stories that help the students make personal or real-world connections to the content. For example, teachers may tie in a personal experience, refer to current television shows or movies, or describe a current event in relation to the content to be addressed.

■ *Have students skim the textbook as a form of advance organizer.* Skimming allows students to preview important information they will encounter later by noting what stands out in the textbook in headings, subheadings, and highlighted information. Students need to see that these features help outline the main information.

■ *Use graphic advance organizers.* By using a graphic organizer, students can become familiar with the information that will be studied along with the relationships among the pieces of information. Graphic organizers give students a visual map of the upcoming information to be studied.

APPLYING THE SIOP MODEL TO STRATEGIES

Meeting the needs of English language learners can be facilitated by the use of the SIOP model to provide more flexibility in the design and delivery of instruction. As outlined in Chapter 1, the SIOP model has eight components, and two of them relate to instructional strategies to promote learning: strategies and practice/application (Echevarria, Vogt, & Short, 2008). While these strategies were originally designed for use with ELLs, they are also helpful in meeting the needs of all learners in the classroom. The excellent content from Echevarria, Vogt, and Short (2008) serves as the foundation for much of the information in this section.

Strategies

Teachers need to give careful and deliberate thought to their choice of instructional strategies and the results they hope to achieve. Using a variety of instructional strategies, providing students with support and assistance with the strategies, and using higher-order questions all require much attention prior to instruction:

1. *Provide ample opportunities for students to use learning strategies.* Students need to be actively involved in their learning, and many instructional strategies provide opportunities for active involvement. However, many ELLs have difficulty assuming active roles because they focus their energies on developing language skills. Therefore, teachers should provide many opportunities for learners to use a variety of learning strategies, and the strategies should be taught through explicit instruction, carefully modeled and supported.

2. *Consistently use scaffolding techniques to assist and support student understanding.* Teachers scaffold instruction when they provide substantial amounts of support and assistance in the earliest stages of teaching a new concept and then gradually decrease the amount of support as the learners acquire experience through multiple practice opportunities.

There are two types of scaffolding. First, verbal scaffolding involves the use of prompts, questioning, and elaboration to facilitate students' movement to higher levels of language proficiency, comprehension, and thinking. This can be done, for example, by paraphrasing a student response to model correct English usage, reinforcing definitions in class discussions or questions, sharing your thinking about an issue, or simply slowing speech and including pauses. Second, procedural scaffolding includes the use of instructional approaches such as partnering or grouping students for reading activities, one-on-one teaching, and small-group instruction.

3. *Use a variety of questions or tasks that promote higher-order thinking skills.* Learning is promoted with higher-order questions that ask students to apply, analyze, and evaluate information. It is important that you carefully plan higher-order questions prior to lesson delivery; it is too difficult to think of them during instruction. Encouraging students to respond with higher levels of thinking requires teachers to consciously plan and incorporate questions at a variety of levels.

Practice/Application

Teachers need to give students a chance to practice with new material, to demonstrate how well they are learning it, and then to apply that new knowledge in new ways. Practice and application is especially important for ELLs' academic language development. Oral and written practice can be achieved through the use of hands-on materials, activities where students apply content and language knowledge, and activities where all language skills are integrated:

1. *Supply hands-on materials for students to practice using new content knowledge.* While all students benefit from guided practice, English language learners make more rapid progress in mastering content objectives when they have multiple opportunities to practice with hands-on materials and manipulatives. Manipulating materials is important for ELLs because it helps them connect abstract concepts with concrete experiences and thus reduces the language load for students. As a general rule, provide short meaningful amounts of material to be practiced, practice for a short time, schedule several episodes of practice close together, and provide specific feedback.

2. *Provide activities for students to apply content and language knowledge in the classroom.* All students learn best when they are involved in relevant, meaningful application of what they are learning. For students acquiring a new language, the need to apply new information is important because discussing and participating in activities helps make abstract concepts concrete. Application can occur when using graphic organizers, participating in discussions, solving problems in cooperative learning groups, or doing a variety of other meaningful activities. Application must also include opportunities to practice language knowledge in the classroom. Opportunities for social interaction promote language development; these include discussion, reporting information orally and in writing, and working with partners and in small groups.

3. *Integrate all language skills into each lesson.* Reading, writing, listening, and speaking are complex cognitive language processes that are interrelated and integrated. Teachers need to create many opportunities for ELLs to practice and use all four language processes in an integrated way. This can be accomplished by designing varied activities that incorporate reading, promote interactions with others, encourage writing about what has been learned, and provide the chance to listen to peers' ideas.

Key Terms

Advance organizers	Cues	Note taking
Classifying	Deductive approaches	Practice
Comparing	Graphic organizers	Reciprocal teaching
Creating analogies	Homework	Summarizing
Creating metaphors	Inductive approaches	Summary frame

Major Concepts

1. There are four common approaches to identify similarities and differences: comparing, classifying, creating metaphors, and creating analogies.
2. Summarizing content and taking notes both require students to distill information.
3. Homework and practice give students opportunities to deepen their understanding and proficiency with the content they are learning.
4. Nonlinguistic representations use images to represent the content.
5. Setting objectives and providing feedback give students direction and help them think about their own learning.
6. Generating and testing hypotheses can be achieved by inductive or deductive approaches.
7. Cues, questions, and advance organizers help students understand and make connections to the content.
8. Instructional strategies can be adapted to meet the needs of English language learners.

Discussion/Reflective Questions

1. From your own school experiences, which of the major strategies presented in this chapter were most helpful in promoting your understanding of the content?

2. What are the benefits of using several approaches when identifying similarities and differences?

3. What are the advantages and disadvantages of occasionally providing students with teacher-made notes?

4. What might be the consequences if teachers do not set objectives and provide student feedback?

5. What have been some effective ways your teachers have used advance organizers to introduce lesson objectives?

Suggested Activities

For Clinical Settings

1. Examine a chapter from a textbook you might use, and determine ways that you could use similarities and differences for part of the instruction.

2. Examine a chapter from a textbook you might use, and prepare several nonlinguistic representations for some of the chapter content.

3. Imagine that you are teaching this chapter. Identify three ways you can use advance organizers to introduce the content to your students.

For Field Experiences

1. Talk with several teachers to see how they use concept maps, forms, or diagrams in their classes.

2. Review the teacher's editions of some textbooks to see whether the suggested instructional activities include some of the approaches discussed in this chapter.

3. Talk with several students about how they summarize and take notes.

Further Reading

Bellanca, J. (2007). *A guide to graphic organizers* (2nd ed.). Thousand Oaks, CA: Corwin Press.

An excellent resource, providing examples of numerous types of graphic organizers that can be used in any subject or grade level.

Chuska, K. R. (2003). *Improving classroom questions: A teacher's guide to increasing student motivation, participation, and higher-level thinking* (2nd ed.). Bloomington, IN: Phi Delta Kappa.

Provides concise, practical guidance for asking better questions, using questions as motivators, designing questions, and using specific questioning strategies.

Hill, J. D., & Flynn, K. M. (2006). *Classroom instruction that works with English language learners.* Alexandria, VA: Association for Supervision and Curriculum Development.

Focuses on nine instructional strategies that are effective in promoting achievement when working with English language learners.

Marzano, R. J., & Pickering, D. J. (2007). The case for and against homework. *Educational Leadership, 64*(6), 74–79.

Reviews the debate over the benefits of homework, the research evidence, and the guidelines for effective use of homework.

8 | Managing Lesson Delivery

Objectives

This chapter provides information that will help you to:

1. Select ways to structure lessons, group students, and hold students academically accountable.

2. Identify ways to handle administrative and instructional responsibilities at the start of a lesson.

3. Identify teacher actions that contribute to effective group management during the middle part of a lesson.

4. Identify actions which teachers take at the end of a lesson to provide for lesson summary and enable students to prepare to leave.

5. Describe ways to manage student work.

6. Select ways to effectively manage whole-group instruction.

7. Describe how lesson delivery can be enhanced for English language learners.

Issues Affecting Lesson Delivery
- Degree of Structure in Lessons
- Grouping Students for Instruction
- Holding Students Academically Accountable

Managing Student Work
- Managing Seatwork Effectively
- Collecting Assignments and Monitoring Their Completion
- Maintaining Records of Student Work
- Managing the Paperwork
- Giving Students Feedback

Managing Parts of the Lesson
- Beginning of a Lesson
- Middle of a Lesson
- Ending of a Lesson

Managing Whole-Group Instruction
- Preventing Misbehavior
- Managing Movement through the Lesson
- Maintaining a Group Focus
- Maintaining Student Attention and Involvement

Applying the SIOP Model to Lesson Delivery
- Comprehensible Input
- Interaction
- Lesson Delivery
- Review and Assessment of Lesson Objectives

When planning for a vacation trip, you often need to plan ahead. Do you want to stay in one place and relax, or do you want to visit a number of areas? Would you like to schedule several events for each day, or would you like to leave the daily schedule very open?

What types of accommodations would you like? To ensure an enjoyable vacation, you need to give these questions attention.

Similarly, you need to give advance thought to the type of classroom that you would like to have. How structured do you want your classroom and lessons? How do you want to group your students for instruction? How will you hold the students academically accountable? How will you handle various aspects of lesson delivery? How will you manage student work? How will you provide for whole-group instruction? How can lesson delivery be enhanced for English language learners (ELLs)? These issues will be explored in this chapter. How you attend to these issues will make a difference in managing instruction and student behavior.

ISSUES AFFECTING LESSON DELIVERY

Preparing daily lesson plans is a vital task for effective classroom management and discipline, because effective, engaging lessons can keep students on task and minimize misbehavior. You need to consider the degree of structure that will occur in each lesson. The grouping planned for the instructional activities will also affect student interaction. Furthermore, students are more likely to stay on task and be engaged in instruction when they know that they will be held academically accountable.

Degree of Structure in Lessons

Many instructional strategies can be used, ranging from teacher-centered, explicit approaches to the presentation of content to student-centered, less explicit approaches. *Teacher-centered approaches* include lectures, demonstrations, questions, recitations, practice and drills, and reviews. *Student-centered approaches* include inquiry approaches, discovery learning and problem solving, role playing and simulation, gaming, laboratory activities, computer-assisted instruction, and learning or activity centers. Various types of grouping and discussion methods may be student or teacher directed, depending on how they are used. Teacher-centered approaches are often more structured than student-centered approaches. As a result, the management issues will vary depending on the approach used.

When deciding on your instructional strategy, you need to weigh the advantages and disadvantages of the various strategies along with the lesson objectives. Effective teachers use several strategies, ranging from teacher directed to student directed. The lesson objectives may determine what type of approach is most appropriate. Some content may lend itself to inquiry and discovery techniques, whereas other content may be better handled with direct instruction. Over time, students should be given the opportunity to learn through a variety of instructional strategies.

Grouping Students for Instruction

You need to consider the type of student grouping that is most appropriate for the instructional strategies and instructional objectives. Focus on a group as a collection of

SAMPLE STANDARDS

Lesson Delivery

There are ten INTASC standards (see page xxi), and each standard includes a list of knowledge, dispositions, and performances to indicate more clearly what is intended in the standard.

Since this chapter deals with lesson delivery, some representative statements for knowledge, dispositions, and performances from INTASC Standard #5 are listed here concerning topics in this chapter.

Knowledge

- The teacher understands how social groups function and influence people, and how people influence groups.
- The teacher knows how to help people work productively and cooperatively with each other in complex social settings.

Dispositions

- The teacher takes responsibility for establishing a positive climate in the classroom and participates in maintaining such a climate in the school as whole.
- The teacher understands how participation supports commitment, and is committed to the expression and use of democratic values in the classroom.

Performances

- The teacher organizes, allocates, and manages the resources of time, space, activities, and attention to provide active and equitable engagement of students in productive tasks.
- The teacher organizes, prepares students for, and monitors independent and group work that allows for full and varied participation of all students.

individuals who learn. Within groups, individual students observe, listen, respond, take turns, and so on. Instructional groups can be large or small. Whole-group instruction, small-group instruction, and independent work are options to consider.

Whole-Group Instruction.   In *whole-group instruction,* the entire class is taught as a group. In the large group, you could (a) lecture, demonstrate, and explain a topic; (b) ask and answer a question in front of the entire class; (c) provide the same recitation, practice, and drill exercises for the entire class; (d) work on the same problems; and (e) use the same materials. Although instruction is directed to the whole group, you can still ask specific students to answer questions, monitor specific students as they work on assigned activities, and work with students on an individual basis. Even with whole-group instruction, give consideration to the individual differences of students.

Small-Group Instruction.   Sometimes instructional objectives can be better met when students work in small groups; this is *small-group instruction.* Small groups enable students to be more actively engaged in learning, and teachers can better monitor student progress. Groups of four students often work well. In a group of more than six, generally not everyone will actively participate.

Since group work helps develop relationships, it is useful to vary the membership of the groups based on gender and ethnicity. Students with disabilities can be placed in groups with nondisabled students to integrate them into the mainstreamed classroom. While there may be good reasons for planning a homogeneous group for certain activities, educators in general recommend the use of heterogeneous groups (Johnson & Johnson, 1999; Slavin, 2009).

There are three types of groupings: cooperative learning groups, ability grouping, and peer tutoring. An explanation of each follows:

1. *Cooperative learning groups.* *Cooperative learning* refers to a variety of teaching methods in which students work in small groups to help one another to learn academic content (Slavin, 2009). One approach is with the use of student team learning methods for which there are team goals, and success is achieved if all team members learn the objectives being taught. Other types of cooperative learning groups include group investigations, jigsaw activities, and complex instruction. All these approaches are discussed more fully in Chapter 6.

As you consider ways to differentiate your instruction, cooperative learning groups serve as an important means to provide instructional variety for your students while relating to various learning styles and student learning preferences. These groups also provide the opportunity to differentiate the content and tasks to meet the diversity of student interests and skills.

2. *Ability groups. Ability grouping* involves the clustering of students who are judged to be similar in their academic ability into classes for instruction. There are two common types of ability grouping: between-class grouping and within-class grouping.

Between-class grouping involves having separate classes for students of different abilities. When reporting research on between-class ability grouping, Slavin (2009) noted that grouping arrangements made on the basis of standardized test scores are not effective in reducing the range of differences that affect the specific class. In addition, the quality of instruction often is lower in lower-track classes, and students feel stigmatized by their assignments to low tracks. They may become delinquent and truant and may eventually drop out of school. The disadvantages of between-class ability grouping suggest that it be avoided when possible (Oakes, 2005). Instead, you might consider within-class ability grouping for a short time, as well as individualized instruction techniques.

Within-class grouping involves creating subgroups within a class, with each subgroup being fairly homogeneous in terms of ability. A small number is better than a large number of groups. In this way, group assignments can be flexible, role models for low achievers are available, teacher morale is higher, and the stigmatizing effect is minimized (Slavin, 2009). Within one classroom, you may group students for various activities or subjects. For example, middle school and secondary teachers may use ability groups for only part of a class period and whole-group activities or other approaches for the rest of the class time. You may group students to work on selected projects or activities.

3. *Peer tutoring.* *Peer tutoring* involves students teaching students. The two types of peer tutoring are (a) cross-age tutoring, by which older students work with younger students, and (b) peer tutoring, by which students within the same class work together.

There are several advantages of peer tutoring (Johnson & Johnson, 1999): (a) peer tutors are often effective in teaching students who do not respond well to adults; (b) peer tutoring can develop a bond of friendship between the tutor and tutee, which is important for integrating slow learners into the group; (c) peer tutoring allows the teacher to teach a large group of students while giving slow learners the individual attention that they need; (d) tutors benefit by learning to teach; and (e) peer tutoring happens spontaneously under cooperative conditions, so the teacher does not have to organize and manage it in a formal, continuing way.

Independent Work.   You might give students opportunities to work on tasks of their own choosing, or you may assign activities that enable students to work alone. This is *independent work.* Good and Brophy (2008) found that one-third of elementary teachers attempt to individualize instruction, as do one-fifth of secondary teachers.

When assigning independent work, you may involve students in any of a number of instructional strategies. In inquiry and discovery instructional approaches, students

Voices from the Classroom

Grouping Students for Instruction

Saralee Wittmer, second-grade teacher, Amarillo, Texas

Students in my room are arranged in small groups of four students according to ability. I shuffle the mix every 4–6 weeks. Students get the chance to work with all other students and can sit close to the teacher, at the back of the room, close to the door, and up by the chalkboards.

Students are encouraged to discuss lessons with each other within their groups. It's amazing how much they learn from each other if we will only give them the opportunities. I can tell what the class might not have gotten from my lesson presentations by listening carefully to them when they are in their groups.

Gladis Diaz, fifth-grade teacher, Reno, Nevada

When preparing to group my students, I have them complete some cooperative activities so that I can see their skills and personalities. This helps me place them in homogeneous groups and establish the roles for each person in a group. Each group has a leader, a recorder, a go-getter, a speller, and an organizer. I choose the leader who remains in that role throughout the school year. The roles of the others rotate four times during the schoolyear. I meet with the group leaders at least twice a week to discuss their role for the week and to be sure everything is running smoothly.

learn about the process of discovery by collecting data and testing hypotheses. Teachers guide students as they discover new meanings, practice the skills, and undergo the experiences that will shape their learning. These approaches include computer-assisted instruction, learning centers, learning stations, laboratories, discovery techniques, and others.

Holding Students Academically Accountable

Procedures to help manage student work must also be selected. *Academic accountability* means that the students must complete certain activities related to the instructional objectives. Teacher responsibilities for holding students academically accountable are displayed in Figure 8.1, some of which are adapted from Emmer & Evertson (2009), Evertson and Emmer (2009), and Jones and Jones (2007).

Consider the following guidelines when holding students academically accountable:

■ *Determine a system of grading* (e.g., letter grades or numerical grades, and measures for nonachievement outcomes). This decision might have been made for you by the school district, as reflected in the report-card format. Use a variety of evaluation measures (e.g., tests, written or oral reports, homework, ratings, projects) throughout the marking period, and describe the grading system to the students.

■ *Make decisions about assignments.* This includes deciding where and how you will post assignments, as well as the requirements and criteria for grading. Students should understand that completed assignments are part of the grading system.

■ *Decide on work and completion requirements.* Students need to have guidelines or work requirements for the various assignments. Details about due dates, late work, and missed assignments due to absence should be explained. The relevant procedures will help students understand expectations held of them and should minimize questions on a case-by-case basis.

■ *Monitor student progress and completion of the assignments.* You may want to use some in-class activities as formative exercises for students but not count performance on these in your grading. The activities may be written, oral, or performance demonstrations. Student progress should be monitored. In many cases, the entire class is at work on the designated activity; this enables you to walk around and observe each student carefully to see how he or she is progressing.

■ *Provide students with feedback about their progress.* Feedback on in-class activities may take the form of statements to the individuals or to the class. Students may exchange papers to evaluate progress on formative exercises. Papers or projects that are to be part of the report-card grade should be collected, graded, and returned promptly. In this way, students receive regular feedback about their progress throughout the marking period. Computer programs available for maintaining a gradebook can easily generate progress reports for both students and teacher.

FIGURE 8.1   Holding Students Academically Accountable

Consider your grade level and subject area as you make decisions on the following issues in an effort to hold students academically accountable.

1. **Grading System**
    a. Select a grading system.
    b. Select types of evaluation measures.
    c. Determine how grades will be assigned.
    d. Address nonachievement outcomes.
    e. Communicate the grading system to students.
    f. Design a gradebook.
    g. Report grades and communicate to parents.

2. **Assignments**
    a. Post assignments.
    b. State requirements and grading criteria for assignments.
    c. Make long-term assignments.

3. **Work and Completion Requirements**
    a. Identify work requirements.
        (1) Use of pencil or pen
        (2) Headings on papers
        (3) Writing on the back of the paper
        (4) Neatness and legibility guidelines
    b. Identify completion requirements.
        (1) Due dates
        (2) Late work
        (3) Incomplete work
        (4) Missed work
    c. Make provisions for absent students and makeup work.
        (1) Have an assignment list or folder.
        (2) Identify a due date.
        (3) Select a place to pick up and drop off absent assignments.
        (4) Provide a regular time to assist students with makeup work.

4. **Monitoring Progress and Completion of Assignments**
    a. Determine when and how to monitor in-class assignments.
    b. Determine when and how to monitor longer assignments, projects, and works in progress.
    c. Determine when and how to monitor in-class oral participation and performance.
    d. Determine which activities will receive a grade and which will be used only for formative feedback for the student.
    e. Select checking procedures that will be used in class.
        (1) Students exchanging papers
        (2) Marking and grading papers
        (3) Turning in papers

5. **Providing Feedback**
    a. Decide what kind of feedback will be provided to students and when it will be provided.
    b. Determine what records students will keep concerning their progress.
    c. Select incentives and rewards.
    d. Record scores in the gradebook.
    e. Post selected student work.

MANAGING PARTS OF THE LESSON

You have finished your planning. You have selected the instructional strategies. You have prepared and gathered the instructional materials. Now it is the day of your lesson. You are all ready to begin, but wait. You also must recognize that you can take certain actions during your instruction that will have an effect on maintaining order in the classroom and on achieving the lesson objectives.

You can use a number of strategies at certain points in a lesson to effectively manage the group, maintain order and control, and fulfill various administrative and academic objectives. If these activities are not handled appropriately, students may be more inclined to be off task and possibly misbehave. As a result, it is important to examine these lesson delivery tasks from the perspective of management and order in the classroom.

Beginning of a Lesson

A successful lesson beginning can greatly contribute to a meaningful learning experience for students. The beginning of a lesson should be designed to capture the students' attention and focus their attention on the learning objectives to be addressed during the lesson. An effective beginning can increase students' ability to focus on the objectives.

Actions you take at the start of a lesson help establish an atmosphere in which students have the "motivation to learn" (Brophy, 2010). *Motivation to learn* draws on the meaningfulness, value, and benefits of the academic task to the learner. For example, math problems may be developed that relate to student interests such as selling products for a youth-group fund-raiser. Thus, the focus is on learning, rather than on merely performing. Often students can be motivated at the beginning of a lesson by emphasizing the purpose of the task or the fact that students will be interested in the task.

Prior to beginning the substance of a lesson, take attendance and get attention. At the beginning of the lesson, your actions include providing daily review, providing a set induction, introducing lesson objectives, distributing and collecting materials, and giving clear, focused directions.

Taking Attendance.   Elementary teachers in self-contained classrooms commonly take attendance first thing in the morning, whereas secondary teachers take attendance at the start of each class. Tardiness also must be noted, and teachers need to follow school policies when recording and responding to tardy students. It is helpful not to hold up the beginning of class to take attendance. You should plan an opening activity for students to do while you take attendance. Some teachers have the first daily activity posted on the board for the students to do while attendance is taken. Have a seating chart for each class; a substitute teacher will find this especially useful.

Getting Attention.   Students should understand that they are expected to give full attention to lessons at all times. A lesson should not begin until you gain their full attention. There should be a predictable, standard signal that tells the class "We are now ready to begin the lesson." The type of signal will vary with teacher preferences. For

Taking Attendance and Handling Opening Activities

Carolyn Steinbrink, middle school American history teacher, Shenandoah, Iowa

I like the class to begin the second the bell rings. This is difficult because there are a dozen little chores that need to be done before actual teaching begins. Attendance must be taken and recorded, make-up work needs to be assigned, and other forms may need to be filled out. While all of this is being done, the students may become chaotic.

To avoid confusion while I take care of the attendance and other items, I have the students review yesterday's learnings. The best approach I have found involves the use of the overhead projector to display directions for a three-minute task using the objectives from yesterday's lesson. Students may be asked to do a quick bit of writing, discuss a question with a partner and be ready to report, take a short 3–5 point quiz, or any of a variety of review techniques.

example, you can raise your hand, ring chimes or a bell, stand in a certain location, or make a statement. After giving the signal, pause briefly to allow it to take effect. Then when you have attention, move quickly into the lesson.

There are a number of ways to get attention at the beginning of a lesson. These approaches are designed to secure the students' attention and reduce distractions that might occur at the beginning of a lesson (Jones & Jones, 2007):

1. *Select a cue for getting students' attention.* Students often need a consistent cue to focus their attention. These cues may include a special phrase chosen by the class to indicate that you want immediate attention, or they may include a nonverbal cue such as closing the door at the beginning of class.

2. *Do not begin until everyone is paying attention.* It is important not to begin a lesson until all students are paying attention to the teacher. Teachers who begin lessons without the attention of all their students spend much more time repeating directions. Also, a teacher who begins a lesson in such a fashion is a poor role model, since it indicates that it is all right to talk while others are talking. Teachers sometimes just stand silent, waiting. Students soon get the message.

3. *Remove distractions.* Some students cannot screen out distracting stimuli. You can help remove distractions by closing the door, having the students remove unnecessary materials from the tops of their desks, adjusting the blinds, or taking other appropriate actions.

Providing Daily Review. A lesson can start with a brief review of previously covered material, correction of homework, and review of prior knowledge that is relevant to the day's lesson. The purpose of daily review is to determine if the students have obtained the necessary prerequisite knowledge or skills for the lesson. This review may last from three to eight minutes, and the length will vary according to the attention span of the learners and the nature of the content. Daily review is especially useful for teaching material that will be used in subsequent learning. Examples include math facts, math computation and factoring, grammar, chemical equations, and reading sight words.

You can conduct a daily review at the beginning of a lesson (a) to provide additional practice and overlearning for previously learned material and (b) to allow the teacher to provide corrections and reteaching in areas where students are having difficulty. Vary the methods for reviewing material.

Checking homework at the start of class is one form of review. Game formats, such as a trivia game, can be used as a means for review. You can conduct review through discussion, demonstration, questioning, written summaries, short quizzes, individualized approaches, and other methods of instruction (Rosenshine & Stevens, 1986). During reviews, students might answer questions at the chalkboard, in small groups, or as a whole class. Some additional techniques include asking questions about concepts or skills taught in the previous lesson, having students meet in small groups of two to four to review homework, and having students prepare questions about previous lessons or homework and ask them of each other or the teacher can ask them of the class.

In addition to daily review, the learning of new material is also enhanced by weekly and monthly reviews. Weekly reviews may occur each Monday, and monthly reviews every fourth Monday. These reviews provide additional checks by the teacher for student understanding, ensure that the necessary prior skills are adequately learned, and also check on the teacher's pace.

Establishing Set.   *Set induction* is the initial activity at the beginning of the lesson that is used to induce students to a state of wanting to learn. This activity helps establish the context for the learning that is to follow and helps students engage in the learning. Typically, the set is brief, lasting only long enough to develop student readiness to accomplish the lesson's objective. Set induction helps students see what the topic of the lesson is in a way that is related to their own interests and their own lives. Madeline Hunter (1994) used the term *anticipatory set* to describe this concept, pointing out that the activity is intended to develop a mental readiness (or "set") for the lesson.

For example, a health lesson on the topic of first aid might begin with the reading of a newspaper report about a recent fire or accident. After reading the article, you could ask the students what they would do if they were the first ones to arrive after the accident. A number of ideas are likely to be generated in this discussion. Then you could bring that opening discussion to a close by saying that today's lesson will be about that exact topic—what type of first aid to administer for various conditions. Then you would move into the first part of the lesson. This set induction activity helps create interest in the lesson in a way that students can relate to their own lives.

Effective set induction activities should meet several criteria:

1. *Get the student interested in what is to be taught during the lesson.* This is referred to as an *initiating activity.* For example, you might begin a lesson on creative writing by turning off the lights in the room and explaining to the students that you will take them on an adventure to a distant planet. As the room remains dark, they are to imagine their trip into outer space.

vibrant is more entertaining to observe than an unenthusiastic teacher. In addition, teacher enthusiasm has also been related to higher student achievement (Good & Brophy, 2008). Enthusiasm has two important dimensions: (a) interest and involvement with the subject matter and (b) vigor and physical dynamism. Enthusiastic teachers are often described as stimulating, dynamic, expressive, and energetic. Their behavior suggests that they are committed to the students and to the subject matter. While teachers often expect students to be interested in *what* they say, students more often react to *how* enthusiastically it is said.

Classroom Case Study

Managing Lesson Delivery

Logan Reynolds's twelfth-grade English class just finished reading George Orwell's *1984,* one of his favorite books to teach. The students participated in panel discussions and debates, and the desks were arranged in a circle to promote discussion. Mr. Reynolds encouraged lively conversations by asking probing questions and engaged his students in role-playing and simulation activities. His animated nature during class discussions motivated the students to become actively involved. Students also responded to a number of journal prompts at the beginning of each class session just prior to discussion. These prompts required students to reflect on the underlying ideas presented in their readings and to make connections to present-day concerns.

The class next moved to a unit on Shakespeare. Although Mr. Reynolds was not particularly interested in the works of Shakespeare, he understood the importance of introducing his class to classics such as *Macbeth.* Since Mr. Reynolds was concerned about the complexity of Shakespeare's works, he decided that lecturing about the material was the best way to promote student learning, and the desks were put into rows for this approach. As a result, student interactions were minimal, with no room for debate, role-playing, and simulation games. Mr. Reynolds felt those activities would only complicate study of an already obscure literary subject. Mr. Reynolds conducted all of his class meetings in a similar fashion, asking students to read a certain number of pages for homework and be prepared for the lectures, with only brief opportunities for discussion. Mr. Reynolds became concerned when his students were not very engaged in the brief class discussions and seemed to lose focus and interest.

Focus Questions

1. What factors contributed to the high level of student involvement in the unit on *1984?* To the low level of student involvement in the unit on Shakespeare?
2. Based on what you know about managing lesson delivery and other instructional factors, what suggestions do you have for Mr. Reynolds when teaching the unit on Shakespeare?

Enthusiasm can be conveyed in a variety of ways. These include the use of animated gestures, eye contact, voice inflection, and movement around the room. A teacher who is enthusiastic in the classroom often manages to develop enthusiastic students. Constant, highly enthusiastic actions are not necessary and in fact may be counterproductive. Instead, a variety of enthusiastic actions, ranging from low to high degrees of enthusiasm, is appropriate.

Ending of a Lesson

As stated earlier, an effective lesson has three important sections: a beginning, a middle, and an end. All three sections must be planned and implemented effectively if a lesson is to be successful. Simply ending a lesson when the bell rings or when you have covered the planned material is not appropriate. In such cases, students are not given the opportunity to place the lesson in a context with other related lessons or are not permitted to ask questions that might clarify a misunderstood point from the lesson. Providing a summary is imperative for a successful lesson. Furthermore, students need time at the end of the lesson to get ready to leave the classroom.

Providing Closure to Part of a Lesson.   *Closure* refers to actions or statements that are designed to bring a lesson presentation to an appropriate conclusion (Shostak, 2006). There are three major purposes for closure:

1. *Draw attention to the end of a lesson segment or the lesson itself.* Often students need to be cued that they have arrived at an important segment of the lesson or that it is time to wrap things up. They might be cued with a statement that it is time to summarize key concepts.

2. *Help organize student learning.* It is the teacher's responsibility to relate the many pieces of the lesson to the whole. Some students are able to do this by themselves while others need the teacher's assistance. To accomplish this purpose, you might provide a diagram, illustration, outline, or other type of summary that indicates how all the content of the lesson is related.

3. *Consolidate or reinforce the major points.* You might emphasize or highlight certain concepts at this point. The major objective is to help the student retain the information presented in the lesson for future use.

Closure is important because students instinctively structure information into patterns that make sense to them. If a learning experience is left with some uncertainties, students may draw inaccurate conclusions as they create their own patterns of understanding from the material, thus detracting from future learning. The second and third purposes involve summarizing, which is addressed later. The time at the end of a lesson segment or the lesson itself can be used to make homework assignments. Between lesson segments, students may be given five to ten minutes to start the homework assignment while you move around the room to answer questions that might arise.

What Would You Decide?   *Providing Closure*

Let's assume that you are teaching a history lesson in which a series of significant dates has been identified and related events have been discussed.

1. How might you bring closure to this part of the lesson in a way that helps students see how all the dates and events are related?

2. How might you involve students in this closure?

3. How might you take into account students' varied learning styles?

Summarizing the Lesson.   Providing a *summary* of the main points of a lesson can help students to gain a better idea of the content or to clarify any misunderstandings. You should plan to stop the lesson several minutes before the bell rings to begin the summation. Make sure that you have the attention of all students before the summary begins. You should avoid merely reiterating the content covered during the lesson. Ask several questions that encourage the students to relate key aspects of the lesson or to evaluate key points. Also, you can ask students for their opinions about what they believe are the key points of the lesson.

To add interest and variety, vary the way that the lesson summary is conducted. Some days may involve simply a series of questions for students. On other days, you may ask several students to go to the chalkboard to solve a problem and discuss the thought process involved. A game format could be used as a means of summary, such as questions out of a hat or a Trivial Pursuit type of approach. Several creative approaches could offer the desired variety of lesson summaries.

The summary should be used to determine whether the students have grasped the main ideas of the lesson. For example, your summary might discover that several students do not understand the key concepts of a math lesson. It would be foolish to teach the next math lesson as though students understood the concept. Therefore, you can use the information gathered during the summary to adjust the next day's lesson plan.

Getting Ready to Leave.   At the end of the lesson, middle, junior high, or senior high school students usually need to leave the classroom and go to their next class. The bell will ring at the end of the class period, and students will have just a few minutes to get to their next class in another room in the building.

You should plan to complete all instruction and lesson summary by the end of the class period so students are not delayed in moving to the next class. You should not teach right up to the bell, because time needs to be allowed for several other events. First, you must allow time for students to return any books, supplies, or materials to the appropriate locations. Also, students need time to throw away any scrap paper and to straighten up the classroom. They need time to put away their own books, papers, pencils, or other materials before leaving. You may plan to reserve from one to four minutes at the end of a lesson to allow sufficient time for these final actions to be completed before the bell rings. Students then should be dismissed on time. You need to schedule this time when planning lessons.

MANAGING STUDENT WORK

Students prepare homework and seatwork as a regular part of their instruction. To effectively manage this student work, guidelines are offered here for managing seatwork effectively, collecting assignments and monitoring their completion, maintaining records of student work, managing the paperwork, and giving students feedback. It is helpful to develop a plan to organize your instructional records, grading and assessment records, classroom management records, parental contact records, and special needs and accommodation records (Mierzwik, 2005).

Managing Seatwork Effectively

Seatwork involves students working on assignments during class that provide practice or review of previously presented material. Students spend hundreds of hours during a schoolyear doing seatwork privately at their desks. It is imperative that you structure seatwork so that it is done effectively while enabling students to experience a high rate of success.

Guidelines for successfully implementing seatwork in the classroom come from a variety of sources (Jones & Jones, 2007; Rosenshine & Stevens, 1986; Weinstein, 2007; Weinstein & Mignano, 2007). The following recommendations represent a synthesis from these sources:

1. Recognize that seatwork is intended to practice or review previously presented material. It is not suited for students to learn new material.

2. Devote no more time to seatwork than is allocated to content development activities.

3. Give clear instruction—explanations, questions, and feedback—and sufficient practice before the students begin their seatwork. Having to provide lengthy explanations during seatwork is troublesome for both you and the student. In addition to procedural directions, explain why the activities are being done and how to do the seatwork.

4. Work through the first few problems of the seatwork together with the students before having them continue independently. This provides a model for completing the work and provides an opportunity for the students to ask questions for clarification about the content or procedures.

5. Decide if you will allow talking during seatwork. It is often desirable to start out with no talking during seatwork to have students work alone. After a month or two, teachers sometimes allow students to talk quietly with others to seek or provide help. Clarify when quiet talking is allowed.

6. Circulate from student to student during seatwork, actively explaining, observing, asking questions, and giving feedback. Monitoring students to provide this positive and corrective feedback is very important.

7. Determine how students will seek help from the teacher. When students are working at their seats and need help, ask them to raise their hands. You can then go to them or signal them to come to you at an appropriate time.

8. Determine when students can get out of their seats. To eliminate unnecessary wandering around the room during seatwork, decide when and for what purpose students can get out of their seats. For example, students may get supplies, sharpen pencils, or turn in papers only when necessary.

9. Have short contacts with individual students (i.e., 30 seconds or less).

10. Break seatwork into short segments, rather than plan one long time slot. Rather than having one lengthy presentation of content followed by an extended period of seatwork, break up instruction into a number of segments followed by brief seatwork after each segment.

11. Arrange seats to facilitate monitoring the students (e.g., face both small groups and independently working students).

12. Establish a routine to use during seatwork activity that prescribes what students will do when they have completed the exercises. Students may complete an additional enrichment assignment for extra credit, or they may use the time for free reading or to work on assignments from other classes.

Collecting Assignments and Monitoring Their Completion

Whether it is homework or seatwork, you need to establish a process for collecting assignments and monitoring their completion:

■ *Have a regular procedure for collecting assignments.* Papers can be collected during class by asking students to pass them in a given direction until you have all papers in your hands. As an alternative, students may be asked to place their completed assignments in certain basket, tray, or drop box at a designated time during class. Once students know this collection procedure, assignments can be gathered quickly and efficiently.

■ *Have a procedure for grouping papers by subject or class session.* In an elementary classroom, assignments on a variety of subjects may be submitted during the day. It is useful to have a separate drop box for each subject. In this way, only papers of a certain subject are in a drop box, and you do not need to spend time sorting through all the papers to pick out just the math papers or just the social studies papers. Similarly, middle and secondary classrooms should have a different drop box for each class period. Thus, students in the fourth hour would place their assignments in the box for their class period.

■ *Have a record of whose papers have been turned in.* If you evaluate the papers quickly, you will know who has or has not submitted the assignments when you record the grades in your gradebook. If there is a delay in grading, you may have a checklist to record who has submitted the assignments. In this way, you can follow up with students who did not submit the materials. Some teachers also have students keep an assignment notebook for homework and seatwork to record the items that were due and what was turned in.

Maintaining Records of Student Work

Records of student progress and completion are entered in your gradebook. For elementary classes, you may organize your gradebook by having a separate section for each subject area. The date and description of the assignment can be entered at the top as a subject heading, and each student's scores can be placed in the appropriate column on the line for his or her name. Similarly, middle-level and secondary teachers can have separate sections of the gradebook for each of their class sections. It is useful to establish a coding system to indicate a student absence or other information related to the assignment. Gradebook software can be used to record the submission of assignments and the scores students receive. Progress reports for individual students can be easily prepared, and these are useful to show the students and parents.

Managing the Paperwork

Homework and seatwork involve a lot of paperwork, and it is easy to get overwhelmed by the volume of papers you deal with on a regular basis. Here are some guidelines to manage your handling of the papers effectively:

■ *Assess, record, and return assignments quickly.* Make a commitment to assess and return all assignments in a day or two. Delays in your return of the assignments often lead to a backlog of assignments to be graded. That situation creates a lot of pressure for you, and it is not fair to the students because they need to receive feedback as quickly as possible.

■ *Be realistic about your grading capabilities.* Plan sufficient time in your schedule to assess and record the assignments. If you are making frequent assignments and getting behind in the grading, it is time to reassess your use of assignments. Strategically space out the assignments that are to be graded. Long assignments take time to assess. The use of short and specific assignments may be effective in monitoring student learning, and they take less time to assess.

■ *Recognize that every seatwork assignment does not need to have a grade.* Every subject or every class period does not need an assignment that must be graded by you every day. Therefore, you do not need to receive papers each day. Students can be assessed in class and given feedback in various ways without asking them to submit the paperwork to you to be assessed. For example, you can assign seatwork and then check each student's work and give feedback during class.

■ *Have a system for coding the papers for each subject or class section.* As mentioned previously, have a system for collecting assignments from your students. Using color-coded folders for each subject or class period can be a helpful technique for organizing the paperwork.

■ *Have a predetermined way to return papers to the students.* When returning papers to students, keep them in labeled folders by the subject or class period. You could organize the papers by rows or groups to facilitate the return. Plan a certain way to return the papers each time. You may choose to use student helpers in returning the papers.

Giving Students Feedback

You will assign seatwork and homework to help students learn, and it is important that students receive feedback about this work. Follow these guidelines for giving students feedback:

■ *Provide frequent and regular feedback.* Students need fairly immediate feedback about their performance so they have an opportunity to correct any errors in their knowledge or skills before going ahead to new material. Thus, plan for ways for students to demonstrate their learning and for ways that you can provide frequent and regular feedback about their learning.

■ *Develop ways to provide feedback to students in class.* To provide prompt feedback and to avoid assigning homework every day, develop ways to provide feedback to students after instruction and practice have taken place in class. For example, you could have students work on problems at the board and give feedback, show answers on an overhead screen, or have students help review each other's work.

■ *Take corrective actions promptly with students who do not perform well.* Don't wait until several poor assignments have been turned in or until it is time to submit the report-card grade before meeting with a student who is not performing well. Some students may need more assistance to learn the content, and this feedback and assistance should come early and without delay.

What Would You Decide?   *Giving Students Feedback*

You regularly use seatwork in your classroom, and you provide prompt feedback. However, three students often have difficulty with the seatwork and need more feedback and guidance.

1. What are some ways that you can provide these students with the extra feedback that they need?

2. How might you use other students in the class to provide this needed guidance and feedback?

MANAGING WHOLE-GROUP INSTRUCTION

In his widely respected book *Discipline and Group Management in Classrooms* (1970), Jacob Kounin reported how instructional techniques contribute to classroom management. The implications from his research can be organized into three areas: preventing misbehavior, managing movement through the lesson, and maintaining group focus. Suggestions are also provided for ways to maintain student attention and involvement.

Preventing Misbehavior

When approaching whole-group instruction, teachers can take a number of actions, based on Kounin's work, to prevent misbehavior:

1. *Exhibit withitness.* Jacob Kounin (1970) is considered the first researcher to systematically study the characteristics of effective classroom managers. He coined the term *withitness* to describe a teacher's disposition (or mental set) to look at all parts of the classroom at all times, notice who is misbehaving, and respond to the misbehavior in an appropriate and prompt manner. Systematic and periodic monitoring of each student in the class is a key part of withitness, because it will help prevent misbehavior from occurring.

2. *Use overlapping.* *Overlapping* refers to teachers supervising or handling more than one group or activity at a time. For example, a teacher working with one group of students can notice and simultaneously address a behavior incident in another part of the classroom. Teachers who are skilled at overlapping are more aware of what is going on; thus, they have good withitness as well. As a result, teachers who overlap can effectively monitor classroom behavior and intervene when needed to keep students on task. When students know their teacher has withitness and is able to overlap, they are less inclined to get off task.

3. *Use desists.* *Desists* are statements by teachers to stop an inappropriate action or a misbehavior by asking or telling a student what to do. To be effective, desist statements should be specific and spoken clearly. A desist might be in the form of an appeal, such as "Shanae, please put away the comb and continue with the class assignment." Or it could be in the form of a command, such as "Wayne, stop talking with your friends and continue with your calculations in the lab activity." Effective use of desists helps keep students on task and minimizes disorder and misbehavior.

4. *Avoid satiation.* *Satiation* occurs when the teacher asks the students to stay on a learning task too long and the students begin to lose interest and get off task. For example, students may enjoy seeing a videotape, writing a creative story, or working in pairs on a project. When these activities are used too often or for too much time, however, students will start to lose interest, become bored, and likely get off task. Satiation can be minimized by (a) highlighting progress toward a learning goal and providing students with feedback; (b) providing variety in the content, group structure, level of difficulty, and instructional materials and activities; and (c) offering a challenging activity to promote a greater sense of purpose and accomplishment.

Managing Movement through the Lesson

To minimize misbehavior and to promote learning, teachers need to have the lesson progress at a reasonable pace and to avoid having the lesson go astray with abrupt changes or shifts. Kounin (1970) described the movement of the lesson in terms of momentum and smoothness, as described here:

1. *Momentum.* *Momentum* refers to teachers starting lessons with dispatch, keeping lessons moving ahead, making transitions among activities efficiently, and bringing lessons to a satisfactory close. Momentum deals primarily with the pacing of the lesson, and the teacher needs to avoid slowdowns in the progression through the lesson. For example, one problem in momentum is *jerkiness,* where the teacher fails to develop a consistent flow of instruction, going too fast at some times and too slow at others.

2. *Smoothness.* *Smoothness* refers to staying on task in the lesson without abrupt changes, digressions, or divergences. Kounin described several problems when trying to maintain a smooth, continuous flow of activities throughout a lesson. Some of these problems include shifting from one topic to another, shifting back to earlier activities or content, and injecting unrelated information into a lesson.

Maintaining a Group Focus

Group focus occurs when a teacher makes a conscious effort to keep the attention of all students at all times. When this occurs, the teacher maintains efficient classroom control and reduces student misbehavior (Kounin, 1970). Group focus includes group alerting, group accountability, and high-participation formats:

1. *Use group alerting.* *Group alerting* refers to taking actions to engage the attention of the whole class when only individuals are responding. This includes a teacher's attempts to involve all students in learning tasks, maintain their attention, and keep them "on their toes." With group alerting, teachers create suspense before calling on a student to answer a question, keep students in suspense regarding who will be called on next, call on different students to answer questions, and alert nonperformers that they might be called upon next.

2. *Maintain group accountability.* *Group accountability* takes place when the teacher lets the students know that their performance in class will be observed and evaluated in some manner. This assessment does not necessarily mean a grade will be recorded, only that the students' performance will be gauged. For example, the teacher might use record-keeping devices such as checklists and task cards. Other strategies include asking students to raise their hands in response to certain questions, asking students to take notes and then checking them, and asking students to write answers and then use various techniques to check them during the class session. Student misbehavior decreases when students know that they are held accountable for their learning and behavior and the teacher knows each student's progress.

3. *Use high-participation formats. High-participation formats* are lessons that have all students performing in some way, even though they may not be involved in answering a teacher's question. High-participation formats occur when each student is expected to manipulate materials, solve problems, read along, write answers, or perform a concurrent task. In this way, students do not simply sit when others are answering questions; they are actively engaged as well.

Maintaining Student Attention and Involvement

To manage a group of students effectively, you need to capture and hold student attention and encourage ongoing involvement. *Attention* means focusing certain stimuli while screening out others. General guidelines and specific techniques for maintaining student attention and involvement are offered here (Eggen & Kauchak, 2007; Good & Brophy, 2008; Jones & Jones, 2007):

1. *Use attention-getting strategies.* You can use certain strategies to capture students' attention at the start of a lesson and throughout the lesson. Overuse of any one approach, however, reduces its ability to arouse and maintain attention. These strategies include the use of stories, physical products, activities, and statements.

2. *Monitor attention during lessons and provide situational assistance as necessary.* Students are much more likely to pay attention if they know you regularly watch them, both to see if they are paying attention and to note signs of confusion or difficulty. Regularly scan the class or group throughout the lesson. When students show signs of losing interest or getting frustrated, you should provide *situational assistance,* which are teacher actions designed to help students cope with the instructional situation and to keep students on task. Situational assistance is discussed more fully in Chapter 10.

3. *Stimulate attention periodically.* Student attention wanders when instruction becomes predictable and repetitive. You can promote continual attention as a lesson or an activity progresses. You can stimulate attention by cueing students through transitional signals that a new section of the lesson is coming up. For example, you might say "We have just spent the last 15 minutes considering what running water erosion is. Now let's look at the ways that farmers and other people try to stop this erosion." Or you can use challenging statements, such as "Now, here's a really difficult (or tricky or interesting) question. Let's see if you can figure it out."

4. *Vary instructional media and methods.* Repeated use of one approach to instruction will soon result in a classroom of bored students. Moreover, student achievement is increased when a variety of instructional materials and techniques are used (Good & Brophy, 2008). Use a variety of media such as an overhead projector, chalkboard, videotapes, and computer. Also use various teaching methods to solicit students' attention through the use of demonstrations, small and large groups, lectures, discussions, field trips, and the like. Not only does variability decrease boredom in students, but it also appeals to the different student learning styles.

5. *Use humor.* Students appreciate a certain amount of humor in the classroom, and it can help maintain students' attention. You may enjoy making silly statements or sharing funny experiences with your students. Be cautious that jokes are not used to tease or demean any student, even if expressed in a funny way, because the student may interpret these statements as being serious.

6. *Maintain individual accountability.* Students should be accountable for being involved in lessons and learning all of the material. It is helpful to ask a question or require the student periodically to make some kind of response. An unpredictable pattern in the way you handle questions or responses helps maintain individual accountability and causes students to be mentally engaged in the lesson and to be more attentive.

What Would You Decide? *Holding Students Accountable*

Let's assume that you are teaching a math lesson and that you are having five students complete sample problems at the chalkboard while the rest of the students remain in their seats.

1. For those who are still in their seats, how might you hold them academically accountable for the material?

2. How could you provide feedback to the students at the board as well as to those still in their seats?

3. How might the lack of a procedure for academic accountability in this setting contribute to a loss of order in the classroom?

---

7. *Pay close attention when students talk and answer questions.* The use of active-listening skills often entails using nonverbal skills that indicate that you are interested in what students are saying. If you do not give attention and show interest when students answer questions, you communicate to them that what they have to say is not very important, which in turn will discourage involvement. Nonverbal expressions of your interest might include nodding, moving toward the student, leaning forward, maintaining eye contact with the student, and showing interest in your facial expression. Verbal expressions of interest may include statements such as "Uh-huh," "I see," "That's a thoughtful answer," and "I appreciate your thorough, insightful answer."

8. *Reinforce students' efforts and maintain a high ratio of positive to negative verbal statements.* Students attend more fully if a positive learning environment has been created. One of the best means for accomplishing this is to respond positively to their efforts. Positive and encouraging statements are very important for all students. Make many more positive and encouraging statements than negative statements. Think about it from the students' point of view: Would you like to be in a classroom where you hear mostly negative statements or positive statements?

9. *Terminate lessons that have gone on too long.* When the group is having difficulty maintaining attention, it is better to end the lesson than to struggle through it. This is especially important for younger students whose attention spans are limited. Nevertheless, some teachers continue lessons to maintain a certain schedule. This can be counterproductive since students may not learn under certain conditions and in any case will have to be taught again. It is always helpful to give advance thought to a backup activity for each lesson. For example, you may select a different instructional technique for covering the same lesson objectives.

APPLYING THE SIOP MODEL TO LESSON DELIVERY

Meeting the needs of English language learners can be facilitated by the use of the SIOP model to provide more flexibility in the design and delivery of instruction. As outlined in Chapter 1, there are eight components of that model, and four components are related to lesson delivery: (a) comprehensible input, (b) interaction, (c) lesson delivery, and (d) review and assessment (Echevarria, Vogt, & Short, 2008). While these strategies were originally designed for use with ELLs, they are also helpful in meeting the needs of all learners in the classroom. The excellent content from Echevarria, Vogt, and Short (2008) serves as the foundation for much of the information in this section.

Comprehensible Input

Information that is understandable to students is referred to as *comprehensible input* (Krashen, 1985). When working with ELLs, teachers need to make verbal communication more understandable by consciously attending to students' linguistic needs and consistently incorporating input techniques into their daily teaching routines:

1. *Speak appropriately for students' proficiency levels.* Students who are at the beginning level of English proficiency benefit when teachers slow down their rate of speech, use pauses, and enunciate clearly while speaking. Teachers also must carefully monitor the vocabulary and sentence structure they use with ELLs to match the students' proficiency levels. Paraphrasing and repetition are useful practices that enhance understanding. Brain research suggests that repetition strengthens the connections in the brain (Jensen, 2005, 2008). Teacher should use simple sentences with beginning students and reduce or eliminate embedded clauses.

2. *Provide clear explanations of academic tasks.* All learners perform better when the teacher gives clear instructions for assignments and activities. For ELLs, it is critical to have instructions presented in a step-by-step manner, preferably modeled or demonstrated. Sample completed projects can be shown to provide further clarity and guidance. Oral directions should be accompanied by written directions so learners can refer back to them.

3. *Use a variety of techniques to make concepts clear and understandable.* High-quality lessons offer students a variety of ways to access the content. With deliberate planning, teachers can incorporate many techniques and activities throughout the week's lessons. A variety of techniques can be achieved through modeling, visuals, hands-on activities, demonstrations, gestures, body language, graphic organizers, and many other approaches that match students' learning styles.

Interaction

Teachers must provide opportunities for students to be actively engaged with the subject matter. Teachers must avoid the tendency to dominate talk in the classroom and permit only limited time for discussion and interaction. The following strategies can be used to deliberately plan more opportunities for student interaction:

1. *Provide frequent opportunities for interaction and discussion.* Reading comprehension skills and writing skills are positively correlated with oral language proficiency in English (Geva, 2006). Thus, teachers need to offer students opportunities to develop these important oral language skills. Effective teachers structure their lessons in ways that promote student discussion, and they strive to provide a balanced exchange with students, rather than dominate talk. Effective teachers also encourage elaborated responses from students when discussing concepts, going beyond simple yes–no answers and short phrases. This can be done by using prompts such as "Tell me more about that" and "Why is that important?"

2. *Group students to support language and content objectives of the lesson.* All students, including English language learners, benefit from instruction that includes a variety of grouping configurations. Effective classrooms have a variety of grouping structures, including individual work, partners, triads, small groups of four or five, cooperative learning groups, and the whole group. Groups also may vary by being homogeneous or heterogeneous by gender, language proficiency, language background, and/or ability. Using a variety of grouping configurations also helps maintain student interest and increases the chance that a student's preferred mode of instruction will be matched.

3. *Consistently provide sufficient wait time for student responses.* Wait time refers to the length of time the teacher waits for students to respond before answering a question himself or herself or calling on someone else to participate. Effective teachers consciously allow students time to reply and to express their thoughts fully, without interruption. Providing sufficient wait time is especially pertinent with ELLs, who need extra time to process questions in English, think of an answer in their second language, and formulate their responses in English.

4. *Give ample opportunities for students to clarify key concepts in their first language.* The National Literacy Panel on Language-Minority Children and Youth found that teaching academic skills such as reading in the first language transfers to the second language (August & Shanahan, 2006). Some ELLs may need a concept or assignment explained or clarified in their first language. This may be accomplished with the use of a bilingual instructional aide or peer or by using materials written in the student's first language.

Lesson Delivery

Although a lesson may be well planned, lesson delivery can go astray if the activities take longer than expected, students do not participate in the expected manner, or a host of other factors occur. The following guidelines will help teachers stay on track in a lesson by identifying and supporting lesson objectives, engaging students in the lesson, and proceeding at an appropriate pace:

1. *Clearly support content objectives by lesson delivery.* Lesson objectives must be stated orally and displayed for students to see. Lesson objectives from professional standards, written in student-friendly terms, convey the purpose and direction for the lesson, provide a structure for classroom procedures, and help students stay on task.

2. *Clearly support language objectives by lesson delivery.* Language objectives are an important part of effective sheltered lessons, where language development is supported. Teachers and students benefit from having a clear language objective written for them to see and review during the lesson. The language objective may relate to an aspect of reading, writing, speaking, or listening.

3. *Engage students during 90 to 100 percent of the lesson.* This means students are paying attention and on task 90 to 100 percent of the class period. This does not mean they need to be highly active in reading, writing, and moving the entire time. Rather, it means they are following the lesson, responding to teacher directions, and performing the activities as expected.

4. *Appropriately pace the lesson to the students' ability levels.* *Pacing* refers to the rate at which information is presented during a lesson. The pace depends on the nature of the lesson's content and the level of the students' background knowledge. Once teachers become familiar with their students, it becomes easier to determine an appropriate pace—one that does not present information too quickly yet is brisk enough to maintain students' interest.

Review and Assessment of Lesson Objectives

Effective sheltered instruction involves reviewing important concepts, providing constructive feedback through clarification, and making instructional decisions based on students' responses. Reviewing and assessing take place throughout each lesson and again when the lesson is concluded. It is especially important for ELLs to receive this review and assessment to find out what is important and where they stand in their comprehension of the lesson:

1. *Provide comprehensive review of key vocabulary.* Language objectives should be identified in lesson plans, introduced to students at the beginning of the lesson, and reviewed throughout the lesson. Multiple exposures to new words also build familiarity, confidence, and English proficiency. The more times students encounter new words, the more likely they are to remember and use them. Key vocabulary words are reinforced if introduced and reviewed through multiple modalities.

2. *Supply comprehensive review of key content concepts.* Just as with key vocabulary, key content concepts must be reviewed for ELLs during and at the end of a lesson. Student learning is supported when teachers stop and briefly summarize, along with students' help, the key content covered to that point. This type of review is informal, but it must be carefully planned. It is important to link the review to the content objectives of the lesson so you and the students stay focused on essential content concepts.

3. *Provide regular feedback to students on their output.* By periodically reviewing language, vocabulary, and content, teachers can provide specific academic feedback to students that clarifies and corrects any misunderstandings. Proficiency in English can be reinforced during these feedback sessions. Teacher can provide feedback verbally, orally, or even nonverbally through facial expressions and body language. Students can also provide feedback to each other through various techniques.

4. *Assess student comprehension and learning for all lesson objectives throughout the lesson.* Assessment must be conducted throughout the lesson to gather and synthesize information about student learning. Assessment must be linked to the instruction and the lesson objectives. Toward the end of the lesson, student progress should be assessed to determine whether it is appropriate to move on or whether it is necessary to review and reteach. As a general rule, multiple assessments should be conducted.

Key Terms

Ability grouping
Academic accountability
Academic learning time
Advance organizer
Anticipatory set
Attention
Between-class grouping
Clarity
Closure
Comprehensible input
Cooperative learning
Desists
Enthusiasm
Fragmentation

Group accountability
Group alerting
High-participation formats
Independent work
Jerkiness
Momentum
Motivation to learn
Overdwelling
Overlapping
Pacing
Peer tutoring
Satiation
Seatwork
Set induction

Situational assistance
Slowdowns
Small-group instruction
Smoothness
Student-centered approaches
Summary
Task orientation
Teacher-centered approaches
Transitions
Whole-group instruction
Within-class grouping
Withitness

Major Concepts

1. The degree of structure in the lesson and the manner in which students are grouped for instruction need to be taken into account when managing instruction and promoting appropriate behavior.
2. Students are more likely to stay on task when they are held academically accountable for their work.

3. When beginning a lesson, teachers need to take attendance, get attention, provide daily review, provide a set induction, introduce lesson objectives, distribute and collect materials, and give clear, focused directions.
4. When conducting the body of a lesson, effective teachers pace the lesson, provide smooth transitions, have a task orientation, ensure

academic learning time, are clear, and exhibit enthusiasm.

5. An effective teacher ends a lesson with a summary of important concepts and allows students time to get ready to leave the room after the lesson.

6. Managing student work involves managing seatwork effectively, collecting assignments and monitoring their completion, maintaining records of student work, managing the paperwork, and giving students feedback.

7. Successful management of whole-group instruction can be achieved by deliberate actions to prevent misbehavior, manage movement through the lesson, maintain a group focus, and maintain student attention and involvement.

8. Several components of the SIOP model can be used to enhance lesson delivery.

Discussion/Reflective Questions

1. What are some merits of whole-group, small-group, and independent work? What might teachers do to minimize misbehavior with each strategy?

2. In what ways might the selection of the various accountability procedures be affected by differences in grade level and subject areas?

3. From your own school experiences, what approaches to review did you find the most successful? What are the merits of using different approaches for review?

4. Recall several examples when your teachers were not clear in providing directions, instructions, or expectations. What effect did this lack of clarity have on you as a student?

5. Why would attention-getting strategies promote student involvement? What precautions could you identify for their use?

Suggested Activities

For Clinical Settings

1. List a number of ways to conduct daily and weekly reviews.

2. List a number of approaches you could use to summarize a lesson. Some of the techniques could be directed by you, and some could involve students in an active way.

3. Reflect on your schooling experiences and identify some strategies that your teachers used to capture and maintain students' interest successfully.

For Field Experiences

1. Talk to teachers about how they hold students academically accountable for each area in Figure 8.1.

2. Talk with several teachers about how they manage seatwork, collect and monitor assignments, maintain records, and manage paperwork. Then outline the ways that you will handle these responsibilities.

3. Ask several teachers how they try to meet the needs of ELLs during lesson delivery.

Further Reading

Good, T., & Brophy, J. (2008). *Looking in classrooms* (10th ed.). Boston: Allyn & Bacon.

Includes thorough review of many aspects of teaching including classroom life, expectations, management, motivation, groupings, and instructional approaches.

Marzano, R. J. (2007). *The art and science of teaching: A comprehensive framework for effective instruction.* Alexandria, VA: Association for Supervision and Curriculum Development.

Provides research-based guidelines for many aspects of lesson delivery, planning, management, student involvement, and assessment.

9 | Classroom Management

We pay attention to the teacher and each other.

We are respectful to others.

We keep our hands and feet to our selves.

Charles Alba
We don't take items that don't belong to us.

Tjaranuki   Emely
Whe are nice to each other and we take turns.

We use nice words when we talk to each other. Jamal   Deion

We do fun things when we behave well.

We keep our classroom clean.

Objectives

This chapter provides information that will help you to:

1. Describe the role of classroom management in creating a learning community.

2. Determine what constitutes order in the classroom.

3. Identify the areas of responsibility for classroom management and discipline.

4. Identify ways to prepare for the schoolyear.

5. Describe ways to organize your classroom and materials.

6. Select and teach classroom rules and procedures.

7. Describe ways to maintain appropriate student behavior.

Classroom Management
- Areas of Responsibility
- Principles for Working with Students and Preventing Misbehavior

Organizing Your Classroom and Materials
- Floor Space
- Storage Space
- Bulletin Boards and Wall Space

Preparing for the Schoolyear
- Making Management Preparations
- Making Instructional Preparations
- Managing Assessments, Record Keeping, and Reporting
- Establishing a Plan to Deal with Misbehavior
- Planning for the First Day

Selecting and Teaching Rules and Procedures
- Rules
- Procedures

Maintaining Appropriate Student Behavior
- Having a Mental Set for Management
- Building Positive Teacher–Student Relationships
- Reinforcing Desired Behaviors

What do award-winning teachers do that makes them so popular and successful? Do they jazz up the curriculum in some way? Do they use especially creative instructional approaches? Do they warm up to the students as if they were their own children? Do they add some magic or sparkle to the classroom experience? The answer is probably a little of each of these suggestions. But it likely goes deeper than that.

217

Successful teachers are often very effective managers of the classroom environment. They create a positive learning community where students are actively involved in their own learning and the management of the classroom. Successful teachers organize the physical environment, manage student behavior, create a respectful environment, facilitate instruction, promote safety and wellness, and interact with others when needed. All these issues relate to classroom management. The main objective is to create a positive learning community and then to take steps to maintain this positive environment by guiding and correcting student behavior.

Problems with student misbehavior are minimized in a learning community where students are actively involved in their classroom and instruction. A learning community is designed to help all students to feel safe, respected, and valued in order to learn new skills. Successful classrooms are those in which students feel supported in their learning and are willing to take risks, challenged to become fully human with one another, and open to new possibilities. Many aspects of classroom management help to promote learning communities.

CLASSROOM MANAGEMENT

Classroom management involves teacher actions to create a learning environment that encourages positive social interaction, active engagement in learning, and self-motivation. Several key questions come to mind about classroom management: How can the physical environment be organized? How can the schoolyear begin effectively? What rules and procedures are appropriate? How can students be held academically accountable? How can appropriate behavior be encouraged and supported? How might order be restored if there are disruptions? How can class time and instruction be managed effectively? How can the safety of students be assured? All these issues are part of classroom management.

Areas of Responsibility

A learning community needs to have order for students to be successful. *Order* means that students are following the actions necessary for a particular classroom event to be successful; students are focused on the instructional tasks and are not misbehaving. Establishing and maintaining order are important parts of classroom management.

It is useful to distinguish between off-task behavior and misbehavior. *Off-task behavior* includes student actions that are not focused on the instructional activities yet would not be considered to be disruptive or be defined as misbehavior. Off-task behavior includes daydreaming, writing notes or doodling, or not paying attention. *Misbehavior* includes behavior that interferes with your teaching, interferes with the rights of others to learn, is psychologically or physically unsafe, or destroys property (Levin & Nolan, 2007). Classroom order is threatened by misbehavior. *Discipline* is the act of responding to misbehaving students in an effort to restore order.

There are several areas of responsibility for classroom management and discipline (see Figure 9.1). An effective classroom manager handles the following seven areas of responsibility (Burden, 2010):

FIGURE 9.1   Areas of Responsibility for Classroom Management and Discipline

1. Select a philosophical model of classroom management and discipline.
2. Organize the physical environment.
3. Manage student behavior.
4. Create a respectful, supportive learning environment.
5. Manage and facilitate instruction.
6. Promote classroom safety and wellness.
7. Interact with colleagues, families, and others to achieve classroom management objectives.

1. *Select a philosophical model of classroom management and discipline.* A number of educators have proposed certain models of classroom management and discipline, such as teaching with love and logic, cooperative discipline, discipline with dignity, and assertive discipline. These models reflect various philosophical views of student development, teaching and learning, and classroom management. Viewing these proposed models on a continuum, they range from low teacher control to high teacher control.

These theoretical models are useful to teachers because they offer a basis for analyzing, understanding, and managing student and teacher behavior. With an understanding of these varied theoretical approaches, you can assess your position on these issues and then select a philosophical model that is consistent with your beliefs. The techniques that you use to manage student behavior should be consistent with your beliefs about how students learn and develop.

2. *Organize the physical environment.* The way the desks, tables, and other classroom materials are arranged affects instruction and influences order in the classroom. To create an effective learning environment, you will need to organize several aspects of the physical space, which are discussed later in this chapter.

3. *Manage student behavior.* Guidelines are needed to promote order in the classroom and to provide a conducive learning environment. Rules and procedures support teaching and learning and provide students with clear expectations and well-defined norms. This, in turn, helps to create a safe, secure atmosphere for learning.

4. *Create a respectful, supportive learning environment.* There are many facets to creating a favorable learning environment, but it is vital for a positive learning community:

- Teachers can take a number of actions to establish a cooperative, responsible classroom by developing positive teacher–student relationships, promoting students' self-esteem, and building group cohesiveness. These actions will help to create an environment where students feel valued and comfortable, thus setting the stage for teaching and learning.
- Teachers can focus student attention on appropriate classroom behavior by helping students to assume responsibility for their behavior, maintaining student attention and involvement, and reinforcing desired behaviors.

- A comprehensive plan can be developed to motivate students to learn, involving decisions about instructional tasks, feedback and evaluation, and academic and behavioral expectations.
- Teachers can be most effective in creating a respectful, supportive learning environment when they have an understanding of the diverse learners in their classroom.

5. *Manage and facilitate instruction.* Certain factors in a lesson have a bearing on classroom order, and teachers need to take these factors into account when planning lessons. These include decisions about the degree of structure of the lesson, the type of instructional groups to use, and the means of holding the students academically accountable.

6. *Promote classroom safety and wellness.* Students need to feel physically and emotionally safe before they can give their full attention to the instructional tasks. Strategies used to manage student behavior, create a supportive classroom, and manage and facilitate instruction all contribute to classroom safety and wellness. In addition, teachers sometimes need to take actions to solve problems and conflicts that threaten classroom order and the learning environment. For this reason, it is helpful to have a set of tools, such as dealing with conflict resolution and anger management, to solve problems.

7. *Interact with colleagues, families, and others to achieve classroom management objectives.* Working with families is another means to help maintain order in the classroom. When the family and teacher communicate and get along together, students will more likely receive the needed guidance and support and will likely have more self-control in the classroom. In addition, teachers may need to consult and interact with colleagues and others when difficulties occur with classroom management and student behavior.

Principles for Working with Students and Preventing Misbehavior

Problem behaviors have a variety of causes, and evidence suggests that some factors are within the school and classroom environment (California Department of Education, 2000; Charles, 2008). To promote classrooms that are conducive to learning and to help prevent problem behaviors, teachers must address certain contextual factors within the classroom. Here are some basic principles for working with students in a manner that establishes a positive, productive classroom in which students learn and have a satisfying educational experience:

1. *Maintain focus on your major tasks in teaching.* Your major tasks are to help students be successful in achieving educational objectives, to promote student learning, and to help students develop the knowledge and skills to be successful in your classroom and beyond.
2. *Understand your students' needs and how to meet them.* Know your students' likes and dislikes, what motivates them, their needs and desires, and what influences their lives. Use that information to create an appropriate learning environment.

3. *Understand and respect ethnic/cultural differences.* With an understanding of the ethnic or cultural background of the students, teachers will be more prepared to facilitate learning and guide behavior.

4. *Know what causes misbehavior and how to deal with those causes.* Take steps to reduce or remove the causes of misbehavior.

5. *Provide clear rules and procedures to guide student conduct.* Rules and procedures need to be clearly identified and taught so students understand the behavioral expectations.

6. *Have a specific plan for responding to misbehavior with a hierarchy of interventions.* Have a specific set of strategies to stop the misbehavior, keep students positively on track, and preserve good relations.

7. *Reduce the use of punitive methods of control.* Coercive or punitive environments may promote antisocial behavior. Other techniques that involve the students in creating a positive learning environment are more desirable.

8. *Take actions to establish a cooperative, responsible classroom.* Use techniques to maintain attention and involvement, reinforce desired behaviors, promote student accountability and responsibility, and create a positive learning community.

9. *Involve students meaningfully in making decisions.* Decisions can involve things such as the selection of classroom rules and procedures, instructional activities and assessments, and curriculum materials. Their involvement generates commitment to the learning process and to the classroom environment.

10. *Teach critical social skills.* Many students lack the social skills necessary to relate positively to peers and to do well academically. Teachers who help students develop these social skills help promote learning and successful classroom discipline.

11. *Involve families to a reasonable degree.* Communicate with families regularly about what you are doing in the classroom and about the progress of their children. Make it clear that you want and need their support.

PREPARING FOR THE SCHOOLYEAR

Imagine that you are going to take a two-week vacation to see the numerous state and national parks in southern Utah and northern Arizona. You gather information about the parks and attractions from a variety of sources, and then you start to plan your itinerary. Next, you make motel reservations and list all the things that you need to take with you, such as hiking shoes, water bottles, sunscreen, sunglasses, camera, and clothing. Before you leave on the trip, you stop your newspaper and mail delivery and make arrangements for your pets for the days that you are gone. All these arrangements, and probably more, are needed to have a fun, trouble-free vacation.

Starting the schoolyear also requires this type of planning. Even before school starts, you can make a number of decisions about instructional and management preparations; plans to promote a positive learning climate; plans for the first day of school; and arrangements for floor space, storage, and other aspects of classroom space. Early planning and decision making on these issues will help to ensure a positive beginning to the schoolyear.

Studies on classroom management have verified that the first few days of the schoolyear set the tone for the entire year (Emmer & Evertson, 2009; Evertson & Emmer, 2009).

To prepare, you can make management preparations and instructional preparations, establish a plan for misbehavior, and also plan for the first day of school. When the schoolyear finally begins, there are certain actions that are appropriate during the first day and over the following few days. A number of these issues are addressed in this section.

A number of resources provide more details than can be discussed in this chapter. Resources are available for the elementary grades (Bosch & Kersey, 2000; Jonson, 2002; Moran, Stobbe, Baron, Miller, & Moir, 2008; Roberts, 2001), secondary grades (Wyatt & White, 2007), and K–12 grades (Guillaume, 2008; Marzano, Gaddy, Foseid, Foseid, & Marzano, 2009; McEwan, 2006; J. G. Thompson, 2007; Wong & Wong, 2009).

SAMPLE STANDARDS

Classroom Management

There are ten INTASC standards (see page xxi), and each standard includes a list of knowledge, dispositions, and performances to indicate more clearly what is intended in the standard.

Since this chapter deals with classroom management, some representative statements for knowledge, dispositions, and performances from INTASC Standard #5 are listed here concerning topics in this chapter.

Knowledge

- The teacher can use knowledge about human motivation and behavior drawn from the foundational sciences of psychology, anthropology, and sociology to develop strategies for organizing and supporting individual and group work.
- The teacher understands the principles of effective classroom management and can use a range of strategies to promote positive relationships, cooperation, and purposeful learning in the classroom.

Dispositions

- The teacher values the role of students in promoting each other's learning and recognizes the importance of peer relationships in establishing a climate of learning.
- The teacher recognizes the value of intrinsic motivation to students' lifelong growth and learning.

Performances

- The teacher creates a smoothly functioning learning community in which students assume responsibility for themselves and one another, participate in decision making, work collaboratively and independently, and engage in purposeful learning activities.
- The teacher maximizes the amount of class time spent in learning by creating expectations and processes for communication and behavior along with a physical setting conducive to classroom goals.

Making Management Preparations

It is important to carefully consider a variety of management issues, such as your school environment, room arrangement, materials, rules and procedures, communication with parents, seating arrangements, and other issues. Based on a study of experienced teachers (Schell & Burden, 2006), you could direct your attention to the following classroom management issues:

   1. *The school environment.* The first step is to become thoroughly familiar with the total environment before school starts: the room, school, facilities, personnel, services, resources, policies and procedures, other teachers, children, and the community. You will then have more information with which to make decisions, will probably feel more confident about your job, and will not need to devote time in the first few weeks to gather this information.

   2. *Gather support materials.* After examining the curriculum guide and textbooks, you might have ideas about activities for a certain unit or lesson. Supplementary materials may be needed when the time comes to teach that lesson. This is the time to gather any additional support materials, such as games and devices, pictures, CDs, ideas for activities, charts, maps, and graphs. The school may have discretionary funds for their purchase. They may be obtained from school supply catalogs, a local teacher store, or even at garage sales.

   3. *Organize materials.* It is useful to set up a filing system for storing district and school communications and other important documents. Papers that should be kept in a filing cabinet include the district's policy handbook; correspondence from the principal, superintendent, or other supervisors; correspondence from professional organizations; lesson plans; and items on curricular content. Some teachers use file folders. A separate file folder may be created for each course unit to hold pertinent notes and resource materials. Textbooks, resource books, manipulative materials, and other types of instructional supplies and materials also need to be organized and stored.

   4. *Classroom procedures.* You can follow various procedures to accomplish specific tasks. Procedures may be identified regarding handing in completed work, sharpening a pencil, using the restroom, or putting away supplies. Before school starts, identify actions or activities requiring procedures that will contribute to a smoothly running classroom, and then decide what those procedures should be.

   5. *Classroom helpers.* Teachers call on students at all grade levels as helpers to perform various classroom tasks. Make a list of tasks that need to be done, and then decide which ones students can perform. Give attention to how task assignment will be rotated to give every student an opportunity to help. Roles are often held for one or two weeks before the assignments are rotated. Depending on the grade level and circumstances, some tasks for students may include line leader, light switcher, pencil sharpener, paper collector, plant waterer, chalkboard eraser, window and blind opener, and supply manager.

   6. *Class lists and rosters.* It is useful to plan a means to record whether students have returned their book orders, picture money, field-trip permission forms, and so on.

Voices from the Classroom

Using a Class List for Various Purposes

Marge McClintock, fifth-grade science and social studies teacher, New Providence, New Jersey

As soon as I am given my class list of students for the year, I assign the students numbers in alphabetical order for each class. The students are told their numbers and are required to put their numbers on all of their work. This has several benefits. When homework or seatwork is handed in, I ask a student to put the papers in numerical order for me. I can see in an instant which numbers are missing and take whatever action is needed.

Another benefit is managing the students on class trips. Although I always carry a class list with me on the trips, it is much faster to have the students call out their numbers in order when they're back on the bus or whenever roll needs to be taken.

A third benefit is in dividing the class into groups. It can be as easy as evens and odds. Or I can require the students to use higher-order math skills by saying, "All the students whose number can be factored by 3, please come to the front of the class. All students whose number can be factored by 2 and who aren't in the '3' group, please go to the back of the room. All the rest, stay where you are."

You can prepare a generic class roster listing the students' names in alphabetical order in the left column, with blank columns on the right to check off the action. It is helpful to input the list on a computer program so that an updated sheet can be easily generated when the roster changes.

7. *School/home communication.* Open communication with families is vital. Before school starts, many teachers prepare an introductory letter to families to welcome them and to inform them about the teacher, the curriculum, grading practices and standards, the homework policy, rules and procedures, and so on. This letter can be sent home with the students on the first day of school. Teachers can also make plans for other types of communication with families, such as phone calls, progress reports, or a back-to-school night.

8. *Birthdays and other celebrations.* Depending on your grade level, you may want to recognize student birthdays. Most schools have very specific policies for celebrating major holidays, such as Halloween, Christmas, Hanukkah, Martin Luther King Jr. Day, and Easter. Inquire about these policies so you will understand what is expected.

9. *Distributing textbooks.* Sometime in the first few days of school, you will need to distribute textbooks. You need to obtain the textbooks and prepare an inventory form on which to record each book number, with a space in which to write the student's name.

Think about when and how the textbooks will be distributed. Since the first day of school often necessitates many announcements and activities, you might want to wait until the second or third day before distributing textbooks, or distribute them just before they are needed for the first time. Attention might be given to the specific means of distribution. One way is to have students line up one row at a time and go to the table where the books are stacked. When giving the book to the student, you can record the student's name on the inventory form.

10. *Room identification.* On the first day of school, students need to locate your classroom. Especially for students new to the building, it is important to have the room clearly labeled. A poster on the outside doorway should include the room number, the teacher's name, the grade level and/or subject (Room 211, Mr. Wagner, World History). This information should also be written on the chalkboard so students see that they are in the correct classroom. Some type of welcoming statement should also be placed on the chalkboard, such as "Welcome! I'm glad you're here."

11. *Room arrangement.* Room arrangement is an issue that can be decided before school starts. Take into account the fixed features in the room, instructional materials and supplies, traffic areas, work areas, boundaries for activity areas, visibility to see all students, and the purposes of various seating arrangements. Determine the arrangement in the classroom for your desk, the students' desks, tables, bookshelves, filing cabinets, and other furniture. The room arrangement that you select should be consistent with your instructional goals and activities. Teacher-led instructional approaches such as presentations and demonstrations require one type of room arrangement, whereas small-group work requires a different type of arrangement.

12. *Seat selections and arrangements.* One teacher may prefer to assign each student's seat, while another may let students select their seats. This decision should be made before school starts. In either case, be sure that there are enough seats for the number of students you expect. You might take the age level and maturity of the students into account as you select the manner of assigning seats. You might change the seating arrangements during the schoolyear to accommodate work groups, to move students who need close supervision to more accessible seats, or simply to provide a change.

13. *Room decoration.* It is important to make your classroom an attractive, comfortable place. Consider having some plants in the classroom or even an aquarium. Displays of pictures, posters, charts, and maps also help cover the walls with informative and appealing materials. Attractive bulletin boards add color. You might prepare one bulletin board listing classroom information and use another one to display seasonal items. After school starts, you can have students prepare bulletin boards.

Making Instructional Preparations

Prior to the start of the schoolyear, carefully consider a variety of instructional issues, such as long-range plans, supplementary materials, student assessment, a folder for substitute teachers, a syllabus, and so on. Based on a study of experienced teachers (Schell & Burden, 2006), you should direct your attention to the following instructional issues:

1. *Long-range plans.* It is helpful to peruse the curriculum guides and other related materials so you can appreciate what should be covered by the end of the schoolyear.

Some tentative decisions need to be made for the amount of time to be spent on each particular unit. Some curriculum guides include recommendations for the number of weeks to spend on each unit.

You may want to solicit advice from other teachers, particularly from those who teach your same subject or grade level. To the extent possible, make these rough schedules conform to the school calendar by taking into account grading periods and holidays. Be careful not to overschedule yourself. Leave some time for review near the end of each unit or chapter, for reteaching as the situation warrants, and for unexpected occurrences, such as school closings due to inclement weather.

2. *Supplementary materials.* For each major curricular topic in your rough long-range plans, start an ongoing list of related supplementary materials or activities. It may include field trip locations, resource people, media, games, assignments, bulletin boards, and additional books. Inquire about library or media center resources, such as films or videotapes, and order and reserve them. You might prepare other supplementary materials to use during the first few weeks of school.

3. *Skeleton plans.* A *skeleton plan* is a brief overview of intended accomplishments. It often includes a weekly list of expected accomplishments. Skeleton plans include more details than the long-range yearly plans but not the detail needed for daily lesson plans. Skeleton plans for the first three or four weeks serve as a guide for preparing the more detailed lesson plans.

4. *Weekly time schedules.* You should establish your weekly schedule before school starts and include a copy in a handy place, such as in your lesson plan book. The weekly schedule is often displayed in a chart, with the weekdays listed at the top and the hours listed on the left-hand column. The class schedule for middle and secondary teachers probably will be determined by the principal or others in the school building, and it will show what grade level and subject are taught during each class period.

5. *Daily lesson plans.* After you have completed the skeleton plans for the first three or four weeks, it is time to prepare the daily lesson plans for the first week of school. Lesson plan formats vary. One that is often used includes boxes for the days of the week and the subjects taught. In these boxes, notes may be included about objectives, a list of topics to be covered or activities to be conducted, materials, and means of assessment. Beginning and probationary teachers are often required to show the principal or assistant principal their weekly lesson plans for the coming week.

6. *Preparing a syllabus.* You need to give students information about each course at the start of the year. You could plan and prepare this information as well as any related materials before school starts. At the middle and secondary levels, teachers often give each student a course syllabus that outlines this introductory information (see Chapter 2). The *course syllabus* includes the course title, the title of the textbook and any other primary resource materials, a brief course description, a list of course objectives, a content outline, course requirements (e.g., tests, homework, projects), how grades will be calculated (e.g., the points for each requirement and the point total needed for certain grades), a description of the homework policy, the attendance and tardiness policy, and a listing of classroom rules and procedures. Some teachers also include a description of the instructional methods and activities that students are to engage in.

7. *Preparing policy sheets.* The syllabus might include all related classroom policies and procedures, although some teachers do not include these items. (Depending on the grade level and circumstances, some teachers do not provide a course syllabus.) As a result, a teacher might prepare a separate policy sheet for the students. The sheet may state the classroom rules and procedures, the policy for attendance and tardiness, and the like. If a course syllabus is not used, this policy sheet might also state the grading policy.

8. *Tentative student assessment.* It is useful to make an initial assessment of the students' understanding and skills at the start of the schoolyear so you can better recognize the abilities and differences within the class. These assessments could be conducted sometime during the first week of school, but you should think about how to plan for the assessment and then make any necessary arrangements before school starts. Assessment procedures might include worksheets, oral activities, observation checklists, pretests, or review lessons. After conducting these early assessments, you should then record the results on a class roster that was drawn up earlier.

9. *Planning for homework.* Give careful consideration to how you will evaluate students and determine report-card grades. One element of student evaluation often involves homework, and preparation for developing a homework policy can be done before school starts. Prepare a homework policy in the form of a letter that is sent home to families at the start of the schoolyear (see Chapter 13).

10. *Backup materials.* It is useful to have some backup materials available when instruction takes less time than anticipated, when a change of plans is necessary, or when students finish their activities early. These backup materials may be related to the particular topics being covered at the time. Many teachers have a collection of puzzles, educational games, discussion questions, brain teasers, creative writing, word searches, and riddles. You can gather these materials before school starts.

11. *Opening class routine.* Students often perform better when they know that a particular routine will be regularly followed at the start of class. You can decide on the particular actions to be taken. You may need to take attendance, make announcements, and attend to other tasks at the start of the class period. The purpose of having a routine is to provide an orderly transition as students enter the room and get ready for instruction. Some teachers have students review vocabulary words or other problems related to the curriculum while other tasks are performed.

12. *Folder for substitute teachers.* A substitute teacher will take your place when you are absent. It is important to prepare materials for substitute teachers to help support what they do, maximize the learning, and minimize any off-task behavior. Many teachers keep a folder for substitute teachers that includes important information. It can be kept on your desk with the plan book.

The type of material in a folder for substitute teachers varies, but the following information would be useful to include: a copy of the daily schedule, times for recess and lunch, a list of the classroom rules, a list of classroom procedures (e.g., morning opening, taking attendance, lunch count, lunch, dismissal, fire drills), a list of reliable students in each class period, hall-pass procedures (to go to the restroom, library, or office), information on where to find certain items (e.g., lesson plans, audiovisual equipment, supplies), others to contact for information or help (e.g., a nearby teacher with room number), and a list and description of students with special needs. Much of this information can be collected before school starts, and additional information can be added as needed.

Managing Assessments, Record Keeping, and Reporting

It is vital to give advance thought to how you will assess student achievement, record student progress and scores, and report the assessment information. Assessment always has been important in teaching, but the No Child Left Behind (2002) act and additional state and local accountability demands for ensuring student learning have placed a higher level of attention on assessment and reporting. Even before the schoolyear starts, you should decide how you will assess student learning, keep records of student performance, and report the assessment data.

Assessments.   While there are many aspects to assessment, you will need to select the means of assessment. Teacher-made tests and quizzes are common. In addition, you may choose to have students demonstrate their learning through the use of performance-based measures with (a) products (e.g., portfolios, work samples, projects, laboratory reports) or (b) performances (e.g., oral presentation, presentation with media, demonstration, debate, athletic demonstration). For each of these assessment approaches, you will also need to determine how you will assess the level of student proficiency. This could be done through an answer key for a test or with the use of rubrics or other rating forms for performance-based measures.

Record Keeping.   Once students have been assessed and you have scored their work, you must keep records in a gradebook. Gradebooks typically have a section for the daily attendance log, achievement scores, and conduct scores. All student assessment scores are placed in the gradebook, so prior thinking about your overall assessment plan will help you design the columns and labels in a useful manner. In addition to scores for performance on test items, portfolios, and other measuring techniques, some teachers have separate charts to record student proficiency for particular knowledge and skills related to the curriculum standards.

Entering the assessment scores in the gradebook is only part of your task. Then you must have a plan to translate all of the performance measures into a grade at the end of the report-card period. For example, in a given subject, will you have a weight of 20 percent for homework, 40 percent for tests, 20 percent for a portfolio, and 20 percent for cooperative group projects? Furthermore, what performance level constitutes an A or a B? You need to think about your grading system before the start of the schoolyear and establish your plan.

Reporting.   Your school district will likely determine a number of aspects of what will be recorded on report cards and how the information will be reported. First, the district determines what achievement and nonachievement (e.g., conduct) progress will be reported. Also, it determines what grading system will be used (e.g., letter grades, pass–fail, checklists). There may be additional ways the district determines how grades are reported.

In addition to report cards, you can communicate students' progress to their families in various ways, such as through parent–teacher conferences, newsletters, and open houses. During a parent–teacher conference, you may want to have a portfolio for each student ready to show representative work. For a newsletter, you may want to share information about the activities and the performance of the entire class. Give advance thought to what information you will be reporting, and develop a plan for the kinds of data and materials you need to gather and report.

Establishing a Plan to Deal with Misbehavior

With an understanding of classroom management and discipline, you will need to develop a plan for dealing with misbehavior in the classroom. A seven-step plan is presented here that begins with establishment of a system of rules and procedures. You need to provide a supportive environment during instruction and also provide situational assistance when students get off task. If the student does not get back on task, you need to move through advancing levels of punishment. If none of these actions works, you may need to involve other personnel.

You should deal with misbehavior in a way that is effective while also avoiding unnecessary disruptions. Researchers and educators have also proposed movement from low to high intervention when developing a plan to address misbehavior (e.g., Charles, 2008; Levin & Nolan, 2007; Wolfgang, 2009). Once the rules and procedures and a supportive classroom environment are in place, the teacher moves from low to high interventions, as described below:

1. *Establish your system of rules and procedures.*   Establish an appropriate system of rules and procedures as a foundation for dealing with discipline. It is vital that you select a system of rules and procedures appropriate to the situation. This system should incorporate reward or reinforcement for desirable behavior and consequences for misbehavior.

No single approach is best for all teachers and all teaching situations. For instance, rules and procedures for a tenth-grade English class would not be appropriate for a third-grade class. Furthermore, the system needs to be consistent with established school and district policies and with your own educational philosophy, personality, and preferences.

2. *Provide a supportive environment during class sessions.*   Once the system of rules and procedures has been established at the start of the schoolyear, you need to maintain a supportive environment. Actions taken in the normal course of instruction are for the purpose of guiding and reinforcing students for positive behavior.

Providing a supportive environment is accomplished primarily through cueing and reinforcing appropriate behavior and through getting and holding attention. Cueing and reinforcing involves stressing positive, desirable behaviors; recognizing and reinforcing desired behaviors; and praising effectively. Getting and holding attention necessitates focusing attention at the start of lessons; keeping lessons moving at a good pace; monitoring attention during lessons; stimulating attention periodically; maintaining accountability; and terminating lessons that have gone on too long. Treat students with dignity and respect, and offer challenging, interesting, and exciting classes.

3. *Provide situational assistance during class sessions.* Students may get off task during a lesson. This off-task behavior may be a form of misbehavior or a lapse in attention. Either way, you need to promptly provide situational assistance. *Situational assistance* denotes actions you take to get the student back on task with the least amount of intervention and disruption possible. Situational assistance can be provided by removing distracting objects, reinforcing appropriate behaviors, boosting student interest, providing cues, helping students over hurdles, redirecting the behavior, altering the lesson, and other approaches (discussed more fully in Chapter 10).

Some inappropriate behaviors are of such short duration and are so insignificant that they can be safely ignored. Your use of situational assistance might be considered a "forgiveness step" for the student by recognizing that the off-task behavior is minor or fleeting and by allowing the student to get back on task without penalty.

What Would You Decide?   *Providing Situational Assistance*

Before using mild responses for off-task behavior, teachers often provide situational assistance to get students back on task.

1. What are the benefits of using situational assistance?

2. How might situational assistance differ for students in the first, seventh, and eleventh grades?

3. How might cultural differences of students affect your decisions about the ways to provide situational assistance?

---

4. *Use mild responses.* If a student continues to be off task after situational assistance is provided, then you need to use mild responses that are intended to correct the student's behavior. These are not intended to be punitive. Mild responses may be nonverbal or verbal (see Chapter 10). Nonverbal responses include ignoring the behavior, using signal interference, using proximity control, and using touch control. Verbal responses include reinforcing peers, calling on the student during the lesson, using humor, giving a direct appeal or command, reminding the student of the rule, and several other approaches.

5. *Use moderate responses.* If students do not respond favorably to mild responses and continue to exhibit off-task behavior, then you need to deliver moderate responses (see Chapter 10). These punitive responses deal with misbehavior by removing desired stimuli so as to minimize the inappropriate behavior. Moderate responses include the use of logical consequences and various behavior modification techniques, such as time-out and loss of privileges.

6. *Use stronger responses.* If moderate responses are insufficient, then you need to move to a more intrusive type of intervention (see Chapter 10). These stronger responses are intended to be punitive by adding aversive stimuli such as reprimands and overcorrection. The purpose of aversive stimuli is to decrease unwanted behavior.

7. *Involve others when necessary.* If all efforts have failed to get the student to behave properly, then you need to involve other persons in the process. This occurs most commonly with chronic or severe behaviors. You may consult or involve counselors, psychologists, principals and assistant principals, teaching colleagues, college personnel, mental health centers, school social workers, school nurses, supervisors and department heads, and families. Their assistance and involvement will vary, depending on their expertise.

Planning for the First Day

Starting the schoolyear effectively is vitally important when establishing a system of classroom management. Marzano and colleagues (2009) report that a strong first day and an emphasis on classroom management in the first few days make a big difference in getting off to a good start. Several principles should guide your decisions about planning the start of the schoolyear and your actions in the first few days of school (Burden, 2010; Emmer & Evertson, 2009; Evertson & Emmer, 2009; Good & Brophy, 2008; Wong & Wong, 2009).

1. Plan to clearly state your rules, procedures, and academic expectations.
2. Plan uncomplicated lessons to help students be successful.
3. Keep a whole-class focus.
4. Be available, visible, and in charge.
5. Plan strategies to deal with potential problems.
6. Closely monitor student compliance with rules and procedures.
7. Stop inappropriate behavior quickly.
8. Organize instruction on the basis of ability levels.
9. Hold students academically accountable.
10. Be clear when communicating information.
11. Maintain students' attention.
12. Organize the flow of lesson activities.

ORGANIZING YOUR CLASSROOM AND MATERIALS

myeducationlab

Go to MyEducationLab, select the topic **Classroom Management,** click "videos," and select "Arranging Furniture and Materials." View the video and reflect.

Decisions about room arrangement must be made before students arrive on the first day of school. Before arranging the classroom, you should consider (a) the movement patterns of students throughout the classroom; (b) the need for students to obtain a variety of materials, texts, reference books, equipment, and supplies; and (c) the need for students to see the instructional presentations and display materials.

Arrange and decorate your classroom in a manner that supports effective classroom management (Marzano et al., 2009). Good room arrangement can help teachers cope with the complex demands of teaching by minimizing interruptions, delays, and dead times. Based on studies of effective classroom managers, there are five keys to good room arrangement (Emmer & Evertson, 2009; Evertson & Emmer, 2009):

1. *Use a room arrangement consistent with your instructional goals and activities.* You will need to think about the main types of instructional activities that will be used in your classes and then organize the seating, materials, and equipment compatibly. Teacher-led presentations, demonstrations, and recitations require students to be seated so that they can see the instructional area. In contrast, small-group work requires a very different room arrangement.

2. *Keep high-traffic areas free of congestion.* High-traffic areas include the space around doorways, the pencil sharpener and trash can, group work areas, certain bookshelves and supply areas, the teacher's desk, and student desks. High-traffic areas should be separated, have plenty of space, and be easily accessible. For example, try not to seat a student next to the pencil sharpener because of the traffic in that area and the possibility for inappropriate behavior.

3. *Be sure students are easily seen by the teacher.* It is important that teachers clearly see students to identify when a student needs assistance or to prevent task avoidance or disruption. Clear lines of sight must be maintained between student work areas and areas of the room that the teacher will frequent.

4. *Keep frequently used teaching materials and student supplies readily accessible.* By having easy access and efficient storage of these materials, activities are more likely to begin and end promptly, and time spent on getting ready and cleaning up will be minimized. Establishing regulated storage areas can help to reduce the occurrence of students leaving materials in their desks or taking them out of the room.

5. *Be certain students can easily see instructional presentations and displays.* The seating arrangement should allow all students to see the chalkboard or overhead projector screen without moving their chairs, turning their desks around, or craning their necks. Place the primary instructional area in a prominent location to help students pay attention and to facilitate note taking.

Floor Space

A classroom typically contains many materials that take up floor space, such as student desks, the teacher's desk, bookcases, tables, and activity centers. Consider the functions of the space and the five keys to good room arrangement to facilitate learning and to minimize interruptions and delays.

A good starting point in planning the floor plan is to decide where you will conduct whole-group instruction. Examine the room and identify where you will stand or work when you address the entire class to conduct lessons or to give directions. This area should have a chalkboard, an overhead projector screen, a table for the overhead projector, a small table to hold items needed during instruction, and an electrical outlet. Consider the following items:

■ *Student desks.* Even if other arrangements are to be used later in the year, you might start the year with student desks in rows facing the major instructional area, since it is easier to manage students with this pattern. Be sure all students can see the major instructional area without having their backs to it and without having to get out of their seats. It is important to keep student desks clear from high-traffic areas. Avoid placing their desks near the door, pencil sharpener, trash can, and supply areas. Leave ample room for aisles between the desks to enable easy movement of students and yourself when monitoring seatwork.

■ *The teacher's desk.* Your desk should be situated so that you can see the students, but it is not essential that the desk be at the front of the room. Placement of your desk at the rear of the room, in fact, may help when monitoring students during independent work. Students facing away from you cannot tell when you are looking at them unless they turn around. This tends to encourage students to stay at their assigned tasks. Instead of sitting at their desks during independent work, many teachers prefer to move around the room to monitor and assist students.

■ *Bookcases and filing cabinets.* These should be placed so students' visibility of chalkboards and relevant displays is not obstructed. These items should also not interfere with your monitoring of students. If a bookcase contains frequently used items such as resource books, dictionaries, or supplies, then it should be conveniently located and monitored. Seldom-used items are best stored in an out-of-the-way place. If there is only one bookcase, it is helpful to use it for frequently used items.

■ *Activity centers or work areas.* An *activity center* is an area where one or more students come to work on a special activity. It may be in the form of a learning center or a computer work area. One or more tables are commonly used as the work surfaces in these areas. When selecting the placement of tables for this area, be sure that you can see all students in the work area, keep traffic lanes clear, and avoid congested areas. A center often will have special equipment, such as tape recorders with headphones, a computer, a filmstrip projector, or other materials and supplies. Enough table and work space must be provided for students to work efficiently. It is useful to place the work area at the side or the back of the room and to the backs of other students.

Storage Space

Teachers and students use a wide variety of instructional materials. All of these materials are not used every day and must be stored when not in use. Therefore, storage space must be provided for textbooks and resource books, frequently used instructional materials, teacher's supplies and instructional materials, equipment, and infrequently used materials. Here are some guidelines:

1. *Textbooks and resource books.* Some textbooks are not kept by students and thus must be stored in the classroom for easy access when needed. In addition, resource books obtained from the school library, public library, or other sources may be available for student use. All of these books should be stored in a bookcase that enables easy access.

2. *Instructional materials.* Materials that students need will vary with the subject area that you teach. These may include rulers, scissors, special paper, pencils, staplers, tape, glue, and other supplies. As with textbooks and resource books, a storage location should be selected to enable easy access to the materials. Clearly labeled containers for each of the supply items are often very helpful in maintaining an orderly supply area. These materials may be stored on shelves of a bookcase or cabinet or on a counter.

3. *Teacher supplies.* Supplies that only you would use should be kept in your desk or in storage areas used only by you. These supplies include items such as hall passes, attendance and lunch count forms, computer disks, computer programs, lesson plan book, tablets, file folders, and chalk. These items should be placed in secure places so students do not have access to them.

4. *Equipment.* An overhead projector, tape recorders, television, and other instructional media are not commonly used every day. Therefore, these items must be stored when not in use.

5. *Infrequently used items.* Some instructional materials are used only one time a year. These include seasonal decorations (e.g., Halloween, Thanksgiving), bulletin board displays, and special project materials. Certain instructional materials may be used for only one unit, as in the case of a model of the human eye for a science class. Some teachers prefer to keep seasonal decorations and other infrequently used materials at their homes.

Voices from the Classroom

Organizing Your Materials and Space

Leila Post, fourth-grade teacher, Reno, Nevada

I find that good organization makes me a better teacher. I organize my daily lessons and activities in five plastic trays lined across a counter, and they are labeled by the day of the week. On top of each tray is another tray for a second week. This allows me to plan and collect related materials for two weeks at a time. This organization also makes it easier for a substitute teacher to locate all the needed materials.

I have student supplies easily accessible on shelves, and I have labeled trays for turning in daily seatwork, homework, and center work. At each cluster of student desks, I have a plastic basket containing glue, erasers, pencils, and crayons. Each student is assigned a number at the start of the schoolyear, and this number is used to identify all folders, mailboxes, scissors, and other items. I find classroom organization of teacher and student materials reduces wasted time, increases productivity, and teaches organizational skills to the students.

Bulletin Boards and Wall Space

Constructive use of bulletin boards and wall space can contribute to a positive classroom environment. This can be achieved by displaying relevant instructional material, assignments, rules, schedules, student work, and other items of interest. Many teachers involve students in the selection of content and the preparation of bulletin boards and the use of wall space. One approach is to select a different group of students to plan and prepare a bulletin board each month.

Some teachers prefer to dedicate a certain purpose for each bulletin board. For example, one bulletin board can be used to post classroom rules, a daily or weekly schedule, classroom helpers, lunch menus, a school map, emergency information, or any other procedural information. Another bulletin board can be used to display student work. A third type of bulletin board can be simply for decoration, with seasonal, motivational, or artistic items. Other bulletin boards can be used to post information and news articles about school or community events. In addition, bulletin boards can also be used to post content-related news articles, posters, or information.

Some of this material, such as a listing of classroom rules, can be placed on posters and displayed on the walls of the classroom if the content is not likely to change during the schoolyear. Designated areas of the chalkboard can also be used to display student assignments or special announcements, because this information is likely to change daily.

SELECTING AND TEACHING RULES AND PROCEDURES

Think about all the traffic laws that govern the use of motor vehicles. Guidelines are set for ways to signal, turn, yield the right of way, pass other vehicles, and numerous other aspects of driving. These laws have been established in each state to ensure the safety of the driver and others. In a similar way, guidelines are also needed in the classroom to govern how the teacher and the students conduct themselves so that learning objectives are achieved and everyone is successful.

Rules and procedures are used to guide and govern student behavior in classrooms. Even in positive learning communities, where students are actively involved in arranging their learning environment, rules and procedures are necessary to guide behavior. Teachers need to carefully consider what rules and procedures are needed to effectively manage the class.

Your philosophical perspective about teaching, classroom management, and discipline will greatly influence how you select rules and procedures. Teachers who prefer to take more control of the classroom decision making will likely select rules and procedures without consulting students. Teachers who prefer to involve students to some degree in the decision making will likely have a discussion with the students and then

myeducationlab

Go to MyEducationLab, select the topic **Classroom Management,** and click "simulations," and select "Addressing Disruptive and Non-Compliant Behaviors." View the simulation and answer the questions.

collaboratively decide on the rules and procedures. Teachers who are very student oriented may turn the discussion over to the students and let them determine the rules and procedures.

As you consider the information on rules and procedures, reflect on your philosophical perspective concerning discipline and classroom management. One model may represent your beliefs about child development and management of student behavior. This, in turn, will give you a perspective about the degree of control that you would want to take when determining rules and procedures.

Rules

Rules refer to general behavioral standards or expectations that are to be followed in the classroom. They are general codes of conduct that are intended to regulate individual behavior in an attempt to avoid disruptive behavior. Rules may be identified to guide the way students interact with each other, prepare for class, and conduct themselves during class. They are commonly stated in positive terms to guide student behavior. In addition to general rules, teachers sometime state rules for specific situations (e.g., gum chewing is not allowed).

Consider these guidelines about creating and enforcing rules:

■ *Examine the need for rules.* Rules provide guidelines for appropriate behaviors so that teaching and learning can take place. They should be directed at organizing the learning environment to ensure the continuity and quality of teaching and learning and not simply be focused on exerting control over students.

Rules are necessary to have teaching and learning take place, and they need to be realistic, fair, and reasonable. Rules that are selected should meet the following purposes: (a) the teacher's right to teach is protected; (b) the students' rights to learning are protected; (c) the students' psychological and physical safety are protected; and (d) property is protected (Levin & Nolan, 2007).

You need to examine the way you teach and the type of classroom environment you would like to maintain when considering rules. A number of factors should be considered, including your educational philosophy, the age and maturity of the students, school rules and expectations, the type of classroom climate to be developed, and the rationale for a particular rule.

■ *Select the rules.* After considering the need for classroom rules, you are ready to select rules that are appropriate for your classroom. Sample rules include (a) follow the teacher's directions; (b) obey all school rules; (c) speak politely to all people; and (d) keep your hands, feet, and objects to yourself. These rules are probably appropriate for all grade levels (K–12).

Due to differences in student maturity and developmental levels, some rules may be needed only for certain grade levels. For example, students in the primary grades (K–3) often need direct guidance on many matters. Some additional rules that would

Voices from the Classroom

Establish the Rules with the Students

Bernadette Hampton, high school math teacher, Beaufort, South Carolina

On the first day of school I conduct an activity where I ask the students, "What do respect, success, and appropriate classroom behavior look and sound like?" Students are asked to pair up and then provide at least three examples for each part of the question. Then we write our resulting ideas on the board and discuss them. Our goal is to establish a consensus for a positive classroom environment. As a result, the climate of the class is set, the classroom rules are established, and we are ready to begin the schoolyear.

be appropriate for these grades may include (a) follow directions the first time they are given, (b) raise your hand and wait to be called on, (c) stay in your seat unless you have permission to get up, and (d) do not leave the room without permission. For departmentalized settings and grade levels, some rules about materials and starting class are often used, such as bring all needed materials to class and be in your seat and ready to work when the bell rings at the start of the period. A number of guidelines for selecting classroom rules are displayed in Figure 9.2.

Consider the degree to which students will be involved in identifying classroom rules. Among other things, student involvement will be affected by the teacher's philosophical perspective. Many teachers do not provide for student choice in rule setting; teachers may clearly present the rules and discuss the rationale for them. Other teachers find that students have more commitment and adhere to the rules if they helped set the rules and consequences in the first place. Teachers can be effective managers whether or not they involve students in identifying classroom rules.

FIGURE 9.2   Guidelines for Selecting Classroom Rules

1. Make classroom rules consistent with school rules.
2. Involve students in making the rules to the degree that you are comfortable and to the degree that the students' age level and sophistication permit.
3. Identify appropriate behaviors, and translate them into positively stated classroom rules.
4. Focus on important behavior.
5. Keep the number of rules to a minimum (four to six).
6. Keep the wording of each rule simple and short.
7. Have rules address behaviors that can be observed.
8. Identify rewards for when students follow the rules and consequences for when they break the rules.

- *Select rewards and consequences.* As previously mentioned, both rewards and penalties need to be identified for the classroom rules. Rewards may include a variety of reinforcers, such as social reinforcers, activities and privileges, tangible reinforcers, and token reinforcers. Students need to be told that these reinforcers will be delivered if they follow the rules. Similarly, students need to be told what consequences will be delivered if they choose to break a rule. When a student gets off task, first provide situational assistance in an effort to get the student back to work. If the student stays off task, then you should deliver mild responses such as nonverbal and verbal actions. If that does not work, you can move to logical consequences and other actions.

- *Teach and review the rules.* After the classroom rules have been identified, teach them in the first class session as if they were subject-matter content. This discussion should include an explanation of the rules, rehearsal, feedback, and reteaching. It is important that the students recognize the rationale for the rules and are provided with specific expectations for each rule. Specific guidelines for teaching and reviewing classroom rules are displayed in Figure 9.3.

- *Obtain commitments.* After teaching the rules to the students, have them express their understanding of the rules and indicate their intention to follow the rules. This can be done in a variety of ways. One of the most effective is to have each student sign a copy of the paper that lists the rules and includes a statement such as "I am aware of these rules and understand them." In this way, each student makes an affirmation of the rules. You can keep these signed sheets. An extra copy of the rules could be given to students for placement in their desks or in a notebook.

As discussed earlier, sending the discipline policy home to the families is another means of obtaining a commitment to the policy. In this way, they are informed of the policy at the start of the schoolyear. Parents can contact you if they have any concerns or questions about the discipline policy. If not, they are asked to sign and return a form that states that they are aware of the rules and understand them (similar to the form their child could sign at school).

FIGURE 9.3   Guidelines for Teaching and Reviewing Classroom Rules

1. Discuss the rules in the first class session.
2. Discuss the reasons for the rules.
3. Identify specific expectations relevant to each rule. Provide examples and emphasize the positive side of the rules.
4. Inform students of consequences when rules are followed and also when they are broken.
5. Verify students' understanding of the rules.
6. Send a copy of your discipline policy home to families and to the principal.
7. Post the rules in a prominent location.
8. Remind the class of the rules at times other than when someone has just broken a rule.
9. Review the rules regularly.

Procedures

Procedures are approved ways to achieve specific tasks in the classroom. They are intended to help students accomplish a particular task, rather than prevent inappropriate behavior, as in the case of rules. Procedures may be identified to direct activities such as handing in completed work, sharpening a pencil, using the restroom, and putting away supplies. The use of procedures, or routines, has several advantages: they increase the shared understanding for an activity between you and students, reduce the complexity of the classroom environment to a predictable structure, and allow for efficient use of time.

As with rules, it is important to clearly state the procedures, discuss the rationale for them, and provide opportunities for practice and feedback, where appropriate:

■ *Examine the need for procedures.* As a first step, you must examine the need for procedures in your classroom. What activities or actions would benefit from having a procedure that would regularize student conduct in the performance of that action? To answer this key question, you might think about all the actions that take place in the classroom and identify those that would benefit from having an associated procedure.

Fortunately, you do not need to start from scratch in doing this assessment, because research studies of classroom management in K–12 classrooms have produced a framework that can be used to examine and identify typical classroom procedures. A number of the specific areas that might need classroom procedures are displayed in Figure 9.4, some of which are adapted from Emmer and Evertson (2009), Evertson and Emmer (2009), Jones and Jones (2007), and Weinstein and Mignano (2007).

■ *Select the procedures.* When examining the items in Figure 9.4, you need to consider the unique circumstances in your classroom. The grade level, maturity of the students, your preference for order and regularity, and other factors may be taken into account when deciding which items will need a procedure. It may turn out that you will select many items from the table, because these items involve fairly standard actions in many classrooms. After selecting the items needing a procedure, decide specifically what each procedure will be.

■ *Teach and review the procedures.* Students should not have to guess if they need to raise their hands during a discussion or interpret subtle signals from you to determine what you want them to do. From the very first day of school, teach and review the various procedures that are needed. Effective teachers spend more time during the first four days of school on management tasks than on academic tasks.

There are several steps that serve as guides when teaching and reviewing classroom procedures with the students:

1. Explain the procedure immediately prior to the first time the activity will take place.
2. Demonstrate the procedure.
3. Practice and check for understanding.
4. Give feedback.

FIGURE 9.4   **Areas Needing Classroom Procedures**

1. **Room Use Procedures**
   a. Teacher's desk and storage areas
   b. Student desks and storage for belongings
   c. Storage for class materials used by all students
   d. Pencil sharpener, wastebasket, sink, drinking fountain
   e. Bathroom
   f. Learning stations, computer areas, equipment areas, centers, and display areas

2. **Transitions in and out of the Classroom**
   a. Beginning the schoolday
   b. Leaving the room
   c. Returning to the room
   d. Ending the schoolday

3. **Out-of-Room Procedures**
   a. Bathroom, drinking fountain
   b. Library, resource room
   c. School office
   d. Playground or school grounds
   e. Cafeteria
   f. Lockers
   g. Fire or disaster drills

4. **Procedures for Whole-Class Activities and Instruction and Seatwork**
   a. Student participation
   b. Signals for student attention
   c. Talk among students
   d. Making assignments
   e. Distributing books, supplies, and materials
   f. Obtaining help
   g. Handing back assignments
   h. Tasks after work is completed
   i. Makeup work
   j. Out-of-seat procedures

5. **Procedures during Small-Group Work**
   a. Getting the class ready
   b. Taking materials to groups
   c. Student movement in and out of groups
   d. Expected behavior in groups
   e. Expected behavior out of groups

6. **Other General Procedures for Secondary Classrooms**
   a. Beginning the class period
      (1) Attendance check
      (2) Previously absent students
      (3) Late students
      (4) Expected student behavior
   b. Out-of-room policies

      c. Materials and equipment
         (1) What to bring to class
         (2) Pencil sharpener
         (3) Other room equipment
         (4) Student contact with teacher's desk, storage, and other materials
      d. Movement of student desks
      e. Split lunch period
      f. Ending the class period

7. Other Procedures
      a. Classroom helpers
      b. Behavior during delays or interruptions

---

  5. Reteach as needed.
  6. Review the procedures with the students prior to each situation for the first few weeks.
  7. Review the procedures after long holidays.

MAINTAINING APPROPRIATE STUDENT BEHAVIOR

When you walk into a classroom where students are actively engaged in learning and cooperating with the teacher and others, you can almost feel the good vibrations given off by the class. Students want to be involved and productive, and they enjoy working together. This type of classroom, however, does not happen by chance. Teachers take deliberate actions to establish a cooperative, responsible classroom where students will choose to cooperate and make efforts to be academically successful. Students need to feel that they are expected to be orderly, cooperative, and responsible. Developing a positive classroom climate is one of the most important ways to establish and maintain student cooperation and responsibility (Burke, 2008).

There are several factors in maintaining appropriate student behavior. These include having a mental set for management, building positive teacher–student relationships, and reinforcing desired behaviors.

Having a Mental Set for Management

A review of research studies on classroom management has verified the importance and effectiveness of having a mental set about managing student behavior (Marzano et al., 2009). In relation to classroom management, a *mental set* is a teacher's heightened awareness of his or her surroundings and involves a conscious effort to control his or her thoughts and behaviors in that setting. That translates into the following actions that you can take in the classroom when attending to student behavior.

Withitness.   Use specific techniques to be aware of the actions of students in your classroom (withitness). Jacob Kounin (1970) is considered the first researcher to systematically study the characteristics of effective classroom managers. He coined the term *withitness* to describe a teacher's disposition (or mental set) to look at all parts of the classroom at all times in order to be aware of what is happening and then to demonstrate this withitness to students by quickly and accurately intervening when there is inappropriate behavior. Reflecting on the old adage, teachers who are "with it" seem to have "eyes in the back of their heads."

Such teachers do these things:

1. *Monitor regularly and react immediately.* To exhibit withitness, you should periodically and systematically scan your classroom, note the behaviors of individual students or groups of students, and respond quickly to inappropriate actions.

2. *Foresee problems.* Another aspect of withitness is the ability to foresee potential problems and make needed adjustments to minimize behavior problems. You should mentally review what might go wrong with specific students in specific classes and consider how you might address these potential problems. When planning certain classroom activities, for example, you might recognize possible confusion or disruption when supplies are being distributed. With this advance thought, you can either modify the way you distribute the materials or take certain precautions when the materials are passed out.

Emotional Objectivity.   Use specific techniques to be emotionally objective with your students. When students misbehave, you may get upset and emotional to some degree. It is important that your disciplinary actions are not seen as an attack on the students involved. You should try to be as objective as possible. *Emotional objectivity* is the ability to interact with students in a businesslike, matter-of-fact manner even though you might be experiencing strong emotions. This is particularly important when you are carrying out negative consequences for inappropriate behavior. Your feelings of anger and frustration are only natural when dealing with misbehavior, but it is not useful to display these emotions when delivering consequences. Look for reasons for the misbehavior, and monitor your own thoughts and attitudes.

Building Positive Teacher–Student Relationships

Research studies on classroom management highlight the importance of having positive teacher–student relationships in promoting appropriate student behavior (Marzano et al., 2009). The level of dominance and cooperation established by the teacher is an important factor in forming good relationships. An optimal teacher–student relationship consists of equal parts of dominance and cooperation.

Level of Dominance.   Effective classroom managers use specific techniques to establish an appropriate level of dominance in the classroom. High dominance is characterized by clarity of purpose and strong guidance in both academic and behavioral aspects of the classroom. Thus, the teacher provides guidance about the content to be addressed and the behavior to be expected in the class. A moderate to high level of dominance and a moderate to high level of cooperation (addressed next) provide the optimal teacher–student relationship for learning (Marzano et al., 2009).

You can express dominance in the following ways:

1. *Establish rules and procedures.* The rules and procedures that you determine will clearly help establish your dominance in the classroom.

2. *Use disciplinary interventions.* When misbehavior occurs, follow it with interventions to stop the inappropriate behavior. Your use of interventions is another expression of your dominance in the classroom.

3. *Exhibit assertive behavior.* One of the best ways to communicate a proper level of dominance is to exhibit assertive behavior. *Assertive behavior* involves standing up for one's legitimate rights in ways that make it less likely that others will ignore or circumvent them. To express assertive behavior, you can use assertive body language, speak in an appropriate tone of voice, and persist until the appropriate behavior is displayed.

4. *Establish clear learning goals.* Another way to express a proper level of dominance is to be very clear about the learning goals to be addressed in a unit, a quarter, or a semester. Clear learning goals can be communicated by establishing learning goals at the beginning of a unit of instruction, providing feedback on those goals, continuously and systematically revisiting the goals, and providing summative feedback regarding the goals.

Level of Cooperation.   Effective classroom managers use specific behaviors that communicate an appropriate level of cooperation. High cooperation is characterized by a concern for the needs and opinions of others and a desire to function as a member of a team as opposed to an individual. A moderate to high level of dominance and a moderate to high level of cooperation provide the optimal teacher–student relationship for learning (Marzano et al., 2009).

You can promote cooperation in the following ways:

1. *Provide flexible learning goals.* While you will determine the learning goals for each lesson and unit, you may provide some flexibility by allowing students to set some of their own learning goals at the beginning of a unit or by asking students what they would like to learn. This conveys a sense of cooperation.

2. *Take a personal interest in students.* All students appreciate the personal attention of the teacher, and anything that you do to show interest in students as individuals has an impact on their learning. For example, you could talk informally with students before, during, and after class about their interests. Or you could compliment students on important achievements in and outside of school, single out a few students each day in the lunchroom and talk with them, or comment on important events in their lives.

3. *Use equitable and positive classroom behaviors.* Teachers should ensure that their behaviors are equal and equitable for all students, thus creating an atmosphere in which all students feel accepted. These behaviors also foster positive teacher–student relationships. This can be done in many ways, such as making eye contact with each student in the room, deliberately moving toward and being close to each student, allowing and encouraging all students to be part of class discussions and interactions, and providing appropriate wait time for all students.

4. *Respond appropriately to students' incorrect responses.* When students respond incorrectly or make no response at all to a question you have posed, they are particularly vulnerable. Your appropriate actions at these critical points go a long way toward establishing a positive teacher–student relationship. You can emphasize what was right, encourage collaboration, restate the question, rephrase the question, give hints or cues, provide the answer and then ask for elaboration, and respect the student's option to pass, when appropriate.

Interacting with Students.   A significant body of research indicates that academic achievement and student behavior are influenced by the quality of the teacher–student relationship (Jones & Jones, 2007). Students prefer teachers who are warm and friendly. Students who feel liked by their teachers are reported to have higher academic achievement and more productive classroom behavior than students who feel their teachers hold them in low regard.

This research suggests that you need to learn and conscientiously apply skills in relating more positively to students. The guidelines listed here will help you build positive relationships (Charles, 2008; Good & Brophy, 2008; Jones & Jones, 2007):

1. *Use human relations skills.* When learning to manage the classroom climate, appropriate *human relations skills* are needed. There are four general human relations skills that apply to almost everyone in all situations: friendliness, positive attitude, the ability to listen, and the ability to compliment genuinely (Charles, 2008). When working with students, also give regular attention, use reinforcement, show continual willingness to help, and model courtesy and good manners.

2. *Enable success.* Students need to experience success. Successful experiences are instrumental in developing feelings of self-worth and confidence toward new activities. Students need to be provided with opportunities to achieve true accomplishments and to realize significant improvements (Charles, 2008). Learning is increased when students experience high rates of success in completing tasks (Jones & Jones, 2007). Students tend to raise their expectations and set higher goals. Failure, however, is met with lowered aspirations.

To establish moderate to high rates of success, (a) establish unit and lesson content that reflects prior learning; (b) correct partially correct, correct but hesitant, and incorrect answers; (c) divide instructional stimuli into small segments at the learners' current level of functioning; (d) change instructional stimuli gradually; and (e) vary the instructional pace or tempo to create momentum.

3. *Communicate basic attitudes and expectations to students, and model them in your behavior.* Students tend to conform not so much to what teachers say as to what they actually expect. You must think through what you really expect from your students and then see that your own behavior is consistent with those expectations. If you expect students to be polite to each other, for example, you should treat your students in the same manner.

4. *Communicate high expectations.* Teacher behaviors that create positive expectations almost always enhance the teacher–student relationship, and behaviors that create negative expectations result in poor relationships and poor student self-concepts and thus reduce learning. For example, students often put forth a solid effort when you say that work may be hard but also express confidence that they will be able to do it.

5. *Be fair and consistent.* Students want to be treated fairly, not preferentially. Your credibility is established largely by making sure that your words and actions coincide and by pointing this out to the class when necessary. If students can depend on what you say, they will be less likely to test you constantly.

6. *Show respect and affection to students.* You must like your students and respect them as individuals. Your enjoyment of students and concern for their welfare will come through in tone of voice, facial expressions, and other routine behaviors. Middle and secondary teachers should make efforts to get to know students personally. Students who like and respect their teachers will want to please them and will be more likely to imitate their behavior and attitudes.

7. *Create opportunities for personal discussions.* Other than through day-to-day activities, teachers often find it helpful to set time aside to get to know their students. Some possible activities include (a) talking with students before and after class; (b) demonstrating your interest in students' activities; (c) arranging for interviews with students; (d) sending letters and notes to students; (e) using a suggestion box; and (f) joining in school and community events (Jones & Jones, 2007).

Reinforcing Desired Behaviors

A *reinforcer* is an event or consequence that increases the strength or future probability of the behavior it follows. Reinforcement is used to strengthen behaviors that are valued and to motivate students to do things that will benefit them.

It is important to recognize the general principle of reinforcement: *Behaviors that are reinforced will be retained; behaviors that are not reinforced will be extinguished.* You need to carefully consider whom to reinforce, under what conditions, and with what kinds of reinforcement. Reinforcement is likely to be effective only to the extent that (a) the consequences used for reinforcers are experienced as reinforcers by the student; (b) they are contingent on the student achieving specific performance objectives; and (c) they are awarded in a way that complements rather than undermines the development of intrinsic motivation and other natural outcomes of behavior (Good & Brophy, 2008).

Several techniques of reinforcement are available, including recognition, activities and privileges, tangible reinforcers, and token reinforcers. Many of these reinforcers can be used with both individual students and the entire class.

Classroom Case Study

Classroom Management

Jasmine Nichols is an experienced fourth-grade teacher in an urban district. Misbehavior is rare in her classroom, because she creates a secure environment that fosters mutual respect. Ms. Nichols and her students generate the classroom rules and their consequences during the first class session of the schoolyear. Each student is asked to sign a copy of the rules and consequences, verifying his or her commitment to them and assuming responsibility for his or her own behavior. The rules and expectations are then posted in the classroom.

Ms. Nichols also gives thought to the classroom arrangement to eliminate distractions for her students. Students' desks are located at a reasonable distance from pencil sharpeners, trash cans, and other such distractions. Infrequently used items are out of the way in a nearby supply closet. Ms. Nichols often moves around the room and monitors her students to be sure they are on task.

Ms. Nichols also implements a token reward system to reinforce desired behaviors. If a student is seen exhibiting positive behavior, he or she is rewarded with a Nichols Nickel. Students know that Nichols Nickels can be used to purchase larger rewards, such as homework passes, colored pencil sets, and other classroom necessities. When Ms. Nichols noticed that one of her students helped a fellow classmate organize his notebook, the student was rewarded with a Nickel. In another instance, when Ms. Nichols had a substitute teacher fill in for the day, she rewarded all of her students with Nickels after the substitute left a note mentioning how well the students behaved.

Focus Questions

1. Identify the classroom management techniques that Ms. Nichols uses to promote and maintain appropriate behavior.
2. What are some additional ways to establish a cooperative, responsible classroom?

Recognition.   *Recognition* is a *social reinforcer* serving as a positive consequence to appropriate behavior. Social reinforcers may be expressed as verbal or written expressions, nonverbal facial or bodily expressions, nonverbal proximity, and nonverbal physical contact. Social reinforcers are especially valued by students when given by people important to them. Social forms of approval are especially useful when reinforcing student behavior if you and the students have a good relationship.

Praise is an expression of approval by the teacher after the student has attained something, and social reinforcers are often used to express this praise. Recognition should always be contingent on performance of appropriate behavior. You should be specific about the behavior that resulted in the praise and the reasons for giving it.

Most social reinforcement should be done privately with the student, but some may be done publicly. You need to carefully consider student characteristics when deciding how to deliver praise. A seventh-grader, for example, might be somewhat embarrassed being praised in front of the class.

Activities and Privileges.   *Activity reinforcers* include privileges and preferred activities. After students complete desired activities or behave in appropriate ways, you can then reinforce them with various activities and privileges. Some of these reinforcers can be various jobs as a classroom helper. Activity reinforcers are often very effective for reinforcing the entire class. A list of sample activities and privileges that can be used as reinforcers is provided in Table 9.1.

It is important to verify that certain behaviors are desirable. When you and students are on good terms, students just performing certain tasks such as straightening the room and cleaning the chalkboards with you can be rewarding. Many other activities and privileges have an intrinsic value that does not depend on a student's relationship to you. Running errands, studying with a friend, going to the library, being first in line, or choosing an activity are likely to be positive incentives that produce satisfaction in their own right. You may have students fill out a sheet at the beginning of the schoolyear to identify activities and reinforcers that they would appreciate.

Tangible Reinforcers.   *Tangible*, or *material, reinforcers* are objects valued in and of themselves: certificates, awards, stars, buttons, bookmarkers, book covers, posters, ribbons, plaques, and report cards. Food also may serve as a tangible reinforcer: cookies, sugarless gum, popcorn, jelly beans, peanuts, candy, or raisins.

If you are interested in using food (M & Ms, cookies, etc.), recognize some cautions. Some families may object to certain foods (such as those high in sugar), and there may be cultural differences related to food. Students may be allergic to certain foods, and health and state regulations may govern dispensing food in schools.

TABLE 9.1   Examples of Activity and Privilege Reinforcers

PRIVILEGES	CLASSROOM JOBS
Playing a game	Distributing or collecting papers and materials
Helping the teacher	Taking attendance
Going to the library	Adjusting the window shades
Decorating a bulletin board	Taking a note to the office
Working or studying with a friend	Watering the plants
Reading for pleasure	Stapling papers together
Using the computer	Erasing the chalkboard
Writing on the chalkboard	Operating a computer or projector
Earning extra recess time	Cleaning the erasers

Since tangible reinforcers serve as external or extrinsic reinforcement, their use should be limited. Other types of reinforcers are generally more available and more reinforcing in natural settings than tangible reinforcers. When you give awards, it is a good idea to distribute them so as to include a good number of the students. Don't give awards only for outstanding achievement; award for improvement, excellent effort, good conduct, creativity, and so on.

Token Reinforcers.   A *token reinforcer* is a tangible item that can be exchanged for a desired object, activity, or social reinforcer at a later time. Tokens may be chips, points, stars, tickets, buttons, play money, metal washers, happy faces, or stickers. The backup reinforcer is the reward for which tokens can be exchanged. Token reinforcement is useful when praise and attention have not worked. Tokens are accumulated and cashed in for the reinforcer.

Key Terms

Activity center	Mental set	Rules
Activity reinforcers	Misbehavior	Situational assistance
Assertive behavior	Off-task behavior	Skeleton plan
Classroom management	Order	Social reinforcers
Course syllabus	Praise	Tangible or material reinforcers
Discipline	Procedures	Token reinforcers
Emotional objectivity	Recognition	Withitness
Human relations skills	Reinforcer	

Major Concepts

1. Classroom management involves teacher actions to create a learning environment that encourages positive social interaction, active engagement in learning, and self-motivation.

2. Maintaining order means that students are performing within acceptable limits the actions necessary for a particular classroom event to be successful.

3. Establishing order begins by preparing for the start of the schoolyear, organizing the classroom and materials, and selecting and teaching rules and procedures.

4. Organizing your classroom and materials involves decisions about floor space, storage space, and bulletin boards and wall space.

5. Rules refer to general behavioral guidelines or expectations that are to be followed in the classroom. Procedures are approved ways to achieve specific tasks in the classroom.

6. Effective classroom managers have a mental set for management, in which they consciously have a high awareness for the actions in the classroom and respond quickly when misbehavior occurs.

7. Recognition, activities and privileges, tangible reinforcers, and token reinforcers can be used to reinforce desired student behavior.

TABLE 10.1   **Three-Step Response Plan to Misbehavior Using the Principle of Least Intervention**

TEACHER RESPONSE	STEP 1: PROVIDE SITUATIONAL ASSISTANCE	STEP 2: USE MILD RESPONSES	STEP 3: USE MODERATE RESPONSES
Purpose	To help the student to cope with the instructional situation and keep the student on task	To take nonpunitive actions to get the student back on task	To remove desired stimuli to decrease unwanted behavior
Sample actions	■ Remove distracting objects. ■ Provide support with routines. ■ Reinforce appropriate behaviors. ■ Boost student interest. ■ Provide cues. ■ Help students over hurdles. ■ Redirect the behavior. ■ Provide nonpunitive time-out. ■ Modify the classroom environment.	Nonverbal responses: ■ Ignore the behavior. ■ Use nonverbal signals. ■ Stand near the student. ■ Touch the student. Verbal responses: ■ Call on the student during the lesson. ■ Use humor. ■ Send an I-message. ■ Use positive phrasing. ■ Remind students of the rules. ■ Give students choices. ■ Ask "What should you be doing?" ■ Give a verbal reprimand.	Logical consequences: ■ Withdraw privileges. ■ Change the seat assignment. ■ Have the student write reflections on the problem. ■ Place the student in a time-out. ■ Hold the student for detention. ■ Contact the family. ■ Have the student visit the principal.

believe the disadvantages of using threats outweigh any possible benefits. Teachers may warn students to alert them to potential consequences, but a threat often expresses more severe consequences than would normally be expected and may be stated when the teacher has lost emotional control.

3. *Nagging.* Continual or unnecessary scolding of a student only upsets the student and arouses the resentment of other students. The teacher may consider these scoldings to be minilectures, but they are seen as nagging from the students' point of view.

4. *Forced apologies.* Forcing a student to express an apology that is not felt is a way of forcing him or her to lie. This approach solves nothing.

5. *Sarcastic remarks.* Sarcastic remarks are statements that the teacher uses to deride, taunt, or ridicule the student. While the teacher may consider such remarks as a means of punishment, they create resentment, may lower the student's self-esteem, and in fact may lower the esteem of the teacher in the eyes of the students.

6. *Group punishment.* *Group punishment* occurs when the entire class or group is punished because of the misbehavior of an individual. The intent is for peer pressure to help modify the behavior of the individual. Group punishment is difficult to use effectively, however, and the undesirable side effects are likely to outweigh the advantages. It forces students to choose between the teacher and one of their classmates. Many students will unite in sullen defiance of the teacher and refuse to blame the classmate if group punishment is used. Even if the students go along with the teacher, the technique engenders unhealthy attitudes.

7. *Assigning extra academic work.* When assigning extra academic work as a punishment, the teacher implies that the work is unpleasant. This extra work is often in the form of homework that is not normally required. The student then associates schoolwork with punishment. This is not the message teachers should convey.

8. *Reducing grades.* Penalizing a student academically for misbehavior again creates an undesirable association. Students who are penalized for misbehaving may develop an attitude of What's the use? toward academic work. Furthermore, reducing grades for misbehavior confounds the grade, which is intended to report only the student's academic progress.

9. *Writing as punishment.* After students misbehave, teachers may have them copy pages out of a dictionary, encyclopedia, or other book or have them write a certain statement ("I will not do such and such again.") a number of times. Unfortunately, this approach leads to hostility by the students, gives the impression that writing is a bad thing (English teachers will get upset about the message being conveyed here), and is not logically linked to what the students may have done.

10. *Physical labor or exercise.* A teacher may use pushups or some other physical action as punishment. However, the teacher may not be familiar with the student's physical abilities, and the student could get hurt. In addition to concerns about the student's safety, having students do extra exercises in physical education in response to misbehavior may cause the student to lose interest in the physical activities when the teacher assigns them as punishment.

11. *Corporal punishment. Corporal punishment* is a strategy in which the teacher inflicts physical pain on the student in an attempt to punish him or her for misbehaving. Paddling, spanking, slapping, and pinching are examples. There are many disadvantages to using physical consequences (Hyman, 1997). Other negative behaviors often emerge, such as escape (running away from the punisher), avoidance (lying, stealing, cheating), anxiety, fear, tension, stress, withdrawal, poor self-concept, resistance, and counteraggression. Because of these disadvantages, *physical consequences should not be used.* Many districts have a policy either prohibiting the use of corporal punishment or establishing specific guidelines for its limited use.

Cautions and Guidelines for Punishment

The later steps of the principle of least intervention may involve punishment. *Punishment* is the act of imposing a penalty with the intention of suppressing undesirable behavior.

You should express confidence in the students' ability to improve, and punish only as a last resort when students repeatedly fail to respond to more positive treatment. Apply punishment as part of a planned response, not as a means to release your anger or frustration.

The following factors are important to consider when effectively using punishment:

1. *Discuss and reward acceptable behaviors.* Acceptable behaviors should be emphasized when classroom rules are first discussed. Make it clear to students why the rules exist. Discuss the reasons for not engaging in behavior considered to be inappropriate. Most students will behave appropriately if they know what is expected.

2. *Clearly specify the behaviors that will lead to punishment.* Clarifying acceptable behaviors for the students may not be enough. To help the students to understand, identify and discuss examples of behaviors that break the rules and lead to punishment.

3. *Use punishment only when rewards or nonpunitive interventions have not worked or if the behavior must be decreased quickly because it is dangerous.* Punishment should be used as a last resort when other techniques have failed.

4. *Administer punishment in a calm, unemotional manner.* If you deliver punishment while still emotionally upset, you may select an overly harsh punishment and may also provoke the student into further inappropriate reactions. Punishment should not be an involuntary emotional response, a way to get revenge, or a spontaneous response to provocation.

5. *Deliver a warning before punishment is applied to any behavior.* The warning itself could reduce the need for the punishment. If the student does not correct the behavior after the warning, punishment should be delivered at the next occurrence.

6. *Apply punishment fairly with everyone who exhibits the targeted behaviors.* You should treat students from both genders the same way and low-achieving and high-achieving students the same way.

7. *Apply punishment consistently after every occurrence of the targeted misbehavior.* Behaviors that reliably receive punishment are less likely to be tried by students than behaviors that occasionally go uncorrected.

8. *Use punishment of sufficient intensity to suppress the unwanted behaviors.* Generally, the greater the intensity is, the longer lasting the effect. But this does not mean that you need to resort to extreme measures. For example, the loss of positive reinforcement because of inappropriate behavior is better than shouting "Don't do that" with increasing intensity.

9. *Select a punishment that is effective, that is not associated with a positive or rewarding experience, and that fits the situation.* Not all aversive consequences that you select may be seen as punishment. Some students, for instance, might think that it is a reward to be placed in a time-out area in the classroom. In this case, a different consequence should be used that is not seen by the student as being positive or rewarding. Also, don't overreact to mild misbehavior or underreact to serious misbehavior. The

Classroom Case Study

Classroom Discipline

Marilyn Schmidt is an experienced middle school music teacher who recently started teaching at a new school after her family relocated. She found the first month at her new school very stressful. On the first day of school, she wanted to show her students how friendly she was by giving them some time to socialize before starting class. As the students came into her classroom, she greeted them and allowed them to move desks around to talk to one another. But when she tried to start class a few minutes later, the students kept talking.

Finally, Ms. Schmidt stood up and yelled for everyone to "Shut up!" The class all looked at one another in shock and then began laughing. Humiliated, Ms. Schmidt made all the students put their heads down for the rest of the period and allowed no talking. One student asked if she could use the bathroom, and Ms. Schmidt explained the class had lost that privilege. The girl began arguing and said that "she really had to go," so Ms. Schmidt gave her a detention. Ms. Schmidt did not like doing that, but she knew she had to demonstrate her authority.

Since that day, the students have not cooperated with Ms. Schmidt. They come into the classroom and immediately begin talking, even after the bell rings for class to begin. Ms. Schmidt thinks the students are intentionally ignoring her. They do not quiet down until she yells several times that class has begun. Throughout the class, students ask to go to the bathroom. The angrier Ms. Schmidt becomes, the more the students laugh. She feels that she has no choice but to hand out more detentions, and now she is also staying after school every day because of it. Ms. Schmidt wishes she were back at her old school, where she had control over the students.

Focus Questions

1. What decisions and procedures did Ms. Schmidt make and use that contributed to the student disorder?
2. What decisions and procedures would have been more appropriate and successful for establishing and maintaining order?

seriousness of the misbehavior, the student, and the context of the situation need to be taken into account.

   10. *Avoid extended periods of punishment.*   Lengthy, mild punishment, such as missing open study time for a week, may have a boomerang effect. Punishment with a short duration is more effective.

THREE-STEP RESPONSE PLAN

When off-task behavior and misbehavior occur, a three-step response plan can be applied as a means to restore order and get the students back on task. The three steps described here are based on the principle of least intervention discussed earlier (see Table 10.1).

You provide situational assistance as the first approach to get the student back on task and then sequentially apply mild and moderate responses. If misbehavior continues after moderate responses are applied, other interventions may be needed. In these cases, it is useful to discuss the situation with the principal and school counselor.

Situational Assistance

Students sometimes pause from the instructional task to look out the window, daydream, fiddle with a comb or other object, or simply take a brief mental break from the work. In these examples, the students are not misbehaving; they are simply off task for a short time. You should take steps to draw the student back into the lesson and to keep the student on task.

To communicate to students that you have noticed off-task behavior, you should first provide *situational assistance*—actions designed to help the students cope with the instructional situation and to keep them on task or to get them back on task before problems worsen. Problem behaviors thus can be stopped early before they escalate or involve other students.

If students remain off task after situational assistance has been provided, move on to *mild responses.* These nonverbal and verbal nonpunitive responses are designed to get the student back on task. The continuum of responses to misbehavior (see Table 10.1) illustrates that situational assistance is the starting point when dealing with off-task behavior. The following techniques can be used to provide situational assistance to help get the students back on task:

1. *Remove distracting objects.* Students sometimes bring objects to school that may be distracting, such as combs, keys, or magazines. When you see that such an object is keeping a student from the assigned tasks, simply walk over to him or her and collect the object. The student should be quietly informed that the object can be picked up after class. Be kind and firm; no discussion is necessary. Inform students that they should store such objects in an appropriate place before school.

2. *Provide support with routines.* Students appreciate and often find comfort in knowing what is going to happen during the class period or during the day. They like to know where, when, why, and with whom they will be at various times. It is helpful to announce and post the daily schedule. Changes in the schedule should be announced in advance, if possible. Even for a single lesson, students often appreciate knowing at the start what activities are planned for the lesson. Knowing the schedule provides students with a sense of security and direction. Routines for entering and leaving the classroom, distributing classroom papers and materials, and participating in group work contribute to this sense of security.

3. *Reinforce appropriate behaviors.* Students who have followed the directions can be praised. This communicates to the student who is off task what is expected. A statement such as "I'm pleased to see that Juan has his notebook ready for today's lesson" communicates to others what is expected. Appropriate behavior is reinforced while simultaneously a signal is given to students who are off task. This approach is

myeducationlab

Go to MyEducationLab, select the topic **Classroom Management,** click "videos," and select "Modeling Mutual Respect, Routines, and Transitions." View the video and reflect.

more commonly used in elementary classrooms; middle and secondary students may consider it to be a little juvenile.

4. *Boost student interest.* Student interest may wane in time as the lesson proceeds. You should express interest in the student's work when he or she shows signs of losing interest or being bored. Offer to help, noting how much work has been completed, noting how well done the completed part of the task is, or discussing the task. These actions can help bring the student back on task. Interest boosting is often needed when students do individual or small-group classwork.

5. *Provide cues.* Sometimes all the students are asked to do one thing, such as to prepare their materials or to clean up at the end of class, and cues can be given in these cases. *Cues* are signals that it is time for a selected behavior. For example, you may close the door at the start of class as a cue that instruction is about to begin and that everyone is expected to have all materials ready. The lights could be flipped or a bell sounded to signal time to begin cleanup or to finish small-group work. You can select an appropriate cue and explain its use to the students. This conveys behavioral expectations and encourages constructive, on-task behavior.

What Would You Decide? | *Using Cues or Signals*

Imagine that your students are working in cooperative learning groups on a seven-day project. When they come into the room, they immediately go to their groups and start work. On some days and during some of the class sessions, you need to give some information to all students.

1. How can you use a cue as a signal for students to stop work at that point and pay attention to you?
2. How can you give a cue that it is time to prepare to leave the class at the end of the class period?

---

6. *Help students over hurdles.* Students who are experiencing difficulty with a specific task need help in overcoming the problem—helping them over a hurdle—to keep them on task. *Hurdle helping* may consist of encouraging words from you, offering to assist with a specific task, or making available additional materials or equipment. For example, in a seatwork activity in which students need to draw several elements, including some straight lines, you might notice that one student is becoming upset that his or her lines are not straight. You could help by handing the student a ruler. In this way, you help before the student gives up on the assignment or becomes disruptive.

7. *Redirect the behavior.* When students show signs of losing interest, you can ask them to answer a question, do a problem, or read as a means of drawing them back into the lesson. Students should be treated as if they were paying attention and should be reinforced if they respond appropriately. It is important not to embarrass or ridicule students by saying that they would have been able to answer the question if they had been paying attention. Simply by asking a content-related question, you will show students that you are trying to draw them back into the lesson. Redirecting student behavior back into the lesson discourages off-task behavior.

8. *Alter the lesson.* Lessons sometimes do not go as well as you would like, and students may lose interest in them for a variety of reasons. The lesson needs to be altered in some way when students are seen daydreaming, writing notes to friends, yawning, stretching, or moving around in their seats. When altering the lesson, select a different type of activity than the one that has proven unsuccessful. For example, if a whole-class discussion proves to be unsuccessful, you might have students work in pairs on a related issue that still deals with the lesson's objectives.

9. *Provide nonpunitive time-out.* Students who become frustrated, agitated, or fatigued may get off task and disruptive. When you notice this happening, provide a nonpunitive time-out. A *time-out* is a period of time that the student is away from the instructional situation to calm down and reorganize his or her thoughts. The student then returns to the task with a fresh perspective. This time-out is not intended to be punishment for the off-task behavior. When a time-out is needed, you can ask the student to run an errand, help you with something, go get a drink, or do some other task not related to the instructional activity. Be alert to students showing signs of frustration and agitation and be ready to respond quickly.

10. *Modify the classroom environment.* The classroom environment itself may contribute to off-task behavior. The arrangement of the desks, tables, instructional materials, and other items in the classroom may give rise to inefficient traffic patterns or limited views of the instructional areas. Other factors include the boundaries between areas for quiet student and group projects and access to supplies. In addition, both your actions and those of your students may affect their behavior. Once misbehavior develops, you may need to separate the students or change the setting in some way. Examine the disturbance and identify the element that contributes to it. Modification in the classroom arrangement may include moving tables, student desks, or the storage area.

Mild Responses

Students may misbehave even after you have developed a system of rules and procedures, provided a supportive instructional environment, and given situational assistance to get misbehaving students back on task. In that case, mild responses should be used to correct the student's behavior. *Mild responses* are nonpunitive ways to deal with misbehavior while providing guidance for appropriate behavior. Nonverbal and verbal mild responses are meant to stop the off-task behavior and to restore order. The three-step response plan shown in Table 10.1 illustrates the movement to more directive responses if situational assistance is not successful.

Nonverbal Responses.   Even with situational assistance, students may get off task. Nonverbal responses are taken as a nonpunitive means to get the student back on task. *Nonverbal responses* may include planned ignoring, signal interference, proximity control, and touch control. These approaches are taken in increasing order of teacher involvement and control.

What Would You Decide?   *Using Nonverbal Responses*

Students are working in small groups on an activity, and you notice that in one group, two students are off task.

1. How can you respond nonverbally to get these two students back on task? What factors might affect your decision about the particular method?

2. At a later time, you are making a presentation to the whole class when you notice two other students off task. What nonverbal responses might you make in that situation?

1. *Ignore the behavior.* Intentionally ignoring minor misbehavior is sometimes the best course of action as a means to weaken the behavior. This is based on the reinforcement principle called *extinction;* that is, if you ignore a behavior and withhold reinforcement, the behavior will lessen and ultimately disappear. Minor misbehaviors that might be ignored are pencil tapping, body movements, hand waving, book dropping, calling out an answer instead of raising a hand, interrupting the teacher, whispering, and so on. Behaviors designed to get your attention or that of their classmates are likely candidates for extinction, or ignoring the behavior.

Ignoring the behavior is best used to control only behaviors that cause little interference to teaching/learning, and it should be combined with praise for appropriate behavior. Extinction is inappropriate for behaviors (e.g., talking out, aggression) reinforced by consequences that you do not control and behaviors (violence) that cannot be tolerated during the time required for extinction to work (Kerr & Nelson, 2006). If the behavior continues after a reasonable period of planned ignoring, you should be more directive.

There are limitations to ignoring the behavior. One risk is that students may conclude that you are not aware of what is happening and may continue the behavior. While you may ignore the behavior and not give the student the desired attention, other students may give such attention. Furthermore, the student may continue the behavior for a while after you ignore it, and thus the time taken for correcting the problem will be too long. Aggressive or hostile behaviors may be too dangerous to ignore.

2. *Use nonverbal signals.* A nonverbal signal can be used to communicate to the disrupting student that the behavior is not appropriate. Signals must be directed at the student. They let the student know that the behavior is inappropriate and that it is time to get back to work.

Nonverbal signal interference may include making eye contact with the student who is writing a note, shaking a hand or finger to indicate not to do some inappropriate action, holding a hand up to stop a student's calling out, or giving the "teacher look." These actions should be done in a businesslike manner. You need to move to the next level of intervention if these disruptive behaviors persist.

3. *Stand near the student.* Using your physical presence near the disruptive student to help him or her get back on task is *proximity control.* This is warranted at times when you cannot get the student's attention to send a signal because he or she is so engrossed in an inappropriate action. For example, a student may be reading something other than class-related material or may be writing a note. While doing this, the student may not even look up at you. As a result, signals will not work. While conducting the lesson, walk around the room and approach the student's desk. The student will then likely notice your presence and put the material away without a word being spoken.

Some proximity-control techniques may be somewhat subtle, such as walking toward the student, while other approaches, such as standing near the student's desk, are more direct. If students do not respond to proximity control, you need to move to a more directive level of intervention.

4. *Touch the student.* Without any verbal exchange, you may place a hand on a student's shoulder in an effort to achieve calm or take a student's hand and escort the student back to his or her seat. *Touch control* involves mild, nonaggressive physical contact that is used to get the student on task. It communicates that you disapprove of the action. Talk to your principal to be certain that you understand the guidelines and legal considerations of appropriate touching.

When deciding whether and how to use touch control, you may take into account the circumstances of the behavior and the characteristics of the students. Students who

---

Voices from the Classroom

Using Body Language and "The Teacher Look"

Lynne Hagar, high school history and English teacher, Mesquite, Texas

I am a small woman, but I can effectively control 30 senior students just by using my voice and my body language. When I want a certain behavior to stop, the first thing I do is to look at the student. Even if that student is not looking at me, he or she eventually becomes aware that I am staring. Then I point at the student and nonverbally indicate that the behavior is to stop. A finger placed on my lips indicates that talking needs to stop.

Often, a questioning or disapproving look or gesture can stop undesirable behaviors right there. I may have to move into a student's personal space or comfort zone to stop a behavior, but a combination of a look and physical proximity are effective about 90 percent of the time. I might even casually rest my hand on the student's desk,

never stopping teaching, and stay put for a minute or so until I'm sure the student is back on task.

My advice is to practice "the look" in the mirror until you get it right. It shouldn't be a friendly look, but it doesn't have to be angry either. Learn to say in your manner, "I am in charge here."

Also, move around the classroom. Getting close to your students is essential, not only when you are correcting them but also when you want to reassure them or reinforce their positive feelings about you and your classroom. A friendly touch on the shoulder as you are helping a student with a problem or a hug when a student has a big success can go miles toward cementing your positive relationship with that student.

are angry or visibly upset sometimes do not want to be touched, and some do not want to be touched at any time. How well touch will be received depends on where it occurs and how long it lasts. A touch on the back, hand, arm, or shoulder is acceptable to many students, whereas a touch to the face, neck, leg, chest, or other more personal area is often not acceptable. Brief touch is considered acceptable; the longer the touch, the more it becomes unacceptable.

Verbal Responses. Although nonverbal mild responses may be effective, verbal responses can be used as nonpunitive, mild responses to misbehavior. Their purpose is to get the student back on task with limited disruption and intervention. Various verbal responses are described here:

1. *Call on the student during the lesson.* You can recapture a misbehaving student's attention by using his or her name in the lesson, such as "Now, in this next example, suppose that John had three polygons that he . . ." You can then ask a question of the student to recapture his or her attention. Calling on the student in these ways allows you to communicate that you know what is going on and to capture his or her attention without citing the misbehavior.

Be cautious: Students' dignity should be preserved. If you call on students in these ways only when they misbehave, they will sense that you are just waiting to catch them misbehaving, and this strategy will backfire by creating resentment (Good & Brophy, 2008).

2. *Use humor.* Humor can be used as a gentle reminder to students to correct their behavior. Humor directed at the situation or even at yourself can defuse tension that might be created due to the misbehavior. It can depersonalize the situation and thus help resolve the problem. You must be careful that the humor is not sarcastic. *Sarcasm* includes statements that are directed at correcting or making fun of the student; these statements are intended to criticize or embarrass the student. Instead, humor is directed at or makes fun of the situation or the teacher. The student may then reconsider his or her actions and then get back on task.

3. *Send an I-message.* An I-message verbally prompts appropriate behavior without giving a direct command (Gordon, 1991). An *I-message* has three parts: (a) a brief description of the misbehavior; (b) a description of its effects on you or the other students; and (c) a description of your feelings about the effects. For example, you might say, "When you tap your pen on the desk during the test, it makes a lot of noise, and I am concerned that it might distract other students."

I-messages are intended to help students recognize that their behavior has consequences for other students and that you have genuine feelings about the actions. Since I-messages leave the decision about changing the behavior up to the student, they are likely to promote a sense of responsibility.

4. *Use positive phrasing.* *Positive phrasing* is used when inappropriate off-task behavior allows you to highlight positive outcomes for appropriate behavior. This usually takes the form of "When you do X (behave in a particular appropriate way), then you can do Y (a positive outcome)." For example, when a student is out of her seat, you might say, "Renee, it will be your turn to pick up supplies when you return to your seat." Through the use of positive phrasing, you redirect students from disruptive to appropriate behavior by simply stating the positive outcomes. In the long run, students begin to believe that proper behavior does lead to positive outcomes.

5. *Remind students of the rules.* Each classroom needs to have a set of rules governing student behavior, along with a set of consequences for breaking them. When students see that consequences of misbehavior are in fact delivered, reminders of the rules can help them get back on task because they want to avoid the consequences. When one student is poking another student, for example, you might say, "Delores, the classroom rules state that students must keep their hands and feet to themselves." This reminder often ends the misbehavior because the student does not want the consequence. If the inappropriate behavior continues, you must deliver the consequence or the reminder will be of little value, because students will recognize that there is no follow-through.

6. *Give students choices.* Some students feel defensive when confronted about their misbehavior. As a result, you can give them choices about resolving the problem. This allows the student to feel that he or she settled the problem without appearing to back down. All the choices that you give to the student should lead to resolution of the problem. If a student is talking to another nearby student, you might say, "Harvey, you can turn back in your seat and get back to your project, or you can take the empty seat at the end of the row." In this way, Harvey has a choice, but the result is that he gets back to work in his seat or in the seat at the end of the row.

7. *Ask "What should you be doing?"* Glasser (1998) proposes that teachers ask disruptive students questions in an effort to direct them back to appropriate behavior. When a student is disruptive, you might ask "What should you be doing?" This question can have a positive effect because it helps redirect the student back to appropriate behavior.

Of course, some students may not answer this question honestly or may refuse to reply at all. In that case, you should make statements related to the question. For example, "Keith, you were swearing and name calling. That is against our classroom rules. You should not swear or call names of others." If the student continues to break the rule, then appropriate consequences should be delivered.

8. *Give a verbal reprimand.* A straightforward way to have the students stop misbehaving is simply to ask or direct them to do so. This is sometimes called a *desist order* or a *reprimand,* and it is given to decrease unwanted behavior. Verbal reprimands are effective with many mild and moderate behavior problems but by themselves are less successful with severe behavior disorders (Kerr & Nelson, 2006).

A *direct appeal* involves a courteous request for the student to stop the misbehavior and to get back on task. You might say, "Martina, please put away the comb and continue with the class assignment." A direct appeal often gives the student a sense of ownership for deciding to get back on task and to do as you requested. The student feels a sense of responsibility.

As an alternative, you could use a *direct command,* in which you take the responsibility and give a direction in a straightforward manner, such as "Wayne, stop talking with your friends and get to work on the lab activity." With the direct appeal and the direct command, the student is expected to comply with your directions. If the student defies your request or command, you must be prepared to deliver an appropriate consequence.

Soft reprimands, audible only to the misbehaving student, are more effective than loud reprimands in reducing disruptive classroom behavior (Kerr & Nelson, 2006). Soft, private reprimands do not call the attention of the entire class to the misbehaving student and also may be less likely to trigger emotional reactions.

Moderate Responses

Following situational assistance and mild nonverbal and verbal responses, students might continue to misbehave. In that case, moderate responses should be used to correct the problem. The three-step response plan shown in Table 10.1 illustrates the movement to more directive responses if mild responses are not successful.

Moderate responses are intended to be *punitive responses* to deal with misbehavior by removing desired stimuli to decrease the occurrence of the inappropriate behavior. Moderate responses include logical consequences and behavior modification techniques. Since student behaviors that warrant moderate responses are more problematic than mild misbehaviors, it is often useful to discuss specific problems with the principal, other teachers, or the school counselor. The family can be contacted at any point to inform them of their child's actions and to solicit their help.

A *logical consequence* is an event arranged by the teacher that is directly and logically related to the misbehavior (Dreikurs, Grunwald, & Pepper, 1998). The consequence should be reasonable, respectful, and related to the student action. For instance, if a student leaves paper on the classroom floor, then he or she must pick it up off the floor. If a student breaks the rule of speaking out without raising his or her hand, you will ignore the response and call on a student whose hand is up. If a student marks on the desk, then he or she will be required to clean the marks off. Students are more likely to respond favorably to logical consequences because they do not consider the consequences mean or unfair.

You may tell the student what the consequence is right after the behavior occurs. For example, "Milton, you left the study area a mess. You need to clean it up at the end of class." As an alternative, you may give the student a choice when inappropriate behavior is noticed. This tells the student that the inappropriate behavior must be changed or, if it is not changed, that a particular consequence will occur. For example, you may say, "Joellen, you have a choice of not bothering students near you or having your seat changed."

When given a choice, students will often stop the inappropriate behavior. This approach can be very effective because the student feels a sense of ownership in solving the problem, and the issue is over quickly. Of course, if the problem behavior continues, you must deliver the consequence that you stated to the student.

At the start of the schoolyear, you should think of two or three logical consequences for each of the classroom rules and inform students of them. Logical, reasonable consequences are preplanned, and you are not under the pressure of thinking up something appropriate at the time the misbehavior occurs. Some examples of logical consequences include the following:

■ *Withdraw privileges.* As a regular part of the classroom activities, you may provide your students with a number of special privileges such as a trip to the library, use of a computer, use of special equipment or a game, service as a classroom helper, or other valued privileges. If the misbehavior relates to the type of privilege offered, a logical consequence would be to withdraw the privilege. For example, if a student mishandles some special equipment, then the student would lose the privilege of using the equipment.

■ *Change the seat assignment.* Students may talk, poke, or interact with other students in nearby seats. Sometimes, a problem occurs because certain students are seated near each other. Other times, just the placement of the seats enables easy interaction. If inappropriate interaction occurs, a logical consequence would be to relocate the student's seat.

■ *Have the student write reflections on the problem.* It is often useful to ask the student to reflect on the situation to help him or her recognize the logical connection

Voices from the Classroom

Using an OOPS Sheet for Reflections

Lisa Bietau, fourth-grade teacher, Manhattan, Kansas

When my students misbehave, I sometimes ask them to fill out an OOPS Sheet to have them reflect on their behavior. OOPS stands for an Outstanding Opportunity for a Personal Stretch. The sheet has a place for their name and date at the top. Then there are several other areas that the student needs to fill in: (1) Describe the problem. (2) What other choices did you have to settle the situation without difficulty? (3) How might you handle this differently if it happens again?

After the student fills out the OOPS Sheet, I meet with the student privately to briefly discuss the situation and to review the options and solutions that the student wrote. This reflection and discussion with me helps the students to understand my expectations and to recognize that they have a responsibility to consider reasonable options when they meet a challenging situation.

I sign the OOPS Sheet and make a copy for my files. The original is then sent home with the student to obtain the parent's signature. All the student's privileges are suspended until the signed sheet is returned. If the sheet is not returned the next day, I call the parents and another copy is sent home, if necessary. I have found that students show more self-control after completing the OOPS Sheet.

between the behavior and the consequences. You may ask the student to provide written responses to certain questions; this might be done during a time-out. These questions may include What is the problem? What did I do to create the problem? What should happen to me? What should I do next time to avoid a problem? Other questions may require the student to describe the rule that was broken, why he or she chose to misbehave, who was bothered by the misbehavior, what more appropriate behavior could be chosen next time, and what should happen to him or her the next time the misbehavior occurs.

■ *Place the student in a time-out.* Sometimes a student is talking or disrupting the class in such a way that interferes with the progress of the lesson. As noted earlier, such a student can be excluded from the group; this is called a *time-out.* Removing the student from the group is a logical consequence of interfering with the group. An area of the room should be established as the time-out area, such as a desk in a corner or partially behind a filing cabinet. As a general rule, a time-out should last no longer than ten minutes.

■ *Hold the student for detention.* *Detention* means detaining or holding back a student when he or she normally would be free to go and do other things. The student is deprived of free time and perhaps the opportunity to socialize with other students. Detention may include remaining after class or staying after school. Detention can be a logical consequence for student behaviors that waste class time. A student might be asked to work on the social studies paper that was not completed during class due to inappropriate behavior. Students will soon see the logic that time wasted in class will have to be made up later, on their own time in detention.

Make sure the student understands the reasons for the detention. It should logically fit the offense, and the time should not be excessive. Twenty to thirty minutes after school would be reasonable. Confer with the student and work out a plan to help him or her avoid detention in the future and move toward self-control.

■ *Contact the family.* If a student shows a pattern of repeated misbehavior, then you may need to contact the family. The logic here is that if all earlier attempts to extinguish the misbehavior do not work, it is appropriate to go to a higher authority. The parents, guardians, or other family members may be notified by a note or a letter to inform them of the problem and to solicit their involvement or support. You may choose to call them instead. If the situation is fairly serious, a conference may be warranted.

■ *Have the student visit the principal.* In cases of repeated misbehavior or serious misbehavior such as fighting, students may be sent to the school office to see the principal. The principal may talk with the student in an effort to use his or her legitimate authority to influence the student to behave properly. Some schools have specific procedures to be followed when students are sent to the principal. When the behavior problems reach this point, additional personnel, including the school counselor or psychologist, and the family need to be consulted to help the student.

DEALING WITH CHRONIC MISBEHAVIORS

Chronic misbehaviors are troublesome behaviors that students repeatedly or compulsively perform. They include tattling, clowning, cheating, lying, stealing, profanity, rudeness toward the teacher, defiance or hostility, and failure to do schoolwork. This behavior is recurring and inappropriate, and teachers can take actions to minimize its presence in the classroom (Gootman, 2008). Strategies to address a number of common chronic misbehaviors are presented here:

1. *Tattling.* Tattling occurs when students report minor infractions or perceived injustices to the teacher. Tattling is not disruptive, but it can become a problem when students commonly report minor, petty complaints. To prevent tattling from occurring in the first place, let students know what kinds of information they should and should not report to you. You need to know about an incident where a student got hurt, for example, but not when some other student is not doing the schoolwork.

Many teachers, especially in the primary grades, have an explicit lesson about tattling. They describe the difference between reporting important information to the teacher and reports that are tattling about minor infractions. Numerous examples can be provided and discussed for each category. Students can offer examples, as well. It is important to convey to students that you will be available to help them with important matters but that you are not interested in minor complaints.

2. *Clowning.* Students who clown behave in silly or funny ways or may play practical jokes. This clowning is disruptive to the class. Figuring out the source of the student's clowning can help determine what to do about it (Gootman, 2008). Some students may use clowning to cover up a deficiency; they may clown during a math lesson because they are weak in math. Clowning also may be a vehicle for a student to achieve success—to gain some recognition, fame, and popularity among other students. Still, clowning may be a way of students venting frustrations and pressures that they may experience from school, home, or other factors.

Keeping a record of who, what, when, where, and how for clowning incidents can help pinpoint the source. Then you can meet privately with the student to discuss the pattern of the clowning behavior and why it is disruptive. Help the student figure out ways to meet his or her needs without being disruptive.

3. *Cheating.* Cheating involves students getting answers or projects from someone else and turning it in as their own. Students may cheat for several reasons. They may cheat if teachers' expectations are too high and they may not be capable of mastering the material. Students then may see cheating as a way out. Other students may simply not be prepared, or they may have test anxiety.

It is best to minimize the temptation to cheat by discussing the difference between helping and cheating, demonstrating expected behaviors for various activities, and having students identify appropriate and inappropriate actions. In addition, it is important to minimize the opportunity to cheat by determining desk placement during tests and by giving attention to policies, procedures, and submission guidelines for other types of student products.

If you catch a student cheating, you can talk to the student privately, present your reasons for suspecting cheating, express concern and try to find out why the student cheated, explain the consequences, and then discuss the consequences for subsequent cheating (Weinstein & Mignano, 2007). Rather than give the student a zero on the assignment, you may ask him or her to complete the test or assignment again under controlled conditions where cheating cannot occur. Some schools have predetermined consequences for cheating, such as parental notification.

What Would You Decide? *Addressing Cheating*

On three successive quizzes in your class, you notice that four students have always received the same score.

1. Under what circumstances would you talk with these four students about their scores?

2. What could you do about the questions and the formatting of the quiz to minimize cheating?

3. What could you do about room arrangement and your monitoring of students during a quiz to minimize cheating?

---

4. *Lying.* Lying involves saying something that is not true in a conscious effort to deceive somebody. Students may have many reasons for lying, such as trying to protect their self-image, to mask their vulnerable points, or to inflate their image in front of others. They may feel afraid, feel insecure, or fear rejection. Students may lie to protect themselves from punishment or if teachers are too strict with them.

The best response is to express concern about the student's need to lie by asking "I wonder why you couldn't tell me what really happened?" This approach makes it easier for the student to talk about the reason he or she felt compelled to lie. Stay calm and encourage the student to discuss his or her reason for telling a lie. In doing so, try not to overreact or get angry with the student. Focus on the student's reasons and feelings that led to the lie. You might encourage the private conversation with a statement such as "If you tell me what really happened, we can figure out what to do about this situation and perhaps I can help you not let this happen again." Encourage students to be honest about their feelings, and use a calm problem-solving approach to help students address the problems that caused them to lie in the first place.

5. *Stealing.* Stealing involves taking something that belongs to somebody else without the owner's permission. Students in early grades may still be learning the difference between sharing and taking what does not belong to them. Students may impulsively steal because they may want something, or they may take something from another student because they are angry with him or her.

If an incident of stealing takes place and you know the culprit, you can have a private conversation with the student about what happened. Describe what you saw and have the student return the item, replace it, or make restitution. Help the student figure out options other than stealing. You may need to respond forcefully depending on the value of the property and the frequency of stealing. In such cases, you may need to contact the principal and the family. Because of legal implications, it is wise to discuss an incident with the principal before conducting a search of backpacks, lockers, or a student's clothing.

6. *Profanity.* Profanity occurs when students use abusive, vulgar, or irreverent language. Age plays a role in the use of profanity. Young children may simply be restating language they heard on television, from family, or from friends with little or no understanding of the meaning. An instructional response is appropriate here, rather than a disciplinary one (e.g., "We don't use words like that in school."). For older students, such language may have become a regular part of their vocabulary, or they may use profanity when they are angry with another person. In such cases, students need to see what is acceptable and unacceptable in school. Stress that using language to hurt others will not be permitted and that there are other acceptable ways to express anger.

7. *Rudeness toward the teacher.* Students may be rude to the teacher by exhibiting disagreeable or discourteous words or actions that are outside acceptable standards. Rudeness may be expressed in talking back, arguing, making crude remarks, or showing inappropriate gestures. It is best to avoid overreacting, arguing, or getting into a power struggle. A low-key, respectful response is more suitable. When rude behavior first is evident, you should inform the student that the behavior is inappropriate, and you might refer to a classroom rule that relates to respectful behaviors. If the actions continue, you should meet with the student privately to identify the reason for the behavior and possibly to deliver consequences. If the rude behavior continues, you may need to consult with the principal or counselors about additional responses.

8. *Defiance or hostility toward the teacher.* Defiance occurs when a student refuses to obey or conform to teacher directions. These actions may be open, bold, or even hostile, and defiance may be in the form of a confrontation with the teacher during a class session. The best way to deal with defiance is to try to defuse it by keeping it in private and handling it individually with the student. Put the student off by saying that you will discuss the situation in a few minutes when you have time. Avoid a power struggle and remain objective. Listen to the student's point of view, but don't engage in an argument. State the consequence clearly and implement it.

Here are some guidelines when students become defiant:

- Stay in control of yourself.
- Direct the rest of the class to work on something while you speak to the student in a private area away from the rest of the students.
- Stand a few feet away from the defiant student (i.e., don't get in his or her face).
- Acknowledge the student's feelings by saying something like "I can see that you are really angry."
- Avoid a power struggle in the conversation (e.g., "I am the boss here, and I am telling you what to do.").

■ As a means to defuse the situation, offer the student a choice of actions for what the student needs to do next (Weinstein & Mignano, 2007).

9. *Failure to do work in class or homework.* You may have some students who regularly do not complete seatwork done in class or homework. You should first examine how you hold students academically accountable in your class and make any needed adjustments to ensure accountability. Next, you should plan to maintain accurate records of the schoolwork and respond early when you recognize students who are regularly not completing their classwork.

You also should examine the nature of the assignments and homework. Is the material too difficult to be completed independently? Is it too boring? Is it too long? Could the material be mastered with a shorter assignment? Was there sufficient preparation in class before students were to do the seatwork or homework? Are there other ways to provide practice and to assess student progress without having seatwork and homework every day? Your reflection on these questions may lead to your adjustment of the assignments and expectations.

Key Terms

Chronic misbehaviors	Hurdle helping	Proximity control
Corporal punishment	I-message	Punishment
Cues	Intervention	Punitive response
Desist order	Logical consequence	Reprimand
Detention	Mild responses	Sarcasm
Direct appeal	Misbehavior	Situational assistance
Direct command	Nonverbal responses	Threat
Extinction	Positive phrasing	Time-out
Group punishment	Principle of least intervention	Touch control

Major Concepts

1. Misbehavior is any student behavior that is perceived by the teacher to compete with or threaten the academic actions at a particular moment.

2. The principle of least intervention states that when dealing with routine classroom behavior, misbehavior should be corrected with the simplest, least intrusive intervention that will work. If that does not work, then move up to a more intrusive approach.

3. Due to inherent problems in the use of punishment, teachers should follow certain guidelines when using punitive responses.

4. A three-step response plan is recommended to address off-task behavior and misbehavior.

5. The first step, situational assistance, is designed to help students cope with the instructional situation and to keep them on task.

6. Next, mild responses are nonpunitive ways to deal with misbehavior while providing guidance for appropriate behavior. Nonverbal and verbal approaches can be used.

7. Moderate responses, the final step, deliver punishment as a means to restore order.

8. Chronic misbehaviors are troublesome behaviors that students repeatedly or compulsively perform. They include tattling, clowning, cheating, lying, stealing, profanity, rudeness toward the teacher, defiance or hostility, and failure to do schoolwork.

Discussion/Reflective Questions

1. How might the cause of the misbehavior affect the teacher's choice of an appropriate response?
2. What are the benefits of providing situational assistance?
3. What justification can teachers offer for the use of punishment?

4. What are the merits and disadvantages of moving in a three-step response plan from providing situational assistance to using moderate responses?
5. What are examples of chronic misbehaviors you have witnessed? How were these behaviors addressed by the teacher?

Suggested Activities

For Clinical Settings

1. Review Table 10.1, and consider additional examples for teacher responses at each of the three steps.
2. Identify examples of student behavior for which mild responses would be appropriate.
3. Consider what types of punishment you might use in your teaching, and identify guidelines that you will follow for their use.

For Field Experiences

1. Find out if there are printed school or district policies about any aspect of classroom discipline (e.g., types of punishments, detention, corporal punishment, suspensions). Read and critique the printed policies.
2. Talk to teachers to identify ways they use situational assistance and mild and moderate responses to misbehavior.
3. Ask teachers what types of chronic misbehavior occur, and discuss how they address these misbehaviors.

Further Reading

Burden, P. R. (2010). *Classroom management: Creating a successful K–12 learning community* (4th ed.). New York: John Wiley & Sons.

Provides a comprehensive K–12 review of ways to establish, maintain, and restore order in the classroom. It carries a practical, realistic view of decisions teachers make about getting organized for management, planning for management, managing when conducting the class, and restoring order after misbehavior.

Burke, K. (2008). *What to do with the kid who . . . : Developing cooperation, self-discipline, and responsibility in the classroom* (3rd ed.). Thousand Oaks, CA: Corwin Press.

Provides many practical ideas for ways to set up a K–12 classroom to minimize misbehavior and presents strategies to deal with misbehavior when it happens.

Sprick, R. S. (2006). *Discipline in the secondary school: A positive approach to behavior management* (2nd ed.). San Francisco: Jossey-Bass.

Offers guidance to set up your classroom management system to support time-on-task and minimize misbehavior.

11 Assessing Student Performance

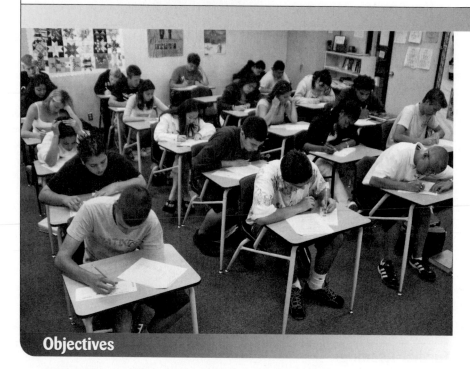

Objectives

This chapter provides information that will help you to:

1. Define the terms *evaluation, measurement,* and *assessment.*
2. Establish a framework for effective evaluation.
3. Identify ways to use formal and informal assessment strategies.
4. Select ways to conduct performance-based evaluation.
5. State guidelines for preparing teacher-made tests.

Evaluation
- Types of Evaluation
- Measurement, Assessment, and Evaluation
- Norm-Referenced and Criterion-Referenced Evaluation
- Characteristics of Good Assessment Instruments
- Adapting Assessment for English Language Learners

Performance-BasedAssessment
- Product Assessments
- Performance Assessments
- Ways to Rate Student Products or Performances

Teacher-Made Tests
- Planning the Classroom Test
- Selecting and Preparing Test Questions
- Assembling the Test
- Administering the Test
- Scoring the Test

Establishing a Framework for Evaluation

Assessing students is necessary to help teachers determine the degree to which educational objectives have been achieved and to help teachers know their students as individuals. As you consider student assessment, consider these questions: What is evaluation? What are the differences among evaluation, measurement, and assessment? How do teachers prepare for evaluation? How can performance-based evaluation be conducted? How can teacher-made tests be prepared and administered? These questions will be explored in this chapter.

EVALUATION

Before teachers conduct evaluation in their classrooms, they need to recognize that there are several types of evaluation; that there are differences among measurement, assessment, and evaluation; and that norm-referenced and criterion-referenced tests can be used.

Types of Evaluation

There are three types of evaluation, each serving a different purpose and each being conducted at different times (Miller, Linn, & Gronlund, 2009). First, *diagnostic evaluation* is necessary at the start to determine students' individual levels of competence, to identify those who have already achieved mastery of the requisite learnings, and to help classify students into tentative small groups for instruction.

Second, *formative evaluation* is used to monitor learning progress during instruction and to provide continuous feedback to students and parents. To obtain the necessary information, you may use commercially prepared tests, your own criterion-referenced tests, observations, or other techniques. Formative evaluation is typically quite comprehensive in the examination of the content. If formative evaluation is to provide useful guidance to the teacher and student, it should include frequent assessment to provide systematic feedback on progress.

What Would You Decide?   *Your Students' Prior Knowledge*

Students in your class will likely have a wide range of prior knowledge about the content in the next unit you will teach.

1. To plan content and experiences in the unit more effectively, how can you determine the students' prior knowledge?

2. How might you enable students to contribute to the planning of the unit?
3. How might the grade level that you teach affect your responses to these questions?

Third, *summative evaluation* is at the end of a unit, marking period, or course and is intended to (a) determine the extent of the students' achievement and competence, (b) provide a basis for assigning grades, and (c) provide the data from which reports to families and transcripts can be prepared. Summative evaluation typically examines the student's broad ability as compared to the detailed examination of each component in formative evaluation.

Measurement, Assessment, and Evaluation

Although measurement and evaluation are related, they are nevertheless different. *Measurement* is the process used to obtain data concerning student learning. For instance, a paper-and-pencil test may be used to measure the achievement of a student, but other types of data collection can be used, such as performance-based measures. The term *assessment* is commonly used as a synonym for *measurement*. Assessment, however, often is viewed by educators as having more emphasis on authentic, alternative, or performance-based measurement as compared to teacher-made tests.

Evaluation is the process in which the teacher uses information derived from many sources to arrive at a value judgment. Evaluation may be based on measurement data but also might be based on other types of data, such as questionnaires, direct observation, written or oral performance ratings, or interviews.

The differences between measurement and evaluation can be illustrated when you determine a grade at the end of a marking period. Throughout the marking period, you will measure student performance by a variety of means. Then you will place these measures within a grading system to determine the student's grade. The grading system actually reflects the value judgment concerning the student's measures.

Norm-Referenced and Criterion-Referenced Evaluation

myeducationlab

Go to MyEducationLab, select the topic **Assessment,** click "videos," and select "Standardized Tests." View the video and reflect.

Norm-referenced evaluation is used to interpret a score of an individual by comparing it with the scores of other individuals. Ranking students is the primary issue. For example, a teacher would use a norm-referenced test to compare the reading abilities of students before forming reading groups. A norm-referenced test finds a student's performance level in relation to levels of others on the same test. Many standardized achievement and aptitude tests are norm-referenced instruments.

In contrast, *criterion-referenced evaluation* is used to interpret an individual's performance by comparing it to some specified criterion, such as a performance standard. Individual mastery is the primary issue. The object is to determine whether the student can or cannot perform at a certain standard. How well others perform on the same standard is not considered.

Characteristics of Good Assessment Instruments

The effectiveness of any measuring device depends on its validity, reliability, and practicality (Airasian & Russell, 2008):

1. *Validity* deals with the extent to which a measuring device measures what it purports to measure. While there are several types of validity, teachers are usually most concerned with content validity. *Content validity* refers to the degree to which an instrument samples the subject matter in the area to be measured or the degree to which it coincides with the instructional objectives to be measured. This is typically the only type of validity used in teacher-made tests and other measures. To determine content validity, you examine the outline of instructional objectives and check the congruence with the test questions. High content validity means that there is a good match between test questions and instructional objectives covered in class. Low content validity means that there is a poor match.

2. *Reliability* deals with the consistency of results. The more consistent the results, the higher the reliability of the test. If you administer a reliable test and shortly after readminister an equivalent form of the same test, students should score roughly the same as they did on the first test.

All measuring devices have some type of error. *Measurement error* may come from errors in the instrument, errors in the use of the instrument, and errors emanating from the subject's response. The more objective the scoring of a test, the more reliable the score. Factors that may act to make a test less reliable are the length of a test (i.e., very short tests are not very reliable), the ambiguity of directions and questions, and an overload of questions that are too difficult or too easy. Variability in the students' responses may also be affected by temporal factors such as poor motivation, lack of interest, improper test environment, poor emotional set, and illness.

3. *Practicality* refers to the ease of administering the measuring device, the time required, the energy expended to collect the data, and the ease with which the data can be interpreted. For instance, an essay test may be easily prepared by the teacher, but the time required to grade it may make such a test impractical. Conversely, an objective test can be graded relatively quickly but may take much longer to prepare.

Adapting Assessment for English Language Learners

English language learners (ELLs) may know the content on which they are being assessed but have difficulty demonstrating their knowledge with standard assessments. These challenges may stem from the vocabulary, reading, and writing that are part of a typical assessment. Given this, teachers must adapt assessments to accurately determine the content knowledge of ELLs.

Echevarria, Vogt, and Short (2008) offer the following suggestions when adapting assessments for ELLs:

1. *Range.* Adapt the number of items that ELLs are expected to complete, such as only the odd or even questions.

2. *Time.* Adapt the amount of time that ELLs have for completing a task, such as providing more processing time or breaking tasks down into manageable chunks. Unless taking a timed test is required, allowing additional time should not affect a student's score.

3. *Level of support.* Adapt the amount of scaffolding provided to English language learners during assessments by asking an aide, peer assistant, or parent volunteer to read or explain the task or even to read the test items aloud. If you are assessing for content knowledge, then it is acceptable to have someone help with reading or clarifying what is expected in the task.

4. *Difficulty.* Adapt the skill level, the type of problem or task, and the process for how ELLs can approach the task, such as allowing use of a calculator, dictionary, or simplified directions. None of these adaptations reduces the expectation of what the student should know; it only makes it easier for him or her to demonstrate understanding.

5. *Product.* Adapt the type of response ELLs are allowed to provide, such as permitting a drawing, a hands-on demonstration, a verbal response, or a translated response, if necessary. These alternatives do not rely on sophisticated English usage.

6. *Participation.* Adapt ELLs' degree of active involvement in assessment, such as encouraging individual or cooperative group self-assessment and assistance in creating rubrics. Content learning is enhanced for all students but especially for ELLs through interaction and group work. English language learners, particularly those in the upper grades, can be involved in assessing their own progress.

ESTABLISHING A FRAMEWORK FOR EVALUATION

Even before instruction begins, you need to establish a framework for student evaluation by addressing the following issues:

1. *Identify the reasons for assessing student performance.* A classroom test, for instance, can serve a variety of purposes, such as judging student mastery, measuring growth over time, ranking pupils in terms of their achievement, and diagnosing student difficulties. Different purposes lend themselves to various evaluation measures. Therefore, it is essential that you know the major use of the evaluation results.

2. *Plan to gather information for both formative and summative evaluation.* Formative evaluation should be conducted frequently to provide feedback about the student's developing knowledge and skills. In fact, all scores for formative evaluation may not need to be recorded for the report-card grade. Summative evaluation is more comprehensive and is conducted at selected concluding points, such as at the end of a chapter or unit. Scores from summative evaluation are tallied as part of the report-card grade.

3. *Identify course content that is to be evaluated.* This content is often included in a course curriculum guide. It will be translated into instructional objectives for daily lesson plans. These objectives will likely be written for the cognitive, psychomotor, and affective learning domains.

4. *Relate the evaluation to the prestated objectives.* Each objective should be evaluated, but the means for gathering evaluation information will vary depending on the stated objectives and the purpose of the evaluation.

5. *Include evaluation measures in all three learning domains.* Instructional objectives should be written for each of the three learning domains, and each objective should be evaluated. Different types of evaluation instruments are often used to measure student performance in each domain. The cognitive domain is often evaluated through the use of (a) tests developed by teachers themselves, (b) achievement tests developed by local, regional, or state agencies, which may or may not be normed, and (c) nationally standardized tests and scales. Skills in the psychomotor domain are evaluated through performance and product tests.

Objectives in the affective learning domain are more difficult to evaluate than objectives in the other domains. Techniques often used include attitude scales, opinion polls, questionnaires, open-ended questions, checklists, observation, group discussion, anecdotal records, interviews, and role-playing. Observation of students in the process of performing a particular task can also provide useful information concerning their attitudes toward the task.

6. *Use multiple approaches when gathering assessment information.* Do not rely only on teacher-made tests. Also use performance-based assessments when appropriate.

7. *Devise an evaluation plan before instruction.* This will guide your planning and preparation for the class sessions. Then communicate the objectives and evaluation criteria to the students.

SAMPLE STANDARDS

Assessment

There are ten INTASC standards (see page xxi), and each standard includes a list of knowledge, dispositions, and performances to indicate more clearly what is intended in the standard.

Since this chapter deals with assessment, some representative statements for knowledge, dispositions, and performances from INTASC Standard #8 are listed here concerning topics in this chapter.

Knowledge

- The teacher knows how to select, construct, and use assessment strategies and instruments appropriate to the learning outcomes being evaluated and to other diagnostic purposes.
- The teacher understands measurement theory and assessment-related issues, such as validity, reliability, bias, and scoring concerns.

Dispositions

- The teacher values ongoing assessment as essential to the instructional process and recognizes that many different assessment strategies, accurately and systematically used, are necessary for monitoring and promoting student learning.
- The teacher is committed to using assessment to identify student strengths and promote student growth rather than to deny students access to learning opportunities.

Performances

- The teacher appropriately uses a variety of formal and informal assessment techniques to enhance his or her knowledge of learners, evaluate students' progress and performances, and modify teaching and learning strategies.
- The teacher monitors his or her own teaching strategies and behavior in relation to student success, modifying plans and instructional approaches accordingly.

PERFORMANCE-BASED ASSESSMENT

myeducationlab

Go to MyEducationLab, select the topic **Assessment,** click "videos," and select "Forms of Assessment." View the video and reflect.

As an alternative to teacher-made tests, teachers can measure student learning by assessing products that students prepare reflecting their learning or by assessing actual student performances designed to demonstrate their learning. This is *performance-based assessment.* Once the student produces the product or conducts the performance, the teacher then needs to use various types of rating scales or checklists to translate the student performance into some type of score.

Since performance-based assessments are seen as alternatives to teacher-made tests, terms such as *alternative assessment, authentic assessment,* and *direct assessment* have been used to describe performance-based assessments. There are two types of performance-based assessments: product assessment and performance assessment (see Table 11.1).

Product Assessments

Instead of completing a traditional paper-and-pencil test, students are asked to prepare a product reflecting their learning, and the teacher then completes a rating scale or composes written comments to assess student learning as reflected in the product. Product assessments include (a) directions that outline the nature of the products that students will develop, (b) the product itself, which students prepare, and (c) a rating scale of some kind that assesses the nature of the student product. There are many types of products that students might be asked to prepare. Some of the more common types of student products are discussed here.

Portfolios. A *portfolio* is a collection of a student's work over time that demonstrates mastery of specific performance criteria against which the tasks in the portfolio can be

TABLE 11.1 **Performance-Based Assessments**

PRODUCTS	PERFORMANCES
Portfolio	Oral presentation
Work sample	Presentation with media
Project or report	Science lab demonstration
Research paper	Athletic demonstration
Science lab report	Musical, dance, or dramatic presentation
Log or journal	Debate
Model	Demonstration of specific tasks
Media products (computer presentation file, audio or videotape)	Participation in an event
	Interview with the student

judged. The student systematically chooses and compiles work products that go into the portfolio. Work products may include items such as reports, letters, drawings, journals, and other documents. Portfolios are intended to actively involve students in learning, develop self-assessment skills, and provide insights to students and teachers on progress and accomplishment (Burke, 2005; Popham, 2008).

You can guide students through portfolio development by identifying the characteristics of good academic work, applying criteria for good work to their own work, using peer-revision groups to refine and assess their work, and selecting work so that the portfolio creates a portrait of the student as a learner. Teachers who have implemented portfolios report that (a) students have a richer, more positive and expanded sense of their progress, (b) assessment becomes collaborative rather than competitive, (c) teachers obtain a richer, clearer view of their students over time, and (d) records of what students are actually doing are available to teachers.

Some teachers think portfolios are only appropriate for use in the elementary grades, but teachers at the middle and secondary levels have also used portfolios successfully. Geometry portfolios, for example, might include work that displays problem solving, communication, or other skills. Language arts and social studies portfolios might include writings and other projects that offer evidence of progress and goal setting.

Work Samples.   Gathering work samples provides a longitudinal record of student progress. Work samples might include (a) written work such as a report, test, or story, (b) artwork, (c) tape recordings, (d) a construction project done in art, industrial arts, or an appropriate subject, or (e) other types of finished products, depending on the subject area. Using work samples probably occurs more in the elementary grades, but teachers in certain secondary subject areas may use work samples as well.

Voices from the Classroom

Evaluating with Work Samples

Joan Spiker, first-grade teacher, Manhattan, Kansas

To evaluate student handwriting and creative writing in first grade, I have kept dated writing samples. I collect monthly samples of handwriting and keep them in individual student folders. The student reviews the samples in the folder, and then I conference with the student to set goals for the next month. The folders are also used to report progress at parent–teacher conferences.

Nearly all the creative writing in first grade is in the form of little books constructed by the students. All the books are dated and kept in special individual writing cubbies (i.e., commercial cardboard shoe keepers). When a little book is completed and shared, it is given a sticker and placed in the student's cubby. All the books through the year are kept and can easily be reviewed by the authors themselves, other students, the teacher, or parents. The collection is reviewed in student conferences and in parent–teacher conferences to evaluate progress and set goals. This strategy works well for handwriting and for creative writing because the students have a dated accumulation of work to use as a basis for self-evaluation.

Experience Summaries.   In so-called experience summaries, students record what they have learned from a particular experience. Teachers and students may do this cooperatively. For instance, after going on a field trip to an art gallery, the class could identify facts and concepts that they learned. This listing would be useful for you to determine the extent of student learning.

Logs or Journals.   While experience summaries are used for one event, logs or journals are kept on a continuing basis. Students might keep a journal to record their insights, conclusions, and feelings about their classroom experiences. The class can log daily progress concerning learning activities in a notebook or on a chart. This provides a running account of work in the unit and can be used to review and check on previous plans and decisions as the unit progresses.

Projects, Reports, or Papers.   Students might prepare various types of projects, reports, or papers that reflect their learning. These products often involve a number of skills and are developed over more than one class period.

Models.   Students may prepare models concerning people, places, or topics being addressed in class. The models may contain information and represent certain aspects of their learning.

Media Products.   Working individually or in groups, students are asked in many classrooms to prepare an audiotape, videotape, or computer-assisted presentation concerning some aspect of the curriculum. The final media product will represent certain aspects of student learning.

Performance Assessments

As with product assessments, teachers will complete a rating scale or compose written comments to assess student learning reflected in a performance that students are asked to conduct. Performance assessments include (a) directions that outline the nature of the products that students will develop, (b) the product itself, which students prepare, and (c) a rating scale of some kind that assesses the nature of the student product. There are many types of performances that students might be asked to conduct. Some of the more common ones are discussed here.

Oral or Mediated Presentations.   Students may be asked to prepare a report on a selected topic and then present it to the rest of the class. Sometimes these reports include instructional media (e.g., overhead transparencies, computer-assisted presentations). The teacher may choose to rate the actual presentation as a way to gauge student learning.

Actual Demonstrations.   Students may be asked to demonstrate their skill in some type of athletic, musical, dance, or dramatic performance. Skills might also be demonstrated in a science lab, a computer class, or any other class where the student's learning is best reflected in actual performance.

Participation in an Event.   Sometimes a group of students or the entire class is involved in an activity in which students exhibit certain knowledge and skills through their participation. A student's knowledge and skill in forensics or debate, for instance, can be seen through participation.

Interviews.   Interviews and individual conferences can be used to evaluate cognitive skills as well as attitudes and values. Students sometimes express ideas and feelings during interviews that they might not otherwise state.

Ways to Rate Student Products or Performances

It is easy to say that it is a great idea to gather student products or to ask students to perform in certain ways as a means to demonstrate their learning. However, teachers may

Classroom Case Study

Performance-Based Assessments

Nadine Espinoza, a sixth-grade teacher, has been introducing her students to a number of algebraic topics in math class. Recently, the students have been studying single-variable equations.

This year, instead of her usual end-of-unit written test, Ms. Espinoza has decided to substitute a performance-based project. She wants to show her students where the concepts they are learning in class can be found in real-life situations. For their end-of-unit project, the students will be asked to collect information about how a family's cutting energy and fuel costs can help them save for a fantasy vacation. Specifically, students will collect data about their families' electricity and automotive fuel consumption and costs for a month.

Using these data, each student will develop an equation to determine the average amount of electricity and fuel his or her family uses on a daily basis. Each student will decide on a reasonable dollar amount that his or her family can put aside each month toward their fantasy vacation. The student will then create an equation to show how much needs to be cut from his or her family's daily electricity and fuel consumption to save that amount. Students will be asked to graph the information they have gathered and to incorporate the graphs and data into a brochure that can be used to persuade their families to reduce electricity and fuel consumption to save for the fantasy vacation.

Focus Questions
1. What advantages do performance assessments have over traditional paper-and-pencil exams? What disadvantages do they have, if any?
2. Think of some examples of performance assessments that might be used in the following content areas: science, language arts, social studies, and/or foreign language.

find it challenging to specify the actual observable criteria that demonstrate student learning and to determine what the actual rating approaches will be. Some guidelines are provided in this section.

Selecting Rating Criteria.   The following guidelines can be used when selecting observable criteria for products or performances (Airasian & Russell, 2008):

1. *Select the performance or product to be assessed and either perform it yourself or imagine yourself performing it.* This step will help you to understand the actual student actions that will need to be completed.
2. *List the important aspects of the performance or product.* The most important behaviors or attributes should be reflected in the rating criteria.
3. *Try to limit the number of performance criteria that can reasonably be observed and assessed.* Each item needs to be assessed, so limit the number of performance criteria to 10 to 15.
4. *If possible, have a group of teachers think through the criteria as a group.* This step will save time and will help to produce a more complete set of criteria than that produced by any single teacher.
5. *Express the criteria in terms of observable student behaviors or product characteristics.* Be specific when stating the criteria.
6. *Avoid vague and ambiguous words.* Avoid wording such as *correctly*, *appropriately*, or *good* that can result in multiple interpretations.
7. *Arrange the performance criteria in the order in which they are likely to be observed.* This will save time when observing and maintain focus on the performance.
8. *Check for existing performance criteria before constructing your own.* Preexisting criteria might be available for your use.

Rating Approaches.   Various approaches can be used to rate student products or performances. The most commonly used approaches are reviewed here:

1. *Rating scales.* A *rating scale* allows a teacher to judge student performance along a continuum, rather than as a dichotomy (present/not present). The rating scale may be numerical (e.g., 1 through 4), descriptive (using a range of words to reflect the criteria), or a combination of the two. Instead of merely indicating the presence or absence of a trait, as in a checklist, a rating scale enables you to indicate the status or quality of what is being rated.

A *rubric* is a type of rating scale used to judge student performance on a continuum. Rubrics can be created in many ways to describe the levels of student performance based on the performance criteria. Rubrics often have more thorough ways of describing each performance level than simple rating scales. The thorough descriptions of performance criteria in rubrics provide considerable guidance for the students as they prepare their products or performances. See Tables 11.2 and 11.3 for examples.

TABLE 11.2   Rubric Template

CRITERIA	RATING			
Criterion 1 *(enter the criterion description here)*	1	2	3	4
Criterion 2	1	2	3	4
Criterion 3	1	2	3	4
Criterion 4	1	2	3	4

Note: Some rubrics have the number rating at the top of the columns and a unique narrative description under each rating for each criterion. This provides more clarity about what is needed for each rating.

2. *Checklists.* A *checklist* is a written list of performance criteria. A teacher reviews the student product or performance to determine which criteria are met. A checkmark indicates that the criterion was met; if it is not, the item is left blank. A checklist enables you to note quickly and effectively whether a trait or characteristic is present, but it does not permit you to rate the quality or frequency of a particular behavior. When that additional information is needed, you may want to use a rating scale or an anecdotal record.

3. *Anecdotal records.* An *anecdotal record* is a written account of events and behaviors that the teacher has observed concerning the student's product or performance. Only those observations that have special significance and cannot be obtained from other assessment methods should be included in an anecdotal record. Anecdotal records should contain factual descriptions of what happened, when it happened, and under what circumstances it happened. The interpretation of the behavior and the recommended action should be noted separately. Each anecdotal record should contain a record of a single incident.

TABLE 11.3   Sample Rubric Rating Scales

NUMERICAL SCALES				
0	1	2	3	4
1	2	3	4	5

NUMERICAL SCALE WITH VERBAL DESCRIPTORS			
1 Weak	2 Satisfactory	3 Very Good	4 Excellent

VERBAL DESCRIPTORS			
Needs improvement Novice	Satisfactory Adequate	Good Competent	Excellent Exemplary

4. *Participation charts.* A *participation chart* is intended only to indicate the degree of involvement and the type of involvement in classroom discussion or activities. A typical form has students' names on one axis and the degree and frequency of involvement on the other axis. The charts are not intended to indicate why students participate.

TEACHER-MADE TESTS

To achieve the purpose of teacher-made tests, you need to carefully plan the test and then select and prepare test questions. Next, you need to assemble, administer, and score the test.

Planning the Classroom Test

The preparation of a classroom test involves many decisions. Advance attention to the following decision areas will likely result in an improved test (McMillan, 2007):

1. *Decide the purpose of the test.* To be helpful, classroom tests must be related to the teacher's instructional objectives and procedures. Classroom achievement tests serve a variety of purposes, such as (a) judging students' mastery of certain knowledge and skills, (b) measuring growth over time, (c) ranking students in terms of their achievement, (d) diagnosing student difficulties, (e) determining the effectiveness of the curriculum, (f) encouraging good study habits, and (g) motivating students. These purposes are not mutually exclusive.

2. *Decide what is to be tested.* What should be tested? The answer depends on the instructional objectives and what has been stressed in class. As noted below, the table of specifications should be determined prior to instruction, and this should serve as the basis for preparing a test. The table of specifications includes instructional objectives and content. The relative emphasis on the three domains of learning should be reflected in the table of specifications. Furthermore, an effective test should include only questions that address important outcomes of instruction.

3. *Prepare a table of specifications showing the content and objectives to be tested.* A *table of specifications* identifies the intended outcomes of instruction; it specifies objectives or behaviors that the student should attain by the end of the instruction and the content related to these objectives. These statements should be precisely stated to clearly convey intentions. Summative evaluation, then, is intended to examine the degree of success with which the objectives were achieved by the students.

When making a test, the table of specifications is intended to identify the scope and emphasis of the test, to relate the objectives to the content, and to construct a balanced test. The table of specifications should be prepared before instruction and can even be distributed to students. The table of specifications displayed in Table 11.4

TABLE 11.4 **Table of Specifications for a Weather Unit in a Middle School Earth Science Class**

OBJECTIVES — CONTENT	KNOWS			UNDERSTANDS	INTERPRETS	TOTAL NUMBER OF ITEMS	PERCENT OF ITEMS
	Basic Terms	Weather Symbols	Specific Facts	Influence of Each Factor on Weather Information	Weather Maps		
Air pressure	1	1	1	3	3	9	15
Wind	1	1	1	10	2	15	25
Temperature	1	1	1	4	2	9	15
Humidity and precipitation	1	1	1	7	5	15	25
Clouds	2	2	2	6		12	20
Total Number of Items	6	6	6	30	12	60	
Percent of Items	10	10	10	50	20		100

Source: Miller, M. D., Linn, R. L., & Gronlund, N. E. (2009). *Measurement and assessment in teaching* (10th ed.). Copyright © 2009. Reprinted by permission of Pearson Education, Inc., Upper Saddle River, NJ.

indicates the number of test questions in each learning domain for each content area in a sample unit in science.

4. *Decide when to test.* The use of the test results will determine the frequency of testing. If used in formative evaluation, students should be given short, criterion-referenced tests frequently to keep you apprised of their performance and identify those in need of additional or remedial instruction. Summative evaluation will be conducted less often.

To some extent, the frequency of testing is affected by institutional regulations on marking and reporting grades to parents. More frequent evaluation is superior to less frequent evaluation. Teachers in secondary schools sometimes communicate with each other in an effort to stagger the days when students are tested, so several tests are not scheduled for the same day.

5. *Decide what kinds of questions to use.* There basically are two item formats: essay and objective (multiple choice, matching, true–false). Some item formats are less appropriate than others for measuring certain objectives. Therefore, carefully consider the advantages and disadvantages of each item format. These will be discussed in greater detail in a later section.

6. *Decide how many questions to include in the test.* The length of a test will vary according to its purpose, the kinds of items used, the reliability desired, the length of testing time available, and the age and ability of the students. Formative tests will be more in-depth and frequent than summative tests. As explained later, the time needed to complete different item formats varies. The longer the test, the more reliable it tends to be, but only so many items can be completed within a 50-minute class period. The age and ability of the students also must be considered.

7. *Decide the level of difficulty for questions included in the test.* The difficulty of a test should depend to a large extent on its purpose. Item difficulty will not be a factor in the selection of test items if the test results are to be used to describe the status of individual students. However, test difficulty is a consideration when the test results are to be used to differentiate among students in terms of their achievement.

8. *Decide the format of the test.* You need to decide about mechanical and formatting features of the test, such as grouping and arranging test items, directions for answering questions, distribution of correct responses, the layout of items, and other aspects. These will be discussed in a later section.

What Would You Decide? *Using a Table of Specifications*

When planning a unit, your preparation of a table of specifications can help you identify instructional objectives in all appropriate learning domains for each content area within the unit.

1. When you prepare a test, how might you use the table of specifications to ensure that

there are test questions covering all the learning domains in all the content areas in the unit?

2. How might this table help you distribute points for the various sections of the test?

Selecting and Preparing Test Questions

There are two categories of test questions: essay and objective. *Essay questions* may include short-answer or restricted responses (about a half page), discussion or extended responses (about two to three pages), or oral responses. *Objective questions* may include multiple choice, matching, true–false, and short answer (a single word or several words). Since some item formats are less appropriate than others for measuring certain objectives, teachers should carefully consider the advantages of each type of item format.

Test questions might be included in the teacher's edition of the textbook, and you might consider using them. Carefully examine test items included in the teacher's edition to be sure they are worded effectively, are at the proper levels of the learning domains being tested, are directed at content that was covered during instruction, and are at the appropriate reading level for your students.

Essay Questions. Two common types of essay questions are the restricted response and the extended response. *Restricted response essay questions* establish limits for the form and scope of the students' answers. Students are often asked to discuss one specific aspect of an issue and to limit their answers to perhaps half a page. Restricted essay questions are useful for measuring comprehension, application, and analysis (Stiggins, 2008).

Extended response essay questions, by contrast, place no limits on the student concerning the points to discuss or the organization used in the answer. Extended response questions require students to call on factual knowledge, evaluate this knowledge, organize the ideas, and present these ideas in a logical, coherent way. Skills in synthesis and evaluation are effectively tested with this type of question.

A variety of mental processes can be evaluated through the use of essay tests. From simple to higher-order skills, these include (a) what, who, when, which, and where; (b) list; (c) outline; (d) describe; (e) contrast; (f) compare; (g) explain; (h) discuss; (i) develop; (j) summarize; and (k) evaluate.

There are advantages and disadvantages to the use of essay questions. Advantages include the fact that they are comparatively easier and less time consuming to prepare than objective tests, require that students supply the answer rather than simply select the answer, measure higher-order thinking, and stimulate creativity and freedom of expression.

But there are also several disadvantages of essay questions. First, they generally sample content in a limited way. Three essay questions may not sample unit content as thoroughly as 50 multiple-choice questions. Therefore, essay tests that have several questions requiring short answers are preferable to a test that has few questions requiring lengthy answers. Second, essay questions are vulnerable to unreliable scoring. This problem of reader reliability can be minimized by careful construction of the test question and by setting up specified scoring procedures. Third, the student may not always understand the question and therefore may be unsure of how to respond, or he or she may be unable to put all appropriate ideas on paper in the given time. Fourth, essay questions require a great deal of time to read and score.

Writing Essay Questions.   To minimize the problems associated with essay questions, it is important to carefully prepare essay questions using the following guidelines:

1. *Reserve adequate time to prepare test questions.* Allow sufficient time to thoughtfully prepare each question and to be certain that each measures the intended objective, is worded in a simple and clear manner, and is reasonable and can be answered by the students.
2. *Precisely define the direction and scope of the desired response.* This can be done by (a) delimiting the area covered by the question; (b) using descriptive, precise words in the question, such as *outline, illustrate, define,* and *summarize* (as compared to the term *discuss*); (c) guiding the student into a certain direction by indicating what should be considered and presented in the answer; and (d) indicating the length of the answer (typically one-half page to two pages per question).
3. *Indicate the point value of each question.* Students need to know the point value of each question to be able to decide how much time to spend on it.
4. *Use essay questions to measure objectives that cannot be measured as well with other item formats.* As compared to other item formats, essay questions are especially useful in assessing students' understanding in the upper levels of the cognitive domain, such as application, analysis, synthesis, and evaluation.
5. *Use many questions requiring relatively brief answers, as compared to just a few questions involving long answers.* Brief answers (about one-half page) provide for a broader sampling of content, tend to discourage bias when some teachers

grade for quantity rather than quality, enable the teacher to read the answers more rapidly and reliably, and also enable the teacher to direct the student to the desired response area.

6. *Take into consideration the time needed for an adequate response and the time available for the testing period.* Students need to have an appropriate amount of time to write out their responses to all questions.

7. *Adapt the length of response and the complexity of the answer to the maturity of the student.* The depth and breadth of the responses from fifth-graders certainly would be different from responses expected from tenth-graders.

8. *Do not provide optional questions on an essay test.* Providing options for the student undermines the basic function of summative tests (e.g., comparing the performance of students in a common area). Furthermore, it is difficult to construct questions of equal difficulty.

9. *Decide in advance how the essay questions will be scored.* In addition to the substance of student answers, decide how grammar, spelling, punctuation, handwriting, composition, and clarity of expression will be scored.

10. *Prepare a scoring key.* When preparing test questions, also identify what topics should be included in student responses to each essay question, and then determine relative points for weak, average, and strong answers.

Evaluating Essay Questions.   The usefulness of a carefully constructed essay test can be undermined by improper grading procedures and standards. Essay tests must be reliably graded with either the analytical method or the rating method. In the *analytical method*, the teacher identifies all the specific points or topics that should be included in an appropriate answer. The student's score is determined by the number of points or topics he or she includes in the response to the essay question.

The *rating method* also involves the teacher identifying the points to be included in the answer, but the wholeness of the response is emphasized. Several student papers are selected to reflect the range of responses on a given question. These papers serve as anchor points as the other papers are read and rated. Papers may be read using a two-point scale (acceptable–unacceptable) up to a five-point scale (with steps going from superior to inferior). With the five-point scale, the teacher will place students' papers in one of these five piles upon reading the students' responses. It is preferable that each paper be read and rated twice. The rating method is effective when a large number of essays are to be read.

When evaluating essay questions, consider the following guidelines.

1. *Check the scoring key against actual responses.* Before scoring actually begins, read a few randomly selected papers to determine the appropriateness of the scoring key. Adjustments might be made in the key based on actual responses. The key should not be changed once actual scoring begins.

2. *If spelling, penmanship, grammar, and writing style of the responses are to be scored, it should be done independently of the subject matter content in the responses.*

3. *Score the students' responses anonymously.* If possible, conceal the student's name as each paper is evaluated in an effort to reduce biases.

4. *Evaluate one question at one time for all students.* This is designed to eliminate the so-called halo effect, a general impression of high, medium, or low quality that might carry over from one response to another for each student. This practice also enables the teacher to more easily keep in mind the standards that are being applied for a particular question.

5. *Shuffle test papers before grading each question.* The ratings given to preceding papers sometimes affect the way teachers rate the next paper to be evaluated. Therefore, shuffle test papers before grading the next test question to try to minimize the effects of the preceding grades.

6. *Try to score all responses to a particular question without interruption.* To keep the standards clearly in mind, the papers should be read without excessive interruption or delay.

7. *Whenever possible, conduct two readings of the test and use the average as the final score.* Two independent readings simply help improve the reliability of the test score. Of course, this may not be realistic at the secondary level if you have 125 student papers to evaluate.

8. *Provide comments and indications of correct answers.* By providing comments, you can provide students with more information about their progress, motivate them, indirectly teach them, and also help to explain the system of grading and determining scores.

9. *Set realistic standards.* Avoid being overly generous or overly demanding as you review student responses.

Objective Questions.   The most common types of objective test items are multiple choice, matching, true–false, and short answer.

Multiple Choice.   A multiple-choice question has two parts: (a) a *stem*, which contains the problem, and (b) a list of suggested answers, or *responses*. The stem is typically in the form of a question or an incomplete statement. The incorrect responses are often called *distracters*. Generally, four or five responses are listed and all but one is a distracter.

From the list of responses provided, the student selects the one that is correct or best. Some questions have only one possible answer that is correct. In other questions, students are asked to identify the most appropriate, or best, answer from the choices given.

The *direct question format* has several advantages. It forces the teacher to state the problem clearly in the stem, it reduces the possibility of giving the student grammatical clues, and it may be more easily handled by younger and less able students because less demand is placed on good reading skills. The *incomplete statement format* can also be effectively used. In this case, the stem must be clear and meaningful and not lead into a series of unrelated true–false statements. A reverse (or negative) version of the direct question format and the incomplete statement format asks the student to select the one incorrect choice from a list of correct choices.

There are several advantages of multiple-choice questions. They (a) can test students in several levels of the cognitive domain, (b) can be scored quickly and accurately, (c) are relatively efficient in terms of the number of questions that can be asked in a given amount of time and the space needed to present the answers, (d) can test a wide range of topics in a short time, and (e) are not significantly affected by guessing.

There are several disadvantages to multiple-choice questions. First, they are very difficult to construct and plausible-sounding distracters are hard to find. Second, there is a tendency by teachers to write only factual recall questions. Of all the selection-type objective tests, multiple-choice items require the most time for the student to respond. Finally, testwise students perform better than do non-testwise students.

Consider the following guidelines when writing multiple-choice questions:

1. Use either a direct question or an incomplete statement as the item stem. A direct question is often preferable.
2. Write items in clear and simple language.
3. Make the response choices as brief as possible.
4. Include only one correct or best answer to every item.
5. With an incomplete statement, place the choices at the end of the statement.
6. Include four to five response choices.
7. State only plausible response choices.
8. List the response choices below the stem in a vertical, easy-to-read format.
9. Use letters for the response choices.
10. Avoid a pattern of answers.

Matching.   Matching questions consist of a set of directions, a list of stems or numbered items (e.g., statements, phrases, words, incomplete sentences), and a list of choices (e.g., words, phrases, numbers). Students are required to make an association between each premise and the choices.

Matching questions are well suited to test knowledge in terms of definitions, dates, names, events, and other matters involving simple relationships. Since they require relatively little reading time, many questions can be asked in a limited amount of testing time. Matching questions are also easy to score. The range of test material can be broad, and guessing is limited.

There are some disadvantages to matching questions. They may encourage serial memorization rather than association. It is also sometimes difficult to get clusters of questions that are sufficiently alike that a common set of responses can be used. It is sometimes difficult to avoid giving clues, and too many items may be confusing to the students. Furthermore, matching questions are not well adapted to measure students' understanding of concepts or their ability to organize and apply knowledge.

The following guidelines will assist you in preparing matching questions:

1. List the homogeneous premises on the left and the options to be matched on the right.
2. List the premises and choices in some logical or systematic order (e.g., alphabetically, chronologically).

3. Keep the list of premises and responses relatively short; the optimum is five to eight items to be matched.
4. Provide extra responses to reduce guessing.
5. The stem should include the longer and more involved statements, and the response choices should be short and simple.
6. Number each stem and use capital letters for each response choice.

True–False.   A true–false item is simply a declarative statement to which the student responds by indicating whether it is true or false. One variation asks the student to correct false statements to make them true; these are often called modified true–false.

.   True–false questions have a number of advantages including the fact that they are good for students who are poor readers; can cover a large amount of content in a given testing period; generally provide high reliability; can be scored quickly and reliably; are adaptable to most subject areas; and can be constructed to measure the higher mental processes of understanding, application, and interpretation.

There are several disadvantages in the use of true–false questions. Scores may be unduly influenced by guessing. True–false items are often susceptible to ambiguity and misinterpretation, resulting in low reliability. The questions lend themselves to cheating more often than do some other types of questions. Some statements are not entirely true or false, and thus specific determiners are often added to the questions.

To help overcome some of the disadvantages, the following guidelines should be used when writing true–false items:

1. Be certain that the item is absolutely true or false, without any qualifications or exceptions.
2. Avoid loosely worded and ambiguous statements.
3. Highlight the central point of the question by placing it in a prominent position in the statement.
4. Avoid negative statements whenever possible.
5. Avoid making true statements consistently longer than false statements.
6. Avoid a disproportionate number of either true or false statements.

Short Answer.   Short-answer or completion questions require students to provide a word or phrase. They are typically in the form of a direct question or a completion statement.

Short-answer questions reduce the chance that the student will guess the correct answer, and test items are relatively easy to construct. On the other hand, short-answer items are more difficult to score than other types of objective tests. There is also an emphasis on vocabulary and recall of information.

Use the following guidelines when constructing short-answer questions:

1. Generally, it is better to use a direct question rather than a completion statement.
2. Use short-answer questions to measure only the recall of important information.

3. Have the statement lead to one or two specific words or phrases.
4. For completion statements, in general, place the blanks near or at the end of the sentence.
5. For completion statements, do not require more than one or two completions to be made in any one test item.
6. When omitting words to make an incomplete statement, leave enough clues so the student knows that the answer selected is correct.

Assembling the Test

The mechanical features of a test—how the questions are grouped and arranged, what directions are given, and how the test is formatted—are no less important than the test items themselves. Careful attention to these aspects will enhance the value of the test as an evaluation tool and will also help save you time and effort.

Grouping and Arranging Test Items.   For most classroom purposes, test items can be arranged by a systematic consideration of the type of items used, the learning outcomes measured, the difficulty of the items, and the subject matter measured. First, all questions of an item format should be grouped because doing so requires the fewest sets of directions, is the easiest for the students because they retain the same mental set throughout each section, and greatly facilitates scoring. Second, when two or more item formats are used in a test, they should be sequenced in the following order (Miller et al., 2009):

1. true–false or alternative response items
2. matching items
3. short-answer items

Voices from the Classroom

Including a Variety of Test Questions

Elicia Ligon, middle school science and English teacher, Ponca City, Oklahoma

When writing a teacher-made test, I try to include questions of all types. There will be short sections of each of the following: multiple choice, true or false, short answer (a sentence or two), an activity (such as a graph or data table), and a short essay question.

I believe this variety helps test all aspects of a student's learning. I also think it puts students at ease to see at least one type of test question that they are comfortable with. These tests take time to prepare, but they seem more like a true measure of student learning in your classroom.

4. multiple-choice items
5. interpretive exercises
6. essay questions

Arranging the sections of a test in this order produces a sequence that roughly approximates the complexity of the learning outcomes measured, ranging from simple to complex.

Third, within each item format, questions related to the same instructional objective should be grouped. Fourth, items within each item format should be arranged in order of ascending difficulty. Therefore, both the sections and the items within the sections are arranged in an ascending order of difficulty throughout the test.

Writing Test Directions.   Directions should indicate what the students should do, how they are to do it, and where they should record their answers. Furthermore, the directions should indicate the time to be allocated to the test, the value of each test item, and whether students should guess at any answers they are unsure of. When determining test directions, teachers can use the following guidelines:

1. Provide a specific set of written directions for each item format.
2. Indicate the basis for the student answering the question.
3. Indicate how the student is to record the answers.
4. Indicate the point value of each question in an item format.
5. Indicate the purpose of the test, the length of time available, and whether students should guess. These issues can be announced verbally as compared to being written on the test paper.

Formatting and Reproducing the Test.   The visual display of the test items on the paper can affect the time and effort the students expend taking the test and also the teacher's time during scoring. Use the following guidelines when formatting, typing, and reproducing a test:

1. Space items so they can be easily read, answered, and scored.
2. Items should be numbered consecutively throughout the test.
3. Make sure all items have generous borders.
4. Keep all stems and options on one page.
5. For matching questions, have the list of premises and choices on the same page.
6. The most convenient method of response in true–false, matching, and multiple-choice questions is circling the correct answer.
7. Avoid a definite response pattern to the correct answer.
8. If no answer sheet is used, one side of the page should be used for responses to all objective questions, regardless of the item format.
9. Use a typewriter or a letter-quality printer to make the most legible-quality print.

Administering the Test

The physical and psychological environment should be conducive for students to demonstrate their achievement of learning outcomes. Bearing this in mind, consider the following guidelines when administering a test:

1. Provide comfortable testing conditions, such as adequate light, ventilation, temperature, quiet, and work space.
2. Do not promote test anxiety by giving warnings about the importance of the test or by threatening the students.
3. Avoid giving a test just before or after a long vacation or some other important school event.
4. During the test, provide reminders about the time remaining.
5. Discourage cheating through careful proctoring and other means.
6. Do not talk unnecessarily before the test.
7. Keep interruptions to a minimum during the test.
8. Avoid giving students hints about any test item.
9. At the start of the test, indicate what the students should do once they complete the test.

Scoring the Test

Guidelines were presented earlier for evaluating essay tests. Scoring objective tests can be done by machine or by hand. Some schools have facilities to score tests by machines that read students' responses off computer cards.

When scoring tests by hand, you have a few options. If the students write their answers on the test sheets themselves, you can simply create an answer key by using a blank test to write the correct answers. It is extremely helpful, as noted earlier, to have all the answers in one column, such as on the left side of the page. In this way, you can hold the answer key next to the student's test and mark the errors. If the student is asked to write the letter of the correct answer, you should draw a line through the incorrect answer and then add the letter of the correct answer. But if all letter choices are given at the left of the question and students are expected to circle the correct answer, you can easily see an incorrect answer and then indicate the error by circling the correct answer. In this way, in one stroke of the pen, the student knows the choice was incorrect and is also given the correct answer.

A scoring stencil can also be used in a similar way to cover all choices except the correct answer. You then can see which items were correctly marked by the students and place a mark on the correct choice when the students have chosen another response.

You could have students place their answers to objective questions (multiple choice, true–false, matching) on computer cards and use scanning systems to score the tests. This can save considerable time, especially when you have many tests to score, such as at the middle and secondary levels. The cards that the students complete are run through a scanning machine and each card is scored. Most scanning systems can generate an item analysis of the questions and a class roster with the score. Some scanning systems allow entering the scores from performance-based assignments (essays, special projects, oral exams, homework) with the machine-scored questions to obtain a combined score. The most sophisticated systems include software to scan, score, handle surveys, and develop a gradebook.

Regardless of the scoring method selected, the scoring key or answer key should be prepared and checked well in advance of the administration of the test. Generally, each item should have equal weight.

Key Terms

Anecdotal records
Assessment
Checklist
Criterion-referenced evaluation
Diagnostic evaluation
Direct question format
Essay questions
Evaluation
Extended response essay
   questions

Formative evaluation
Incomplete statement format
Measurement
Norm-referenced evaluation
Objective questions
Participation chart
Performance-based assessment
Portfolio
Practicality
Rating scale

Reliability
Restricted response essay
   questions
Rubric
Summative evaluation
Table of specifications
Validity

Major Concepts

1. There are three types of evaluation: diagnostic, formative, and summative. Each serves a different purpose, and each is conducted at different times.

2. Measurement or assessment is the process used to obtain data concerning student learning. Evaluation is the process of making a value judgment about student learning based on the measurement and assessment data.

3. Even before beginning instruction, teachers need to establish a framework for student evaluation.

4. When using performance-based assessment, teachers must specify the criteria by which the student products or performances will be

rated, and then they must prepare the actual rating forms.

5. A table of specifications identifies objectives in all three learning domains that the student should attain by the end of instruction and also the content related to these objectives.

6. Student evaluation should be related to instructional objectives that are included in the table of specifications.

7. Guidelines for planning the classroom test, selecting and preparing test items, assembling the test, and administering and scoring the test can aid in effective measurement.

Discussion/Reflective Questions

1. Recall times in your own schooling when you took part in diagnostic, formative, and summative evaluation.
2. Why is it useful to have a variety of assessment measures when evaluating student learning?
3. List factors that help maintain high reliability of a test. Similarly, list factors that help maintain high validity of a test.

4. What are the advantages and disadvantages of using products and performances to assess student learning?
5. What are the advantages of using a table of specifications when preparing a test?

Suggested Activities

For Clinical Settings

1. Prepare a table of specifications for this chapter that includes learning objectives and content.
2. Prepare three questions for each of the following for a test on this chapter: true–false, short answer, multiple choice, and essay questions.
3. Construct a rubric that could be used in assessing students' understanding of a short story.

For Field Experiences

1. Ask one or more teachers to discuss the way they evaluate students. Analyze their responses in relation to the framework for evaluation discussed in this chapter.
2. Talk with several teachers about the ways that they conduct product or performance assessments. Ask specifically about rating criteria and rating forms.
3. Obtain one or more teacher-made tests, and critique them based on the guidelines discussed in this chapter for planning the test, selecting and preparing test items, and assembling the test.

Further Reading

Burke, K. (2005). *How to assess authentic learning* (4th ed.). Thousand Oaks, CA: Corwin Press.

In a workbook format, it addresses learning standards and multiple ways to assess students, including portfolios, performance tasks and rubrics, teacher-made tests, logs and journals, checklists, and conferences.

Butler, S. M., & McMunn, N. D. (2006). *A teacher's guide to classroom assessment: Understanding and using assessment to improve student learning.* San Francisco: Jossey-Bass.

A comprehensive guide that shows step-by-step ways to integrate assessment in the classroom. Considers meeting standards, setting expectations, gathering assessment evidence, making sense of the data, and linking assessment to instruction.

Gronlund, N. E., & Waugh, C. K. (2009). *Assessment of student achievement* (9th ed.). Boston: Allyn & Bacon.

Serves as a practical guide for assessing the intended outcomes of instruction. Emphasis on teacher-made assessments and performance assessments.

Miller, M. D., Linn, R. L., & Gronlund, N. E. (2009). *Measurement and assessment in teaching* (10th ed.). Upper Saddle River, NJ: Merrill/Prentice-Hall.

Provides thorough coverage of all aspects of measurement and assessment. Many examples and guidelines are included.

12 Grading Systems, Marking, and Reporting

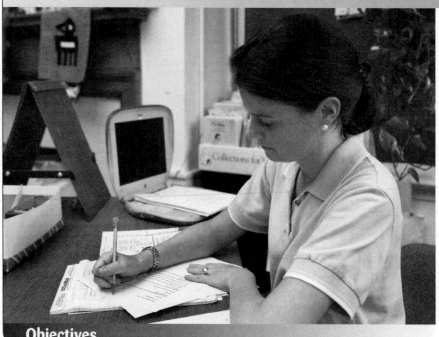

Objectives

This chapter provides information that will help you to:

1. State the purposes of grading.
2. Describe the features of the various types of grading systems.
3. Determine the steps to take when assigning grades.
4. Identify nonachievement outcomes and determine how they can be measured and reported.
5. Describe the information that needs to be recorded in the gradebook and how it can be formatted in an efficient manner.
6. Determine ways to report grades and effectively communicate to families.

Purposes of Grading
- Functions of Grades
- Confounding the Achievement Grade

Grading Systems
- Percentage Grades
- Letter Grades
- Descriptive Evaluations
- Pass–Fail Grading
- Checklists of Objectives

Assigning Letter Grades
- Determining What to Include in a Grade
- Creating a Composite Score
- Selecting a Frame of Reference for Grading
- Determining the Distribution of Grades
- Calculating Semester and Annual Grades

Nonachievement Outcomes
- Rating Scales
- Checklists
- Special Reports

Designing a Gradebook
- Daily Record
- Achievement Scores
- Summary Charts

Reporting Grades and Communicating to Families
- Report Cards
- Cumulative Record Files
- Newsletters
- Open Houses
- Parent–Teacher Conferences
- Contacts with Individual Families

General Principles in Grading and Reporting

It is not sufficient to simply gather information about student performance through teacher-made tests, portfolios, work samples, and other approaches. You must also determine the grade for the student's work, place that grade within a grading system, and then report the grade to the student's family.

Marks or *grades* are summative, numerical, or quasi-numerical symbols that represent a student's performance in a marking period or a course and become a part of the student's permanent records. The terms *mark* and *grade* are frequently used interchangeably.

It is important to differentiate a mark or a grade from a score. A *score* is assigned for a specific report, homework assignment, or test that is done while instruction is still taking place; this is formative evaluation. *Grades* are used in summative evaluation to represent the extent of the student's achievement and competence after instruction has occurred.

You will decide the type of information to gather to evaluate students, how heavily to weigh each source of information, and which frame of reference (i.e., criterion-referenced, norm-referenced, or potential standards) to use in assigning the grades. This information may come from homework, tests, quizzes, written or oral reports, or other measures. The choice of the grading system is often made by the school district and is reflected in the format used on the report cards.

When addressing the issue of grading student performance, you will need to make decisions about a number of factors: What are the purposes of grading? What types of grading systems can be used? How are grades to be assigned? How are nonachievement outcomes reported? How can a gradebook be formatted, and how can information be recorded in it? How is student progress to be reported to families? These factors will be examined in this chapter, along with some general principles about grading and reporting.

PURPOSES OF GRADING

Grades convey information concisely, without needless detail. They also must be able to communicate information to a number of diverse audiences who use the grades for different purposes. The major audiences include students, parents, school administrators, counselors, other schools, college admission officers, and prospective employers. Each of these audiences uses grades in a somewhat different manner.

Functions of Grades

Grades and other reports of student progress serve several functions (Airasian & Russell, 2008; Carey, 2006). The two major purposes of grades are to provide information and to aid in making administrative decisions within the school, but there are other purposes as well:

1. *Informational functions.* Grades are used to inform students and families about the student's academic progress. This feedback should enable students to judge their performance, lead to modification of their behavior, differentiate strong and weak areas of their performance, and serve as reinforcement for jobs well done. Grades inform families about their child's performance and also may provide the basis for questions to ask the child's teacher. This information enables families to give their children needed emotional support and encouragement. These summary reports also give families the basis for helping the children make sound educational plans.

2. *Administrative functions.* Grades are used for a variety of internal administrative purposes by the institution where they are assigned. They are used for determining promotion and graduation, awarding honors, deciding on admission to special courses and programs, and determining eligibility for scholarships and extracurricular activities, including athletic competition.

3. *Guidance functions.* By looking at a student's entire record, the student and a counselor may determine strengths, weaknesses, and interests. Counselors use this information to help students develop better self-understanding and make more realistic educational and vocational plans. This information could be used to make decisions about enrollment in certain courses or programs and about potential careers.

4. *Sorting and selecting functions.* Grades are often used when choosing individuals for academic honors, fellowships and awards, employment, advanced education in colleges and universities, and participation in various professional institutional activities. These decisions are competitive, and the decision makers are typically from an institution other than the one where the grades were assigned. Employers and admission officers from colleges and universities use grades to determine whether an individual will be hired or admitted.

5. *Motivational functions.* Periodic progress reports can contribute to student motivation by providing short-term goals and knowledge of results. How motivating the reports are likely to be, however, depends on the nature of the report and how it is used. If a single letter grade is used and students are threatened with low grades unless they study harder, the results are likely to be negative. However, when the reports are viewed as opportunities to check on learning progress, they are likely to have positive motivational effects.

6. *Research functions.* An often overlooked function of grades is the role they play in educational research. In research on student selection, grades are used as the criterion against which a predictor variable is validated (e.g., using high school grades as a predictor of success in college). Grades are also sometimes used in curriculum research and evaluation by using student success as an index of student performance.

Regardless of the purpose, all student work should be graded and returned promptly.

Confounding the Achievement Grade

When trying to create a comprehensive index of student progress, some teachers might combine scores on conduct and achievement, thinking that improves the accuracy of students' grades, but the exact opposite occurs. The combining of these variables *confounds,* or mixes up, the meaning of the grade. Therefore, the meaning of the grade for achievement is compromised, and valid interpretation becomes difficult.

There are four common ways that teachers confound achievement grades (Carey, 2006). You should avoid the following practices:

1. *Treating practice tests and homework as summative evaluation.* As discussed in Chapter 11, diagnostic, formative, and summative evaluation serve different purposes. You would not consider using diagnostic evaluation data as the basis of a report-card grade, since that information is used to make placement and planning decisions. In a similar way, formative evaluation data are intended to give the students and teacher feedback about student performance while instruction is still taking place. Unfortunately, teachers often combine formative evaluation data with summative evaluation data to determine the grade for the marking period or course. This combination of formative and summative evaluation data confounds the meaning of the grade.

Since the purpose of practice tests, homework, and related assignments used in formative evaluation is rehearsal, they are premature measures of achievement. Consequently, students' scores on practice tests tend to be lower than their scores on legitimate posttests. Teachers who confound practice and achievement in this way usually attempt to minimize this negative influence by reducing the percentage that practice tests or homework contribute to the composite score, eliminating the lowest practice test score, providing opportunities for extra credit, or a combination of these three strategies.

2. *Administering unannounced posttests.* Some teachers use unannounced posttests, called *pop quizzes,* as a means to keep students studying on a regular basis rather than cramming before a scheduled test. Unfortunately, this practice confounds actual achievement and study habits. Student scores tend to be lower on unannounced tests as compared to their performance on scheduled tests. Teachers who use unannounced tests generally need to develop strategies to counter their negative influence.

3. *Reducing posttest scores due to misbehavior.* This practice confounds achievement with conduct. Unacceptable student behavior may include cheating on a test, talking or being disruptive during a test, or submitting assignments late. Teachers usually alter the earned score to teach the student that such misbehaviors will not be tolerated. Instead of reducing earned scores, alternative strategies should be used for encouraging honesty, consideration, and promptness. Many districts have a separate area of the report card to record behavior and citizenship.

4. *Using extra-credit assignments to alter grades.* Extra-credit assignments are those not required of all students in the regular conduct of the classroom, and these assignments may be used as the basis for altering the student's grade. This practice, however, confounds student achievement and effort. A higher grade that a student would earn through the use of extra-credit assignments actually masks the student's actual mastery level. Some teachers view extra-credit assignments as opportunities for the student to show added mastery or special skills.

SAMPLE STANDARDS

Assessment

There are ten INTASC standards (see page xxi), and each standard includes a list of knowledge, dispositions, and performances to indicate more clearly what is intended in the standard.

Since this chapter deals with assessment, some representative statements for knowledge, dispositions, and performances from one or more INTASC standards are listed here concerning topics in this chapter.

Knowledge

- The teacher understands the characteristics, uses, advantages, and limitations of different types of assessments for evaluating how students learn, what they know and are able to do, and what kinds of experiences will support their further growth and development. (INTASC #8)
- The teacher knows how to select, construct, and use assessment strategies and instruments appropriate to the learning outcomes being evaluated and to other diagnostic purposes. (INTASC #8)

Dispositions

- The teacher values ongoing assessment as essential to the instructional process and recognizes that many different assessment strategies, accurately and systematically used, are necessary for monitoring and promoting student learning. (INTASC #8)
- The teacher respects the privacy of students and confidentiality of information. (INTASC #10)

Performances

- The teacher maintains useful records of student work and performance and can communicate student progress knowledgeably and responsibly, based on appropriate indicators, to students, parents, and other colleagues. (INTASC #8)
- The teacher makes links with the learners' other environments on behalf of students, by consulting with parents, counselors, teachers of other classes and activities within the schools, and professionals in other community agencies. (INTASC #10)

GRADING SYSTEMS

Effective grading and reporting should provide the type of information needed by the reports' users and present it in an understandable form. Depending on the purpose of the grade, as described earlier, some users of grades prefer comprehensive and detailed

Creating a Learning Community

Discussing Purposes of Grading with Your Students

With a learning community, it is not the teacher *against* the students; it is the teacher *with* the students. In a learning community, everyone works together to promote student learning. One way to do that is to discuss the reasons for actions that are taken in the classroom.

Students know that assessment has to take place, but you can build understanding and commitment to assessment by discussing the reasons for assessment and the ways that the students might benefit. For example, formative assessment measures student learning as you proceed through a unit and provides feedback about areas of strength and weakness in student performance prior to the final, summative assessment. Formative assessment performance is recorded but may not be used to calculate the report-card grade. (Scores from unit tests and projects may be used for the final, summative evaluation.) Once students know the reasons for formative assessment and re-

alize that it shows their development and will not be used for the report-card score, they will feel less pressured and more willing to participate.

In addition, there may be various ways to involve students in the development of assessments in an effort to build their understanding and commitment to assessment in a learning community.

1. How might you go about discussing the reasons for formative and summative assessment in your classroom?
2. How might you ask for your students' preferences for the types of assessments to be used in your classroom? How might you ensure that you follow up by using their recommendations?
3. How might you actually involve your students in the preparation of various types of assessments?

reports, while other users prefer a single mark. As a consequence, most grading systems represent a compromise between the detailed information and the concise report.

A *grading system* is the manner in which the students' achievement is reported (McMillan, 2007). There are several commonly used grading systems, as discussed in the following sections (Miller, Linn, & Gronlund, 2009). Regardless of the procedure used, you should inform your students of the grading system that you will be using and clearly describe what your grading procedures and requirements will be.

Percentage Grades

In a percentage grading system, the teacher assigns a number between 0 and 100; often this number is supposed to correspond to the percentage of the material that the student has learned. A disadvantage of this approach is the difficulty in making distinctions of less than 4 to 7 points out of the 100. Consequently, during the 1930s and 1940s, many school districts switched from numerical to letter grades.

Letter Grades

Letter grades have become the most commonly used grading system to represent students' achievement. In this system, a single letter (e.g., A, B, C, D, F) is used to represent a student's achievement. There are at least two variations of the A-to-F grading system. One involves the use of a single number (e.g., 5, 4, 3, 2, 1) to represent the same meaning as the A-to-F. Another variation is the use of only two letters such as S (satisfactory) and U (unsatisfactory). This approach is most commonly used in elementary schools.

While concise and convenient, this system has shortcomings: (a) the meaning of the grades is often unclear because they are a collection of such factors as achievement, effort, and good behavior; (b) interpretation is difficult; and (c) letter grades have resulted in an undesirable emphasis on grades as ends in themselves (Miller et al., 2009).

But the letter grade system does have a number of benefits. First, it is relatively easy to translate from letter grading to percentage grading and back. This conversion is convenient for the teacher who is able to record all student information on a numerical basis, weigh and average this information, and then assign letter grades accordingly. Second, the symbols + and − may be used to represent more specificity in the grade. Third, letter grades can easily be averaged to form a summary index called a *grade point average (GPA)*.

Descriptive Evaluations

Descriptive evaluations are qualitative descriptions of learning, skills, and abilities that characterize a student's work. These may be in the form of written reports that are sent to families or are included in the student's cumulative record folder. These reports enable greater flexibility in reporting student progress to families by indicating strengths, weaknesses, learning needs, and suggestions for improvement.

Criticisms of this grading system center on (a) the need to wade through extensive documentation in an effort to differentiate students, (b) the validity of the descriptions being affected by the style and personality of the student, and (c) the time and effort involved in writing the descriptions. Some grade cards, including computerized versions, provide a space for brief comments.

Pass–Fail Grading

Some high schools have permitted students to take courses on a pass–fail basis, rather than on the traditional A-to-F system. Because the pass–fail grade is not included in students' grade point average, this system encourages them to explore new areas of study without the fear of lowering their grade point average. As a grade reporting system, this approach offers less information than the A-to-F system.

Checklists of Objectives

For more informative progress reports, some schools have replaced or supplemented the letter or percentage grading systems with a list of major objectives to be checked or rated. This approach is most commonly used at the elementary level. For instance, five

Informing Students about Grading Procedures

Jeanne Pohlman, high school mathematics teacher, Wichita, Kansas

At the start of the schoolyear, I give my students a handout that describes my grading procedures and expectations. The handout outlines the weight for tests, quizzes, and homework. Procedures are described for obtaining extra help and for using a three-ring notebook. I also include information about materials needed in class and procedures that we will use when beginning class. The policies on tardiness and cheating are also included. I think it is important to clearly state all these guidelines and expectations.

major objectives might be listed for each subject area, with a checklist for each objective indicating the level of performance (e.g., outstanding, satisfactory, needs improvement).

ASSIGNING LETTER GRADES

Since most schools use the A-to-F grading system, you will need to determine what will be included in a grade and then establish a way to determine a composite score for each student. Next, you will need to select the frame of reference that is used in grading and then determine a method of distributing the grades for all the students in the class. Finally, you will need to calculate semester and annual grades.

Determining What to Include in a Grade

Letter grades will be most meaningful and useful when they represent achievement only. The interpretation of grades becomes confused when extraneous factors such as effort, conduct, study habits, and practice are included with achievement. Descriptions of student learning and development will be more precise if only achievement is used in determining the grade.

Grades should be valid measures of achievement. An *evaluation measure* is the means by which a teacher gathers information about the students' achievement. Evaluation measures may include tests, quizzes, reports, homework, and other approaches. Tests and other evaluation measures should actually measure student learning outcomes of the course objectives. Letter grades should reflect the extent to which students have achieved the learning objectives specified in the course objectives, and these should be weighted according to their relative importance.

Creating a Composite Score

At the end of a marking term, you will need to combine evaluation measure scores into a score that reflects each student's achievement throughout the term. This summative evaluation score for the marking term is called a *composite score*. A composite score is created by combining two or more scores obtained from the evaluation measures.

No single method should be used to calculate composite scores; instead, a variety of approaches are used by teachers. Regardless of the specific approach taken, teachers need to consider the four following steps as they develop a procedure that works best for them when creating a composite score (Carey, 2006; Miller et al., 2009):

1. *Select evaluation measures that will be used in determining the student's grade.* Measures of student achievement can be obtained through a variety of means, such as tests, written or oral reports, homework, ratings, laboratory performance, and projects.

2. *Analyze the relationship between the evaluation measures.* Some evaluation measures may be worthy of carrying more weight as the grade is determined. Therefore, first examine characteristics of the evaluation measures. When considering the complexity of an evaluation measure, look at its scope and the difficulty level of goals it measures. The scope can be compared using the number of goals measured and the

---

Voices from the Classroom

Creating a Composite Score

Leslie Berman, middle school science and language arts teacher, Dania, Florida

In my school, we are told to have at least two grades per week for each student and to be able to justify all our judgments about these grades. As a result, I have developed the following point system for grading.

I grade on a scale of 10 points as follows: 0 = nothing handed in; 1 point = a blank paper with a name on it and handed in; 2 to 5 points = minimal work completed and handed in; 6 to 10 points = gradable work completed and handed in.

I grade every piece of work that I assign; some I grade for correctness and some for simple completion. After 10 assignments, I list all of them on the board and give the students two days for make-up completion. Then I total the grades for the 10 assignments and close out the book on them. I even highlight the total in my gradebook for easier identification and later averaging. For each marking period, I average about 30 to 40 assignments. More important items, such as book reports, count in multiples of 10, such as 20 or 30. Tests are averaged separately.

At parent conferences, it is impressive to show so many grades and so many opportunities for success. The system is geared to help the students succeed, and it is based on immediate feedback. With this system, grades are less intimidating, and it helps alleviate some classroom pressure.

length of time between instruction and testing. Difficulty can be compared using the relative complexity of the goals measured by each evaluation measure.

When considering scope, quizzes administered immediately following instruction that measure only one instructional goal are the least complex. Unit tests measuring more goals and spanning more time are more complex. Based on differences in complexity, a teacher might decide that a comprehensive final should contribute more to the composite score than any midterm exam; a midterm exam should contribute more than any unit test; and a unit test should contribute more than any quiz (Carey, 2006).

The difficulty of the goals being measured also has to be taken into account. Based on differences in skill level, you might decide to assign more weight to tests that measure more difficult goals. One test that measures several less difficult goals may be considered comparable in overall complexity to another test that measures fewer but more difficult goals.

3. *Determine the percentage to be contributed to the composite score by each evaluation measure.* You need to calculate the percentage that each individual evaluation measure will contribute to the composite score. For example, if there were six unit tests and the teacher has identified that unit tests would contribute a total of 33.3 percent to the composite score, then you would divide the percent of contribution by the number of unit tests. In this case, each of the six tests would contribute 5.55 percent to the composite score (6 tests × 5.55 percent = 33.3 percent). In a similar way, each of two midterm exams would be worth 16.65 percent if the total weight of midterm exams were to total 33.3 percent. Then, the final exam would be worth 33.3 percent. Figure 12.1 displays a sample for the way these percentages would be allocated for each evaluation measure. The example shown in Figure 12.1 includes only tests; teachers may want to include other measures, such as homework and projects, as part of the composite score.

Usually, it is a matter of professional judgment when deciding on the percentage to allocate to each of the evaluation measures that are part of the composite score. Some districts, however, have grading policies that prescribe the percentage to be allocated to final exams.

4. *Combine scores from evaluation measures into a composite score.* Although teachers may calculate a composite score in various ways, the objective is to combine the scores from each evaluation measure into a composite score. The complicated part is to devise a system to have the scores from each evaluation measure reflect the appropriate relative weight when calculating the composite score. This composite-score calculation can be done in several ways.

One way is to use a commercially prepared computer program to aid in these calculations. Grade analysis software such as this can automatically calculate composite scores using the relative weights that teachers specify for each evaluation measure. Such software can analyze and report data in a variety of ways. Second, you

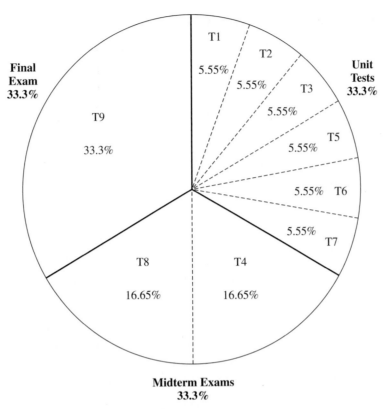

FIGURE 12.1 **Percentage Contributed to the Term Composite Score by Each Test Category and Individual Test**

Source: Carey, L. M. (2006). *Measuring and evaluating school learning* (4th ed.) (p. 420). Boston: Pearson Custom Publishing. Reprinted with permission of the author.

may calculate the average score for each type of evaluation measure and then calculate the composite score from these averages.

Third, at the start of the marking term, you may assign points for each individual evaluation measure that reflects the appropriate weight of the composite score. In this way, you need only to add up the total points at the end of the term to calculate the composite score. A drawback of this approach is that you will need to predetermine the exact type and number of evaluation measures to be used throughout the term. Fourth, you may identify a weight factor for each evaluation measure, calculate weighted scores for each measure, and combine weighted scores into a composite score. Fifth, you may devise a number of variations to these approaches or use completely different approaches in an effort to calculate a composite score.

Selecting a Frame of Reference for Grading

Teachers should consider three frames of reference when determining students' grades (Miller et al., 2009):

1. *Criterion-referenced standards.* Assigning grades on a criterion-referenced basis involves comparing a student's performance to prespecified standards set by the teacher, usually indicated in percentages of material learned. Setting standards for criterion-referenced grading is a matter of professional judgment. With this approach, you would select score ranges for A to F that reflect outstanding, very good, satisfactory, very weak, and unsatisfactory achievement.

To some extent, this approach does involve comparisons with other individuals because standards have to be realistically set; they should be based on previous evidence of student performance. If the standards are set too high, many students will fail; if they are too low, students will achieve invalidly high grades. However, when preset standards are used, students do not compete with one another as they may when peer comparisons are made.

The criterion-referenced system of grading is more complex than it first appears. To use an absolute level of achievement as a basis for grading requires that (a) the domain of learning tasks be clearly defined, (b) the standards of performance be clearly specified and justified, and (c) the measures of student achievement be criterion referenced (Miller et al., 2009).

2. *Norm-referenced standards.* Assigning grades on a norm-referenced basis involves comparing a student's performance with that of a reference group, typically one's classmates. Therefore, the grade is determined by the student's relative ranking in the total group, rather than by some absolute standard of achievement. Because grading is based on relative performance, the grade is influenced by both the student's performance and the performance of the group.

3. *Potential standards.* Grading students with respect to their potential involves several considerations: their apparent ability levels, their past performances, and the efforts they have made. Under this system, students will receive high marks if they perform well relative to their apparent abilities, improve considerably, or appear to be making extensive efforts.

Teachers often have difficulty in grading effectively using the potential standard method. Making reliable estimates of learning potential, with or without tests, is a challenging task because judgments of potential are likely to be contaminated by achievement to some unknown degree. It is also difficult to estimate improvement over a short span of time. Consequently, grades based on potential are not dependable due to the lack of reliability in judging achievement in relation to potential and due to problems in judging the degree of improvement.

Determining the Distribution of Grades

Once the frame of reference has been selected, teachers need to decide how to distribute grades within that frame of reference. A number of guidelines exist for this task.

Criterion-Referenced Grading.   When criterion-referenced grading is used, conditions for grading on an absolute basis must be met. These conditions include identifying the domain of learning tasks to be achieved, defining the instructional objectives in performance terms, specifying the standards of performance to be attained, and measuring the intended outcomes with criterion-referenced measurements.

The letter grades in a criterion-referenced system may be defined as the degree to which the objectives have been attained as illustrated here:

> A = Outstanding. The student has mastered all of the course's major and minor instructional objectives.
>
> B = Very Good. The student has mastered all of the course's major instructional objectives and most of the minor objectives.
>
> C = Satisfactory. The student has mastered all of the major instructional objectives but just a few of the minor objectives.
>
> D = Very Weak. The student has mastered just a few of the course's major and minor instructional objectives and barely has the essentials needed for the next highest level of instruction. Remedial work is desirable.
>
> F = Unsatisfactory. The student has not mastered any of the course's major instructional objectives and lacks the essentials needed for the next highest level of instruction. Remedial work is needed.

Using these definitions as a guide, a point range must be determined for each letter grade. Some school districts have identified the point range for each letter grade. Often, it is left up to the professional judgment of the teacher.

There are a number of possibilities when determining the point range for each letter grade. For instance, you might determine the lowest passing score and then have an equal range of points for each letter grade, as illustrated in the samples in Table 12.1. The three samples show the lowest passing score of 60, 65, and 70, and each sample illustrates a fairly even number of points for each letter grade. Sometimes teachers prefer to have fewer points for an A or have a decreasing range of points as the grade gets higher. Again, the range of points that a teacher selects is a matter of professional judgment.

With criterion-referenced grading, the distribution of grades is not predetermined. If all students perform well, all will receive high grades. If some students demonstrate low levels of performance, they will receive lower grades. Therefore, the distribution of grades is not determined by the student's relative position in the group but rather by each student's level of performance.

TABLE 12.1   **Sample Grading Standards**

GRADE	COMPOSITE SCORE AND THE RANGE OF POINTS		
	Sample 1	*Sample 2*	*Sample 3*
A	90–100 (11 pts.)	92–100 (9 pts.)	93–100 (8 pts.)
B	80–89 (10 pts.)	83–91 (9 pts.)	85–92 (8 pts.)
C	70–79 (10 pts.)	74–82 (9 pts.)	77–84 (8 pts.)
D	60–69 (10 pts.)	65–73 (9 pts.)	70–76 (7 pts.)
F	Below 60	Below 65	Below 70

Source: Adapted from Carey, L. M. (2006). *Measuring and evaluating school learning* (4th ed.) (p. 424). Boston: Pearson Custom Publishing. Reprinted with permission of the author.

Norm-Referenced Grading.   Norm-referenced grading involves the ranking of students in order of their overall achievement and assigning letter grades on the basis of each student's rank in the group. A common method for assigning norm-referenced grades has two steps:

1. *Determine what proportion of the class will receive each letter grade.* This task is not as simple as it first might appear, because the teacher needs to take a number of factors into account as the selection of the proportions is made. As the starting point of these decisions, the normal bell-shaped curve can be used. Grading on the normal curve results in an equal number of As and Fs, and Bs and Ds.

In a classroom of 20 to 30 students, the use of norm-referenced grading may not be desirable because (a) the groups are usually too small to yield a normal distribution, (b) classroom evaluation instruments are usually not designed to yield normally distributed scores, and (c) the student population becomes more select as it moves through the grades and less-able students fail or drop out of school (Miller et al., 2009). Consequently, teachers who use norm-referenced grading consider additional factors such as the type of class (e.g., introductory or advanced), the type of student (e.g., gifted, average, or slow learning), and others. After considering these factors, teachers may use their professional judgment to adjust the percentages for each letter grade.

Recognizing that a variety of factors need to be considered, you can use the following as a guide when selecting the proportion of students to receive each letter grade (Miller et al., 2009).

A = 10–20% of the students
B = 20–30% of the students
C = 30–50% of the students
D = 10–20% of the students
F = 0–10% of the students

These percentage ranges are for illustration only. There are no simple ways for determining the ranges for a given situation.

2. *Make grade assignments based on the students' ranked scores.* There are three steps to this process. First, using the percentage of students that you selected in the first step, determine the number of students that are to receive each letter grade. Second, rank students in the order of their achievement. This can be done by listing the scores in descending order and indicating a frequency tally by each score. And finally, assign the grade for each student based on his or her score and on the letter grade designation for that score based on the previous steps.

Calculating Semester and Annual Grades

At the end of two or more marking terms, term grades are combined into a semester grade. At the end of the year, semester grades are then combined into an annual grade. Teachers often calculate semester and annual grades in a way similar to that which they used to calculate the composite scores for each marking term. As noted previously, there is a great deal of variability among teachers in the way this is done.

One way to calculate semester and annual grades is to use a computer program to aid in grade analysis and record keeping. Second, you can take the average of the marking term grades to calculate the semester grade or take the average of the marking term grades and the final exam to calculate the annual grade. Third, you can identify a weight factor for the marking terms, semester grades, and final exam; calculate weighted scores for each measure; and combine weighted scores into a composite score. Fourth, you can devise a number of variations to these approaches or use completely different approaches in an effort to calculate semester or annual grades.

NONACHIEVEMENT OUTCOMES

In addition to reporting achievement, teachers are often expected to measure and report student conduct. *Nonachievement outcomes* involve student conduct in areas such as effort, study habits, attitude toward learning, and citizenship. Most commonly, the report card used by the district will indicate the categories to be reported along with the manner in which the report will be made. Nonachievement outcomes typically reported include rating scales, checklists, and special reports; these same approaches may be used for recording achievement outcomes.

Rating Scales

Probably the most popular method of reporting judgments of effort, work habits, character traits, and other nonachievement information is a *rating scale.* For example, work habits, effort, and initiative can be rated as "superior," "average," or "unsatisfactory." Other items such as the respect for rights, property, and feelings of others can be rated on a three-step scale with "shows great respect," "shows proper respect," and "shows little respect." Rating scales on report cards may include three to five intervals for such traits as honesty, dependability, and leadership.

There are some disadvantages to the use of rating scales. First, ratings require considerable teacher time. Second, ratings are subject to the halo effect, which is the tendency of raters to consistently rate certain individuals positively and other individuals negatively regardless of the trait or characteristic being rated. This is a special danger when the teacher does not know the student well and consequently relies on general impressions of the student in making ratings of specific traits or when a teacher lacks objectivity.

Checklists

A second procedure for reporting nonachievement outcomes is the *checklist.* A listing of specific behaviors or behavior patterns related to the traits to be judged is typically presented. While the checklist may include both desired and undesirable behaviors, it is more common for items to be stated all positively or all negatively.

For example, items listed under the heading of work habits might include positive statements such as "Uses time effectively," "Organizes work well," "Follows directions," "Uses resource materials appropriately," and "Demonstrates the capacity for independent study." In contrast, a list of negative statements for work habits might include "Makes poor use of time," "Does not organize work well," "Distracts others," "Does not follow directions," "Fails to use resource materials appropriately," and "Lacks the capacity for independent study." Positive statements have the advantage of praising desired behavior. On the other hand, it is probably more informative to students and their families to know what weaknesses in study habits a teacher perceives so that steps can be taken to remedy them.

Special Reports

An alternative to rating scales and checklists is the use of special report forms to communicate with families and for use in cumulative student records. These are used when a teacher considers a student's behavior to (a) merit special commendation or (b) warrant a formal reprimand or warning. Special reports take less teacher time and energy than do ratings forms or checklists. To be used fairly and consistently, it is helpful to have a guide prepared by the district to assist teachers in making such reports. It is important that the reports not be viewed by students simply as a system for recording disciplinary problems.

What Would You Decide?   *Nonachievement Outcomes*

Nonachievement outcomes may include items such as effort, study habits, attitude toward learning, and citizenship.

1. What additional nonachievement outcomes might be related to particular subject areas (e.g., physical education, social studies, science, art)?

2. What kind of information will you need to gather for each nonachievement outcome, and how will you record it in your gradebook?

Voices from the Classroom

Each Student Has a Gradebook

Alice Dwyer, third-grade teacher, Guthrie, Oklahoma

Each student in my class keeps a gradebook, which is a folder where they record their own scores for the assessments they take. There is a simple line graph for the students to record the scores for their addition, subtraction, and multiplication facts. There are also several blank laminated sheets for students to place the stickers that they got on returned papers. It also contains a log where students write their scores from computer-ized reading tests. Students record their scores immediately after receiving their returned papers.

The purpose of this student gradebook is to instill ownership in their own learning, provide immediate and regular feedback, and promote motivation. I want my students to compete with themselves instead of their peers. Students are also able to communicate better with their parents since their grades are accessible and not a mystery.

DESIGNING A GRADEBOOK

A *gradebook* includes three types of student behavior that teachers are usually expected to monitor and report: achievement, attendance, and conduct. Consequently, a gradebook documents students' progress throughout the schoolyear. While teaching assignments and information requirements vary, most teachers need a daily record of students' attendance and other information related to classroom management, a record of achievement scores, and a record of conduct scores.

Your gradebook design should reflect the nature of your teaching assignment. A teacher who is assigned five different groups needs a gradebook that contains a daily log, a record of achievement scores, and a conduct record for each class. On the other hand, an elementary teacher who teaches five different subjects to the same group needs to create one daily log, one conduct record, and then a different achievement record for each subject.

While commercially produced gradebooks are available, many provide inadequate space for good documentation and are not formatted in ways that are the most efficient for the teacher. Consequently, you may be more satisfied with a gradebook that you construct using a large loose-leaf notebook; large block, two-sided graph paper; and divider pages with tabs. After students' names are recorded on the first page, subsequent pages can be trimmed so the names remain visible as new pages are added. With this design, you can add new pages as needed, remove and store information from previous semesters, and insert records you might generate using the various computer programs available for gradebooks.

While there will be some variation due the nature of the your teaching assignment, an efficiently designed gradebook should have three sections to record (a) the

TABLE 12.2   Sample Symbols and Format for Recording Behaviors

SAMPLE SYMBOLS FOR RECORDING BEHAVIORS

ATTENDANCE	*Study Habits*	*Participation*	*Conduct*
/ = Absent	H = Homework	M = Materials not present	A = Aggressive
(/) = Unexcused absence	(H) = Homework accurate	C = Clothing inadequate	D = Disruptive
X = Tardy	XH = No homework	P = Did not participate	CT = Cheating on test
(X) = Unexcused tardy	IH = Inaccurate homework	T = Time wasted	
	CH = Homework not complete		
	LH = Late homework		

SAMPLE DAILY RECORD OF CONDUCT

Dates	9–1	2	3	4	5		8		9	10	11		12
Students								H				**Trip**	
Allen, B.					(/)		X	IH	X	P		ok	
Baker, J.								H	/			ok	

Adapted from Carey, L. M. (2006). *Measuring and evaluating school learning* (4th ed.) (pp. 435–436). Boston: Pearson Custom Publishing. Reprinted with permission of the author.

daily record, (b) achievement scores, and (c) summary charts for the semester and the schoolyear.

Daily Record

The *daily record* is used to document information about attendance, homework and classroom assignments, particular instances of conduct that you want to record, and other school matters (Carey, 2006). To prepare this section, select the information you will document, choose symbols that represent each type of information, create a legend for the symbols, list the class dates, and record the selected behaviors. A sample list of symbols for recording behaviors is shown in Table 12.2 along with an illustration of how to record these symbols in the daily log. The sample shown in Table 12.2 includes only symbols for negative behavior; teachers often include symbols for positive behavior as well.

You will also need a summary section for the marking term in which you record the frequency of each behavior over the term. A sample summary section of the daily record is displayed in Table 12.3.

Achievement Scores

The gradebook should also contain a section to record and summarize students' achievement scores on posttests (e.g., tests conducted after instruction). Again, the

TABLE 12.3   **Sample Summary Section of the Daily Record**

Students	ATTENDANCE				STUDY HABITS					PARTICIPATION				CONDUCT		
	/	⟨/⟩	X	⟨X⟩	Ⓗ	XH	IH	CH	LH	M	C	P	T	A	D	CT
Allen, B.	0	1	1	0	12	2	1	0	0	1	0	0	0	0	0	1
Baker, J.	3	0	1	0	2	4	6	1	2	7	0	2	0	0	1	0

Adapted from Carey, L. M. (2006). *Measuring and evaluating school learning* (4th ed.) (p. 437). Boston: Pearson Custom Publishing. Reprinted with permission of the author.

amount and type of information that needs to be recorded will vary with the teacher's assignment. In general, the more complete the information recorded, the easier it is to determine the student's grade for the marking term, semester, and schoolyear. A format is needed in the gradebook to systematically record necessary information.

Summary Charts

Another section of the gradebook is needed to record summary information for the semester and the schoolyear. Selected information and summaries from the sections for daily records and for achievement scores will be transferred to this summary section. The summary section, therefore, will include summary information on the daily record, on the semester summary of achievement scores, and on the annual summary of achievement scores.

REPORTING GRADES AND COMMUNICATING TO FAMILIES

Families need to know how their children are progressing in school. In addition to reporting information about achievement and nonachievement outcomes, families often want information about course content, instructional activities, grading procedures and student requirements, and special activities. By properly communicating with families, you (a) fulfill your responsibility in telling them of their children's progress, (b) explain the academic program to them and solicit their understanding and assistance, and (c) enlist their help in educating their child.

Information about course content, instructional activities, grading procedures and student requirements, and special activities can be conveyed through the use of newsletters, open houses, and parent–teacher conferences. Achievement and nonachievement outcomes are communicated through report cards and sometimes individualized letters to families and parent–teacher conferences. A cumulative record file for each student is also maintained in the school as a source of information for the teacher and families.

Report Cards

Report cards serve as the primary means to report to families about their child's achievement and nonachievement progress (Stiggins, 2008). The district determines a number of aspects of what will be reported on the report cards and how the information will be reported:

1. The district determines what achievement and nonachievement progress will be reported.
2. It determines what grading system will be used to report achievement progress. This may be in the form of letter grades, percentage grades, pass–fail, description evaluations, checklists of objectives, or other approaches.
3. It may determine the frame of reference (criterion-referenced or norm-referenced grading) to be used when assigning grades.
4. It may determine guidelines when calculating term or annual grades. For example, this may be in the form of a requirement to count a semester exam as 25 percent of the semester grade.
5. It may determine the percentages that should be used for each letter grade.

All of these decisions are beyond your control, and you need to be prepared at the end of the marking term to record information on the report card in the manner the district dictates. Some districts send progress reports to families halfway through the marking period. Beginning teachers, especially, should examine the district's report card for their grade level to see what information they are expected to report at the end of the marking term. Take this into account as you devise the evaluation system for your classroom.

Report cards differ in the way that nonachievement progress is reported. These reports vary considerably among districts and also by grade level. Report cards for the elementary grades, especially the primary grades of K–3, often have a number of nonachievement measures such as social development, work habits, effort, citizenship, academic readiness, and other areas. Report cards for the intermediate grades (4–6) have less emphasis on these items and have fewer items for teachers to report. Likewise, report cards for middle school, junior high school, and high school students have fewer items for reporting nonachievement information.

Cumulative Record Files

The school maintains a *cumulative record file* for each student as a source of information for the teacher and families. The file for each student commonly contains one or more cumulative record cards recording the following information: (a) personal information (home address and telephone number, parents' names, parents' work addresses and phone numbers, the name of a person to contact in an emergency, and other useful background information); (b) information for each schoolyear and in each subject area concerning the student's attendance, achievement (often including grades for each marking term, each semester, final exams, and final annual grades), nonachievement areas (often related to work habits, citizenship, and conduct); (c) the student's scores on various achievement tests and other standardized tests taken over the years he or she has been in school; (d) health; and (e) honors or participation in special activities. In addition, the cumulative record file often includes information about specially scheduled parent–teacher conferences and other anecdotal information.

The responsibility for updating the cumulative files for each student for each year varies among districts. For certain types of information, the school's secretarial staff sometimes enters the information. For other information, it is the classroom teacher's responsibility to have the file completely updated at the end of the schoolyear. The balance of responsibility often depends on the situation in each individual school.

Cumulative record files serve several important purposes. First, the file provides the official record of a student's attendance, achievement, promotions, and graduation. It constitutes the basis for the student's transcript when transferring to another school. Second, the academic information can assist in determining each student's appropriate assignment to grade level or to specific classes. For instance, reading levels indicated for a student during second grade can help the classroom teacher make the appropriate reading group assignment when the student starts third grade.

Third, the data recorded in these records can help teachers understand the student's academic and social behavior. By examining these records, you may be able to identify special needs, distinguish between transient and permanent behavior tendencies, find out when a problem started, and discover clues concerning causal factors underlying a student's difficulties. And fourth, this record can help families and teachers achieve a more objective and accurate picture of the student's achievements, special abilities, and special problems. Cumulative record files are also accessible to families.

Newsletters

At the start of the schoolyear or a new course, teachers sometimes prepare a newsletter that will go to the families of all the students in the class. This newsletter often includes information about the course content, instructional activities, and grading procedures and student requirements. Of course, the nature of the initial newsletter will vary with the grade level and the type of teaching assignment. As a guide, though, the newsletter may include a description of the following:

1. Course title or subject area(s)
2. Brief course or subject area description
3. Course objectives
4. A brief content outline
5. Typical learning activities
6. Grading procedures. This could include a listing of the types of evaluation measures to be used and the proportion of the marking term grade that each measure

will carry. For example, tests (40 percent), homework (20 percent), projects (20 percent), and quizzes (20 percent). In addition, the grading scale could be included indicating the percentages for each letter grade.

7. Materials that the student will need
8. Behavioral guidelines and expectations
9. The school telephone number. This is included as a convenience for the parents in the event they need to contact you.

It is important that you convey this information to the students as well. Students especially need to know grading procedures and guidelines and also behavioral expectations. During the schoolyear, additional newsletters might be sent to all families with information about special events, programs, or opportunities.

Open Houses

Many schools plan an open house near the beginning of the schoolyear, inviting families to come to the classroom and meet the teacher. Teachers commonly make a presentation to all the families at one time and use this opportunity to convey the same type of information that was outlined in the newsletter described earlier. In fact, it is very helpful to have this same information printed and ready to distribute to families when they arrive at the open house. The sheets that families receive can then serve as the outline for the teacher's presentation at the open house.

The open house is typically not a time when teachers meet with individual families about their child's progress. Some schools plan additional open houses later in the schoolyear, but it is more common to have one open house at the start of the schoolyear or the start of the semester.

Parent–Teacher Conferences

Many districts schedule parent–teacher conferences to permit teachers to explain students' grades and answer questions parents might have about their child's achievement, conduct, or attendance. At the elementary level, many districts have regularly scheduled parent–teacher conferences at least once and perhaps two or three times throughout the schoolyear. These conferences are much less common at the secondary level. In addition to parent–teacher conferences scheduled by the district, teachers or parents may initiate a conference to address some aspect of the student's progress.

When preparing for and conducting parent–teacher conferences, consider the following guidelines:

1. Prepare for the conference.
2. Give the parents some idea in advance of the topic to be discussed.
3. Allow enough time for the conference.
4. Begin with a positive statement regarding the student.

Classroom Case Study

Conferences with Parents

David DeFranco, an eleventh-grade chemistry teacher, noticed a drastic decrease in the work effort of one of his most consistent students, Jake. To express his concern, Mr. DeFranco scheduled a parent–teacher conference with Jake's parents.

When Mr. DeFranco notified Jake's parents that he would like to meet with them, he didn't state a reason for the conference. But when Jake's parents arrived for the meeting, three days later, they immediately began to worry. They found the school's vice principal and Mr. DeFranco looking at the gradebook. Mr. DeFranco was repeatedly tapping his fingers.

Mr. DeFranco looked up and said, "Hello, you must be Jake's parents."

"Yes," Jake's father replied. "So, why did you call this meeting?"

Mr. DeFranco let out a sigh. "Well, I've noticed a recent downtrend in Jake's work. Can you explain why?"

"No," Jake's father quickly retorted. "Jake has always done well in school. Do you think there might be something different about your class?"

Mr. DeFranco became obviously perturbed. "Jake had an A average during the first semester, and my teaching style hasn't changed a bit. That's why I think there is something going on outside school."

Jake's mother interrupted and asked, "Are you suggesting my son is hiding something from us?"

"Well, I know the change in Jake's performance has nothing to do with my teaching," Mr. DeFranco said.

Jake's father, although irritated, was still focused on finding the explanation. He asked, "Well, do you have any suggestions for how we can help improve Jake's performance?"

Mr. DeFranco looked at his watch and said, "I'll think about all of this. I hate to cut this conference short, but I have to go coach tennis now. Please contact me at your earliest convenience."

Mr. DeFranco never heard back from Jake's parents.

Focus Questions

1. What things would have to change for this conference to be successful?
2. What should Mr. DeFranco do differently to prepare for and conduct a parent–teacher conference?

5. Present the documentation for the grades.
6. Avoid becoming defensive when parents question the teacher's judgment.
7. Maintain an open mind to parents' ideas.
8. Listen to all that parents are saying (verbally and nonverbally) before responding.
9. Avoid overwhelming parents with the presence of other school personnel.

10. Avoid overwhelming parents with irrelevant material or use of jargon.
11. Avoid physical barriers such as a desk or uncomfortable chairs.
12. Follow up on commitments made during the conference. (Some teachers ask the parents to call back in a week or so.)

Contacts with Individual Families

Teachers commonly contact individual families through telephone calls or letters, and there are several reasons for doing this. First, you may want to invite the families to a particular class activity or function, one in which their child is playing a significant role. Second, you may provide the families with information about their child's academic work. Often, this concerns difficulties the student is having, and you may wish to discuss the issue with the family to enlist their assistance and support. Do not overlook the importance of sending letters to the family that provide good news about the child's academic work. Many schools have forms or certificates that can be used to convey positive news. These do not take much of the teacher's time but make a big difference in the relationship that is established with the student and the family.

Third, you may provide information about the conduct of the child. As with the letter concerning academic progress, these letters to the family should not be just for problems. Letters should also be sent that convey positive information concerning the child's conduct. Similarly, forms and certificates are often available for conveying good news concerning conduct. Fourth, you may send a letter asking that a parent–teacher conference be scheduled to discuss some aspect of the student's progress.

GENERAL PRINCIPLES IN GRADING AND REPORTING

The following general principles can serve as the basis of your system of grading and reporting:

1. Describe the grading requirements to the students. This includes providing information about the types of evaluation measures that will be used, the proportion of the marking term grade that each measure will carry, and the percentages required for each letter grade.
2. Grades should represent academic achievement only. Do not alter grades due to student misbehavior.
3. Evaluate students at all levels of the cognitive domain.
4. Evaluate frequently throughout the marking term so that sufficient data concerning student achievement are obtained to determine the grades.
5. Communicate clearly to students what they will be evaluated on each time an evaluation is to occur.

6. Use many different evaluation measures. There should be a good balance of homework, classwork, quizzes, major tests, projects, and other appropriate evaluation measures.
7. Keep students informed about their progress throughout the marking term.
8. Devise an efficient format for the gradebook to accurately record all evaluation data and to simplify the task of calculating marking term, semester, and annual grades.

Key Terms

Composite score
Criterion-referenced standards
Cumulative record file
Daily record
Evaluation measure

Gradebook
Grades
Grading system
Marks
Nonachievement outcomes

Norm-referenced
   standards
Potential standards
Scores

Major Concepts

1. Grades convey information about a student's progress to students, families, school administrators, counselors, other schools, college admission officers, and prospective employers. They serve informational, administrative, guidance, and sorting and selecting functions.

2. A grading system is the manner in which grades are reported. Grading systems include percentage grades, letter grades, descriptive evaluations, parent–teacher conferences, pass–fail grading, and checklists of objectives.

3. To assign grades, teachers must determine what to include in a grade, create a composite score, select the proper frame of reference for grading, and determine the distribution of grades.

4. Assigning grades on a criterion-referenced basis involves comparing a student's performance to prespecified standards set by the teacher. Norm-referenced grading involves comparing the student's performance with that of a reference group, typically one's classmates.

5. Teachers are often expected to measure and report on student's conduct in such areas as effort, study habits, attitude toward learning, and citizenship. These are often reported in rating scales, checklists, and special reports.

6. A gradebook should be designed and formatted for efficient recording and use of the daily record (e.g., attendance, homework and classroom assignments, conduct), a record of achievement scores, and summary charts for the semester and the school year.

7. Besides reports cards, teachers can communicate to families through newsletters, open houses, parent–teacher conferences, and contacts with individual parents. The student's cumulative record file can also serve as a source of information.

8. Teachers should describe the grading requirements to the students. This includes providing information about the types of evaluation measures that will be used, the proportion of the marking term grade that each measure will carry, and the percentages required for each letter grade.

Discussion/Reflective Questions

1. List the advantages and limitations for the types of grading systems: percentage grades, letter grades, and descriptive evaluations.
2. Why should teachers use a variety of evaluation measures during a marking term?
3. What are the advantages and limitations of assigning grades on a criterion-referenced basis?
4. For the grade level and/or subject area that you intend to teach, what type of non-achievement outcomes (e.g., conduct) would be appropriate to report? How would you measure these outcomes and report them?
5. What advantages would there be if the teacher prepared and distributed a newsletter at the start of the schoolyear for families concerning course content, learning activities, grading procedures, and student expectations?

Suggested Activities

For Clinical Settings

1. Select the types of conduct (e.g., effort, study habits, attitude toward learning, citizenship, or others) that you would want to measure and report on the report card for the grade level you intend to teach. Design a gradebook format to record information about this conduct. This should include a key for the information, a way to record the daily log, and a way to provide a summary of this information at the end of the marking term.
2. For your grade level and subject area, select evaluation measures for achievement you would use during a marking term and identify information concerning these that you would need to record in the gradebook. Next, design a gradebook that would enable you to record the required information and prepare marking term summaries.
3. Identify the percentages for each letter grade that you would use in the grade level and/or subject you intend to teach. State the rationale for the lowest passing percentage and for the range of points at each letter grade.

For Field Experiences

1. Talk with one or more teachers to determine what evaluation measures they use, how they create a composite score for the marking term, what frame of reference they use when grading, and how they determine the distribution of grades within the class.
2. Examine the report card for a school district to see what achievement and nonachievement information is reported and how it is reported. Critique the report card for positive and negative aspects.
3. With the permission of the teacher, examine the cumulative record files for the students in one class. Notice the type of information recorded, and identify ways this information could be used.

Further Reading

Burke, K. (2005). *How to assess authentic learning* (4th ed.). Thousand Oaks, CA: Corwin Press.

In a practical, workbook format, it addresses learning standards and multiple ways to assess students, including portfolios, performance tasks and rubrics, teacher-made tests, logs and journals, checklists, and conferences.

Gronlund, N. E., & Waugh, C. K. (2009). *Assessment of student achievement* (9th ed.). Boston: Allyn & Bacon.

Serves as a practical guide for assessing the intended outcomes of instruction. Emphasis on teacher-made assessments and performance assessments.

McMillan, J. H. (2007). *Classroom assessment: Principles and practice for effective instruction* (4th ed.). Boston: Allyn & Bacon.

Shows how assessment principles apply to the full range of teacher decision making. Includes emphasis on high-quality assessments, assessing mainstreamed students, and assessments in each learning domain.

Popham, W. J. (2008). *Classroom assessment: What teachers need to know* (5th ed.). Boston: Allyn & Bacon.

Includes material dealing with the day-to-day decisions teachers make about assessment.

13 Working with Colleagues and Families

Objectives

This chapter provides information that will help you to:

1. Identify the reasons you would turn to colleagues for assistance.
2. Identify the reasons for contacting and interacting with families.
3. Describe the reasons some families resist involvement.
4. Determine ways to work through cultural and language differences.
5. Determine ways to communicate with families.
6. Describe ways to effectively prepare for and conduct parent–teacher conferences.

> **Working with Colleagues**

> **Working with Families**
> - Reasons for Working with Families
> - Why Some Families Resist Involvement
> - Working through Cultural and Language Differences

> **Contacting and Communicating with Families**
> - Ways to Communicate with Families
> - Parent–Teacher Conferences

Can you imagine how challenging it must have been to teach in a one-room school-house? There were so many responsibilities and challenges with the curriculum, instructional materials, and student behavior, and no one to turn to for help. Fortunately, teachers today have a number of colleagues whom they can turn to for assistance concerning a variety of issues.

Families can also be contacted for assistance when working with their children. In addition, teachers must take a variety of steps to contact and communicate with families about the school program and the progress of their children. This chapter addresses ways to work with both colleagues and families.

WORKING WITH COLLEAGUES

Teachers often need to turn to others for assistance when dealing with problems about student behavior, reading or language problems, media and instructional technology, students with special needs, curricular issues, instructional strategies, and numerous other issues. Depending on the issue, teachers may turn to one or more of these colleagues and resource people:

- principals
- counselors or psychologists

331

- reading specialists
- special education resource teachers
- librarians
- media specialists
- curriculum specialists
- school or district committees
- district or community agencies
- school secretaries
- custodians

When dealing with a student who has significant misbehavior problems, for example, it is wise to consult with the principal, school counselor, and/or psychologist to obtain information and advice as you work with this challenging student. Sometimes, however, students do not respond to any of your strategies, and the misbehavior may continue to be chronic and serious. Deviant and disruptive behavior warrants referrals to outside help. In such cases, you may need to refer this student to the school counselor or psychologist when you recognize that a developing problem is beyond your professional expertise. Remember that you have not been trained to be a psychologist, counselor, or social worker, and you should not view yourself as a failure when referring the student to receive help from someone with appropriate training.

Before problem student behavior gets serious enough for these referrals, it is often helpful to have telephone calls and conferences with families to inform them of the student behaviors and your actions and to solicit their assistance. In addition, the principal can counsel or intervene in various ways when handling a challenging student.

In serious cases, district and community agencies might need to be contacted to work with the school and the family. Many districts or city governments have an office of substance abuse and violence prevention and intervention, and its resources may be useful. Social workers are available in various community agencies. Other types of offices and organizations within the district or community might be contacted for help.

You may have a student with a disability or with special needs. In this case, you would contact the special education resource teacher for guidance and assistance. Or you might have a student who has limited English proficiency. Or you may want to integrate instructional technology into your instruction. Or you may have an interest to use a particular instructional approach, such as problem-based instruction. In all these cases, you would likely seek out colleagues in your school or district for assistance. Useful resources are available about working with paraprofessionals and support staff (Ashbaker & Morgan, 2006; Campbell & Fairbairn, 2005; Sausen, 2004).

Teaching should not be a solitary profession; you strengthen yourself when you turn to others for assistance. Keep in mind that your students will be ultimate beneficiaries of your willingness to seek out this assistance.

WORKING WITH FAMILIES

Imagine that you are a parent and you and your family have just moved into the community during the summer. You have one child in third grade and another in seventh grade. Because you moved from another state, you are concerned that the curriculum might be quite different in this new district, and you wonder how your children will adjust to the new community and their new school and teacher. Wouldn't you want to talk to the teachers to share some of these issues? Wouldn't you like to hear about the curriculum and how the teachers will handle instruction? Wouldn't you like to maintain ongoing contact throughout the school year? Yes, of course!

Good communication with families should be a priority, because it keeps teachers and families informed about what is happening. It also builds trust so that there can be

SAMPLE STANDARDS

Parents and Partnerships

There are ten INTASC standards (see page xxi), and each standard includes a list of knowledge, dispositions, and performances to indicate more clearly what is intended in the standard.

Since this chapter deals with parents and partnerships, some representative statements for knowledge, dispositions, and performances from INTASC Standard #10 are listed here concerning topics in this chapter.

Knowledge
- The teacher understands schools as organizations within the larger community context and understands the operations of the relevant aspects of the systems within which she or he works.
- The teacher understands how factors in the students' environment outside of school (e.g., family circumstances, community environments, health and economic factors) may influence students' life and learning.

Dispositions
- The teacher is willing to consult with other adults regarding the education and well-being of his/her students.
- The teacher is willing to work with other professionals to improve the overall learning environment for students.

Performances
- The teacher can identify and use community resources to foster student learning.
- The teacher establishes respectful and productive relationships with parents and guardians from diverse home and community situations, and seeks to develop cooperative partnerships in support of student learning and well-being.

a working partnership in the event that there are difficulties with the students. Although a teacher's primary responsibility is to work with students, it is important to communicate and interact with the students' families throughout the schoolyear. The reason for the communication will often determine the timing of the contact and the means by which the contact will be made.

At the start, we must recognize that children come from many types of family settings. While some students come from traditional or nuclear families (47 percent), others come from single-parent families (27 percent), blended families (16 percent), extended or multigenerational families (6 percent), or other types of families, such as gay and lesbian families, families headed by grandparents, families with adopted or foster children, and even homeless families (Barbour, Barbour, & Scully, 2008; Diffily, 2004). Some children are cared for by a combination of community caregivers, not in a traditional home.

As a result of these various family settings, the term *parent* is used sparingly in this chapter and in a broad sense to represent the adult or adults who have parental responsibility. Thus, this definition of a parent could include the biological parents, foster or stepparents, a grandparent, an aunt or uncle, an older sibling, or a guardian.

Families want their children to succeed in school and generally appreciate teachers' efforts to keep them informed and involved about academic and behavioral issues (Berger, 2008). Families' reactions to problems vary widely. Reactions are largely determined by individual experiences, life experiences, education and training, expectations, socioeconomic circumstances, and other factors. The reactions of the child, the teacher, and others also have a bearing on how the problem will be handled (Walker, Shae, & Bauer, 2007).

It is important to listen carefully to families to identify their concerns and suggestions. Trust is developed when they know that their ideas are recognized and understood. The full benefits of parent–school relationships are not realized without this interaction and collaboration. Fortunately, a number of useful resources provide guidance when working with families (e.g., Canter & Canter, 2001; Diffily, 2004; National PTA, 2000; Rudney, 2006).

What are the reasons for working with families? Why is it important to understand them and their point of view? When should families be contacted? What are the ways that teachers might communicate with families? We will examine these questions in this chapter.

Reasons for Working with Families

myeducationlab

Go to MyEducationLab, select the topic **Cooperative Learning and the Collaborative Process,** click "videos," and select "Involving Parents." View the video and reflect.

Students ultimately benefit from good communication and effective working relationships between the school and home. Families' involvement in their children's schooling has been associated with better attendance, more positive student attitudes and behavior, greater willingness to do homework, and higher academic achievement.

You should communicate with families for several reasons:

1. *To create open, two-way communication and to establish friendly relations.* Having positive contacts with families early in the year helps families establish positive, friendly relations. In this way, families and teachers do not see each other as adversaries but as allies in helping the student be successful. Two-way communication can be fostered, and that will result in appropriate school–community relations that will benefit everyone involved.

2. *To understand the student's home condition.* Information about a student's home condition can help you decide on an appropriate course of action with the student. You may learn the parents are having marital problems, have limited ability to read or speak English, exert excessive pressure for the child to excel academically, or tend to be abusive to the student when there are problems at school. Such factors can be important as you decide how best to help each student academically and behaviorally.

3. *To inform families of academic expectations and events as well as student performance.* Families appreciate knowing your policy concerning homework, late papers, and grading guidelines. They also like to know what content will be covered, when the quizzes or tests are scheduled, and what special events are scheduled. Introductory letters or a Back-to-School Night are helpful, as are newsletters devoted to special events, units to be covered, or the academic schedule. Finally, families want to know how their children are doing. Report cards and conferences provide information periodically, but many families appreciate learning about early indications of academic difficulties.

4. *To enlist help from families about academic issues.* Teachers often seek help from families at the start of the year. They may send a list of needed classroom and instructional supplies home to the families to supplement purchases made by the school district. You may want to identify family members who might be available to serve as classroom aides or chaperones for regular or special events. This assistance may include preparing materials for bulletin boards, assisting during a field trip, and the like.

5. *To inform families of disciplinary expectations and actions.* At the start of the year, teachers often inform families of their disciplinary policy and their expectations for student conduct. As with the academic information at the start of the year, this communication is often accomplished through an introductory letter or a newsletter, or at the Back-to-School Night. If a student misbehaves, you may need to inform the family of the situation without having to seek additional support and assistance from them.

6. *To enlist help from families about dealing with their children.* When a student has difficulties, the family should be contacted to identify ways they might help. When a student has misbehaved, the family should be contacted so that you can work together to help the student stay on task and be successful. Families exert much influence on their children, and they can cooperate and support your actions.

You and the family may both agree on strategies to help the child and to build the child's cooperation and commitment to address any problems. A behavior-modification program may be agreed on; as part of the plan, the family may withhold privileges or offer rewards at home. The family has access to more attractive rewards than does the school, such as a videotape rental, a trip to the pool, or the purchase of an item of clothing. Establishing a plan of action with the student as an active participant and with the support of the family is crucial for successful progress.

Why Some Families Resist Involvement

As much as you would like the cooperation and support of families when dealing with a student with academic or behavioral difficulties, you may find some families apathetic or resistant to involvement. There are several possible reasons for resistance (Diffily, 2004; McEwan, 2005):

■ As students, some adults may have had unhappy experiences. They may view school as being oppressive and not a place of hope for their children. These families may consider it unlikely that school personnel can solve problems.

■ Families of children who have a history of misbehavior may adopt coping mechanisms in an effort to deal emotionally with the problems (Walker et al., 2007). Their responses may point to self-doubt, denial, withdrawal, hostility, and frustration. These families may resist involvement with all school personnel.

■ Some families view teachers, principals, counselors, and other school personnel as the experts in addressing issues such as misbehavior (Turnbull, Turnbull, Erwin, & Soodak, 2006). Consequently, they may resist involvement because they do not want to interfere with the actions taken by the teacher or other officials.

■ Some families are threatened by the school itself and the bureaucracy. They may be intimidated by the size of the school, the need to report to the school office when visiting the school, the busy nature of the school, the lack of private areas for discussion, and other physical aspects of the school. As a result, these families may resist involvement because they have a sense of discomfort about the school.

■ Diversity among the population and the sense of being different from school personnel may make families uncomfortable in seeking contact with teachers or administrators. For example, Asian immigrant parents may think that communication with teachers is considered to be "checking up on them" and an expression of disrespect. Members of other ethnic groups may likewise feel out of place.

■ Some families do not know what is expected of them or how they might contribute to their child's education. They may withdraw or become angry or frustrated when the school seems to be failing to meet their child's needs. They do not realize that the school would value their involvement.

■ Some families do not become involved with the school for practical reasons. They may not speak English or have limited competency in English. They may not drive a car or have limited access to transportation. They may not have access to a babysitter or cannot afford one. Or they simply may be too tired after long days at work themselves.

■ Teachers or administrators may have done things in the past to upset family members, and now they may not want to get involved or may participate in an angry manner.

In previous interactions, educators may have failed to communicate with the family, held stereotypes, broken promises, or been rude, condescending, dishonest, or unprofessional in various ways (McEwan, 2005).

■ Schools may have not met the family's expectations for various reasons, and this may influence their involvement. Some families' concerns may be about a lack of student learning in the school, poor behavior in the school, a lack of competent teachers, erosion of values, a lack of safety, or even a feeling of having to settle for financially poor schools (McEwan, 2005).

■ Some families may have personal problems themselves, and these factors may interfere with good communication and involvement with the school. There may be separated or divorced parents or problems such as abuse, addiction, dysfunction, and mental illness. There are also some parents who simply must complain (McEwan, 2005).

What Would You Decide? *Families Not Attending*

Let's assume that you teach in a school that has much ethnic diversity and that some families do not attend the Back-to-School Night or the parent–teacher conferences at the end of the report-card periods.

1. How can you find out why the families do not attend?

2. How can you communicate to these families that it is acceptable to attend such sessions and that their child will ultimately benefit from their attendance?

3. What support might you seek from the principal in communicating with families?

Working through Cultural and Language Differences

An increasing number of students are from culturally and linguistically diverse families. It is imperative that you make adjustments in how you approach and interact with the families to develop successful home–school communication and partnerships (Grant & Ray, 2009):

myeducationlab

Go to MyEducationLab, select the topic **Diversity: Cultural and Linguistic,** click "videos," and select "Incorporating the Home Experiences of Culturally Diverse Students." View the video and reflect.

1. *Learn about the cultures of the families of students.* Information is available about families of different cultures. For example, Lynch and Hanson (2004) provide detailed cultural descriptions on families with Anglo American, American Indian, African American, Latino, Asian, Filipino, and Middle Eastern roots. *Involving Latino Families in Schools* (Gaitan, 2005), *Teaching Hispanic Children* (Jones & Fuller, 2003), and *Educating Immigrant Students in the Twenty-First Century* (Rong & Preissle, 2009) are examples of books addressing specialized cultures.

2. *Acknowledge and adapt to cultural differences in social etiquette and ways of communicating and expressing respect.* If you do not speak the same language as the family, your nonverbal messages become more important. Use positive body language

when you meet family members at an open house or other school event. Greeting families at the door, for example, expresses respect. Any notes, letters, or newsletters sent home should be translated into the home language.

3. *Have early and frequent teacher–family contacts.* Initiate positive home–school contact and dialogue by chatting, making phone calls and home visits, talking with community workers, and arranging for afternoon homework help or tutoring to promote student success.

4. *Provide families with information about the school.* Keep families informed (in the home language, if possible) about important classroom, school, and community events, help available in the school or from community-based organizations, and sources of academic support. Communicate through student-produced newsletters, telephone calls, and other notices. Provide materials in the home language.

5. *Encourage family participation at the school and in the home.* Encourage and welcome families to come to school meetings and social events and even to come to the classroom. Encourage family members to come to class to share skills or to discuss their culture. Provide suggestions for ways families can enable their students' learning by supporting homework and creating a positive learning environment at home.

6. *Adjust how you conduct family–teacher conferences.* Schedule a time for the conference that is convenient for family members, and show them a portfolio of the student's successes. By also including the student, this three-way conference can promote a dialogue about schooling. The use of an interpreter is sometimes necessary, and this shows respect for the home language of the family. Watch for any facial expressions, voice intonations, and body movements to extend communication (Diaz-Rico, 2008).

CONTACTING AND COMMUNICATING WITH FAMILIES

As discussed previously, there are several reasons for working with families. The timing of the contact will depend on the reason for it. There are three points to consider when contacting families:

1. *Initial contact with all families* should occur at the start of the year. This contact should be designed to inform families about the academic program, grading guidelines, the homework policy, rules and procedures, and other academic and behavioral expectations. Requests for additional classroom supplies and for volunteers for activities are generally made at this time. You can make these contacts through an introductory letter, a newsletter, Back-to-School Night, or other means.

2. *Ongoing contact with all families* occurs throughout the year to provide information about content being covered in class, the schedule for tests or other evaluation requirements, field trips, the progress of the students, and so on. You may need additional volunteers throughout the year and may contact family members at various times as the need arises. These ongoing contacts can be made through a newsletter or information sheet, an open house, report cards, or other means.

3. *Contact with selected families* needs to occur to inform them about unique concerns about their child's progress. These contacts may occur when there is either positive or negative news to report. You will often contact families when there is a problem, yet it is easy to overlook contacting them when there is good news to report. Families especially appreciate reports of good news. If a problem arises later, they are often more willing to support and cooperate with the teacher. Guidebooks are available for advice on working with parents of students with special needs (e.g., Dardig, 2008) and even for working with parents of bullies and victims (e.g., Roberts, 2008).

Ways to Communicate with Families

There are many ways to communicate with families, and the method may be affected by its purpose. To discuss a serious act of misbehavior, for example, you would probably not wait for a parent–teacher conference scheduled at the end of a report-card period to contact the family but would likely call them immediately.

Much communication with families occurs at the start of the year in the form of an introductory letter, a letter about classroom management and discipline, a Back-to-School Night, and information sheets. Ongoing communication may be through an open house, newsletters, notes and letters, phone calls, special events and informal contacts, sending home student work, report cards, home visits, and parent–teacher conferences. To contact a family about their child's academic work or behavior, you could call them or arrange for a special conference.

Figure 13.1 is a summary of the ways to communicate with families that are discussed in the following sections.

Introductory Letter.   Teachers sometimes send an *introductory letter* home with the students to give to their parents during the first week of school prior to the Back-to-School Night. This letter is intended to serve as a brief welcome to the new year, include some

---

FIGURE 13.1   **Ways to Communicate with Families**

1. Introductory letter
2. Letter about classroom management and discipline
3. Back-to-School Night
4. Information sheets
5. Open houses
6. Newsletters
7. Assignment sheets
8. Individual notes and letters
9. Phone calls
10. Websites and e-mail
11. Special events and informal contacts
12. Sending home student work
13. Report cards
14. Home visits
15. Parent–teacher conferences

Voices from the Classroom

Introductory Letter to Families

Sherry Bryant, middle school social studies teacher, Rochester, New Hampshire

Have a letter ready to send home with the students on the first day of school to introduce yourself to parents and explain your goals for the year. Ask for parental support. Have them discuss with their child the goals, when and where they will do homework, and other aspects of the schoolwork. Explain to parents that they are their child's main educators. Discuss the importance of their role in their child's life, and mention that you value them. Ask the parents to fill out a questionnaire that will help you know what the parents' hopes are for their child. Give your phone number. Let the parents know that you welcome their calls, and let them know that you want to work with them so that this is a good year for their child.

basic information about the class, and invite family members to the Back-to-School Night that will soon follow.

The letter may include some information about the schedule, homework, absences, and the curriculum. You may mention in the letter that more will be said about these and other issues at the Back-to-School Night. A sample introductory letter to families is displayed in Figure 13.2. You can adapt this letter for your particular situation.

Letter on Classroom Management and Discipline.   You need to share your plan for classroom management and discipline with the families and the principal. If you expect them to be involved when you need them, they need to know that you have a plan and to be aware of your rationale for rules, positive recognition, and consequences.

At the start of the schoolyear, you need to discuss rules, consequences, and other aspects of management with the students. A copy of this information sheet should be given to the students to take home to their parents. The letter should provide details of the classroom management and discipline plan and explain why it is important. Ask the parents to discuss the plan with their children, sign the plan, and return the signature portion to you. A sample letter to parents on classroom management and discipline is displayed in Figure 13.3. You may adapt that letter for your particular situation.

If the Back-to-School Night is scheduled early in the year, you may ask the families to return the signature portion at that time. Or you may prefer to wait and present the letter to the families at the Back-to-School Night and get the signatures at that time. Letters can then be sent home to families who did not attend that evening.

Back-to-School Night.   Many schools schedule a *Back-to-School Night* or Family Night during the first or second week so families can receive information about the academic program, grading guidelines, the homework policy, rules and procedures, and other expectations. Requests for additional classroom supplies and for volunteers for activities are generally made at this time.

FIGURE 13.2   **Sample Introductory Letter to Families**

September 4

Dear Parents:

Now that the schoolyear has begun, I'd like to introduce myself. I am Melissa Riley, and I am your child's ninth-grade algebra teacher this year. I have taught in this school district for 14 years, and have taught pre-algebra, algebra, geometry, and trigonometry. I completed my undergraduate work at the University of Illinois and my master's degree at Kansas State University.

I want this to be a successful schoolyear for you and your child. To ensure this success, it is important that we maintain open communication. Please do not hesitate to contact me if you have any questions or concerns. You can call me at school after dismissal between 3:30–4:30 p.m. at 555-7308. Or you can call anytime during the day and leave a message for me to call you back. My e-mail address is mriley@hotmail.com.

At various times throughout the schoolyear, I will be sending a newsletter home with your child to provide information about classroom activities and special events. On a regular basis, your child will bring home graded assignments for you to look at. I also look forward to seeing you at the conference session, which we schedule at the end of each report-card period.

The annual Back-to-School Night for this school is scheduled for next Thursday, September 12, from 7:30–9:15 p.m. On that evening, you will have the opportunity to go through your child's schedule of classes in shortened 10-minute class periods. When you meet me during algebra class, I will share information about the curriculum, my approach to instruction, my academic expectations and procedures, my policy on discipline, and other issues. The books and materials that we will be using this year will also be on display. I encourage you to attend the Back-to-School Night because it will give you an opportunity to understand the mathematics program and become better acquainted with me.

Working together and keeping in good contact, I'm confident that this will be an exciting and successful schoolyear. I look forward to meeting you at the Back-to-School Night.

Sincerely,

Melissa Riley

Melissa Riley

Some schools do not schedule a Back-to-School Night, or if they do, it comes later than the first or second week of school. Given this, you may find other ways to communicate with families, since it is important to establish contact as early as possible. For example, a letter about classroom management and discipline might be expanded to include information that is commonly covered at a Back-to-School Night.

FIGURE 13.3 **Sample Letter to Families on Classroom Management and Discipline**

Dear Parents:

Now that the schoolyear has begun, I'd like to introduce myself and give you some information about how I conduct my classes. My name is Keith McKinsey, and I am your child's fifth-grade teacher. I have taught in this school district for eight years. I completed my undergraduate work at Florida State University and my master's degree at Kansas State University.

To maintain an appropriate learning environment, I have established the following classroom rules, which all students are expected to follow:

1. Follow the teacher's directions.
2. Keep your hands, feet, and objects to yourself.
3. Do not swear or tease.

To encourage students to follow the rules, I will recognize appropriate behavior with praise, various types of reinforcement, and notes or calls home to you. If students choose to break the rules, I have established an escalating series of responses ranging from gentle prompts and reminders, to the use of logical consequences, and to detention. In class, we have discussed these rules, the reinforcement for following the rules, and the consequences if the students choose to break the rules. My goal is to ensure success for your child. Working together, I'm confident that it will be an enjoyable and productive schoolyear.

Please indicate that you understand this discipline plan by signing your name below and indicating the phone numbers where you can be reached during the day and evening. You might also discuss the rules to make sure your child understands them.

Please do not hesitate to contact me if you have any questions or concerns. You can call me at school after dismissal between 3:30–4:30 p.m. at 555-6188. Or you can call anytime during the day and leave a message for me to call you back. My e-mail address is kkeith@hotmail.com.

Sincerely,

Keith McKinsey

Keith McKinsey

(Tear off and return the part below to Mr. McKinsey)

- -

I have read and understand Mr. McKinsey's classroom management plan, and I have discussed it with my child.

Parent/Guardian Signature _____   Date _____

Comments:

The scheduling of the Back-to-School Night is handled in different ways. For middle, junior high, and senior high schools, families are often given their child's schedule, and they follow it just as the student would but in shortened class sessions of 10 to 15 minutes. In this way, the family sees every teacher in the way that their child would during the schoolday. Teachers often use this time to present information to families about academic and behavioral guidelines and expectations.

Preparing for Back-to-School Night.   Back-to-School Night is often your first contact with families, so thorough preparation is necessary. There are many ways to prepare for this evening:

- *Prepare your own introductory letter to families about the Back-to-School Night in your classroom.* (See the sample introductory letter that mentions Back-to-School Night in Figure 13.2.) Do not rely only on notices that the school sends home. Some teachers like to have their students prepare special invitations for their own families.

- *Make sure that the classroom looks attractive and neat.* Post your name and room number prominently on the door and the front chalkboard. Display samples of work by all students. Display copies of the textbooks and other instructional materials.

- *Prepare a list of any instructional supplies or materials that families might be able to provide.* This list will vary depending on the subject and grade level. It may include items such as rulers, buttons, a box of facial tissue, or other supplies. Have enough copies of the list to give to all families.

- *Prepare separate sign-up sheets for families.* These may concern the need for a private follow-up conference about their child, volunteers to help at special events such as field trips, volunteers such as guest speakers in class, or volunteers to provide various instructional supplies requested by the teacher.

- *Plan a well-organized, succinct presentation.* Families want to hear about your background and experience, behavioral and academic expectations, procedures for issues such as homework and absences, and other policies. Be sure to plan for time at the end of the presentation for questions.

- *Prepare handouts for your presentation.* Families will receive these handouts at the Back-to-School Night. Have enough copies of this material to give to all of them. A sample content outline of the presentation is shown in Figure 13.4. Your handout should include details about issues such as those listed in that figure. On the front page of the handout, include your name, the school phone number, and the times that you can be reached at the school at that phone number. Attach other related materials to this handout; these materials may include a sheet showing the daily or weekly class schedule, a sheet of needed instructional materials and supplies, or a sheet concerning the classroom management and discipline policy. To simplify distribution, staple all the handouts together as one set of materials sequenced in the order that you will cover the material during the presentation.

FIGURE 13.4   Sample Content Outline for the Back-to-School Night Presentation

1. **Background about yourself**
   a. College training and degrees earned
   b. Professional experience, including length of teaching service, grade levels taught, where taught
   c. Personal information (e.g., family, hobbies, special interests or experiences)
2. **The curriculum, academic goals, and activities**
   a. Overview of the curriculum and the topics to be covered (refer to the textbooks and related instructional materials on display in the room)
   b. Your approach to instruction
   c. Instructional activities and any special events, such as field trips or unique programs
3. **Academic expectations and procedures**
   a. Grading guidelines and procedures (how grades are determined)
   b. Grading requirements (e.g., tests, quizzes, homework, projects)
   c. Homework (purposes, how often, makeup policy, absences)
   d. When report cards are delivered
   e. Parent–teacher conferences
4. **Discipline**
   a. Classroom rules
   b. Positive rewards
   c. Consequences for breaking the rules
   d. Incremental steps taken when misbehavior continues
   e. When parents will be contacted
   f. Parents need to sign the sheet concerning the classroom management and discipline policy
5. **Ask families to sign up for selected issues**
   a. For a private follow-up conference about their child
   b. For parent volunteers for providing instructional materials and supplies
   c. For parent volunteers to help at special events such as field trips
   d. For parent volunteers such as guest speakers in class
6. **Express an interest to hear any ideas and concerns from families at any time**
7. **Allow time for questions at the end of the session** (save several minutes if possible)

Conduct the Back-to-School Night.   Take several guidelines into account when conducting the Back-to-School Night. Since your presentation is usually limited, possibly to only 10 to 15 minutes, it is important to plan how to conduct yourself.

Greet families at the door, introduce yourself, and ask them to be seated. Begin your presentation using the handout that you previously prepared concerning your background, the daily and weekly schedule, the curriculum, academic goals and activities, academic expectations and procedures, discipline, and other issues. At the start, hand a copy of the handout to each family member.

Have parents sign up for individual follow-up conferences if they want to talk with you at length about their child. Back-to-School Night is not intended to deal with concerns about individual students. Allow time for family members to ask questions. This will be an opportunity for you to provide clarification about issues and to hear families' concerns.

Information Sheets.   Not all schools schedule a Back-to-School Night, and not all families attend a scheduled night. In both cases, you can prepare a packet to send home that provides information about the curriculum, grading expectations and requirements, rules and procedures, the discipline plan, and other matters. The sheets may be the same as those given to families who attend the Back-to-School Night or shortened versions.

Open Houses.   Once or twice a year, most schools schedule an open house for families to visit the classrooms during a particular evening to see their child's teacher, observe the classroom and samples of student work, and learn about books and materials being used. Some districts do not have a Back-to-School Night but instead schedule the first open house in mid to late September. At open house, teachers may give a formal presentation about the program, or schools may allow families to drop in at any time during open house to informally discuss issues with the teacher.

Since open houses are conducted well into the schoolyear, materials and projects that students have prepared can be displayed. A science fair, for example, may be scheduled at the same time as an open house to provide an opportunity for families to see students' science displays. Since some of the families attending the open house may not have attended the Back-to-School Night, it is often useful to have extra copies of the handout provided at the Back-to-School Night to describe your policies.

Newsletters.   A newsletter periodically sent to all families contains information about special events, content to be covered in the curriculum, tests or quizzes that are coming up, student projects, and other issues. Newsletters may be as brief as one page or longer, according to need. You can report accomplishments of the class and of individual students. Computers can be used to prepare the newsletters. Students can prepare the newsletter as a group or class project, under suitable circumstances.

Assignment Sheets.   Another way to communicate with families is through an assignment sheet, which describes the assignments for the next week or two. Students are asked to show it to their parents. Some teachers may prefer that the parents sign the sheet and have it returned to school. This makes students fully aware of what needs to be turned in for evaluation, and they can make needed arrangements in their schedules. The parents also are aware of what is happening.

What Would You Decide?   *Communicating with Families*

Sending notes or letters home to families is one way to communicate with them.

1. What types of information might you convey in the notes or letters?
2. What guidelines will you establish for yourself about the content, the writing form, the frequency, and other factors?

3. How might you modify your procedures if a number of parents have limited English proficiency or several ethnic groups are represented?

Individual Notes and Letters.   Notes and letters are written to individual parents to discuss some particular issue about their child. You can use them to request that a conference be arranged with you, to invite family members to class functions, to inform them about their child's work, or to offer suggestions.

Notes should be carefully written. They should be free of errors in spelling, grammar, and sentence structure. Furthermore, they should be brief, clear, honest, and factual. Educational jargon should not be used. Notes and letters are especially useful for contacting families who are hard to reach by telephone.

Make sure that you address the letter with the correct names, since the parent and child may not have the same last name. If the family does not read English, try to take steps to write the letter or note in their native language. Avoid writing a letter when you are upset about a classroom event; calm down first. Try to end with a positive statement about working together for the benefit of the child.

Be cautious about sending notes home to families only when there is bad news to deliver. Certainly, there are times when such notes need to be sent. You should also send notes home to families with good news about the child's academic work or behavior. Brief, positive notes take only a few minutes to write to express pleasure about the child's performance. By systematically writing one or two notes to different parents each day, you will provide good news and help build positive relationships with them. Parents will usually talk with their child about the note, and the child may come to school the next day with a more positive attitude.

Phone Calls.   Like notes and letters, telephone calls are made to families to discuss a particular issue. The phone call could request that a conference be arranged with you, invite the family to class functions, inform them about their child's work, or offer suggestions. As with notes and letters, be cautious about calling families only when you have bad news. Also call them when there is good news to report.

Phone calls can be quite brief, because you need to have only two or three positive statements to share. They are not intended to be lengthy discussions about students. The parents should be asked to tell the child about the phone call.

There are times when you need to contact the family about the child's misbehavior. You need to plan ahead before making the call. The call should begin with a statement of concern, such as "Mrs. Erickson, I care about Kristina and I feel that her behavior in the classroom is not in her best interest." You then should describe the specific problem and present any pertinent documentation. You should go on to describe what you are doing and have done to deal with the misbehavior. At this point, it is helpful to invite the family's input by asking questions such as "Has Kristina had similar problems in the past? Why do you think she is having these problems at school? Is there something going on at home that could be affecting her behavior?"

It is then useful to get input about how to solve the problem. State what you will do to help solve the problem, and explain what you want the parent to do. Before ending the telephone conversation, you should let the family know that you are confident that the problem can be worked out and tell them that there will be follow-up contact from you. Then recap the conversation.

Making "Good News" Phone Calls to Families

Bernadette Hampton, high school mathematics teacher, Beaufort, South Carolina

To build positive relationships with parents and students, I call home for the top three students after a quiz or a test. I do this to encourage and motivate the student to excel. You can also select other criteria for the phone calls, such as most improved, most creative, or others to include most students over time.

Parents are often surprised to receive this phone call, especially when they usually receive phone calls with negative news. Students return to school with much appreciation for the good news call. The student's self-esteem is increased, and support is gained from the parent. If I need to call the parent about difficult behavior or another troublesome issue, I then have the support of the parent. The "good news" phone calls help me develop a positive relationship with the parents as well as the students.

Websites and E-Mail.   Many schools have websites, and these may include links to a website for each teacher in the school. In these cases, teachers can place information on the site to communicate to students and families about homework, class projects, grading policies, and many other issues.

As computer use has become more common, many families have e-mail capability. Teachers can provide students and families with their e-mail addresses to open this type of communication. Families can contact the teacher with questions or comments through e-mail, and teachers can report student progress and other information to parents through e-mail.

Special Events and Informal Contacts.   Throughout the year, teachers and families may attend many special events. These may include sporting events, concerts, plays, carnivals, craft displays, and others. Contacts with family members at these events may provide brief opportunities to share a few words about their child's work. These contacts are especially useful as progress reports and as a means of discussing a particular issue.

Sending Home Student Work.   You can inform families about their child's academic progress by sending home completed and graded student work. They can see what you have covered, the child's work, and any notes or remarks you have made.

Sending home only completed worksheets may not be very enlightening for families. It is useful to send home a variety of materials, including worksheets, tests, quizzes, homework, projects, lab reports, writing samples, artwork, and other types of student products. Be sensitive about notes or remarks you place on the papers. These

SPOTLIGHT on Technology

Using Technology for Communication

Increasingly, schools are using computer technology and webpages to make information available to parents, students, and the public. Webpage information about the school might include the school calendar; directories for teachers, administrators, and the staff; school policies; special events; and other information. Some schools make provisions so that each teacher has a webpage for use for his or her classroom. Teachers may post their syllabi, rules and procedures, notices about special events, listing of assignments or homework, Web links to useful resources, and much more.

In addition, e-mail may be provided, opening up the capability to communicate within the school and also to students and families at their homes.

1. If you had a webpage available for your use for your classroom, how might you use it? What information might you post?
2. When considering e-mail, what types of communication might you consider with students and families? What provisions for communication will you make for families that do not have Internet access?

---

notes are evaluative statements, but they should also include comments about good points and improvement as well as about areas still needing attention.

Papers that are sent home with students to show their parents may not even get home, and those that do get home may not be shown to the parents. To overcome these problems, you might devise various ways to have parents sign a sheet to indicate that they have seen the material. For example, a parent response sheet might list the material being sent home, with a blank space for parents to sign and date. The student then returns the response sheet to you.

Report Cards.   Families are informed of their child's academic performance when report cards are distributed. Most report cards have an area where you can either write a statement or indicate a code for a statement concerning effort and citizenship. As with notes, letters, and phone calls, you should be cautious about making only negative notes on report cards. Deserving students should receive positive notes.

When warranted, include notes on the report card to indicate the need to improve. Families may call teachers shortly after report cards have been delivered if they have any question about them. Have documentation ready to justify what you have noted.

Home Visits.   Another means for personal contact with families is through home visits, especially for families who are reluctant to visit the school. This type of communication is not as popular as it once was due to changing social conditions and concerns about safety to the visiting teachers. Nevertheless, home visits allow you to inform the family about the academic program and the child's progress. You may choose to make home visits to those families who did not attend the Back-to-School Night or parent–teacher conferences. The handout prepared for the Back-to-School Night could be given to these families. Visiting the student's home gives you insight into the family environment.

Some school districts have a home-visitation coordinator or a parent educator who is responsible for regularly visiting students' homes to discuss the child's progress in school, important events in the family's life, and ways families can support and extend their child's learning.

It is important to know the community before making home visits because of concerns about safety. When the visits may prove beneficial, two teachers may visit the student's home together, or a teacher and a security guard may make the visit.

Classroom Case Study

Working with Colleagues and Families

Hui Chen is an eighth-grade mathematics teacher at a middle school. At a grade-level team meeting about six months into the schoolyear, Ms. Chen and her colleagues discussed issues of concern. They noted that one of their students, Miranda, had been struggling in all of her classes all year. Miranda was on the verge of failing three of these classes, and she would likely have to repeat the eighth grade unless her performance improved. Even when the teachers had discussed Miranda in previous team meetings, they had agreed that her poor organizational and study skills contributed to her current academic standing.

Ms. Chen and her colleagues scheduled a student–teacher meeting with Miranda, where they discussed ways to improve her organizational and study skills. Miranda was given a booklet to record her homework assignments, and she was encouraged to attend after-school homework sessions. Despite these efforts, Miranda continued to struggle in all of her classes, and her grades worsened. After determining that Miranda was on the verge of being held back, Ms. Chen and her colleagues decided to contact Miranda's family.

When Ms. Chen telephoned Miranda's family, the conversation was tension filled and awkward. Miranda's parents were frustrated that they had not been contacted sooner. They stated that Miranda had never performed at the top of her class but that she always earned passing marks. Even though Ms. Chen attempted to address the issues and schedule a meeting about the concerns, Miranda's parents refused and declared that they would go straight to the school administration to discuss their daughter's situation.

Focus Questions

1. What errors did the teachers make in handling the situation with Miranda?
2. How could the teachers have handled the situation differently to establish better communication and collaboration with Miranda's parents from the start?

Parent–Teacher Conferences

Another important way of communicating with families is through *parent–teacher con-ferences* to report information about progress, academic performance, or behavior. Many school districts schedule a day or two at the end of each report-card period for parent–teacher conferences so parents can meet individually with the teachers. Confer-ence days are typically scheduled only for elementary grades; all parents are invited to attend these individually scheduled conferences.

Many middle schools, junior high schools, and high schools do not schedule parent–teacher conferences but instead arrange for a block of time on one day at the end of the report-card period for families to visit with each teacher on a drop-in basis. The ways to prepare for and conduct this session will be somewhat different than that used at the elementary level, but the general principles discussed here for preparing for this contact still apply.

In addition to the conferences conducted at the end of report-card periods, parent–teacher conferences are held with particular parents as the need warrants. When a student persistently misbehaves or has academic problems, you may ask the family of that child to come to the school for a conference. Prior to having such a conference, you may want to meet with the student to work out a plan to address the problem. If this meeting with the student does not lead to resolution, then a meeting with the family is warranted, and the student may be asked to also attend.

To have effective parent–teacher conferences, teachers should thoroughly prepare for the conference, take certain actions when conducting the conference, and provide appropriate follow-up. Guidelines discussed in the following sections center primarily on parent–teacher conferences to address academic issues. These guidelines would need to be adapted somewhat to address individually scheduled parent–teacher confer-ences concerning academic or disciplinary issues.

Preparing for the Conference.   Preparation for a drop-in conference with the family at the end of the report-card period will be different from preparation for an individu-ally scheduled parent–teacher conference. Administrators in middle schools, junior high schools, and high schools commonly take steps to inform families about the day and time for the drop-in conferences at the end of the report-card periods. Since these teachers have responsibility for many students, it is usually not feasible to have sample materials available for all of them. Instead, teachers often have the gradebook on hand along with sample tests, quizzes, homework, and projects that students have completed throughout the marking period.

If an individual parent–teacher conference is needed, the teacher often calls the family to select a day and time. Before the conference, the teacher may gather pertinent materials about the student and the situation. If it is an academic issue, the teacher may collect the gradebook and a sample of work done by the student, including tests, proj-ects, and homework to be shown to the family during the conference. If it is a behavioral issue, anecdotal record sheets and other documentation may be gathered.

Whether for a drop-in conference at the end of the report-card period or for an in-dividually scheduled conference, the physical environment needs to be prepared for the session. You can arrange for these materials: (a) a table for the conference, (b) three or four adult-sized chairs for the table, and (c) a clean, tidy room.

Conducting the Conference.   Discussion and questions in the conference should be sequenced to develop rapport, obtain information from the family, provide information to them, and summarize follow-up. The following guidelines include a technique to sandwich your main messages between good news or positive statements at the start and at the end of the conference. The parents who hear good comments at the start will be in a comfortable frame of mind. As the conference comes to a close, it is useful to summarize your main points and then conclude with additional positive statements.

Consider these guidelines:

1. *Begin the conference in a positive manner.* Walk up to the parents, introduce yourself, and welcome them into the room. Start the conference with a positive statement about the student, such as "Emily really enjoys providing leadership for students in her small group when working on projects."

2. *Present the student's strong points before describing the matters needing improvement.* Highlight the student's strengths as you move into a discussion about his or her performance. Show samples of the student's work to the family. Later, identify matters that need further improvement.

3. *Encourage the family to participate and share information.* Allow opportunities to ask questions and share information about the student. Pose questions to parents at various points of the conference to encourage their input.

4. *Plan a course of action cooperatively.* If the student needs to work on a particular issue, discuss the possible actions that you or the parents could take. Come to agreement about the course of action that each of you will take.

5. *End the conference with a positive comment.* Thank the family for coming, and say something positive about the student at the end of the conference.

6. *Use good human relations skills during the conference.* To be effective, you should be friendly and informal, positive in your approach, willing to explain in understandable terms, willing to listen, willing to accept parents' feelings, and careful about giving advice. You should avoid arguing and getting angry; asking embarrassing questions; talking about other students, teachers, or families; bluffing if you do not know an answer; rejecting parents' suggestions; and being a "know it all" with pat answers (Miller, Linn, & Gronlund, 2009).

Handling Conference Follow-Up.   During the conference, it is useful to make a list of follow-up actions. These actions may include providing more thorough feedback to the student during the next marking period, recommending additional readings to some students, providing certain families with periodic updates on their child's performance, or a host of others. It is important to follow up in the ways that were identified during the parent–teacher conference.

Key Terms

Back-to-School Night
Introductory letter

Parent
Parent–teacher conferences

Major Concepts

1. Teachers often need to turn to others for assistance when dealing with problems about student behavior, reading or language, media and instructional technology, students with special needs, curricular issues, instructional strategies, and numerous other issues.

2. Teachers work with families to (a) understand the student's home condition; (b) inform parents of academic expectations and events as well as student performance; (c) enlist family members' help with academic issues; (d) inform them of disciplinary expectations and actions; and (e) enlist their help in dealing with their children.

3. Families' resistance may be due to (a) their unhappy experiences when they were students; (b) their coping mechanisms in dealing with ongoing problems with their children; (c) their view that educators are the experts; or (d) their intimidation by the school and the bureaucracy.

4. To accommodate differences in culture and language, teachers must adjust how they approach and interact with families to develop successful home–school communication and partnerships.

5. The timing of the contact with the family will be determined by the reason for the contact. The three main points of family contact are (a) initial contacts with all families at the start of the schoolyear; (b) ongoing contacts with all families throughout the schoolyear; and (c) contact with selected families concerning their child's academic or behavioral progress.

6. Initial communication with the family occurs at the start of the schoolyear in the form of an introductory letter, a letter about classroom management and discipline, a Back-to-School Night, or information sheets.

7. Ongoing communication throughout the schoolyear may occur with an open house, newsletters, notes and letters, phone calls, special events, informal contacts, sending home student work, report cards, home visits, and parent–teacher conferences.

8. To contact individual families about their child's academic work or behavior, teachers often call the parents and sometimes arrange for a special parent–teacher conference to address the issues.

Discussion/Reflective Questions

1. How might information about a student's home condition help you as a teacher decide on an appropriate course of action with him or her? How might this information create some problems for you?

2. When is an appropriate point to contact the family if a student is exhibiting mild misbehavior? Moderate misbehavior?

3. In what ways did your teachers in the middle and secondary grades contact and interact with your family?

4. What are some ways that teachers can communicate with families about academic expectations and events?

5. How can you communicate with families who do not show up for Back-to-School Night or parent–teacher conferences?

Suggested Activities

For Clinical Settings

1. Prepare an introductory letter that you might send to families at the start of the schoolyear.
2. Assume that you will send four newsletters to families during the schoolyear. For each newsletter, select the month it will be sent and list the type of content that you might report in it. (Would you have regular features in each newsletter? What content might be unique to each issue?)
3. Prepare a letter that you might send to families prior to a parent–teacher conference.

For Field Experiences

1. Talk with several teachers about experiences they have had with families who resist involvement. How did these teachers still communicate with these families? What suggestions do they offer?
2. Ask several teachers to describe the ways that they prepare for and conduct the Back-to-School Night. What recommendations do they have to aid your preparation?
3. Talk with several teachers about their experiences preparing for and conducting parent–teacher conferences. What suggestions do they offer for your handling of the conferences?

Further Reading

Canter, L., & Canter, M. (2001). *Parents on your side: A teacher's guide to creating positive relationships with parents* (2nd ed.). Bloomington, IN: Solution Tree.

Provides thorough, practical guidance about ways to communicate, establish positive relationships, and solve problems that may occur.

Diffily, D. (2004). *Teachers and families working together.* Boston: Allyn & Bacon.

Discusses strategies to communicate with and involve families, types of families, and barriers and benefits of family involvement.

Stein, J., Meltzer, L., Krishnan, K., Pollica, L. S., Papadopoulos, I., & Roditi, B. (2007). *Parent guide to hassle-free homework.* New York: Scholastic.

Offers guidance about the home study environment, ways to support the child, motivation, and communicating with the teacher.

Trumbull, E., Rothstein-Fisch, C., Greenfield, P. M., & Quiroz, B. (2001). *Bridging cultures between home and school: A guide for teachers.* Mahwah, NJ: Lawrence Erlbaum Associates.

Includes guidance for parent and family involvement, with special emphasis on addressing the cultural differences that may exist between the educators and the parents.

References

Airasian, P. W., & Russell, M. (2008). *Classroom assessment.* (6th ed.). New York: McGraw-Hill.

Allen, M. (2003). *Eight questions on teacher preparation: What does the research say?* Denver: Education Commission of the States.

American Association for the Advancement of Science. (1993). *Benchmarks for science literacy: Project 2061.* New York: Oxford University Press.

Anderson, L. W., & Krathwohl, D. R. (Eds.). (2001). *A taxonomy for learning, teaching, and assessing: A revision of Bloom's taxonomy of educational objectives.* Boston: Allyn & Bacon.

Arends, R. I. (2007). *Learning to teach* (7th ed.). New York: McGraw-Hill.

Ashbaker, B. Y., & Morgan, J. (2006). *Paraprofessionals in the classroom.* Boston: Allyn & Bacon.

August, D., & Shanahan, T. (Eds.). (2006). *Developing literacy in second-language learners: A report of the National Literacy Panel on Language-Minority Children and Youth.* Mahwah, NJ: Erlbaum.

Auwarter, A., & Aruguete, M. (2008). Effects of student gender and socioeconomic status on teacher perceptions. *Journal of Educational Research, 101*(4), 242–246.

Banks, J. A. (2006). *Cultural diversity and education: Foundations, curriculum, and teaching* (5th ed.). Boston: Allyn & Bacon.

Banks, J. A. (2007). Approaches to multicultural curriculum reform. In J. A. Banks & C. A. M. Banks (Eds.), *Multicultural education: Issues and perspectives* (6th ed.) (pp. 242–261). New York: John Wiley & Sons.

Barbour, C., Barbour, N. H., & Scully, P. A. (2008). *Families, schools, and communities: Building partnerships for educating children* (4th ed.). Upper Saddle River, NJ: Pearson/Prentice Hall.

Bellanca, J. (2007). *A guide to graphic organizers* (2nd ed.). Thousand Oaks, CA: Corwin Press.

Berger, E. H. (2008). *Parents as partners in education: Families and schools working together* (7th ed.). Upper Saddle River, NJ: Merrill/Prentice Hall.

Berk, L. (2008). *Infants and children* (6th ed.). Boston: Allyn & Bacon.

Berk, L. (2007). *Development through the lifespan* (4th ed.). Boston: Allyn & Bacon.

Bloom, B. S. (1981). *All our children learning.* New York: McGraw-Hill.

Bloom, B. S. (1982). *Human interactions and school learning.* New York: McGraw-Hill.

Bloom, B. S. (Ed.). (1984). *Taxonomy of educational objectives. Handbook I: Cognitive domain.* New York: Longman. (Originally published in 1956)

Bomer, R., Dworin, J. E., May, L., & Semingson, P. (2008). Miseducating teachers about the poor: A critical analysis of Ruby Payne's claims about poverty. *Teachers College Record, 110*(11). Retrieved July 30, 2008, from www.tcrecord.org/PrintContent.asp?ContentID=14591

Books, S. (2004). *Poverty and schooling in the U.S.: Contexts and consequences.* Mahwah, NJ: Erlbaum.

Borich, G. (2007). *Effective teaching methods* (6th ed.). Upper Saddle River, NJ: Merrill/Prentice Hall.

Bosch, K. A., & Kersey, K. C. (2000). *The first-year teacher: Teaching with confidence (K–8)* (rev. ed.). Washington, DC: National Education Association.

Brophy, J. (2010). *Motivating students to learn* (3rd ed.). New York: Routledge.

Bruner, J. S. (1966). *Toward a theory of instruction.* Cambridge, MA: Harvard University Press.

Burden, P. R. (2000). *Powerful classroom management strategies: Motivating students to learn.* Thousand Oaks, CA: Corwin Press.

Burden, P. R. (2010). *Classroom management: Creating a successful K–12 learning community* (4th ed.). New York: John Wiley & Sons.

Burke, K. (2005). *How to assess authentic learning* (4th ed.). Thousand Oaks, CA: Corwin Press.

Burke, K. (2008). *What to do with the kid who . . . : Developing cooperation, self-discipline, and responsibility in the classroom* (3rd ed.).Thousand Oaks, CA: Corwin Press.

Butler, S. M., & McMunn, N. D. (2006). *A teacher's guide to classroom assessment: Understanding and using assessment to improve student learning.* San Francisco: Jossey-Bass.

Byrd, D. M., Foxx, S., & Stepp, S. L. (1990, April). *Journal writing: An analysis of levels of reflection.* Paper presented at the annual meeting of the American Educational Research Association, Boston.

California Department of Education. (2000). *Classroom management: A California resource guide.* Sacramento, CA: Author.

California Department of Education. (2004). *Statewide Stanford 9 test results for reading: Number of students tested and percent scoring at or above the 50th percentile.* Retrieved Feb. 23, 2004, from www.dq.cde.ca.gov/dataquest

Campbell, A., & Fairbairn, G. (2005). *Working with support in the classroom.* Thousand Oaks, CA: Sage.

Campbell, B. (2008). *Handbook of differentiated instruction using the multiple intelligences.* Upper Saddle River, NJ: Pearson/Prentice-Hall.

Campbell, L., Campbell, B., & Dickinson, D. (2004). *Teaching and learning through multiple intelligences* (3rd ed.). Boston: Allyn & Bacon.

Canter, L., & Canter, M. (2001). *Parents on your side: A teacher's guide to creating positive relationships with parents* (2nd ed.). Bloomington, IN: Solution Tree.

Capps, R., Fix, M., Murray, J., Passel, J. S., & Herwantoro, S. (2005). *The new demography of America's schools: Immigration and the No Child Left Behind Act.* Washington, DC: Urban Institute.

Carey, L. M. (2006). *Measuring and evaluating school learning* (4th ed.). Boston: Pearson Custom.

Center for Applied Special Technology. (2008). *Universal design for learning guidelines.* Wakefield, MA: Author. Retrieved July 30, 2008, from www.cast.org/publications/UDLguidelines/version1.html

Chamot, A. U., & O'Malley, J. M. (1994). *The CALLA handbook: Implementing the cognitive academic language learning approach.* Reading, MA: Addison-Wesley.

Charles, C. M. (2008). *Building classroom discipline* (9th ed.). Boston: Allyn & Bacon.

Chuska, K. R. (2003). *Improving classroom questions: A teacher's guide to increasing student motivation, participation, and higher-level thinking* (2nd ed.). Bloomington, IN: Phi Delta Kappa.

Clark, C. M., & Yinger, R. J. (1987). Teacher planning. In D. C. Berliner & B. V. Rosenshine (Eds.), *Talks to teachers* (pp. 342–365). New York: Random House.

Cooper, H. M. (2007). *The battle over homework: Common ground for administrators, teachers, and parents* (3rd ed.). Thousand Oaks, CA: Corwin Press.

Cooper, J. M. (2006). *Classroom teaching skills* (8th ed.). Boston: Houghton Mifflin.

Council for Exceptional Children. (2005). *Universal design for learning: A guide for teachers and educational professionals.* Arlington, VA: Author.

Council of Chief State School Officers. (1992). *Model standards for beginning teacher licensing, assessment, and development: A resource for state dialogue.* Washington, DC: Author. Retrieved July 30, 2008, from www.ccsso.org/content/pdfs/corestrd.pdf

Crane, J. (2002). *The promise of value-added testing.* Washington, DC: Progressive Policy Institute.

Cruickshank, D. R. (1985). Uses and benefits of reflective teaching. *Phi Delta Kappan, 66*(10), 704–706.

Danielson, C. (2007). *Enhancing professional practice: A framework for teaching* (2nd ed.). Alexandria, VA: Association for Supervision and Curriculum Development.

Dardig, J. C. (2008). *Involving parents of students with special needs.* Thousand Oaks, CA: Corwin Press.

Darling-Hammond, L., & Baratz-Snowden, J. (2007). A good teacher in every classroom: Preparing the highly qualified teachers our children deserve. *Educational Horizons, 85*(2), 111–132.

Davis, B. M. (2006). *How to teach students who don't look like you: Culturally relevant teaching strategies.* Thousand Oaks, CA: Corwin Press.

Dewey, J. (1933). *How we think: A restatement of the relation of reflective thinking to the educative process.* Boston: Heath. (Originally published in 1909)

Diaz-Rico, L. T. (2008). *Strategies for teaching English learners* (2nd ed.). Boston: Allyn & Bacon.

Diffily, D. (2004). *Teachers and families working together.* Boston: Allyn & Bacon.

Drapeau, P. (2009). *Differentiating with graphic organizers: Tools to foster critical and creative thinking.* Thousand Oaks, CA: Corwin Press.

Dreikurs, R., Grunwald, B. B., & Pepper, F. C. (1998). *Maintaining sanity in the classroom: Classroom management techniques* (2nd ed.). Philadelphia: Taylor & Francis.

Echevarria, J., Short, D. J., & Vogt, M. (2008). *Implementing the SIOP model through effective professional development and coaching* (3rd ed.). Boston: Allyn & Bacon.

Echevarria, J., Vogt, M., & Short, D. J. (2008). *Making content comprehensible for English learners: The SIOP model.* Boston: Allyn & Bacon.

Educational Research Service. (2004). *Helping struggling learners in the elementary and middle grades.* Arlington, VA: Author.

Eggen, P. D., & Kauchak, D. P. (2007). *Educational psychology* (7th ed.). Upper Saddle River, NJ: Merrill/Prentice-Hall.

Emmer, E. T., & Evertson, C. M. (2009). *Classroom management for middle and high school teachers* (8th ed.). Boston: Allyn & Bacon.

Evertson, C. M., & Emmer, E. T. (2009). *Classroom management for elementary teachers* (8th ed.). Boston: Allyn & Bacon.

Falk, B. (2002). Standards-based reforms: Problems and possibilities. *Phi Delta Kappan, 83*(8), 612–620.

Ferguson, R. F. (1998). Teachers' perceptions and expectations and the Black-White test score gap. In C. Jencks & M. Phillips (Eds.), *The Black-White test score gap and can schools narrow the Black-White test score gap?* (pp. 273–374). Washington, DC: Brookings Institution Press.

Ferguson, R. F., & Ladd, H. F. (1996). How and why money matters: An analysis of Alabama schools. In H. F. Ladd (Ed.), *Holding schools accountable: Performance-based reform in education.* Washington, DC: Brookings Institution Press.

Fetler, M. (1999, March 26). High school staff characteristics and mathematics test results. *Education Policy Analysis Archives, 7*(9). Retrieved December 22, 2005, from http://epaa.asu.edu/epaa/v7n9.html

Fogarty, R. J., & Stoehr, J. (2008). *Integrating curricula with multiple intelligences* (2nd ed.). Thousand Oaks, CA: Corwin Press.

Freeman, D., & Freeman, Y. (2007). *English language learners: The essential guide.* New York: Scholastic.

Freiberg, H. J., & Driscoll, A. (2005). *Universal teaching strategies* (4th ed.) Boston: Allyn & Bacon.

Gagné, R. M. (1985). *The conditions of learning and theory of instruction* (4th ed.). New York: Holt, Rinehart & Winston.

Gagnon, G. W., & Collay, M. (2006). *Constructivist learning design: Key questions for teaching to standards.* Thousand Oaks, CA: Corwin Press.

Gaitan, C. D. (2005). *Involving Latino families in schools: Raising student achievement through home-school partnerships.* Thousand Oaks, CA: Corwin Press.

Gaitan, C. D. (2006). *Building culturally responsive classrooms: A guide for K–6 teachers.* Thousand Oaks, CA: Corwin Press.

Gardner, H. (1983). *Frames of mind: The theory of multiple intelligences.* New York: Basic Books.

Gardner, H. (1995). Reflections on multiple intelligences: Myths and messages. *Phi Delta Kappan, 77*(3), 202–209.

Gardner, H. (1999). *The disciplined mind: What all students should understand.* New York: Simon & Schuster.

Gay, G. (2000). *Culturally responsive teaching.* New York: Teachers College Press.

Gay, G. (2005). Politics of multicultural teacher education. *Journal of Teacher Education, 56*(3), 221–228.

Geva, E. (2006). Second-language oral proficiency and second-language literacy. In D. August & T. Shanahan (Eds.), *Developing literacy in second-language learners: Report of the National Literacy Panel on Language Minority Children and Youth.* Mahwah, NJ: Erlbaum.

Gillies, R. M. (2007). *Cooperative learning: Integrating theory into practice.* Thousand Oaks, CA: Sage.

Glasser, W. (1998). *The quality school: Managing students without coercion* (rev. ed.). New York: HarperPerennial.

Goldenberg, C. (2008, Summer). Teaching English language learners: What the research does—and does not—say. *American Educator,* 8–23, 42–44. Retrieved July 30, 2008, from www.aft.org/pubs-reports/american_educator/index.htm.

Gollnick, D. M., & Chinn, P. C. (2009). *Multicultural education in a pluralistic society* (8th ed.). Boston: Allyn & Bacon.

Good, T. L., & Brophy, J. E. (2008). *Looking in classrooms* (10th ed.). Boston: Allyn & Bacon.

Gootman, M. E. (2008). *The caring teacher's guide to discipline: Helping students learn self-control, responsibility, and respect, K–6.* (3rd ed.). Thousand Oaks, CA: Corwin Press.

Gordon, T. (1991). *Discipline that works: Promoting self-discipline in children.* New York: Plume.

Gorski, P. (2008). The myth of the "culture of poverty." *Educational Leadership, 65*(7), 32–36.

Grant, K. B., & Ray, J. A. (2009). *Home, school, and community collaboration: Culturally responsive family involvement.* Thousand Oaks, CA: Sage.

Gregory, G. H. (2005). *Differentiating instruction with style: Aligning teacher and learner intelligences for maximum achievement.* Thousand Oaks, CA: Corwin Press.

Gregory, G. H., & Chapman, C. (2006). *Differentiated instructional strategies: One size doesn't fit all* (2nd ed.). Thousand Oaks, CA: Corwin Press.

Grigg, W., Daane, M., Jin, Y., & Campbell, J. (2002). *The nation's report card: Reading 2002.* Washington, DC: U.S. Department of Education.

Gronlund, N. E., & Brookhart, S. M. (2009). *Gronlund's writing instructional objectives* (8th ed.). Upper Saddle River, NJ: Pearson/Prentice-Hall.

Gronlund, N. E., & Waugh, C. K. (2009). *Assessment of student achievement* (8th ed.). Boston: Allyn & Bacon.

Guillaume, A. M. (2008). *K–12 classroom teaching: A primer for new professionals* (3rd ed.). Upper Saddle River, NJ: Pearson/Prentice-Hall.

Gurian, M., & Henley, P. (2001). *Boys and girls learn differently: A guide for teachers and parents.* San Francisco: Jossey-Bass.

Gurian, M., & Stevens, K. (2005). *The minds of boys: Saving our sons from falling behind in school and life.* San Francisco: Jossey-Bass.

Gurian, M., Stevens, K., & King, K. (2008). *Strategies for teaching boys and girls: Elementary level.* San Francisco: Jossey-Bass.

Haager, D., & Klingner, J. K. (2005). *Differentiating instruction in inclusive classroom: The special educator's guide.* Boston: Allyn & Bacon.

Hale, M. S., & City, E. A. (2006). *The teacher's guide to leading student-centered discussions.* Thousand Oaks, CA: Corwin Press.

Hanushek, E. A., Kain, J. F., & Rivkin, S. G. (1998, August). *Teachers, schools, and academic achievement.* (NBER Working Paper No. w6691). Cambridge, MA: National Bureau of Economic Research.

Harmin, M., & Toth, M. (2006). *Inspiring active learning: A complete handbook for teachers.* Alexandria, VA: Association for Supervision and Curriculum Development.

Harrow, A. J. (1972). *A taxonomy of the psychomotor domain: A guide for developing behavioral objectives.* New York: Longman.

Hill, J. D., & Flynn, K. M. (2006). *Classroom instruction that works with English language learners.* Alexandria, VA: Association for Supervision and Curriculum Development.

Howard, G. R. (2007). As diversity grows, so must we. *Educational Leadership, 64*(6), 16–22.

Hunter, M. (1976). *Improved instruction.* El Segundo, CA: TIP.

Hunter, M. (1981). *Increasing your teacher effectiveness.* Palo Alto, CA: Learning Institute.

Hunter, M. (1984). Knowing, teaching, and supervising. In P. L. Hosford (Ed.), *Using what we know about teaching* (pp. 169–192). Alexandria, VA: Association for Supervision and Curriculum Development.

Hunter, M. (1994). *Enhancing teaching.* New York: Macmillan.

Hunter, R. (2004). *Madeline Hunter's mastery teaching: Increasing instructional effectiveness in elementary and secondary schools* (rev. ed.). Thousand Oaks, CA: Corwin Press.

Hyman, I. A. (1997). *School discipline and school violence.* Boston: Allyn & Bacon.

Interstate New Teacher Assessment and Support Consortium (INTASC). (1992). *Model standards for beginning teacher licensing, assessment and development: A resource for state dialogue.* Washington, DC: Council of Chief State School Officers.

Interstate New Teacher Assessment and Support Consortium (INTASC). (1998). *Next steps: Moving toward performance-based licensure in teaching.* Retrieved July 30, 2008, from www.ccsso.org/intasc.html

Irvine, J. J., & Armento, B. J. (2001). *Culturally responsive teaching: Lesson planning for elementary and middle grades.* New York: McGraw-Hill.

Jacobsen, D. A., Eggen, P. D., & Kauchak, D. P. (2009). *Methods for teaching* (8th ed.). Upper Saddle River, NJ: Merrill/Prentice-Hall.

James, A. N. (2007). *Teaching the male brain: How boys, think, feel, and learn in school.* Thousand Oaks, CA: Corwin Press.

Jensen, E. (2005). *Teaching with the brain in mind* (2nd ed.). Alexandria, VA: Association for Supervision and Curriculum Development.

Jensen, E. (2008). *Brain-based learning: The new paradigm of teaching* (2nd ed.). Thousand Oaks, CA: Corwin Press.

Jensen, R. A., & Kiley, T. J. (2005). *Teaching, leading, and learning in pre K–8 settings: Strategies for success* (2nd ed.). Boston: Houghton Mifflin.

Johnson, D. W., & Johnson, R. T. (1999). *Learning together and alone: Cooperative, competitive, and individualistic learning* (5th ed.). Boston: Allyn & Bacon.

Jolliffe, W. (2007). *Cooperative learning in the classroom: Putting it into practice.* Thousand Oaks, CA: Sage.

Jones, T. G., & Fuller, M. L. (2003). *Teaching Hispanic children.* Boston: Allyn & Bacon.

Jones, V. F., & Jones, L. S. (2007). *Comprehensive classroom management: Creating communities of support and solving problems* (8th ed.). Boston: Allyn & Bacon.

Jonson, K. F. (2002). *The new elementary teacher's handbook* (2nd ed.). Thousand Oaks, CA: Corwin Press.

Joyce, B., & Weil, M. (2009). *Models of teaching* (8th ed.). Boston: Allyn & Bacon.

Karges-Bone, L. (2000). *Lesson planning: Long-range and short-range models for grades K–6.* Boston: Allyn & Bacon.

Karnes, F. A., & Stephens, K. R. (2008). *Achieving excellence: Educating the gifted and talented.* Upper Saddle River, NJ: Pearson/Prentice-Hall.

Kauchak, D., & Eggen, P. (2008). *Introduction to teaching: Becoming a professional* (3rd ed.). Upper Saddle River, NJ: Pearson/Prentice-Hall.

Kellough, R. D., & Carjuzaa, J. (2009). *Teaching in the middle and secondary schools* (9th ed.). Upper Saddle River, NJ: Merrill/Prentice-Hall.

Kellough, R. D., & Kellough, N. G. (2008). *Teaching young adolescents: A guide to methods and resources* (5th ed). Upper Saddle River, NJ: Merrill/Prentice-Hall.

Kerr, M., & Nelson, C. (2006). *Strategies for addressing behavior problems in the classroom* (5th ed.). Upper Saddle River, NJ: Merrill/Prentice-Hall.

Kindler, A. (2002). *Survey of the states' limited English proficient students and available education programs and services. 2000–01 summary report.* Washington, DC: Clearinghouse for English Language Acquisition.

Kober, N. (2006). *A public education primer: Basic (and sometimes surprising) facts about the U.S. education system.* Washington, DC: Center on Education Policy.

Kounin, J. S. (1970). *Discipline and group management in classrooms.* New York: Holt, Rinehart & Winston.

Kralovec, E., & Buell, J. (2000). *The end of homework: How homework disrupts families, overburdens children, and limits learning.* Boston: Beacon Press.

Krashen, S. (1985). *The input hypothesis: Issues and implications.* New York: Longman.

Ladson-Billings, G. (1997). *The dreamkeepers: Successful teachers of African American children.* San Francisco: Jossey-Bass.

Lazear, D. (2003). *Eight ways of teaching: The artistry of teaching with multiple intelligences* (4th ed.). Thousand Oaks, CA: Corwin Press.

Lee, J. S., & Bowen, N. K. (2006). Parent involvement, cultural capital, and the achievement gap among elementary school children. *American Educational Research Journal, 43,* 193–218.

Levin, J., & Nolan, J. F. (2007). *Principles of classroom management: A professional decision-making model* (5th ed.). Boston: Allyn & Bacon.

Lou, Y., Abrami, P. C., Spence, J. C., Paulsen, C., Chanvers, B., & d'Apollonio, S. (1996). Within-class grouping: A meta-analysis. *Review of Educational Research, 66*(40), 423–458.

Lynch, E. W., & Hanson, M. J. (Eds.). (2004). *Developing cross-cultural competence: A guide for working with children and their families* (3rd ed.). Baltimore: Paul H. Brookes.

Macionis, J. (2007). *Society: The basics* (9th ed.). Upper Saddle River, NJ: Pearson/Prentice-Hall.

Mager, R. F. (1997). *Preparing instructional objectives* (3rd ed.). Atlanta, GA: Center for Effective Performance.

Marlowe, B. A., & Page, M. L. (2005). *Creating and sustaining the constructivist classroom* (2nd ed.). Thousand Oaks, CA: Corwin Press.

Marzano, R. J. (1998). *A theory-based meta-analysis of research on instruction.* Aurora, CO: Mid-Continent Research for Education and Learning. (ERIC Document Reproduction Service 427 087)

Marzano, R. J. (2007). *The art and science of teaching: A comprehensive framework for effective instruction.* Alexandria, VA: Association for Supervision and Curriculum Development.

Marzano, R. J., Gaddy, B. B., Foseid, M. C., Foseid, M. P., & Marzano, J. S. (2009). *A handbook for classroom management that works.* Upper Saddle River, NJ: Pearson/Prentice-Hall.

Marzano, R. J., & Kendall, J. S. (2008). *Designing and assessing educational objectives: Applying the new taxonomy.* Thousand Oaks, CA: Corwin Press.

Marzano, R. J., Norford, J. S., Paynter, D. E., Pickering, D. J., & Gaddy, B. B. (2005). *A handbook for classroom instruction that works.* Upper Saddle River, NJ: Merrill/Prentice-Hall.

Marzano, R. J., & Pickering, D. J. (2007). The case for and against homework. *Educational Leadership, 64*(6), 74–79.

Marzano, R. J., Pickering, D. J., & Pollock, J. E. (2005). *Classroom instruction that works: Research-based strategies for increasing student achievement.* Upper Saddle River, NJ: Merrill/Prentice-Hall.

McCombs, B. L. (2003, April). *Defining tools for teacher reflection: The assessment of learner-centered practices.* Paper presented at the annual meeting of the American Educational Research Association, Chicago.

McEwan, E. K. (2005). *How to deal with parents who are angry, troubled, afraid, or just plain crazy* (2nd ed.). Thousand Oaks, CA: Corwin Press.

McEwan, E. K. (2006). *How to survive and thrive in the first three weeks of school.* Thousand Oaks, CA: Corwin Press.

McMillan, J. H. (2007). *Classroom assessment: Principles and practice for effective instruction* (4th ed.). Boston: Allyn & Bacon.

Mierzwik, N. D. (2005). *Classroom record keeping made simple.* Thousand Oaks, CA: Corwin Press.

Miller, M. D., Linn, R. L., & Gronlund, N. E. (2009). *Measurement and assessment in teaching* (10th ed.). Upper Saddle River, NJ: Pearson/Prentice-Hall.

Minott, M. (2007). *The extent to which seasoned teachers in the Cayman Islands use elements of reflective teaching in their lesson planning, implementing, and evaluation: Implication for teacher education and training globally and locally.* Report International University of the Caribbean. (ERIC Digest Document Reproduction Service ED495112.)

Moje, E. B., Collazo, T., Carrillo, R., & Marx, R. W. (2001). "Maestro, what is quality?": Language, literacy, and discourse in project-based science. *Journal of Research in Science Teaching, 38*(4), 469–496.

Monk, D. H. (1994). Subject matter preparation of secondary mathematics and science teachers and student achievement. *Economics of Education Review, 13*(2), 125–145.

Moore, K. D. (2007). *Classroom teaching skills* (6th ed.). Boston: McGraw-Hill.

Moran, C., Stobbe, J., Baron, W., Miller, J., & Moir, E. (2008). *Keys to the elementary classroom: A teacher's guide to the first month of school* (3rd ed.). Thousand Oaks, CA: Corwin Press.

Morine-Dershimer, G. (1977, April). *What's in a plan? Stated and unstated plans for lessons.* Paper presented at the annual meeting of the American Educational Research Association, New York.

Morine-Dershimer, G. (1979). *Teacher plan and classroom reality: The South Bay study: Part 4* (Research Series No. 60). East Lansing, MI: Institute for Research on Teaching, Michigan State University.

Morrison, G. R., Ross, S. M., & Kemp, J. E. (2007). *Designing effective instruction* (5th ed.). New York: John Wiley & Sons.

Murnane, R. J., & Steele, J. L. (2007). What is the problem? The challenge of providing effective teachers for all children. *Future of Children, 17*(1), 15–43.

National Board for Professional Teacher Standards (NBPTS). (2005). *What teachers should know and be able to do: The five core propositions of the National Board.* Retrieved July 30, 2008, from www.nbpts.org/about/coreprops.cfm

National Center for Education Statistics (NCES). (2005). *Dropout rates in the United States: 2005.* Washington, DC: Author. Retrieved July 30, 2008, from www.nces.gov/pubs/dropout05

National Clearinghouse for English Language Acquisition (NCELA). (2004). *Data on languages spoken by U.S. students.* Washington, DC: Author and Language Instruction Educational Programs. Retrieved July 30, 2008, from www.ncela.gwu.edu/stats/4_toplanguages

National Clearinghouse for English Language Acquisition (NCELA). (2005). *ELL demographics by state, 2000–2005.* Washington, DC: Author and Language Instruction Educational Programs. Retrieved July 30, 2008, from www.ncela.gwu.edu/ stats/3_bystate.htm

National Clearinghouse for English Language Acquisition (NCELA). (2006). *How has the English language learner population changed in recent years?* Washington, DC: Author and Language Instruction Educational Programs. Retrieved July 30, 2008, from www.ncela.gwu.edu/expert/faq/08leps.html

National Council for Accreditation of Teacher Education. (2008). *Professional standards for the accreditation of teacher preparation institutions.* Washington, DC: Author.

National Council of Teachers of English & International Reading Association. (1996). *Standards for English Language Arts.* Urbana, IL: Authors.

National Council of Teachers of Mathematics. (1989). *Curriculum and evaluation standards for school mathematics.* Reston, VA: Author.

National Institute of Mental Health. (2006). *Attention deficit hyperactivity disorder.* Washington, DC: Author. Retrieved July 30, 2008, from www.nimh.nih.gov/healthpublications/adhd/summary.shtml

National Parent Teachers Association (NPTA). (2000). *Building successful partnerships: A guide for developing parent and family involvement programs.* Bloomington, IN: Solution Tree.

No Child Left Behind. (2002). U.S. Department of Education. Available online at www.ed.gov/nclb/landing.jhtml

Oakes, J. (2005). *Keeping track: How schools structure inequality* (2nd ed.). New Haven, CT: Yale University Press.

Olsen, G. W., & Fuller, M. L. (2008). *Home–school relations: Working successfully with parents and families* (3rd ed.). Upper Saddle River, NJ: Pearson/Prentice-Hall.

Orlich, D. C., Harder, R. J., Callahan, R. C., Trevisan, M. S., & Brown, A. H. (2007). *Teaching strategies: A guide to effective instruction* (8th ed.). Boston: Houghton Mifflin.

Ormrod, J. E. (2008). *Educational psychology: Developing learners* (6th ed.). Upper Saddle River, NJ: Pearson/Prentice-Hall.

Osterman, K. F., & Kottkamp, R. B. (2004). *Reflective practice for educators: Professional development to improve student learning* (2nd ed.). Thousand Oaks, CA: Corwin Press.

Pajak, E. (2001). Clinical supervision in a standards-based environment. *Journal of Teacher Education, 52*(3), 233–243.

Payne, R. K. (2005). *A framework for understanding poverty* (rev. ed.). Highlands, TX: aha! Process.

Payne, R. K. (2008). Nine powerful practices. *Educational Leadership, 65*(7), 48–52.

Phi Delta Kappa. (n.d.). *Reflective teaching.* Bloomington, IN: Author.

Popham, W. J. (2008). *Classroom assessment: What teachers need to know* (5th ed.). Boston: Allyn & Bacon.

Posner, G. J., & Rudnitsky, A. N. (2006). *Course design: A guide to curriculum development for teachers* (7th ed.). Boston: Allyn & Bacon.

Price, K. M., & Nelson, K. L. (2007). *Planning effective instruction: Diversity responsive methods and management* (3rd ed.). Belmont, CA: Thomson Wadsworth.

Public Agenda. (2008). *Lessons learned: New teachers talk about their jobs, challenges and long-range plans* (Issue No. 3: Report from the National Comprehensive Center for Teacher Quality and Public Agenda). New York: Author.

Roberts, M. P. (2001). *Your mentor: A practical guide for first-year teachers in grades 1–3.* Thousand Oaks, CA: Corwin Press.

Roberts, W. B. (2008). *Working with parents of bullies and victims.* Thousand Oaks, CA: Corwin Press.

Robins, K. N., Lindsey, R. B., Lindsey, D. B., & Terrell, R. D. (2006). *Culturally proficient instruction: A guide for people who teach.* (2nd ed.). Thousand Oaks, CA: Corwin Press.

Romero, M., Mercado, C., & Vazquez-Raria, J. A. (1987). Students of limited English proficiency. In V. Richardson-Koehler (Ed.), *Educators' handbook: A research perspective.* New York: Longman.

Rong, S. L., & Preissle, J. (2009). *Educating immigrant students in the twenty-first century: What educators need to know* (2nd ed.). Thousand Oaks, CA: Corwin Press.

Rosenshine, B. (1987). Explicit teaching. In D. C. Berliner & B. V. Rosenshine (Eds.), *Talks to teachers* (pp. 75–92). New York: Random House.

Rosenshine, B., & Stevens, R. (1986). Teacher functions. In M. C. Wittrock (Ed.), *Handbook of research on teaching* (3rd ed.) (pp. 376–391). New York: Macmillan.

Rothenberg, C., & Fisher, D. (2007). *Teaching English language learners: A differentiated approach.* Upper Saddle River, NJ: Pearson/Prentice-Hall.

Roy P. (2005, February). A fresh look at follow-up. *Results.* Retrieved July 30, 2008, from www.nsdc.org/library/publications/results/res2–05roy.cfm

Rudney, G. L. (2006). *Every teacher's guide to working with parents.* Thousand Oaks, CA: Corwin Press.

Ruiz-de-Velasco, J., & Fix, M. (2000). *Overlooked and underserved: Immigrant students in U.S. secondary schools.* Washington, DC: Urban Institute.

Sadker, D. M., & Silber, E. S. (2007). *Gender in the classroom: Foundations, skills, methods, and strategies across the curriculum.* Mahwah, NJ: Erlbaum.

Sanders, W. L., & Rivers, J. C. (1996). *Cumulative and residual effects of teachers on future student academic achievement.* Knoxville, TN: University of Tennessee Value-Added Research and Assessment Center.

Sausen, J. (2004). *Working with paraprofessionals.* Thousand Oaks, CA: Corwin Press.

Schell, L. M., & Burden, P. R. (2006). *Countdown to the first day of school* (3rd ed.). Washington, DC: National Education Association.

Schoenfeldt, M. K., & Salsbury, D. E. (2009). *Lesson planning: A research-based model for K–12 classrooms.* Upper Saddle River, NJ: Pearson/Prentice-Hall.

Serdyukov, P., & Ryan, M. (2008). *Writing effective lesson plans: A five-star approach.* Boston: Allyn & Bacon.

Shen, J., Poppink, S., Cui, Y., & Fan, G. (2007). Lesson planning: A practice of professional responsibility and development. *Educational Horizons, 85*(4), 248–258.

Shostak, R. (2006). Involving students in learning. In J. M. Cooper (Ed.), *Classroom teaching skills* (8th ed.) (pp. 77–99). Boston: Houghton Mifflin.

Shulman, L. S. (2004). *The wisdom of practice: Essays on teaching, learning, and learning to teach.* San Francisco: Jossey-Bass.

Siegel, H. (2002) Multiculturalism, universalism, and science education: In search of common ground. *Science Education, 86,* 803–820.

Silver, H. F., Strong, R. W., & Perini, M. J. (2000). *So each may learn: Integrating learning styles and multiple intelligences.* Alexandria, VA: Association for Supervision and Curriculum Development.

Skowron, J. (2006). *Powerful lesson planning: Every teacher's guide to effective instruction* (2nd ed.). Thousand Oaks, CA: Corwin Press.

Slavin, R. E. (1995). *Cooperative learning* (2nd ed.). Boston: Allyn & Bacon.

Slavin, R. E. (2009). *Educational psychology* (9th ed.). Boston: Allyn & Bacon.

Slavin, R. E., Cheung, A., Groff, C., & Lake, C. (2004). Effective reading programs for middle and high schools: A best evidence synthesis. *Reading Research Quarterly, 43*(3), 290–322.

Smutny, J. F., & von Fremd, S. (2009). *Igniting creativity in gifted learners, K–6.* Thousand Oaks, CA: Corwin Press.

Sousa, D. A. (2006). *How the brain learns* (3rd ed.). Thousand Oaks, CA: Corwin Press.

Sprick, R. S. (2006). *Discipline in the secondary school: A positive approach to behavior management* (2nd ed.). San Francisco: Jossey-Bass.

Steffy, B. E., Wolfe, M. P., Pasch, S. H., & Enz, B. J. (Eds.). (2000). *Life cycle of the career teacher.* Thousand Oaks, CA: Corwin Press.

Stein, J., Meltzer, L., Krishnan, K., Pollica, L. S., Papadopoulos, I., & Roditi, B. (2007). *Parent guide to hassle-free homework.* New York: Scholastic.

Steinberg, A., & Almeida, C. (2004). *The dropout crisis: Promising approaches in prevention and recovery.* Boston: Jobs for the Future.

Stiggins, R. J. (2008). *An introduction to student-involved assessment for learning* (5th ed.). Upper Saddle River, NJ: Merrill/Prentice-Hall.

Taggart, G. L., & Wilson, A. P. (2005). *Promoting reflective thinking in teachers: Fifty action strategies* (2nd ed.). Thousand Oaks, CA: Corwin Press.

Teaching Commission. (2004). *Teaching at risk: A call to action.* New York: The Teaching Commission. Retrieved December 22, 2005, from www.theteachingcommission.org/press/FINAL_Report.pdf

Thompson, G. L. (2004). *Through ebony eyes: What teachers need to know but are afraid to ask about African American students.* San Francisco: Jossey-Bass.

Thompson, G. L. (2007). *Up where we belong: Helping African American and Latino students rise in school and life.* San Francisco: Jossey-Bass.

Thompson, J. G. (2007). *The first-year teacher's survival guide* (2nd ed.). San Francisco: Jossey-Bass.

Tomlinson, C. A. (2005a). *How to differentiate instruction in mixed-ability classrooms* (2nd ed.). Upper Saddle River, NJ: Pearson/Prentice-Hall.

Tomlinson, C. A. (2005b). *The differentiated classroom: Responding to the needs of all learners.* Upper Saddle River, NJ: Pearson/Prentice-Hall.

Tomlinson, C. A., & Allan, S. D. (2000). *Leadership for differentiating schools and classrooms.* Alexandria, VA: Association for Supervision and Curriculum Development.

Trumbull, E., Rothstein-Fisch, C., Greenfield, P. M., & Quiroz, B. (2001). *Bridging cultures between home and school: A guide for teachers.* Mahwah, NJ: Erlbaum.

Tsui, M. (2007). Gender and mathematics achievement in China and the United States. *Gender Issues, 24*(3), 1–11.

Turnbull, A. P., & Turnbull, H. R. (2007). *Exceptional lives: Special education in today's schools* (5th ed.). Upper Saddle River, NJ: Merrill/Prentice-Hall.

Turnbull, A. P., Turnbull, H. R., Erwin, E., & Soodak, L. (2006). *Families, professionals, and exceptionality: Positive outcomes through partnership and trust* (5th ed.). Upper Saddle River, NJ: Merrill/Prentice-Hall.

Villegas, A. M., & Lucas, T. (2007). The culturally responsive teacher. *Educational Leadership, 64*(6), 28–33.

Vogt, M., & Echevarria, J. (2008). *Ninety-nine ideas and activities for teaching English language learners with the SIOP model.* Boston: Allyn & Bacon.

Walker, J. E., Shae, T. M., & Bauer, A. (2007). *Behavior management: A practical approach for educators* (9th ed.). Upper Saddle River, NJ: Merrill/Prentice-Hall.

Walsh, J. A., & Sattes, B. D. (2005). *Quality questioning: A research-based practice to engage every learner.* Thousand Oaks, CA: Corwin Press.

Weinstein, C. S. (2007). *Middle and secondary classroom management: Lessons from research and practice* (3rd ed.). New York: McGraw-Hill.

Weinstein, C. S., & Mignano, A. J., Jr. (2007). *Elementary classroom management: Lessons from research and practice* (4th ed.). New York: McGraw-Hill.

Wiggins, G., & McTighe, J. (2006). *Understanding by design* (expanded 2nd ed.). Upper Saddle River, NJ: Pearson/Prentice-Hall.

Wilen, W. W. (1991). *Questioning skills, for teachers* (3rd ed.). Washington, DC: National Education Association.

Wolfgang, C. H. (2009). *Solving discipline and classroom management problems* (7th ed.). New York: John Wiley & Sons.

Wong, H. K., & Wong, R. T. (2009). *The first days of school: How to be an effective teacher* (4th ed.). Mountain View, CA: Harry K. Wong.

Woolfolk-Hoy, A. (2007). *Educational psychology* (10th ed.). Boston: Allyn & Bacon.

Wormeli, R. (2005). *Summarization on any subject: Fifty techniques to improve student learning.* Alexandria, VA: Association for Supervision and Curriculum Development.

Wormeli, R. (2007). *Differentiation: From planning to practice, grades 6–12.* Portland, ME: Stenhouse.

Wyatt, R. L., & White, J. E. (2007). *Making your first year a success: A classroom survival guide for middle and high school teachers* (2nd ed.). Thousand Oaks, CA: Corwin Press.

York-Barr, J., Sommers, W. A., Ghere, G. S., & Montie, J. K. (2006). *Reflective practice to improve schools: An action guide for educators* (2nd ed.). Thousand Oaks, CA: Corwin Press.

Name Index

Subject Index

Photo Credits

Text Credits